Children's Writer

Guide to 2005

THE WRITER'S
BOOKSTORE

Editor: Susan M. Tierney

Contributing writers:

Pegi Deitz Shea
Mark Haverstock

Nancy Markham Alberts
Pamela Holtz Beres
Judy Bradbury
Kristi Collier
Kelly Easton
Sue Bradford Edwards
Gail Minett Eltringham
Marjorie Flathers

Lizann Flatt
Jan Goldberg
Jane Landreth
Louanne Lang
Ellen Macaulay
Janine Mangiamele
Paula Morrow
Mary Northrup
Jennifer Reed
Stephen Roos
Catherine Welch

Copy Editor: Cheryl de la Guéronnière

Editorial and Research Assistants:
Janine Mangiamele
Marni McNiff

Cover Art and Production: Joanna Horvath

Publisher: Prescott V. Kelly

Printed and bound in Canada.

Table of Contents

Book Publishing

The Truth Is in the Deals

By Pegi Deitz Shea

The spirit of Monty Hall and *Let's Make a Deal* is kicking around publishing these days. But instead of choosing between door number one, two, or three, some publishers are taking all of them.

Publishing giants such as Scholastic, the Penguin Group, HarperCollins, and Houghton Mifflin are making deals with smaller companies to compete better in some of the largest growth categories: middle-grade and young adult fiction, licensing, and graphic novels. Some publishing executives think that it is easier to ally with specialty companies than to grow the specialty in-house.

Midsized companies are also making deals to court older readers. The strategy at Harry Abrams Books and Boyds Mills Press was to team up with other companies; Charlesbridge and Candlewick have taken hiring steps to initiate or to expand their fiction line in-house.

Compared with fiction, the picture book market is still pretty flat. But publishers are aggressively going after the older end of that market with new or refurbished easy reader programs. As for preschool books, licensed characters and concepts are helping to keep sales steady.

Tweens & Teens Are Still Reading

Studies show that kids over the age of 10 may not be reading books that have been in the classics canon for 200 years, but they're gobbling up books made just yesterday.

Figures released for the last fiscal year show that the children's and young adult market grew by 19 percent, according to the Association of American Publishers. The Harry Potter fans are embracing more fantasy. Having been raised in the lap of luxurious American picture books, these readers are sticking with the visuals by glomming onto graphic novels. It's these same consumers—weaned from Pokémon—who are fueling the demand for *manga*. These mostly paperback-sized comic books are

Graphic Novels

Responding to the traditional publishers' moves into graphic books, comics companies are infiltrating the world of traditional novels. Formerly at Scholastic, Ruwan Jayatilleke now heads Marvel Press, a new imprint of Marvel Comics. In 2005, the press is publishing 12 character-based novels in three lines: grade school, young adult, and adult.

Dark Horse Comics is also operating in this sort of reverse mode, by issuing novels from its new imprint, M Press. And CDS Books has teamed up with Sony Online Entertainment to publish books based on the EverQuest multiplayer online game. R. A. Salvatore, a best-selling science fiction author, is the in-house editor.

And other companies are starting up: Creators of the *Matrix* movies have launched a comics and graphic novels publishing enterprise, Burlyman Entertainment. An older comics publishing house that was highly successful in the 1970s and 1980s and that failed in the mid-1990s, Now Comics, has restarted, with five paperback collections and plans for up to 10 new books a year. Keenspot.com used its base of Web comics to publish about a dozen titles, with about 20 in 2005. Capstone Press is directing its line, Graphic Library, to reading levels for grades three and four.

derived from Japanese cartoon series (*anime*) or original print series. The upshot is that the distinctions between print media categories have never been so fuzzy—make that *fizzy* with opportunity.

Let's look at some of the recent developments and what they may spark in 2005.

The Penguin Group for Young Readers had an impressive fiscal year in the last year for which figures are available, with children's book sales rising about 7 percent. The group's imprints include Dial, Dutton, Puffin, Putnam, Viking, and Grosset & Dunlap. Doug Whiteman, President of Penguin Books for Young Readers, says, "Grosset & Dunlap showed the greatest growth, nearly 50 percent over the year before. This was a result of a major commitment Grosset made to go into the licensing business quite aggressively. Several of the projects they bought into had enormous success: Strawberry Shortcake, the Bratz dolls, and Wiggles being most prominent."

Whiteman guesstimates that licensing revenue accounts for around 10 to 12 percent of the division's revenues at this point. That figure is poised to rise with Penguin's new venture with BBC Worldwide. A new imprint, BBC Children's Books, will bring out 60 to 80 books a year, featuring British TV characters including the *Teletubbies* and the *Tweenies*.

Penguin is shooting for about 3 percent growth in revenues overall for 2005, says Whiteman, similar to the growth in 2004. "Our industry is not seeing substantial growth right now, and these numbers reflect that. The truth, however, is that we hope and expect to do better than these targets would suggest."

Penguin has taken several significant measures to expand its teen readership. It began a new imprint, Razorbill, for readers 12 and up. According to Senior Vice President and Publisher Eloise Flood, the imprint will publish a mix of "commercial, good quality fiction" along with "celebrity bios, media tie-ins, and nonfiction." In August, the company entered into a three-year deal with Digital Manga to publish YA manga books that will cross over into the adult market.

Whiteman explains the thinking behind these two deals: "Razorbill tends to go for highly commercial topics and treatments. I see Digital Manga, which is part of Razorbill's program, as a natural extension of this, since manga and graphic novels in general are the fastest growing components of our industry right now."

Puffin Graphics is yet another expansion into the young adult market for the company. It debuts its first graphic novel versions of classic titles in the summer. Already planned are versions of *Black Beauty, Call of the Wild, Dracula, Frankenstein, Macbeth, The Red Badge of Courage, Treasure Island,*

and *The Wizard of Oz.* They are being done in conjunction with Byron Preiss Visuals.

Most of the Penguin imprints publish some books for older readers. This year, Dial is publishing the last book in a trilogy by Zizou Corder that began with *LionBoy,* for ages nine and up. But books for teens are only a modest compo-

nent of the overall publishing program, according to Whiteman. "The difference with Speak (a literary imprint launched in 2002) and Razorbill is that they are *completely* focused on the teen market. They bring a whole different sensibility, and in fact have a spillover impact on the other imprints, who see how cutting edge one can be with teen publishing and learn from it."

When asked about the near future, Whiteman foresees more deals in the coming year. "I don't think they'll necessarily be product acquisition deals, but might be more focused on opening new distribution channels or developing joint relationships with companies in other forms of entertainment, such as gaming or movies. I feel very good about the number of titles we're producing at this point, and I certainly don't think we want to increase that number in any meaningful way for the next year or two, at least."

Scholastic, which saw a 14 percent increase in sales of children's books in fiscal year 2004, has also been dealing. It's teaming up with other media companies, launching an imprint, and entering into distribution agreements. Jean Feiwel, Publisher and Editor in Chief of Scholastic, heads Graphix, the new imprint for graphic novels. Spring brings their publication of *Bone*, a

fantasy adventure by Jeff Smith. Smith first self-published the series and sold over 400,000 copies.

The fall Scholastic list includes chapter books, graphic novel-style storybooks, and activity books for the Trollz brand owned by DIC Entertainment. DIC is paving the way earlier in the year with other media products. Books with licensed characters such as these account for 5 to 10 percent of Scholastic's children's book and distribution revenues, which in turn comprise 67 percent of the company's entire revenues, including magazines and other products.

Scholastic also has a new deal with the LEGO Company. It's been publishing books featuring LEGO's Bionicle action figures since 2003. A new contract allows Scholastic to publish a variety of books about LEGO's Knights Kingdom characters and sets. The Director of LEGO global licensing, Stephanie Lawrence, says that Scholastic was the only choice for extending the LEGO brand in publishing. Future projects include titles based on Clikits, a girls' fashion and craft property, the Alpha Team adventure sets, and Duplo preschool building sets.

Let's Get Together

As opposed to the wholesale swallowing of small publishers by the giants that categorized the 1990s, this round of deal-making seems more creative, synergistic, and flexible. These deals are just as likely to occur among individuals, small presses, and midsized publishers, as they are with huge corporations.

Front Street Books, formerly associated with Carus Publishing, has joined Boyds Mills Press, the trade book division of Highlights for Children, Inc. "The association with Front Street," says Kent Brown, Jr., Publisher of Boyds Mills, "gives us more of an ability to serve middle-grade and young adult readers." Front Street Publisher and President Stephen Roxburgh brings about 100 backlist titles to Boyds Mills, which usually publishes about six novels a year. The Boyds Mills backlist of 400 books primarily features picture books, nonfiction, poetry, and activity books. The company recently launched a new historical fiction and nonfiction imprint, Calkins Creek Books.

In three recent cases, notable editors and executives have joined midsized publishers to build lists for older readers. Judy O'Malley, Executive Editor, will help grow Charlesbridge Publishing from their base in picture books, up through easy readers and chapter books. Editor Marc Aronson will develop YA titles for Candlewick Press. President and Chief Executive Officer Michael Jacobs and Editor Susan Van Metre launched the new Abrams Books for Young Readers middle-grade and teen novel imprint, Amulet Books; it also publishes a nonfiction line of advice books, Sunscreen.

Charlesbridge hired O'Malley to spearhead a major expansion into the middle-grade market. Most recently Editorial Director of children's books at Houghton Mifflin, and previously Editor at Cricket Books and Editor of the American Library Association (ALA) magazine *Book Links*, O'Malley will be acquiring a new list of transitional books that will bridge from the company's fiction and nonfiction picture books to books for older readers.

The first list is scheduled to appear in fall 2006 and will include fiction and nonfiction in early reader, chapter, and middle-grade book formats.

"We're particularly interested in innovative topics or themes for these young readers," says O'Malley.

"Humor and subjects that are especially intriguing to boys are certainly of great interest, but we're not limited to any narrow categories."

Yolanda LeRoy, Editorial Director of Charlesbridge, says, "Judy's familiarity with the school and library market will be valuable to us as we continue to create high-

BLONDE AMBITION
AN A-LIST NOVEL
ZOEY DEAN

quality books that connect to the classroom, library, and home." LeRoy adds that the expansion should bring Charlesbridge's output from 28 books a year to 32.

Aronson, an author of historical nonfiction in his own right, expects to acquire three or four older YA novels a year for Candlewick. "I tend to go for great writing, intelligence, beauty of language, more than by-the-book *teenage*. I am interested in crossing between cultures, within America or around the world. I respond well to voice. I'm always looking for humor. I think not enough is written for intelligent teenage boys."

Aronson eagerly awaited Candlewick's most recent lists. He is publishing Paul Fleischman's play, *Zap*, which is actually seven different plays, being performed at the same time. "Only Paul could pull this off, and he does, magnificently. I will also publish Holly-Jane Rahlens's novel *Prince William, Maximilian Minsky, and Me,* which won the equivalent of the Newbery or Printz in Germany. Her great comic voice, and very probing insights into what it is to be Jewish in modern Berlin convinced me—and the award jury."

Jacobs left Scholastic last year to head up Abrams Books for Young  Readers. Explaining the launch of Amulet Books, he says, "We felt that we could grow our children's presence and business by publishing terrific middle-grade and young adult fiction which, up to this point, didn't have a logical home on the rest of our children's lists. Additionally, we have a very talented editor, Susan Van Metre, who brought experience, contacts, and author relationships with her and it seemed like a great opportunity for us to branch out as the market for these books was growing."

Amulet Books literally burst onto the scene in 2004 with the novel *TTYL,* by Lauren Myracle, which reached more 75,000 copies in print. "It's our single best-selling title so far this year across the entire company," says Jacobs. Forthcoming are another Myracle novel and one by William Sleator, plus paperbacks, and the nonfiction Sunscreen line.

Jacobs says graphic novels are in the company's future. "And there are more likely to be humorous and/or edgy books that defy clear categorization—new formats and designs and much more visual kinds of books that tell stories. I want Abrams to be known for beautiful quality books that kids, parents, and teachers want to read, buy, and give as gifts." Jacobs adds that Abrams's books sell well in non-trade venues such as museums, gift stores, and craft stores.

Surging Ahead

Another company looking to grow more in the middle-grade market is Chronicle Books, which recently acquired SeaStar Books, and which distributes for North-South Books, Innovative Kids, Handprint Books, and Ragged Bears. Chronicle has a few nonfiction titles for older readers, such as the forthcoming *Middle School: How to Deal* (by five middle-school girls). Its Deptford Mice Trilogy, published by SeaStar, has found many older fans of fantasy.

Chronicle has several new early chapter books lined up for 2006. "We'd love some fiction projects for middle-grade and young adult readers," says Associate Publisher Victoria Rock. "But they need to be projects that feel right for Chronicle, something just a bit different and likely with a visual component of some sort." Rock points to the

YA Remains on the Rise

Harry N. Abrams, Amulet Books: 115 West 18th St., New York, NY 10011. www.abramsbooks.com. Just over a year old, the Amulet imprint for preteens and teens debuted with titles such as award-winning YA author William Sleator's *The Boy Who Couldn't Die.*

Candlewick Press: 2067 Massachusetts Ave., Cambridge, MA 02140. www. candlewick.com. Teen fiction has become a focus of Candlewick over the last fews years, from its highly successful 2002 title *Feed*, to its new *Vegan Virgin Valentine,* for ages 14 and up.

HarperCollins: 1350 Ave. of the Americas, New York, NY 10019. www.harperteen.com. **HarperTempest** is dedicated to contemporary teen fiction, while the **Eos** line offers science fiction and fantasy. The company also publishes romance and YA nonfiction. The website demonstrates the range and the strength of the HarperCollins approach to teens.

Henry Holt: 115 West 18th St., New York, NY 10011. Shortly after Holt's purchase of Roaring Brook Press last year, a new graphic novel line by Roaring Brook was announced. The audience age range is 11 to 16.

Houghton Mifflin: 222 Berkeley St., Boston, MA 02116. www. houghtonmifflinbooks.com. The new imprint **Graphia** does original and reprint paperbacks for older teens, with fiction, nonfiction, and poetry. The Kingfisher Publications imprint is publishing nonfiction with the *New York Times* for preteens and young teens.

Llewellyn Worldwide: P.O. Box 64383, St. Paul, MN 55164-0383. www.llewellyn.com. This New Age publisher has expanded its materials for tweens and teens in fiction and nonfiction. One of its newest series is Diadem: Worlds of Magic.

Penguin: 345 Hudson St., New York, NY 10014. www.penguin.com. **Speak** is a paperback line just a few years old dedicated to older readers. Penguin had increased its YA fiction for the line. Even newer for teens at Penguin is **Razorbill**, which publishes good quality commercial fiction; it looks for coming-of-age titles, mysteries, science fiction and most recently, in a new deal with a company called Digital Manga, graphic novels.

Smooch: Suite 2000, 200 Madison Ave., New York, NY 10016. www.smoochya.com. Smooch is a new small press publishing fiction in the genres of paranormal, horror, fantasy, contemporary, humor, and romance titles for teen girls. It published 12 titles last year.

Best-Selling Books

Among the best-selling titles on the Publishers Weekly list in the last year were the following. Seasonal titles are not included.

- *The Amulet of Samarkand,* Jonathan Stroud (Hyperion).
- *Black Water,* D. J. Machale (Aladdin).
- *Dragon Rider,* Cornelia Funke (Scholastic/Chicken House).
- *Eragon,* Christopher Paolini (Knopf).
- *Girls on Film,* Zoey Dean (Little, Brown).
- *The Grim Grotto,* Lemony Snicket (HarperTrophy).
- *Hoot,* Carl Hiaasen (Knopf).
- *Inkheart,* Cornelia Funke (Scholastic).
- *Molly Moon's Incredible Book of Hypnotism,* Georgia Byng (HarperTrophy).
- *Peter and the Starcatchers,* Dave Barry (Disney).
- *Rakkety Tam,* Brian Jacques (Philomel).
- *Shadowmancer,* G. P. Taylor (Putnam).
- *The Supernaturalist,* Eoin Colfer (Hyperion).
- *Teen Idol,* Meg Cabot (HarperCollins).
- *The Wrath of Mulgarath,* Holly Black (Simon & Schuster).
- *Zombie Butts from Uranus!,* Andy Griffiths (Scholastic).

Batchelder Honor Book *The Man Who Went to the Far Side of the Moon* as an example.

Exciting projects for publishers sometimes come from abroad, much to the chagrin of homegrown authors. Sometimes U.S. authors have ridden the best-selling coat-tails of Roald Dahl, Brian Jacques, J. K. Rowling, and the millions of copies sold for Orchard Books's Charlie Bone series, by British novelist Jenny Nimo. Random House will be releasing books four, five, and six in the British 10-book series The Edge Chronicles, by Paul Stewart and Chris Riddell.

Japan has its own impact on American publishing, with DC Comics importing, translating, and distributing manga titles under its CMX line. New this year are special releases to build the female readership: *Phantom Thief Jeanne,* about a reincarnated Joan of Arc; *Musashi #9,* about a 16-year-old girl who fights terrorism and crime; and *Gals!,* about an urban girl gang.

A surprise entry into the YA market is Brown Barn Books, a new division of Pictures of Record, a publisher of archaeology teaching materials. On its recent first list, Brown Barn Books released five trade paperback novels, and the company hopes to publish ten a year. When asked how she made the jump to this readership, Brown Barn owner and Editor in Chief Nancy Hammerslough says, "Young adult fiction can take readers outside their own lives. I think kids are too often bounded by people they know, the environment they live in, and the lives they see. We can widen their lives through fiction and bring some of their fantasies to life." She continues, "*Home to the Sea* does just this: illuminating the fantasy of many girls to be a mermaid, in the context of the real world."

Hammerslough cites the views of Sarah Herz, author with Donald R. Gallo of *From Hinton to Hamlet: Building Bridges between Young Adult Literature and the Classics* (Greenwood Press). "I'm convinced of Sarah Herz's take on YA—that it can be a stepping-stone to the classics, and that kids have to enjoy reading stories with which they can identify before they can enjoy reading *David Copperfield* and *Pride and Prejudice.*"

Brown Barn means to put into readers' hands books that aren't formulaic and don't fall into easy categories or have stereotypic protagonists. Hammerslough cites Michelle Taylor's *What's Happily Ever After Anyway?* She also feels that YA novels, in general, should avoid graphic sex, "but I hesitate to make any rules at all about the creative process."

With the company's background in archaeology, Hammerslough says, "I'd love to publish more novels set in other times, either prehistoric or more recent." But she warns she's a stickler for "authenticity in any fiction—whether it is set in 2005 or in 12,000 B.C. or possibly in 3000 A.D.—that shows the author has done some meaningful research to which he or she brings a new, imaginative perspective. That's one reason we're publishing *The Secret Shelter,* by Sandi LeFaucher, which takes place in the 1940 blitz of London—not exactly archaeology, but certainly good historical fiction."

Henry Holt's YA and middle-grade fiction has always had high literary value, whether in historical fiction or other genres. 2005 will see *Shakespeare's Secret,* by Elise Broach, a literary mystery and first novel; and *Wing Nut* by M. J. Auch, among other titles. "We've always published a consistent number of YA each season," says Christy Ottaviano, Executive Editor.

Pop!

Pop books, the antithesis of literature, are also faring well. Based on the success of its Smooch imprint and a contest it held for teen readers last summer, Dorchester Publishing expects to release more fun

Help Yourself to a Nonfiction Niche

Publishers of self-help books for children and teens include:

Bureau for At-Risk Youth: 135 DuPont St., P.O. Box 760, Plainview, NY 11803. www.at-risk.com. Classroom materials on overcoming life's challenges.

Creative Bound: P.O. Box 424, 151 Tansley Drive, Carp, Ontario K0A 1L0 Canada. www.creativebound.com. A small press that offers books on personal growth.

Frederick Fell: Suite 305, 2131 Hollywood Blvd., Hollywood, FL 33020. www.fellpub.com. Spiritual growth embraces books on a broad range of self-help topics for this small press.

Free Spirit: Suite 200, 217 Fifth Ave. North, Minneapolis, MN 55401. www.freespirit.com. Self-understanding is the underlying purpose of Free Spirit's publications.

Hazelden Foundation: P.O. Box 176, Center City, MN 55012. www.hazeldenbookplace.org. Hazelden focuses on addiction self-help materials.

Magination Press: 750 First St. NE, Washington, DC 20002. www.maginationpress.com. A small specialty publisher of self-help for children to age 12.

New Harbinger: 5674 Shattuck Ave., Oakland, CA 94609. www.newharbinger.com. Workbooks with self-techniques and exercises, for psychological health.

Newmarket Press: 15th floor, 18 East 48th St., New York, NY 10017. www.newmarketpress.com. Self-help and parenting books.

Parenting Press: P.O. Box 75267, Seattle, WA 98175. www.parenting-press.com. Practical life skills for children and parents.

PowerKids Press: 29 East 21st St., New York, NY 10010. www.powerkidspress.com. Guidance and curriculum-based books for kindergarten to grade eight.

Red Wheel: 368 Congress St., Boston, MA 02210. www.redwheelsweister.com. Self-help and inspirational books.

Small Horizons: P. O. Box 669, Far Hills, NJ 07931. www.newhorizonspressbooks.com. For adults helping children deal with stress, divorce, depression, anger, peer pressure.

Sourcebooks: Suite 139, 1935 Brookdale Road, Naperville, IL 60563. www.sourcebooks.com. Self-help for parents and families.

Starseed Press: P. O. Box 1082, Tiburon, CA 94920. www.nwlib.com.

titles next summer. Smooch publishes contemporary, paranormal, horror, and romance fiction, primarily for girls 12 to 16. Kate Seaver is Editor. Among its titles are *The Taming of the Dru,* by Katie Maxwell; *My Alternate Life,* by Lee McClain; and *Boy Down Under,* by Sally Odgers. Dorchester has been an independent mass-market publisher since 1971. Among its other lines of pop books are Making It, offering *chick lit,* and Vortex, a fantasy imprint, which debuted with *The Adventures of Charley Tooth* by L. B. Richards.

Little, Brown has two best-selling series on its hands, rather, in girls' hands: Cecily von Ziegesar's Gossip Girl Novels, and Zoey Dean's A-List Novels. Bookstore owners have called these books "eye candy," and there will be more to come in the year ahead.

Dial Books is turning to a collection of YA short stories to illuminate issues for guys: *Every Man for Himself . . . Being a Guy,* edited by Nancy Mercado. Editor Cecile Goyette says, "Dial has signed up more novels, and more older-skewing YA, while not ignoring the middle-grade readership either. We'd like to take on some less totally angst-ridden tales for teens—stories that are funny but smart and meaningful."

Weighing in with Nonfiction

"Funny but smart and meaningful" can apply to nonfiction, too, according to Free Spirit Publishing Publicity Director Amy Dillahunt.

In particular, as one can deduce from many popular titles, books promising to be *guides* or containing helpful lists are two nonfiction forms that entertain as well as educate today's busy young readers.

As long as there are teens, there will be teen issues to address. Dillahunt cites several 2005 self-help books for teen boys and girls: *Too Stressed to Think? A Teen Guide to Staying Sane When Life Makes You Crazy,* by Annie Fox and Ruth Kirschner; *Respect: A Girls' Guide to Getting Respect and Dealing When Your Line is Crossed,* by Courtney Macavinta and Andrea Vander Pluym; and *100 Things Guys Need to Know,* by Bill Zimmerman.

Amulet will be publishing nonfiction teen paperbacks under the Sunscreen line, which was adapted from the Oxygen series published by Abrams's French parent company, La Martinière. "They are advice books for kids on subjects

that most adolescents deal with— shyness, divorce, sex and body image, dealing with your parents and friends, etc.," Jacobs explains. "We launched the list this past year and are building its presence both in trade and institutional markets."

Hot public issues and history are the business of the Thomson Group, which includes the nonfiction imprints Greenhaven Press, Lucent Books, Blackbirch Press, and Kid-Haven Press. Thomson sells most of its titles in series to libraries and schools. After all, students in almost every grade level are required to write papers based on research—research that is more reliable than the information found on most websites.

Here is a handful of 2005 titles, provided by Editor in Chief Chandra Howard: Greenhaven will tackle *How Should the United States Treat Prisoners in the War on Terror,* written by Lauri S. Friedman. *Ovarian Cancer,* by Barbara Sheen, will come out in Lucent's series on Diseases and Disorders. KidHaven Press offers younger readers books like *What Makes Me a Muslim,* by Catherine Petrini. And Blackbirch will publish *Giants of Science: Robert Goddard, Rocket Pioneer,* by Kaye Patchet.

Encouraged and requested by teachers, science-related books seem to be the "new math." Holt looks at the history of trail-blazing scientists and their often risky endeavors. *Guinea Pig Scientists: Bold Self-Experimenters in Science and Medicine* was written by Leslie

Dendy and Mel Boring. This 2005 volume, addressing the call for more visual stimuli, is also illustrated by C. B. Mordan.

Picture Books Pick-me-up

Publishers' lists of picture books may be shorter these days, but editors say the books make up for it with outstanding quality and innovation and some are predicting an upturn in another year

In the unique quality column, Holt is counting on famous designer Nancy Wolff's *Tallulah in the Kitchen* finding fans among the thousands of people who purchase Wolff's cards, journals, and prints. For Dial, a Penguin Group imprint, an added quality comes in the person of African-American poet Carole Boston Weatherford with her book *Freedom on the Menu,* illustrated by Jerome Lagarrique.

Penguin Group's Whiteman has high hopes for the future. "My instincts tell me that 2006 will see the beginning of another upsurge in picture book sales. I believe that we're at the beginning of another small baby boom right now. But even beyond that, it appears to us that the state budget outlook is much better once we get past 2005, and that has a huge impact on picture book sales, especially in

and **tango** makes **three**

by Justin Richardson and Peter Parnell
illustrated by Henry Cole

Picture Book Sales Stars

Picture book publishers, with best-sellers from last year:

▓ **Candlewick Press:** 2067 Massachusetts Ave., Cambridge, MA 02140. www.candlewick.com. 200 titles last year. Publishes for all ages. *Dr. Ernest Drake's Dragonology: The Complete Book of Dragons,* Ernest Drake et al. *And Here's to You,* David Elliott.

▓ **Child Welfare League of America:** 3rd floor, 440 1st St. NW, Washington, DC 20001. www.cwla.org/pubs. 5 children's books last year. Fiction and nonfiction. *The Kissing Hand,* Audrey Penn.

▓ **Harcourt:** 15 East 26th St., New York, NY 10010. www.harcourtbooks.com. 185 titles last year. All ages, all genres. *How I Became a Pirate,* Melinda Long. *Tails,* Matthew Van Fleet.

▓ **HarperCollins:** 1330 Ave. of the Americas, New York, NY 10019. www.harperchildrens.com. 100 titles last year. Fiction only, for all ages. *Hard to Be Five: Learning How to Work My Control Panel,* Jamie Lee Curtis (Joanna Cotler Books). *The Little Old Lady Who Was Not Afraid of Anything,* Linda Williams (HarperTrophy). *Diary of a Worm,* Doreen Cronin.

▓ **North Atlantic Books:** 1435A Fourth St., Berkeley, CA 94710. www.northatlanticbooks.com. An alternative press with a small number of children's books. *Walter the Farting Dog,* William Kotzwinkle.

▓ **Penguin Putnam:** 345 Hudson St., New York, NY 10014. www.penguinputnam.com. The divisions of Penguin Putnam include Dial, Dutton, Puffin, Viking, and others, annually publishing 100s of books in all genres, for all ages. *The Umbrella,* Jan Brett (Grosset & Dunlap). *Mister Seahorse,* Eric Carle (Philomel).

▓ **Random House:** 1745 Broadway, New York, NY 10019. www.randomhouse.com. Preschool to young adult, in divisions that include Bantam, Crown, Knopf, Wendy Lamb, some of which publish as few as 10 books a year, and some several hundred. *Wild About Books,* Judy Sierra.

▓ **Roaring Brook Press:** 2 Old New Milford Road, Brookfield, CT 06804. Purchased last year by Henry Holt, from the Millbrook Press, which went into bankruptcy. *The Man Who Walked Between the Towers,* Mordicai Gerstein.

▓ **Simon & Schuster:** 1230 Ave. of the Americas, New York, NY 10020. www.simonsayskids. Hundreds of titles last year by imprints such as Atheneum, Margaret K. McElderry, Little Simon, and others. *Duck for President,* Doreen Cronin.

paperback," because of funding for library and school purchases.

At Simon & Schuster Books for Young Readers, Editorial Director David Gale is excited about the new talents hitting the market. First-time children's authors Justin Richardson and Peter Parnell are coming out with *And Tango Makes Three,* illustrated by Henry Cole. "This is a warm and loving picture book based on the true story of two male penguins at the Central Park Zoo who hatched an egg and raised a chick," says Gale. "It reinforces the bonds that create all kinds of families."

Talking about family books, Simon & Schuster is also publishing *Let George Do It!,* written by former pro boxer George Foreman and Fran Manushkin, and illustrated by newcomer Whitney Martin. Gale says it's "a very funny picture book about the complications that ensue when a man named George has five sons named George," as is true in Foreman's real family.

Whiteman is not the only publisher seeing bluer skies for picture books. DK Publishing will be ready for the boom with titles in three new series for babies and preschoolers. Editor Elizabeth Landis Hester says, "All will be clearly marked with age-grading information, as will other series in the new preschool line." The sense of hearing and touch will be appealed to in *Baby Talk* and *Noisy Farm,* two new titles in the birth- to-18-month series, Baby Fun Flaps. In the Sparkly Book series, kids aged 18 months to 3 years will be introduced to Sparkly Ballerina and Sparkly Princess. For readers three to five, Hester singles out the Make Believe series as a sample of all the interaction DK books invite. "Children can pick out sparkly wands, lift flaps to reveal surprises, touch featured textures, and cast a magic spell" with the Princess and Fairy titles.

Four-year-old Red Rock Press has enough faith in the coming market to launch children's imprint Red Pebble Press. Strong in the adult gift-book market, Red Pebble will package some of its titles with craft materials. "Generally speaking, Red Pebble Books is more interested in works that spur children's imaginations than books centering on youngsters with bleak problems," says Creative Director Ilene Barth.

When asked how the company will compete in such a currently tight market, Barth explains, "We also aim to sell Red Pebble Books at nontraditional venues including street fairs and gift shops, some specifically geared to a particular book's content, such as balloon and party-favor shops for *Where Do the Balloons Go?*" This book, by Elena Davis August and illustrated by Anna Jurinich, was the imprint's inaugural release.

Barth adds that a small company lacks deep pockets: "Ergo the challenge is to develop memorable authors and books. There are more miracles in children's books than in adult ones. Harry Potter aside, the true miracle is when a child grows up, becomes a parent, and then

Animals All-Around

Stories about animals have a universal appeal for children. The next year is bringing a flock of picture book titles about animals:

Though Executive Editor Judy O'Malley will be focusing more on new books for older readers at Charlesbridge Publishing, she singles out several interesting picture books on the list. *Picasso and Minou,* by P. I. Maltbie and illustrated by Pau Estrada, is based loosely on a real incident. The painter's clever cat Minou gets Picasso out of his sad Blue period by leading him to a troupe of circus performers. "Pau Estrada's watercolor illustrations, infused with hues from Picasso's Blue and Rose periods, bring alive the people and places of early twentieth-century Paris."

Another animal-driven picture book from Charlesbridge is *Fluffy: Scourge of the Sea,* by Teresa Bateman and illustrated by Michael Chesworth. Fluffy is a pampered poodle set upon by scurvy pirate dogs. "Hilarious art makes this motley crew memorable," says O'Malley.

Charlesbridge also publishes nonfiction picture books. Two new titles are *Amelia to Zora: 26 Women Who Changed the World,* by Cynthia Chin-Lee, and illustrated by Megan Halsey and Sean Addy; and *The Bumblebee Queen,* by April Pulley Sayre and illustrated by Patricia J. Wynne.

Animals also figure in releases from Chronicle Books, says Editor Melissa Manlove, including *Romeow & Drooliet,* by Nina Laden; *Little Pea,* by Amy Krause Rosenthal and illustrated by Jen Corace; *Stanley Mows the Lawn,* by Craig Frazier; and *Little Miss Liberty,* by Chris Robertson.

presents a book she or he once loved to the child."

And all publishers, whether huge or humble, still strive to achieve that miracle.

Jacobs calls the new picture books at Abrams Books "beautiful and fun, instant classics." Look for *Piglet and Mama,* and *Puppies, Puppies, Puppies.* Abrams is also publishing "a kids' edition of a book on Toulouse-Lautrec, tying into a museum exhibition. Also terrific are new Hello Kitty and Babar books, two properties we continue to nurture."

Tilbury House is proud to release *Playing War,* by Kathy Beck-with and illustrated by Lea Lyon. Editor Jennifer Bunting explains, "Playing war—with sticks for guns and pine cones for grenades—is the game of choice for these neighborhood kids until a newcomer, a boy from another country, shares his experience with real war and puts their game in a new light." Bunting adds, "Lyons's bright, fluid style is just right for these sort of edgy books."

At Walker Books, according to Editor Timothy Travaglini, current releases are led by some very well-known names, including Kathleen Krull and *Houdini: World's Greatest*

Mystery Man and Escape King, illustrated by Eric Velasquez. Author Kevin O'Malley and illustrator Patrick O'Brien team up for *Captain Raptor and the Moon Mystery.* Late in the year comes the release of *Earth Mother,* written by Ellen Jackson and illustrated by Leo and Diane Dillon.

License to Sell

Face it, licensed characters and brands have become a permanent and dependable fixture in children's books. Penguin has the Teletubbies; Charlesbridge has the M&Ms; Chronicle has the *Nickelodeon Jr.* characters; HarperCollins has My Little Pony; and Scholastic has licensed characters coming out of its ears—*Clifford*, *Shrek*, and *Star Wars* figures to name a few. Revenues from these licensed book products can account for up to 10 percent of these children's publishers' total sales, according to a Scholastic spokesman.

"Our licensed books are part of an overall balanced approach to publishing," says Yolanda LeRoy, Editorial Director at Charlesbridge. "We publish approximately two licensed books per year out of 30 frontlist titles." The *M&M Subtraction Book* is one new title.

Since 1998, Chronicle has been enjoying a profitable relationship with the Caterpillar company— home of the construction toys boys most covet. The Caterpillar books, contributing 3.5 percent of Chronicle's children's book sales, are nonfiction concept books, with photographs of construction equipment in use. Books featuring Nickelodeon TV characters, added in three years ago, make up about 9.5 percent of sales. The *Nick Jr.* line ranges from concept and activity books to easy readers. The line veers into an older age group, a target area Chronicle wants to grow into.

In fact, while picture book market growth is down the horizon, many publishers are redesigning and releasing, or publishing original easy readers. Random House, Grosset & Dunlap, Harcourt, and Simon & Schuster are all revamping their lines. New easy reading products are coming from Orca Young Readers, HarperCollins, Pleasant Company. Orca plans to target six-to eight-year-olds with early chapter books, under the imprint of Orca Echoes. Harper is debuting a line of photographic nonfiction readers in conjunction with the Wildlife Conservation Society. Only a year old, Pleasant Company's Hopscotch Hill School imprint for girls four to six published five titles, and has more on the way.

In 2005 and beyond, children's book publishers—and authors, illustrators as well—must seize opportunities in every type of media to create and sell products. Print is far from dead. On the contrary, print is enjoying new incarnations. And readers are expecting writers to deliver.

Profile

Bloomsbury Welcomes Cecka

By Judy Bradbury

When an editor moves to a new house, it's always news. Why the move? What's her new title? How have her needs changed with the move? Who will follow her? Is she accepting submissions? What should we know about her new home?

Big news last year was the move of longtime Viking Children's Books Editor Melanie Cecka to Bloomsbury Children's Books to take on the position of Executive Editor. Prior to her decade at Viking, Cecka worked at Knopf Books for Young Readers and Villard Books, an adult imprint at Random House.

In retrospect, Cecka notes, "I've always loved books and writing. I was a writing major in college and I minored in art history, but while I technically had the building blocks for a career in children's publishing, I had my heart set on adult fiction. My first job out of college was working with a commercial adult publisher, and although it was glamorous and exciting (we did lots of celebrity autobiographies), I found I didn't really connect with the books themselves."

Of that first experience in publishing, Cecka says, "It wasn't until I edited a series of illustrated gift books that I figured out there was another—and very different—path available to me. Though meant for adults, we hired a children's illustrator to do the interiors, and I found myself so wrapped up in the process of bringing text and art together that I knew my days in adult trade were numbered. I quickly transferred into the children's division and submerged myself in picture books and fiction, where it seemed that everything I loved about books came together in a way that was meant to endure and make a difference."

In portraying Bloomsbury, Cecka says, "They are a relative newcomer to the American children's book market. Bloomsbury opened offices in the states just three years ago, but has fairly significant roots in Britain as the original publishers

The Shape of Cecka's Tastes

"I can't boast an extensive reading list from childhood," says Bloomsbury Children's Books Executive Editor Melanie Cecka. "I went from classic picture books (*Madeline, Corduroy, Harry the Dirty Dog, The Little House*) to young favorites from my mother's childhood (*The Boxcar Children; Betsy, Tacy, and Tib; The Girl of the Limberlost*). I moved on to middle-grade books by more contemporary authors of the time: *Bridge to Terabithia, The Witch of Blackbird Pond,* and *Island of the Blue Dolphins*. Young adult literature wasn't nearly the rich territory it has since become, so aside from a couple of titles, I moved from middle-grade into adult pretty early on."

Advice to Writers

"Be sure to do your research, which means going out to bookstores and libraries and reading the best and newest in children's books. Too many of the manuscripts we receive are like something else out there. As the marketplace gets more and more competitive, having a creative edge to your voice or story becomes more important than ever before."

Cecka advises writers to "find a good writers' group and work with them to get your stories in the best possible shape. You've got to write a lot, and these days you've got to steel yourself for a lot of rejection. All the more reason to have people you trust share the ups and downs with you. It's no fun to be a writer in a vacuum."

of J. K. Rowling (the Harry Potter books are licensed to Scholastic in the U.S.). Bloomsbury is a small independent publisher—just 11 staff members—and because we work very closely with our U.K. colleagues as well as with our German office, Berlin Verlag, you'll see a lot of British and European authors on our list. It's a true transatlantic operation."

Cecka is quick to point out, however, "This doesn't mean we're looking for *British* books. In fact, we are adding more and more books by U.S.-based authors and illustrators all the time—so much

so that our staff has nearly doubled in the last two months to keep up with our expanding list. We publish approximately 60 original trade books a year, plus some paperback reprints, ranging from board books to young adult fiction. Our website (www.bloomsburyusa.com) is updated regularly and offers a good look at recent titles, authors, and illustrators."

Magic Unfolding

In her 10 years at Viking, Cecka had the opportunity to work with some of the best in the field of children's books. "Every author and illustrator I've worked with has in some way shaped my understanding and appreciation for children's literature," notes Cecka. Of the books she has worked on, Cecka claims *Keeper of the Doves,* by Betsy Byars, as a personal favorite. "It's spare and lovely and elegant, and Betsy is a class act." *Strange Mr. Satie,* by M. T. Anderson with illustrations by Petra Mathers, is another special book. "It's about the French composer Eric Satie, who's not necessarily a household name among the picture book set. However, Tobin [Anderson] knew precisely how to make a figure like Satie come alive for readers, and it was a dream come true to work with Petra Mathers. I feel like I just sat back and watched the magic unfold with that book," recalls Cecka.

"But it was probably my first two bosses who influenced my tastes and approach to editing the most," says Cecka. "Anne Schwartz, who I worked with at Knopf, is arguably the best picture book editor in the industry. I'm always jealous of her books. I'll go into a bookstore and see some gorgeous title, and half the time it's got her name on it. Regina Hayes, the publisher at Viking, is a graceful and succinct editor. She somehow knows how to get straight to the heart of a problem in a novel and ask just the right questions to set the author on his way. She also has an instinct for publishing's big picture that I really admire." Cecka believes Hayes "understands the balance between a book that is loved by kids, cherished by librarians, and sells well with booksellers—something every editor aspires to, but only a few know how to do well."

Cecka is equally excited and optimistic about the lasting value of her current projects. "I'm working on a big and varied list that includes a young adult novel set in a sleepy Louisiana town, a sassy middle-grade mystery, a very young, nearly wordless picture book about a newborn chick, and a picture book about Marie Antoinette and her pug."

Open for submissions, Cecka is looking for "contemporary fiction and engaging, well-researched historical fiction." Cecka warns readers that although "Bloomsbury publishes some extraordinary fantasy, it's not something I'm actively looking for."

On the other hand, she says, "Picture books with very strong, narrative hooks and solid characters" are of interest to her. "Although everyone in the industry seems to

25

be facing the same problems when it comes to picture books," Cecka makes the point that "it's important to remember that children's literature is more sensitive to demographic changes than almost any other type of literature. Picture books are in a down cycle now because kids aged 10 and up make for the largest percentage of young readers. But that's not to say editors are just going to stop publishing picture books outright. We will always want new talents, new stories, new illustrators. I like to think the bar has been raised that much higher on the quality of the picture books that are coming out."

by M. T. Anderson
Illustrated by Petra Mathers

Like most editors these days, Cecka is looking for novels, "particularly middle-grade and young adult." She feels they "will continue to be a major growth area."

Unique Editorial Paths

Clearly, Cecka loves all of it, from picture books to teen novels. "There's nothing like working in a creative environment. The unique perspective that art and editorial teams bring to the life of a book never ceases to fascinate me. I love watching a book go from inception to first review, and knowing that no one story will ever be the same as

any other. The editorial path of every book is unique, so the novelty of what I do never wears thin."

The least favorite aspect of her work, Cecka notes, is "the inevitable rejection letters you have to write. It's never easy to turn down a story, no matter how many times you've done it." Also difficult, she says, "There's never enough time to read, and the reading material never stops coming in. Whether it's a new manuscript, a review, or magazine, or a book published by a competitive house, it's next to impossible to stay on top of it all. As much as you want to read, read, read [submissions] and find something terrific, it's often a daunting, Sisyphean process." Even so, Cecka says, "I can't imagine not being involved with writing or books."

Look around her office and you'll get a sense that Cecka's in the game for the long run. Beside a schedule of yoga classes, photos of family and friends, and an occasional fortune from a cookie, you'll find sketches and postcards from illustrators with whom Cecka has worked or whose work she admires. An orchid on the windowsill is from an author Cecka has edited. "She sent it to me on my first day on the job here. I know orchids are delicate, and I warned her from the beginning that I would probably kill it, but somehow it's still alive."

Bloomsbury Submissions

Bloomsbury currently accepts unsolicited manuscripts. Says Cecka, "We welcome picture book manuscripts and queries for longer works, whether fiction or nonfiction. We publish picture books, chapter books, easy readers, middle-grade and YA novels, science fiction, fantasy, and some nonfiction. With queries, please include a synopsis of the book and the first 10 pages or the first chapter or so."

Send an appropriate SASE. Cecka is emphatic. "We will not return submissions without one!" She also asks writers, "Please make sure that everything (including the SASE) is stapled, paper-clipped, or rubber-banded together." Allow up to 20 weeks for a reply. The address is: Bloomsbury Children's Books, 175 Fifth Avenue, Suite 712, New York, NY 10010. Check the website for current publications: www.bloomsburyusa.com.

Profiles

Up & Comers: Career Paths of 3 Writers on the Rise

By Judy Bradbury

Jon Scieszka in his address to participants at the annual Society of Children's Book Writers and Illustrators' (SCBWI) annual conference in Los Angeles noted that there are no rules to getting published. Then he went on to list all the common faux pas he committed on his path to publication—and how they led to his enviable success. At the same conference, Gordon Korman related how a manuscript he wrote as a teen was driven by a forklift to the right editor's desk at just the right time.

Serendipity? Yes, there's no denying that there's a chunk of that at play when a writer strives for published author status. But, as politicians and pundits love to say, make no mistake. There's also the enduring, no-nonsense, unglamorous, consistent hard work that absolutely must be at the core of our dream. And there's an elusive quality. Some call it voice. Whatever its label, it takes courage coupled with the confidence of a honed craft to celebrate your uniqueness and allow it to be reflected in your work.

Here, three rising stars describe how their own combination of spit and polish allowed them to shine, and how they work tirelessly at their craft to continue to produce work they are proud of and that their readers and editors seek out. Luck? Sure, there's that. But there's more, much more than that. Plugging away, having guts, being a terrific collaborator, a good listener, understanding economy of language, having a sense of humor, being honest, tough, and tenacious. Not the résumé of the fainthearted. But you knew that, and still you love the pen. So read these histories, take heart, and write until you shine.

▪ Leslie Connor Chose a Pen

"They've been so kind!" Leslie Connor exclaims. Her reaction was a reflection on the rave reviews she received since Houghton Mifflin released her first picture book, *Miss*

Bridie Chose a Shovel, illustrated by Caldecott winner Mary Azarian.

These days, although Connor hopes one day to illustrate her own books, she is glad she chose a pen over a paintbrush when she responded to Miss Bridie's call. Connor says the line that eventually became the title kept coming to her. She now thinks of Bridie, the Irish nickname for Bridget, "almost as a term of endearment and respect."

Connor's success with *Miss Bridie Chose a Shovel* did not happen overnight. "I had the story around for a while," she recalls. "I didn't shop it much." Until, that is, she attended the *Highlights* Writers Workshop held in Chautauqua, New York, where an editor from a well-known house smiled when he read the manuscript and went on to ask "interesting questions" about the main character. Connor considered those questions and went to work revising her story. She gave Miss Bridie "some troubles" because, she realized, "a character needs problems." Connor went on to submit the revamped version to Connecticut's Tassy Walden Award for New Voices in Children's Literature.

She won that contest—in more ways than one. In the corps of judges was agent Jennie Dunham, who saw promise in the story. "I heard Leslie read it as the first-place picture book text winner," recalls Dunham. "I was immediately drawn to the strong voice." Dunham approached Connor, suggesting she represent the author. Three weeks after they signed a contract, Connor was signing another one with Houghton Mifflin.

"I offered to represent Leslie, and then I told her I was going to submit the manuscript to one editor, Ann Rider, at Houghton Mifflin," recalls Dunham. "Three weeks later I got a call from Ann saying how much she liked it. She asked if Leslie would be open to suggestions for revising it, and I said that I felt pretty sure she would. Ann then said she'd like to make an offer with the understanding that the two of them would work on the text to make it shine." Dunham was confident Connor would agree.

"Coincidentally, I had scheduled a visit with Leslie's critique group not a week later, so I decided to wait and give her the news in person. I met Leslie and another client for dinner. Before we started eating, I said I wanted to talk about Miss Bridie. I outlined the suggestions Ann had given me to convey to Leslie, who said she agreed with them all and that she saw how they'd help strengthen the story. Then I said, 'I have to tell you that Ann has made an offer.' Leslie was thrilled, of course. We opened a bottle of champagne to celebrate."

Ever humble, Connor feels indebted to her agent. She is convinced that "Jennie knew just who to give it to." Of herself, Connor says, "I'm shy. I find conferences overwhelming. I look at all those success stories and think, 'This is impossible for me,' but I just keep plugging away, reminding myself that this is my work."

Trust Story Power

In many ways, Connor's path to publication is a perfect example of writing what you know and love. The idea for her picture book came from the experience of building her home into a hillside in Connecticut 17 years ago.

She also has a deep interest in historical fiction: "early pioneers, strong people, women especially, who were the backbone of the farm and heroic in hard times." Yet she has other stories to tell as well. Her contemporary young adult novel for ages 13 and up, tentatively entitled *Dead at Town Line,* is due to be released by Dial Books. Connor says, "It's a sad, spooky murder story complete with the ghost of a dead girl who wants to be found and wants the crime solved."

Dial Senior Editor Cecile Goyette says of this project, "From the onset, the pages showed me an author who trusted the power of her story and style of telling and didn't feel the need to clutter it up. In addition to demonstrating talent,

there was an assurance in her writing. During revision, Leslie proved herself to be open, flexible, and receptive without sacrificing any of her own strength and convictions. We didn't always agree, but that isn't at all necessary. It's far more important that we're both pretty good listeners and that the result is a fruitful dynamic. Leslie has guts and is a terrific collaborator."

At Houghton Mifflin, Rider agrees. She says *Miss Bridie Chose a Shovel* "was perhaps unusual in that it left me very little to do as an editor. We worked a bit on adding conflict so there would be a point where Miss Bridie and her shovel would not be so very strong and useful and independent." Connor credits the editor: "There was no fire in my original text. Ann pulled it out of me."

But the manuscript's strengths were also apparent, says Rider. "Leslie's lovely spare writing was immediately remarkable to me, but I also liked the feeling in the manuscript of making choices and facing change. I believe children know that feeling of possibly being ill-equipped to face the world—of perhaps having brought the wrong thing, made the wrong choice, and having done so, how can they face the world? I also loved the strength and independence of this woman, so well represented by the shovel. I believe the story works on several different levels."

In retrospect, Rider says, "everything about this book—text and art —seemed to flow along on its own correct course. Mary Azarian [who

How Connor Caught the Eye

Jennie Dunham, agent:
"In *Miss Bridie Chose a Shovel*, Leslie Connor captures one woman's hopes and struggles as she immigrates to America to start a new life. I like that the shovel is an unusual item to choose as a sentimental connection to her old life, and yet it's the perfect item to help Miss Bridie at every stage during her life. It's practical, and to me it hearkens back to the pioneer heartiness of early settlers. The clincher is that the voice is perfect for the strong character and her story of triumph through adversity."

Ann Rider, Editor, Houghton Mifflin:
"Connor's images and writing are very accomplished, but fine writing isn't enough for her: She *must* try to communicate something important to her. And she certainly has."

Cecile Goyette, Senior Editor, Dial Books:
Connor caught this editor's attention with "that voice, a relatable plainspoken grace that talked about circumstances both extreme and ordinary in a way that invited you in and didn't force the inherent drama."

Mary Azarian, illustrator:
"My editor sent me the manuscript of *Miss Bridie* to consider and I liked it immediately. I liked the very spare text, which allowed me to consider all of the things inferred but not stated about her. The fact that no one else is ever named in the text was striking. After completing the illustrations, she had become a real person to me. "

illustrated the book] seemed the obvious choice to me from the very beginning, and all of her images were just right for the story. Not many books come together so easily. It's a joy to watch them when they do."

Making Choices, Facing Change

Initially, Connor thought of herself as an illustrator. "Art's my thing," she maintains. She first joined the SCBWI to learn more about illustrating for children. When she found she was having difficulty illustrating a 32-page book, she decided it was time to take a writing course. She enrolled in an adult education class and found that "telling stories to kids of all ages" seemed to happen "automatically." She never looked back.

"Writing is so fulfilling," says Connor, "and the surprises when they come are like those brown paper-wrapped gifts from Grandma we discover in the mail. I love writing stories, and it's great to know that others care what I have to say."

As an author, artist, wife, and mother, Connor's writing workday involves a simple but satisfying routine that suits her. She is "on the trail" with her border collie mix pup every morning as soon as her three children board the bus. "The dog and I go, and often I carry a pencil and an index card in my pocket." Once she returns, she sits down and "goes through a bucket of tea" putting pen or pencil to paper.

Connor admits to not being one to outline or plan. "I believe story structure is one of my weak points. I keep learning as I go along." And she sketches, drawing and writing side by side in notebooks without lines. From these jottings she turns to the computer. "I love chasing the story down the page," she reflects. "I love to see it blossom and grow." And she loves being able to delete paragraphs. "If it's terrible, I push a button, and it's as if it was never there!"

Connor carts her laptop computer to the library or a coffee shop or the home of a member of a critique group with whom she meets twice a month. "They have everything to do with where I am today," says Connor of her writing mates. "I have complete trust in them." The critique group has a rule about not refuting each other's opinions. Connor shares a similar insight with aspiring writers about the process a manuscript will go through once a publisher accepts it. "Be open-minded," she advises. "The publishers will change your book. You can no longer think of it as *my* project. Once it's accepted, it's *our* project." In all cases so far, however, Connor believes that the changes she has made to manuscripts as a result of editorial input have resulted in "a more interesting read." She believes Miss Bridie "came to life" in the rewrites.

"Many people, especially non-writers, think that writing a picture book is easy. After all, it's short, right? It is, but a picture book is a very specific format. It's hard to tell a story with humor and heart using so few words. It has to capture the short attention spans of readers between three and seven years old. The description must be conveyed through action, and the story still needs to rise in tension to a climax that resolves in a satisfying way. In *Miss Bridie Chose a Shovel*, Leslie does all of this flawlessly," says Dunham.

In Connor, Dunham finds qualities much sought after. "Leslie has a knack for hearing a character's voice and writing a story that matches that voice perfectly. She works hard by rolling up her sleeves and revising when she needs to. She listens to constructive comments from her critique group and her editor. She's got a sense of humor too."

And Connor has the quality of gratitude as well, in addition to her gifts and hard work: "I've been understood, and for that I feel very, very lucky."

■ Sara Pennypacker: True to Voice & Self

A sign above Sara Pennypacker's desk reads, "Trust your voice." That she does faithfully, as she becomes Stuart with his magic cape, Pierre in love, or a six year old living in

Maoist China. "I have the best job in the world," gushes Pennypacker. "I am so lucky. I get to live different lives and do research on things that interest me," and refers to the novel she is currently developing that is set in Occupied Holland during World War II.

Pennypacker admits to working in her pajamas and writing when she wants to write. "I am so spoiled," she believes, "no one would hire me for any other type of job!" That's just fine with her agent, Steven Malk, who signed on with Pennypacker because of her "distinct voice, great sense of character, wit, and sensitivity." While Pennypacker may feel indulged, Malk says, "Sara works harder than almost any author I know."

Writing for children was not Pennypacker's first job. An artist for most of her life, she became fascinated with children's books and "what they had come to" when she was homeschooling her children in the early 1990s. She wrote *Dumbstruck*, a novel published in 1994 by Holiday House. Her current early chapter books have received wide acclaim among teachers, parents, and young readers alike. *Stuart's Cape* and its sequel, *Stuart Goes to School,* are delightful and fresh. They center on a second grader with a magical cape made from 100 men's ties. Two more installments to the series are in the works; *Principal Stuart* is scheduled for release by Orchard Books/Scholastic.

Says Malk, "There's a lot of stuff out there for this age range, but Sara managed to create a completely unique, endearing, and funny character who's going through things that any kid can relate to."

These books of fewer than 100 pages are just right for newly independent readers. Illustrated in a comic style by the late Martin Matje, they are humorous, fantastical, and a perfect match for the interests and angst of many seven to nine year olds. As a worrywart, Stuart fears his new school, imagines (and then is) trapped in the boys' lavatory, and wrings his hands over myriad mishaps. Typical kid, typical issues. He also, however, floats above the house when he eats angel food cake and is rescued only when Auntie has the wherewithal to feed him (heavy) pound cake. He makes a bed from leftover toast and his cat drives a dump truck. "Stuart is droll," says Pennypacker, "and one rule every day lightens up for him. It's a different thing every day, but it's always one thing," and that's something the reader can count on—and look forward to.

Stuart came to be through a short story contest that a friend urged Pennypacker to enter. Limited to 500 words, it was the original story of what was eventually Stuart's second day with his cape. The cape itself grew out of a nephew's complaining that he was bored and would like his Aunt Sara to make him a cape. Pennypacker did not win that contest, but she did make the cape, and she went on to write more about this zany worrywart.

Later, Pennypacker submitted her manuscript for critique at a New England SCBWI retreat. Enter Amy Griffin, who was Senior Editor at Orchard Books: "Sitting on my bed in a pile of manuscripts, Sara's immediately struck me because of its quirky sense of humor and economy of language. And of course the element of surprise: What was going to happen to this kid next?!" Griffin loved the story and made an offer.

Friends, a Team

"If I had one piece of advice to give to writers, it would be to attend SCBWI conferences and pay the $50 or $60 to get a polished manuscript critiqued," advises Pennypacker. "What better way do we have to meet and get to know an editor? You have an opportunity for one-on-one for 20 to 30 minutes with a real, live editor!" exclaims

---

A Funny Thing Happened on the Way to a Book

Editor Amy Griffin recalls of author Sara Pennypacker and her Stuart books, "When [the late] Martin Matje, the French-speaking artist who illustrated the Stuart books, read Sara's line, 'What if there were man-eating spiders in his new bedroom closet?' he interpreted it as 'a man who eats spiders' rather than as the huge, hairy, man-eating spiders Sara (and Stuart and I) were imagining. But when we saw that illustration, we thought, 'We must find a way to make it work!' And that wasn't hard at all. Sara just added a line, 'Or, a man eating spiders' and that was all it took! That image was mentioned in one or two of the reviews, so I'm happy we decided to work it into the story rather than having Martin illustrate those man-eating spiders we'd been expecting."

Pennypacker. She and Griffin began as editor and author, and have become great friends as well.

And how to get an agent? "Once I had the contract, I wanted the best, so I started at the top," explains Pennypacker. She contacted Malk and asked him to represent her in the negotiations with Orchard Books for *Stuart's Cape*. He accepted, and they've been a team ever since. "I'm always interested in a great voice, whether it's funny, sad, angsty, or otherwise," says Malk, "and Sara has a strong voice that's very fresh."

Although the search for an agent seemed to be effortless for Pennypacker, she had polished her work and caught the interest of an editor at a well-known and highly respected house before approaching Malk. Pennypacker believes it's tougher and tougher for an author to get work looked at without an agent. "Once your work is ready, exhaust yourself to get an agent," urges Pennypacker. "Let your agent deal with the rest of the business while you deal with the writing."

Pennypacker is usually doing just that, working hard on one of her many current projects. Although she used to write in longhand "using an onyx Uniball Roller and only that pen," she now relies on her computer. She begins the morning with a daily walk around scenic Chatham, on the elbow of Cape Cod, using the time to think through plot issues. Back at home, she sits down at the computer and reads what she wrote the day before to help herself "get into the voice." She is happy to report that she spends her days "being eight years old and worried or six years old in Maoist China, and" says Pennypacker, "like Stephen King, I don't like a day when I'm not writing."

Pennypacker claims to be a "slow writer," but she had to work quickly on a recent project. Dream-Works wanted a storybook to go along with the film *Shark Tale*.

Scholastic got the job to produce it and they asked Pennypacker to do the adaptation, which, she reveals, "really amounted to choosing bits of dialogue from the screenplay and then weaving narrative around them." Pennypacker recalls, "The challenge was to tell the story in an abbreviated form without actually changing dialogue—just cutting it." *Shark Tale: The Movie Storybook* was published by Scholastic in conjunction with the movie last fall.

"I was given visuals of the characters and told who would be doing the voices, but I never saw cuts from the movie. I had to force myself to write quickly to meet their deadline and the strict word limit, which made me pay attention to economy of words—good lessons for me."

Book Bravery

Overall, Pennypacker is comfortable with her writing process. A Stuart book takes "eight months to write and a year to complete, considering editorial involvement."

Malk notes, "Although the Stuart books are relatively short, they take her a long time to complete. There's so much work and emotion packed into those pages, which is ultimately what makes them so wonderful and why they stand out from other books."

In that time when Pennypacker is crafting her stories, her critique groups offer advice and feedback. She belongs to two "main" groups. One is composed of seven to eight children's writers who keep an eye on the market, children's interests, and the like. The other group is composed of a handful of writers who publish in a wide range of genres. This latter group keeps her quality up, Pennypacker says. She believes "there's no difference between adult and children's writing in terms of quality." The writing group, she says, trusts her choices of children's "subject matter, but they hold my writing to the highest standard. There are no cheap sentences."

Pennypacker offers this advice to aspiring writers: "Don't work at writing what you think children should hear. Just fly. Trust your instincts. Tell the truth about human beings because they are wonderful. Sweetness is better if it's not saccharine. Like people, books have toughness, bravery. Most new writers aren't courageous enough. Go get braver. Go out on a limb."

Griffin believes Pennypacker does this exceptionally well. "Sara is someone who listens very carefully to every child she meets. She is determined that her stories have real kid appeal, yet they are sophisticated enough to appeal to parents too. Her books work on many levels." In retrospect, Pennypacker believes the one thing she's done that's made a difference is to trust herself. "That's what makes something successful. Don't second-guess. Trust your voice."

▪ Introducing … Lucky
Eddie de Oliveira

Ask an editor, "What's hot?" and the answer, if he's not holding a double espresso, most likely will be, "YA." Or "teen," as Scholastic/ PUSH Editor David Levithan prefers to call the genre. From dead in its tracks in the 1990s to a full-blown craze causing new imprints to pop up almost monthly, teen lit is *it*.

And it's lit like we've never seen before. Or have we? The details are different, but the content is the same. It's all about finding a place, finding heart, figuring it out. From Robert Cormier's *The Chocolate War* to Laurie Halse Anderson's *Speak* and Virginia Euwer Wolff's *True Believer,* teen literature is concerned with that fearful and frantic leap into adulthood, and what happens in midair.

Leading the pack in establishing new imprints for teen books was Scholastic. PUSH, its three-year-old imprint, features first-time authors of teen material. PUSH books, says the website, "tell it like it really is. No preaching. No false endings. No stereotypes or contrivance. Just an honest dose of reality. These books are funny, observant, heartbreaking, and heartstopping. Just like life." (www.thisispush.com)

Founding Editor and Director of the imprint, and an author himself, Levithan believes, "Connecting the right book at the right time in a person's life is an amazing thing." He thinks *Lucky*, a first novel by Eddie de Oliveira about self-discovery, sexual identity, and friendship, may be one of those books. From his first look at de Oliveira's work, Levithan was struck by his "humor and his honesty. And certainly his keen eye for social detail."

Fringe

Lucky started out as a one-act play. Of how the play came to be a teen novel, de Oliveira says, "I wrote and directed *Lucky* at the Edinburgh Festival Fringe, and it received a fair bit of media coverage. Levithan read about the play in an American magazine [*The Advocate*]. A few months later, I think he Googled me, or used some highly secretive espionage tactics to track me down. He suggested I adapt *Lucky* into a YA novel."

Levithan recalls, "I do love the way we met. An article leads to a website that leads to an email address that leads to a random email from an editor to a playwright who'd never thought of writing a novel. These things couldn't have happened—at least not so quickly—10 years ago. Luckily, I had already planned a trip to London when our correspondence started, so we got

to meet in person before we really started to work on the novel. We went to see a Noel Coward revival starring a big British TV star who I'd never heard of. Eddie had to explain her significance to me."

De Oliveira admits, "I had never considered writing a book before," but he decided to give it a try. "All my material focuses on young people. I am young and I'm writing about what's going on around me. I could try my hand at a piece about middle-aged butchers and bakers, but I'm not sure it'd ring very true," he quips.

Inevitable Outsider

De Oliveira was born in London in 1979 "to an Argentinean mother of Italian stock and a Brazilian father with ancestors from Scotland." This "aristocratic footballing ethnicity," says *Lucky*'s back cover notes, "has given him a combined total of 10 World Cup wins to celebrate (none of them Scottish)." He studied English Literature at University College, London. "Since then I have worked as a teacher, a script reader at a film production company, a DJ, an actor, and a *Yellow Pages* delivery boy (among other things)," says the 25 year old. Of his latest career, however, he admits that one of the best things about it is "being able to say to people, 'I'm a writer.'"

He recalls, "I have always been into writing and acting; as a kid I wrote a few little plays I performed with school friends. I edited a satirical magazine at school. Then when I was 18 I co-wrote a play for the

Edinburgh Festival Fringe, which is a big international arts festival held every year in Scotland. The biggest, in fact. That went well, and I followed it up with three other plays I wrote and directed between 1999 and 2001. The easiest way to get my plays produced was to direct them myself. I was lucky enough to find brilliant actors, many of whom helped me develop the scripts. Since my last play three years ago, I've written and directed a short film and been published for the first time." Not bad for this self-described "left-handed, color-blind kid with weird hair."

De Oliveira claims he follows that "very simple advice" to write what you know. "But what you know isn't necessarily limited to what you have experienced." He believes that "everything I've ever done has played its part" in his writings, from "the tiniest experiences" to "the momentous ones." As examples, he lists "all the old movies I watched as a very young boy, particularly the Marx Brothers and Inspector Clouseau; traveling; bad television; cookery and food," and of course that hair. But perhaps most of all, he jokes, is "being born. Closely followed by the Mexico '86 Soccer World Cup."

When asked to name one person who has most influenced his career, de Oliveira does not hesitate. "I can go one better and name two—my mum and my dad." The son of parents who left their home countries, de Oliveira feels, "This inevitably makes you something of an outsider, viewing the country you were born and raised in with different eyes."

Flesh & Vessels

That perspective is at work as de Oliveira writes late into the night. "I've never been a morning writer. I plan out chapters and most characters in advance, but never the dialogue or the minutiae. That tends to just come as I write. I'll always let myself go off on tangents—it's better to have too much than too little. So I give myself a framework—a skeleton, if you will—around which I add the flesh and vessels. Sometimes the vessels will flow, sometimes they'll spurt. It's the editor who helps me work out which are flowing and which are spurting. It's important for me not to feel restricted by my own plans; the scenes and chapters I map out are more of a guide dog than a husky," explains de Oliveira.

"I tend to set aside a couple of weeks, or a couple of days, to work really hard, rather than do it in drips and drabs as the months go by. This method seems to work for me. Sure, I'll be thinking about the piece all the time, and making notes on train tickets or discarded hamburger containers. But the proper writing is done in concentrated chunks." He recalls, "I wrote a whole first draft of *Lucky* before the green light was given and we got to work."

Of his latest project, teen novel *Johnny Hazzard*, de Oliveira says, "the idea was formulated in August

What's Next for de Oliveira?

Johnny Hazzard is due to be released by PUSH/Scholastic later this year. Author Eddie de Oliveira says it is about "a 15-year-old skateboard aficionado from Austin, Texas, who spends his summers in London visiting his divorced dad. This particular summer he falls in love for the first time. There is, inevitably, a little twist or two. It's a story about what it's like being an American—a Texan even—in Europe in these strange times. It demonstrates that anti-Americanism is now the only acceptable bigotry." He goes on to say that in the book, "there is also a comic book—holiday to Belgium, Brazilian corny love music, cocktails, Beastie Boys—thing going on."

2003, when I also wrote a plot synopsis. I outlined the chapter content in September. I finally began writing it solidly for two weeks in January 2004, then went off to do some research in Texas in February."

It was in the writing of the second book that, de Oliveira says, he discovered the idea of research. "This involved a trip to Austin, a trip to Belgium, various interviews with various people, and a meal at a Spanish restaurant with wonderful flamenco dancers." He hesitates. "Okay, so it's not proper work, but

taking endless notes does dim the enjoyment slightly (and the costs add up). It was an unconscious decision to write a novel that required so much research," notes de Oliveira, "but I'm very happy it worked out that way. I'm discovering new things and the ideas come from what I'm learning. I hope the new book will, as a result, be richer."

He was back at the desk in March when he "wrote for another two weeks. I added bits and pieces and did another solid few weeks at the end of August, start of September. When my drafts go to my editor, he works with me on improving what I've done and suggesting new bits to add."

The theme of luck is strong editorial for de Oliveira. "I've been lucky with my editor, in as much as we agree on almost everything. It can sometimes be hard being so far away (me in England, he in New York). But when I received the first set of notes on *Johnny Hazzard,* it all made perfect sense."

In turn, Levithan says, "I love how truthful his writing is and how funny some of it is. Usually writers tackle subjects like sexuality with very straight faces. Eddie realizes there is as much humor as gravitas for teens when they talk about relationships and sex, and that really comes through in his writing." De Oliveira adds, "I think my sense of humor shoots through both books. Sarcasm and irony are probably evident in both. They both contain Beastie Boys, too, as well they might."

No Pussyfooting

While he doesn't feel qualified to comment on the state of the teen book publishing market, de Oliveira does say, "I think the U.S. has a more developed YA market than the U.K., so it seems to be a good time [to be writing in this genre] in terms of having people interested in buying what you write." He advises aspiring writers of teen fiction, "If you're older, think back to when you were 13, and 15, and 17, and 18, and try to recapture something of the joy/misery/loneliness/hope/confusion/paranoia/excitement of that time. Perhaps," he adds, "you're 45 and still feeling all those things, which probably sucks, but could be very useful for your writing!"

Serious, he adds, "Write honestly. It's no good pussyfooting around the more explicit elements and pretending teens are something that they're not.

"Think of people you know and knew, and mix up elements of them with elements of you. Don't be afraid of offending." Finally, de Oliveira cautions writers, "Do *not* be inspired by characters from *Dawson's Creek* or *The O.C.* Be inspired by characters from the café, the football ground, the bus, or, if you must, the mall." Once the book is written, de Oliveira believes you must "keep going. Never take no for an answer. Rejections will come thick and fast, but they ought to make you more determined to succeed. Develop a very thick skin and take any critic's review—good or bad—with a pinch of salt." And, of course, as new as he is to the life of a published writer, he knows, "Self-publicizing is a good idea."

Magazine Publishing

Changing, Surviving, Growing

By Mark Haverstock

"It is not necessary to change. Survival is not mandatory," said renowned statistician and a management guru, W. Edward Deming. As 2005 progresses, the only constant is change and the magazine industry is more than surviving. It is adapting and perhaps even revitalizing. The economy has been making a slow and mostly steady rebound, with consumers and business people starting to spend again. The educational market appears to be on an upswing. Launches and retargetings of publications seem to show a sound awareness of reader needs and tastes.

Trend Summary

In the magazine industry, advertising money is trickling in, reversing a three-year trend of decreased spending. In June of last year, the number of advertising pages increased more than 3 percent, showing an 8.4 percent year-to-date increase over the preceding year, according to the Magazine Publishers of America (MPA). "A combination of growing consumer and advertiser confidence continues to play a key role in magazine advertising's improvement," says Ellen Oppenheim, MPA Executive Vice President and Chief Marketing Officer. The number of consumer magazine titles also continues to rise.

Charlene Gaynor, Executive Director of the Association of Educational Publishers (EdPress), observes that in the home or lifestyle market, as in past years, more spin-offs from established adult magazines are reaching down to the children's and teen markets. She cites *ELLEgirl* and the new *Cargo*, a kind of *Consumer Reports* on gadgets and men's fashion that appeals to teens and twentysomethings. "Stepping down one level from your target age group is one trend I see. This is something that's also been going on for a while in the school market," as with *Time For Kids* and *Sports Illustrated For Kids,* and is now extending to other markets.

"Another trend is leveraging your brand in the children's and teen markets—movie, television, and character tie-ins, for example," explains Gaynor. "However, creating a new brand in this market is a more daring undertaking for a magazine start-up."

Optimistic news appears in the market in general, although Gaynor characterizes the current children's and teen market as still somewhat cautious. "I can only think of a handful of start-ups in the children's market last year," says Gaynor. "You can't take on a magazine blithely, and publishers need to understand it's a long haul to create a successful publication."

But start-ups do continue even as established magazines for adults and children are working hard to continue their strength and some to carve new slants—including *Twist, Sweet 16,* and *Teen.* New publications range from *Justine* for teen girls to *Tessy & Tab* for preschoolers, from Canada's *Shameless* (again for teen girls) to the Christian music magazine *Young Believers in Christ.* Despite boys' reputation for reading less than girls, the list of the years' launches directed primarily to guys is longer this year: *Cargo, Skateboard Mag, Snowboard Journal, Golf Punk, American Adrenaline, Hype, Refuel.*

Essential to creating a successful publication, new or old—or to writing for one—is to be true to your target audience and serve their wants and needs.

Models of Success

For models of success, one can look to the "old-timers" such as *Boys' Life* and *Highlights for Children,* magazines that have been in the children's market for more than 50 years and still boast circulations in the millions. "Producing quality editorial that is engaging to your audience: That is the essential skill," says Gaynor. "Folks who know how to do it know how to do it well. They stay in touch with their readers and the times, and know how kids change as well as how they stay the same. I think that's a testimonial to good, basic editorial judgment, and magazines such as *Boys' Life* and *Highlights* truly understand the editorial process."

Keeping a fresh perspective is important. "You have to learn to challenge one another, you have to listen to your readers, and you have to remind yourself that you can do better," says Kent Brown, Jr., Editor in Chief of *Highlights.* "Our Editor, Christine French Clark, is constantly looking at ways to improve the magazine. One of the pitfalls of having a successful magazine with a long history is that you can get complacent and don't try to improve it or add new features."

Paula Morrow, Editor of *Babybug* and *Ladybug*, says the Cricket Magazine Group editors review their magazines monthly and annually. "We're always looking for new artists and new writers. We're committed to keeping things fresh," she explains. "But at the same time, we will never replace all the good and reliable aspects of our magazines just for the sake of being new. We have some tried-and-true authors whom we know our readers love, so we look for a balance between the old and the new."

Listening to what readers say helps the Cricket Magazine Group stay up to speed. "Through feedback via reader letters, we're always trying to improve our publication. For example, in response to comments, we've offered more reader art and added brief biographies of poets and authors in each issue of *Cicada*," says Tracy Schoenle, Senior Editor of the literary magazine for ages 14 and up. "For *Cricket*, we keep our eyes open for excellent submissions and reprint articles on topics that readers frequently ask to see more about." The 30-year-old *Cricket* targets ages 9 to 14.

Publications from the Cobblestone Group, begun in 1980 and acquired by the Cricket Group five years ago, pride themselves on providing kids with material they can learn from while they are enjoying the reading experience. "One of the things we're seeing is there's so much more competition today and kids are expecting so much more in terms of what interests them and what attracts them," says Lou Waryncia, Managing Editor of *Cobblestone*. "If you can't grab their attention, no matter how good your content is, they're probably going to put your magazine down and pick up something else. Our goal is to make our magazine more accessible without compromising our integrity as an educational publication."

> The climate for educational publishing is on the upswing. . . . [It] has been a financial sleeper for the last three years, growing at a rate of nearly 5 percent or more a year. "It's one of the best-kept secrets of the magazine economy."

Getting an Education

According to Gaynor, the climate for educational publishing is on the upswing. Supplemental educational publishing, which includes titles from the children's and teen markets, has been a financial sleeper for the last three years, growing at a rate of nearly 5 percent or more per year. "It's one of the best-kept secrets of the magazine economy," Gaynor says. Some of the more recognizable names in the industry include Weekly Reader, Time Inc.'s *Time For Kids* Media Group, and Scholastic magazines.

Gaynor says the future also includes more potential for acquisitions, like the recent purchase by School Specialty of part of McGraw-Hill's children's publishing business.

She thinks consolidation among educational publishers will continue. "Another thing I see more of is more large consumer companies reaching down into the children's market—especially the educational market," she explains. "If any new giants are going to be created in the children's market, they're likely to be giants expanding from other arenas, perhaps the toy or broadcast industries."

State and national literacy initiatives, such as No Child Left Behind (NCLB), will continue to have their influence on educational publishing. "A smart person operating in the children's market right now will be aware of NCLB and how it's affecting schools, parents, and kids," says Gaynor. "It will have an impact on material written for kids, and that impact will continue to be felt for years to come."

Astute writers will recognize and respond to these educational needs. Children's magazines of all kinds—classroom or those not immediately directed to the classroom but educational—will continue to be key supplementary resources to help kids read, to get kids interested in reading, and to help build some of the core reading competencies.

Because of today's enormous emphasis on reading and writing for proficiency tests, Ira Wolfman, Senior Vice President of Editorial for Weekly Reader Publications, says some schools push kids to learn things as an *end:* They really need to learn to read, to write a declarative sentence, how paragraphs are put together. "Instead, we see it as a *means:* the learning that they do is really opening all kinds of doors to enjoyment and fun, achievement and success. We're there to show them why it's exciting and useful to read and write well."

Wolfman believes the role of educational magazines is to engage, excite, and entertain with learning as the basis. Magazines have an advantage because they can cover current topics—unlike textbooks, which are written with a long lead time and are often used in classrooms for five to ten years before they are replaced. "Our publications are delivered within weeks of completion," he says. "Unlike textbooks, we can incorporate popular culture."

"We're hoping that our magazines are helping students to meet standards," says Cobblestone Publishing's Waryncia. "We've had teachers and curriculum developers say that they are using our product specifically for that need and we know of at least one major school system in the U.S. that is using our magazine specifically for that purpose." Teachers have told Waryncia that they're routinely using ancillary materials such as magazines to get kids to read and bring information to them in ways that are more accessible and entertaining.

Though the Cricket Magazine Group markets primarily to home subscribers, "We're delighted that our publications are being used in schools," says Schoenle. "From

Selected Educational Markets

The following publications are for students, teachers, or parents, and use educational materials. Frequency, circulation, and percentage written by freelancers is indicated for each title.

M = monthly   Q = quarterly   W = weekly

ADDitude: 6x/yr. Circ. unavailable, 80%.

American Journal of Health Education: 6x/yr. 8,000. 100%.

American String Teacher: Q. 11,500. 75%.

Art Education: 6x/yr. 20,000. 100%.

Art & Activities: 10x/yr. 20,000. 95%.

Biography Today: 6x/yr. 9,000. 50%.

Christian Home & School: 6x/yr. 68,000. 75%.

The Clearing House: 6x/yr. 1,500. 100%.

CollegeBound Teen: M. 755,000. 60%.

College Outlook: 2x/yr. 710,000. 60%.

Connect: 5x/yr. 2,000. 90%

Current Health 1 & 2: 8x/yr. 163,793/232,000. 90%.

Current Science: 16x/yr. 1 million. 40%.

Dimensions: Q. 165,000. 60%.

Educational Leadership: 8x/yr. 170,000. 90%.

Education Week: W. 50,000. 8%.

English Journal: 6x/yr. 40,000. 80%.

eSchoolNews: M. Hits unavailable. 20%.

Gifted Education Press Quarterly: Q. 1,500. 75%.

Green Teacher: Q. 7,000. 90%.

Gumbo: 6x/yr. 25,000. 15%.

Home Education: 6x/yr. 60,000. 90%.

Homeschooling Today: 6x/yr. 30,000. 90%.

Instructor: 8x/yr. 250,000. 75%.

Journal of Adolescent & Adult Literacy: 8x/yr. 16,000. 100%.

Journal of School Health: 10x/yr. 5,000. 90%.

Kansas School Naturalist: irregular. 9,300, 75%.

Know Your World Extra: M. 80,000. 40%.

Language Arts: 6x/yr. 22,000. 85%.

Leadership for Student Activities: 9x/yr. 51,000. 67%.

Learning and Leading with Technology: 8x/yr. 12,000. 90%.

Learning Guide: Q. 10,000+. 85%.

Library Media Connection: 7x/yr. 15,000. 100%.

Momentum: Q. 24,000. 90%.

Multicultural Review: Q. 5,000. 90%.

MultiMedia & Internet Schools: M. 12,000. 90%.

Music Educators Journal: 5x/yr. 80,000. 90%.

New York Times Upfront: 18x/yr. 250,000. 10%.

ParenTeacher: 6x/yr. 35,000. 20%.

Principal: 5x/yr. 36,000. 90%.

Read: 18x/yr. 250,000. 60%.

The Reading Teacher: 8x/yr. 61,000. 99%.

Reading Today: 6x/yr. 80,000. 30%.

SchoolArts: 9x/yr. 20,000. 90%.

School Library Journal: M. 42,000. 80%.

Science & Children: 8x/yr. 23,000. 99%.

The Science Teacher: 9x/yr. 29,000. 100%.

Science Weekly: 14x/yr. 200,000. 100%.

Social Studies and the Young Learner: Q. 15,000. 95%.

Student Leader: 3x/yr. 130,000. 10%.

SuperScience: 8x/yr. 250,000. 75%.

Teacher: 6x/yr. 120,000. 40%.

Teachers & Writers: 6x/yr. 2,000. 70%.

Teaching PreK-8: 8x/yr. 107,000. 43%.

Technology & Learning: 11x/yr. 85,000. 50%.

Time For Kids: W. 3.5 million. 5%.

Picture This

Jamstart Publishing cofounders Judy MacDonald Johnson and Rosie Welch believe that to build the best foundation for reading, children first need to have fun experiences with print. Their offering is the *Tessy & Tab* Reading Club.

The idea to make *Tessy & Tab* a picture book magazine came from looking at the current magazine market for preschoolers. "All of the current ones seemingly trickle down to preschoolers from existing magazines," says Johnson. "If you look at *Cricket* and the National Wildlife magazines, they started with products for older kids and later developed younger versions." (The National Wildlife magazines are *Ranger Rick, Backyard Buddies,* and *Wild Animal Baby*.)

Instead, Johnson and Welch wanted to start with this very young age group and develop something a three year old could "read" alone with minimal parent intervention.

"We tell the parents, let the child read it to you. This is going to be a little unusual the first time because the child is used to you reading to him," says Johnson. "You ask the child to tell you what is going on and you respond, 'Yes that's right. And then what happened?' Within three or four pages they get it and realize they're telling you the story." Every time they sit down to read you the story, they tell it in the same way. Though their story may not exactly match any of the few words on the page, they feel like they're reading and it gives them that confidence while they're learning words. When they get older, they gain a renewed interest in looking at *Tessy & Tab* because they can now figure out the words.

Each issue is just one story, taken from an experience you might have as a three-year-old child, such as going to the store or going to the library. Even if there isn't a parent available to sit and read with the child, he can read it to himself because it's all in the pictures. That gets the child to feel like a reader. "In our mind, that's the important thing. If you feel you can read, you will be more likely to read because you think it's fun," says Johnson. "We believe reading pictures is a valid form of reading. And if you think about it at some level, letters and words are pictures too—ones that someone invented ages ago to represent things and meanings."

reader feedback and surveys we've conducted in the past, we know that our publications are used by homeschoolers, too."

School-age kids are not the only ones of interest to educational publishers. Magazines like *Babybug*, *Wild Animal Baby,* and *Turtle* target early reading skills and try to foster a love of reading. One of the newer entries to this niche market is the *Tessy & Tab* Reading Club, from Jamstart Publishing. Cofounders Judy MacDonald Johnson and Rosie Welch set out to help preschoolers build a foundation for reading.

The *Tessy & Tab* issues are small in size and they're 16 pages long, targeted for a three year old. "Most magazines for kids are 10 or 12 times a year, but we found through national surveys that if you get it every two weeks, three year olds would start to develop an anticipation for it," says Johnson. The publishers make clear, however, that they're not trying to teach children how to read. "If you try to pressure a kid at three to read, it could backfire," she says. "We feel our contribution is to make reading fun."

Teen Scene

The teen market exploded in the late 1990s, and the seas are still calming. "There was tremendous growth based on what was going on in pop culture," says Damon Romine, Deputy Editor of *Teen*. "Magazines rode the wave of *NSYNC, the Backstreet Boys, and Britney to great success."

Now that this wave has crested,

the magazines are struggling to find ways to keep reaching readers in a crowded and rapidly changing market. Though the universe is big and continues to grow—32.4 million people between the ages of 12 and 19—teen magazines are still finding their own place in that particular ocean. Some of the strategies have included mergers, refocusing editorial content, changing frequency of publication, and redefining their target audiences.

Teen merged with *Seventeen* magazine, and is now publishing quarterly specials along with their popular *TeenPROM* issue. "To avoid treading on *Seventeen*'s toes or those of our other Hearst sister magazine *CosmoGirl!*, we've made moves to skew *Teen* to a younger audience," says Romine. "Since we're gearing our magazine for the 11 to 14 window, we provide a safe haven for this age. We're not talking about sex. We're leaving that for our sister mags, and we cover subjects that *Seventeen* and *CosmoGirl!* wouldn't be interested in, like younger teen stars and hip shows on Nickelodeon and The N. The focus of *Teen* continues to be more lifestyle and service and less focused on celebrity, because we are published quarterly."

While *Teen* is courting the younger set, *YM* had tried targeting older readers to attract a more sophisticated audience. "Instead of trying to be all things to all teens, we're focusing on the 19-year-old mind-set, encompassing older teens and sophisticated younger teens who want to aspire up," said Linda Fears, Editor in Chief. The idea was to be successful by staying ahead of the curve. Unfortunately, the strategy didn't work and *YM* recently ceased publication.

Twist has undergone a transformation into a service magazine for teens. "*Twist* has differentiated itself in the teen market by moving away from the more traditional lifestyle magazines. We examine the lives of our readers' favorite stars and combine our reporting with service and advice to which they can relate. Our service essentially comes through the voice of today's hottest celebrities, and the result is fun and fresh," says Betsy Fast, Editor in Chief.

Guideposts for Teens is now reborn as the bimonthly *Sweet 16,* along with a change in format that targets girls ages 11 to 19. Guideposts Publishing offers inspirational magazines and books based on the power of positive thinking and achieving individual spiritual potential. "We really wanted to reach teens who aren't being reached in more traditionally religious ways," says Mary Lou Carney, Editor in Chief. "It's the *Guideposts* way to be inclusive, not exclusive. We wanted

to create a product that was more inclusive and would consequently let us serve more readers."

Carney sees their redesigned magazine as a place for tweens to go, after they've outgrown *American Girl, Girls' Life* [now known as *GL*], or other magazines aimed at a younger age. She says of *Sweet 16,* "It's inspirational and uplifting, but we also acknowledge that kids live in the real world. There are pop culture references, celebrity covers, fashion, beauty, in the magazine. But at the same time it's positive and acknowledges the faith side of life. We're all about real girls—and real girls are about both those things."

Newcomer *Justine* appeared on the newsstands in midsummer, filling a void in the market, according to Editor and Publisher Jana Pettey. "I'm the mom of a teenager and our other publisher also has a teenage daughter. We both felt there was another voice missing from the teen market," she explains. "Our target market is girls who are college-bound and are working hard to make something of themselves. It seems that much of the content in some teen magazines focuses on only one element: celebrity idolization, rather than speaking to a well-rounded kid. Sure, we have fashion and beauty, but we also offer pieces on how to study for the SATs or cool places you might consider studying abroad."

Justine also strives to address self-esteem issues for teen girls. "So many of the problems teens have,

Preteen & Teen Religious Magazines

Brio and *Brio and Beyond:* Focus on the Family, 8605 Explorer Dr., Colorado Springs, CO 80920. www.briomag.com. Monthly. Girls, 12-15 and 16-20, respectively.

Breakaway: Focus on the Family, 8605 Explorer Dr., Colorado Springs, CO 80920. www.breakawaymag.com. Monthly. Boys, 12-18.

Cadet Quest: Calvinist Cadet Corps, P.O. Box 7258, Grand Rapids, MI 49510. www.calvinistcadets.org. 7x/yr. Boys, 9-14.

Club Connection: Assemblies of God, 1445 Boonville Ave., Springfield, MO 65802. www.clubconnection.ag.org. Quarterly. Girls, 6-12.

The Conqueror: United Pentecostal International. 8855 Dunn Road, Hazelwood, MO 63042. www.pentecostalyouth.org. 6x/yr. 12-18.

Devo'Zine: P.O. Box 340004, 1908 Grand Ave., Nashville, TN 37203. www.devozine.org. 6x/yr. Teen devotional magazine.

Encounter and *InSight:* Standard Publishing, 8121 Hamilton Ave., Cincinnati, OH 45231. Weekly. 13-19 and 14-41, respectively.

Guide: Review and Herald Publishing, 55 West Oak Ridge Dr., Hagerstown, MD 21740. www.guidemagazine.org. Weekly, 10-14.

High Adventure: Assemblies of God, 1445 Boonville Ave., Springfield, MO 65802. www.royalrangers.ag.org. Quarterly. Boys, 6-12.

InTeen: P. O. Box 436987, Chicago, IL 60643. www.urbanministries. com. Quarterly. African American inner-city teens, 15-17.

On Course: Assemblies of God, 1445 Boonville Ave., Springfield, MO 65802. www.oncourse.ag.org. Quarterly. 12-18.

On the Line: Mennonite Publishing, 616 Walnut Ave., Scottsdale, PA 15683. www.mph.org/otl. Monthly. 9-14.

Partners: Christian Light Publications, P. O. Box 1212, Harrisburg, VA 22803. Monthly. 9-14.

PrayKids!: P. O. Box 35004, Colorado Springs, CO 80935. www.praykids.com. 6x/yr. 8-12.

The Rock: Cook Communications, 4050 Lee Vance View, Colorado Springs, CO 80918. www.cookministries.org. Weekly during school. 10-14.

Sharing the Victory: Fellowship of Christian Athletes, 8701 Leeds Road, Kansas City, MO 64129. www.fca.org. 9x/yr. Athletes, coaches, grade 7 up.

Shine Brightly: P.O. Box 7259, Grand Rapids, MI 49510. www.gemsgc.org. 9x/yr. 9-14.

Spirit: Sisters of St. Joseph of Carondelet, 1884 Randolph Ave., St. Paul, MN 55105. 28x/yr. Teens.

With, the Magazine for Radical Christian Youth: P.O. Box 147, 722 Main St., Newton, KS 67114. 6x/yr. 15-18.

be it eating disorders or even more drastic problems, so much of it goes back to low self-esteem and peer pressure," says Pettey. "Instead of having an article on how to bribe your boyfriend back, we'd have an article on how to feel good about yourself so you can attract good guys. It's a little different spin on essentially the same issues."

Although *Justine* targets an older audience, girls 16 to19, and covers some tough issues, keeping the content nonoffensive is important to the publishers. "If a 10- or 11-year-old sister picks it up, we want to make sure she can read it too."

GL Publisher Karen Bokram predicts that as much as the teen market for female readers changes on the surface, the same themes will still be playing in the future. "You're going to have the same old fashion books, the same old service books, the racier side, like *Cosmo-Girl!,* and the more conservative titles like ours," she says of the magazine for ages 10 to 15. It has been publishing for more than 10 years and its circulation is 400,000.

Bokram does suggest, however, that the market is ripe for sports-related titles, as a result of the increased participation of teen girls in sports.

It's a Guy Thing

That sports market has always been as dominated by boys as the rest of the teen market has seemed to cater to female readers. Publishers still attempt, with mixed results, to target teen guys. You might re-member *Dirt,* published by the same company as *Sassy*, and both folded. Then *Men's Health* introduced a junior version of their magazine, *MH-17,* later titled *MH-18,* but it didn't make the cut under either name.

Breakaway is one of the few magazines for teen guys that has survived. "In one sense, we're a general purpose magazine, but in another sense, we're very segmented because we are a Christian magazine," says Editor Michael Ross. "Guys look to us for stories on sports, adventure, music, and girls, but they also look to us for faith, the foundation of *Breakaway.* They look for advice and spiritual growth."

Ross notes that teen boys typically don't read magazines as frequently as teen girls. The ones who do will look toward magazines that cover their very specific interests or needs, such as sports, skateboarding, or video games. "Teen boys are more segmented in their interests. If they're interested in skateboarding, they'll plug into a skateboarding magazine or website. If they're interested in adventure, they'll plug into those kinds of magazines."

Often, male teens reach up demographically to grab special interest magazines such as *Sports Illustrated* or *Car and Driver.* New entries like *Cargo* may catch their eyes with the latest in technology and gadgets, as well as grooming and clothes, once a male teen starts to care about the way he looks.

Other magazines new to the teen market include the *Skateboard*

Mag, a monthly started by several editors who left Time Warner's Transworld *Skateboarding.* According to the editors, "*The Skateboard Mag* seeks to maintain the independent nature and integrity of the skateboard culture at all levels, provide readers with a broad, accurate, and knowledgeable view of skateboarding, and advance skateboard publishing through excellence in photography, writing, and design."

Snowboarders will find in-depth articles on their sport in the *Snowboard Journal,* while young golfers can score with *Golf Punk. American Adrenaline* dedicates its pages to prekindergarten through eighth-grade wrestlers and their families, coaches, and fans.

The new bimonthly hip-hop magazine *Hype* covers all aspects of hip-hop culture for fans, with a special emphasis on the music. Christian music fans can look to *Young Believers in Christ* for the latest in CDs, relationship advice, and faith stories. And last year's Bible magazine for teen girls, *Revolve,* now has a male counterpart, *Refuel.* Formatted like a sports or entertainment magazine, this New Testament Bible-in-a-magazine comes to life with teen-relevant applications.

Family Matters

While national publications like *Parenting* or *Child* may be more well known, the 120-plus regional parenting publications have the greatest reach when it comes to readers. "In the Dallas area, for example, the local parenting publica-

tion is reaching 10 to 15 times as many parents as the national publication is in the same market," says James Dowden, Executive Director of the Parenting Publications of America (PPA). "The typical parent magazine at the national level is only selling to one in a thousand households in the region."

Regional parenting publications are often a first step for writers in juvenile and family markets because many of them rely heavily on  freelance submissions—especially from local authors who know the region and the needs of the particular audience. "When you're local, you can put a local spin on a parenting issue. Localize it and make it pertinent to our readers," says Liz White, Editor of *Atlanta Parent.* "The national publications for the most part can't do that. They rely on nationally known experts; we try to use local sources. For example, if you're reading an article about kids and cancer in Atlanta, they'd be mentioning the AFLAC Cancer Center at Children's Hospital in Atlanta."

The regional parenting market retains its strength, even growing a little because of increasing ad rev-

Finding Your Own Voice

If you don't like what's on the newsstand, start your own magazine. That's what Melinda Mattos and Nicole Cohen did.

Mattos and Cohen, journalism students at Canada's Ryerson University, first hatched their magazine idea two years ago when they were asked to create a prototype as part of an assignment. They envisioned a progressive magazine for teenage girls who they thought were under-represented in the mainstream media. On graduation, the duo worked to bring their prototype to life.

Shameless, their new publication for teen girls, was born out of their frustration with the teen magazines they read while growing up. "Most mainstream teen magazines teach girls to be ashamed— to be ashamed of their bodies, of their minds, and of their sexuality," says Mattos. "We feel that girls should be shameless. Be proud of who you are and what you're doing and be outspoken about it."

According to their website, www.shamelessmag.com, *Shameless* has a tone unlike other teen magazines. It doesn't talk down to girls or come off acting like a know-it-all big sister. "I always get the sense that those other magazines are edited by women in their thirties and forties telling their readers what they should want," says 22-year-old Mattos. She would rather have their 15- to 19-year-old readers think of *Shameless* as "trusted friend or co-conspirator"—a strong, smart, sassy girl like themselves.

Will you find supermodels or teen icons on the cover? No way. Tips on how to lose weight or deal with boyfriends? Not likely. Instead you'll find politics, pop culture, music, arts and crafts, technology, and stories of successful female role models.

The premiere issue hit the stands last summer on a shoestring budget of $5,000 raised through concerts, dances, and a lone anonymous donor. Numerous artists and writers donated their talents to fill the pages. Along with their Art Director, Jason Paré, Cohen and Mattos composed the publication on their home computers.

The *Shameless* crew realizes that it's going to be a tough sell in a market where many new launches die a painful death in their first few months. Nevertheless, they plan to publish three times a year and hope they won't have to rely on donations to fund subsequent issues. "If you have enough passion for something, you can make it work," says Mattos.

enues—their bread and butter. "For every regional parenting magazine that's gobbled up by a bigger entity or ceases publishing, someone else comes in and takes their place," says White. "The biggest change I'm seeing is that 10 or more years ago, they were started by entrepreneurs—a mom with a good idea starting at the kitchen table." Now most of the new regional parenting magazines are being started by people who are already in the publishing business, at weeklies and dailies that recognize there is a niche for these publications.

Regional parenting publications are also realizing they can address sub-audiences. "In your core publication, you try to address as many age groups as possible," says White. "But we're also on the bandwagon for producing publications for special needs markets." *Atlanta Parent* also publishes *Atlanta Baby* four times a year to address the needs of families of newborns and toddlers.

Taking a cue from the event calendars in most regional parenting magazines is *Time Out New York Kids*. The quarterly targets parents of kids from birth to14 who want to turn the cultural capital of the world into their personal playground. They feature a comprehensive listing of events for busy families who want to know what's happening in the Big Apple, but don't have time to spend searching for themselves.

Other niche magazines will continue to appear in various forms. Rosie O'Donnell announced plans for another shot at the magazine market this year with a new magazine tentatively titled *R Family,* targeting gay and lesbian parents. It joins one other title serving this audience, *And Baby,* a bimonthly founded in 2001 that lists a circulation of more than 100,000. Based on O'Donnell's name recognition, no interference from Gruner + Jahr, and the fact that more than 3.1 million children live with gay, lesbian, or bisexual parents, the publication stands a better-than-average chance of success.

Healthy Family, a bimonthly launched last year, doesn't expect to reinvent the wheel in the editorial sense. The magazine plans to offer the typical range of family-oriented features, equally divided between more weighty topics like serious health issues and lighter ones like home and travel. "There is no national consumer magazine that focuses on the health of the entire family," says Publisher Richard Bulman. "We think we can be the user's manual for raising a healthy family in today's world."

Two new magazines address various ages of motherhood. *Mamalicious* bills itself as "an independent magazine for youthful, passionate, street-smart moms" that reflects the diverse lives led by moms and their kids today. The magazine promises to be a bit edgier than the typical moms' mag. On the other end of the spectrum is *Plum*, a new magazine geared to the over-35 crowd who are having children later in life. "This magazine is intended to help women to relax and

Online Markets

Able Ezine: www.able-ezine.org. Teens living with a disability. 5x/year. Publishes 150-200 freelance submissions a year.

America's Moms: www.parentinguniverse.com. Practical information for expectant parents. Monthly. 1,000 submissions/year.

Busy Family Network: www.busyfamilynetwork.com. Includes several publications, including *Natural Family, Busy Parents, Busy Homeschool*. Monthly. 140 submissions/year.

Connect for Kids: www.connectforkids.org. Building healthy communities for kids and families. Weekly. 12 submissions/year.

Drink Smart: www.drinksmart.org. Alcohol and addiction-related issues for teens. 150-200 submissions/year.

Eclectic Homeschool Online: www.eho.org. Christian homeschooling. Monthly. 30 submissions/year.

ePregnancy: www.epregnancy.com. Any issue related to pregnancy, including health, fashion, relationships, careers. Monthly. 300 submissions/year.

eSchoolNews: www.eschoolnews.com. Technology for educators. Monthly. 6-8 submissions/year.

GeoParent: www.geoparent.com. Parenting information. Weekly. 50 submissions/year.

Go-Girl: www.go-girl.com. Girls' social and school needs. 6x/year. 100 submissions/year.

Going Forth: www.goingforth.net. For Christian youth. Quarterly. 15-35 submissions/year.

enjoy pregnancy," says Rebekah Meola, Publisher. "By the time you're 40, you just have a different life than you do when you are in your twenties."

Grand Magazine plans to tap into a huge market, more than 70 million strong, providing a modern resource for a new generation of grandparents. "I believe that baby boomers are going to reinvent grandparenting," says Publisher Christine Crosby. "They're going to want to do it bigger and better than any previous generation and *Grand Magazine* wants to be the resource

that helps them do that."

See more on regional markets in "Our Town: Writing for Regional Magazines," page 99.

Magazines.com

While Internet usage in general is increasing, online publishing in the children's and parenting markets has not grown significantly.

"I haven't seen as many emagazine launches as in past years, with the exception of those for existing periodicals," says Gaynor. "When you look at the economics of publishing on the Web, it

Online Markets

Guideposts for Kids Online: www.gp4k.com. Stories, articles, activities for ages 6 to 12. 150 submissions/year.

Kids Domain: www.kidsdomain.com. Entertaining educational site for kids, parents, and educators. Weekly. 10 submissions/year.

Parents and Children Together Online: www.reading.indiana. edu/www/famres. Literacy learning. 50-80 submissions/year.

Real Sports: www.real-sports.com. Women's sports.

SheKnows.com: www.sheknows.com. Parenting. Monthly. 150 submissions/year.

Teenage Christian Magazine: www.teenagechristian.net. Teens bringing faith to the forefront of life. 12-25 submissions/year.

Teen Countdown: www.jdrf.org. Teens with Type 1 diabetes. 2x/year. 25 submissions/year.

Teenwire.com: www.teenwire.com. Planned Parenthood site about sexual health for teens. 110-150 submissions/year.

The Universe in the Classroom: www.astrosociety.com. Astronomy site for teachers to use with children. Quarterly. 4 submissions/year.

Vegetarian Baby & Child and **Vegetarianteen.com:** www.vegetarian-baby.com. Health and vegetarianism for parents and for teens. Monthly. 100-150 submissions/year.

Wee Ones: www.weeonesmag.com. Stories, articles, activities, poems for ages 5 to 10. 6x/year. 200 submissions/year.

looks so attractive compared to print, but if you really don't have the publishing expertise and you don't know how to engage readers, it's not as easy as it looks. Also, if you have no brand and you're trying to create that brand on the Internet, it's very difficult."

Jennifer Reed, Editor of *Wee Ones* and a pioneer in the online market, agrees. "As far as online publishing goes, I don't think it's caught on as much as people would have liked," she says. "I frequently get people emailing me about wanting to start an emagazine. I tell them it's a hard business to start, get going, and hard to earn any kind of reputation."

According to Reed, the biggest problem with online magazines is that it's difficult to make any profit. Readers still balk at paying subscriptions to use a website because it's not a tangible object like a print magazine. Most visitors are still used to getting free Internet content. "Advertising doesn't really work either, and we didn't want to bombard children with ads," she says. "So we have to find other creative ways to bring in money. Most sites that are currently self-supporting are companions to existing print magazines and derive their revenue from them."

Though most websites aren't money-makers, they're still sometimes the best way to get a message across. "Our website and email forms of communication allow us to reach a broader audience more frequently, more efficiently and less expensively," says Claire Green, President of the Parents' Choice Foundation.

Another benefit is interactivity and a sense of community among those who frequent a publication's website. "We try to make *Breakaway*'s website an interactive community. We host contests, such as a music cut-a-demo contest where the winner gets to hang out in Nashville with a major Christian band," says Ross. "In everything we do, we try to be involved in their lives and give them a place where they can interact and communicate with us and other teens. They might be reluctant to go to their parents or their youth pastor for advice, so they can come to our website and talk about serious struggles they're having."

Cicada uses writing to get readers involved in their community. "Currently, we offer 'The Slam' (think *poetry slam*) for teens and young adults, a portion of the *Cicada* website dedicated to contributors' poetry and microfiction, which is updated about once a week," says Schoenle. "These young adult poets and authors can also receive feedback on their work from fellow writers in posted critiques."

One of the new entries in the online market is BusyFamilyNetwork.com. The Busy Family Network began as one site, Busy Parents Online, and branched out into others. According to the site description, "Busy Family Network is an innovative company that's continually growing and moving, just like your busy family and small business. We're serving parents on their terms." The site also offers a subscription email newsletter.

Websites are not the end-all to electronic publishing, and the technology continues to evolve. Instead of being tied to a computer, Reed suggests that soon you really can take it with you. "We're looking at other technologies so that readers could read our magazine almost as if it were a book—e-readers are devices a reader opens up like a book," she says. "You download a magazine, book, or whatever and read it from page to page on a very portable, thin, and flexible display." These units, unlike earlier e-books, offer ink-on-paper readability under all lighting conditions. They're already available in Asia, but have not arrived in the U.S. as yet.

Dealing with Competition

Collectively, hundreds of print and online magazines are available in the children's, teen, and family markets, but the real competition is not coming from within the market but from without.

"This is a difficult arena to be playing in right now. I'm not breaking new ground by mentioning how all kids' magazines are competing with a multitude of alternative sensory experiences that our readers have access to," says Mike Goldman, Senior Editor of *Boys' Life.* "To be successful, we need to continue to provide the intriguing, entertaining, and relevant content that will keep readers turning to us and not to TV, the Internet, or Playstation."

Today's editors are more aware of content and packaging than ever before. "Readers want to know what they're going to get: 'how much of a commitment do I have to make to read this article?'" says Wolfman. "One of the things that we find is important in an environment where people are barraged with thousands of messages a day is to choose our articles carefully, to figure out what is going to connect with kids, what are the educational objectives behind them, and to work hard to package them so kids and teachers can tell at a glance why they'd want to read it."

Wolfman says the Weekly Reader Publications are working hard on headlines, decks, and captions, and other components of the articles they publish. "It's not enough just to write a wonderful piece. Now you have to write a wonderful piece and show what it is about the piece that's wonderful enough so the reader really wants to read it. Otherwise he may not get to it because there are 43 other urgent things going on," says Wolfman. "Kids will engage with print if you connect with them, if you make it compelling, and you package it in a way that speaks to them, their needs and their interests."

There's no question that articles are getting shorter and tighter. In the transition from *Guideposts for Teens* to *Sweet 16,* the typical first-person story word count shrank from 1,500 words to just less than 800, to stay in tune with reader preferences. "It's shorter, but meatier content in *Boys' Life,*" says Goldman. Articles are "bite-sized nuggets. That's the way the industry is going, whether it's newspapers or magazines."

The trend of the shrinking article has been going on for some time as Meg Weaver of Wooden Horse Publishing notes. Industry-wide, magazines launched in the 1990s and 2000s have been out to capture even younger audiences than in past decades. To draw these young readers, magazines are publishing shorter material. When Weaver investigated article lengths, she found the average minimum word count that editors requested from their writers ranged from a high of 738 words in the magazines founded in the 1960s to an average of 478 words in magazines launching today.

Missing in Action

Baby Years ceased publication with the February/March 2004 issue due to the lack of advertising support.

Beautiful Girl, trendy teen Christian magazine published quarterly since December 2003, "is going through some transitional changes right now and the print magazine will be on hiatus until further notice," says Editor Scarlett Williams. "However, our website isn't going anywhere, so you can still read archived articles, listen to Christian music, chat with friends on the *Beautiful Girl* message board or say hello from anywhere in the world on our *Beautiful Girl* Guest Map."

Boy Crazy!, the publication written by teen boys for teen girls, offering insider tips on dating and relationships, appears to have ceased publication with its June/July 2003 issue. The website, however, is functional as of this writing.

Beckett Publications' *Best of Dragon Ball Z* appears to have ceased publication with issue #41, April 2004. Its website is still up and running.

Child Care Business still has a working website, but has no information beyond its February/March 2004 issue.

College shut down after two issues due to lack of financing.

The Crystal Ball is currently on hiatus.

Dallas Family ended publication in February 2004.

Dream/Girl is not accepting new subscriptions as of March 2004. According to the website, "The magazine has always been a labor of love for us, but it gets harder to find the time every year. We're currently working to find a nonprofit group to take over publication of the magazine and have decided not to make any promises we aren't sure to keep in the meantime."

Just Weird Enough, a quarterly print and online publication featuring fantasy and science fiction for young readers, ceased publication.

Our Kids Atlanta ended publication in February 2004, according to the parenthood.com website.

Another kind of competition involves magazines versus the Internet for advertising dollars. According to a study from Jupiter Research, by 2008, advertisers will be spending more money on the Internet than on print titles. The study predicts that magazine ad revenue will increase from $12.2 billion to $13.8 billion, a modest 13.1 percent. During the same period, Internet ad revenue will grow from

Missing in Action

▓ Online publication *r*w*t* left the following note to readers: "Thank you for your years of readership. Unfortunately, we are unable to continue publishing *r*w*t* magazine."

▓ *Team NYI* webzine is off the Web, but its parent site, nyitoday.org, continues to serve readers.

▓ *Teenpreneur* is no longer in print, though its parent magazine, *Black Enterprise,* is still publishing and maintains a website.

▓ *Writes of Passage* still maintains its website but is not currently accepting any new submissions. They suggest contributors check back for updates over the next few months.

▓ *YM* ceased publication in October 2004.

The following magazines have ceased publication temporarily, permanently, or are on hiatus without any further information available at this time:

▓ *Black Parenting Today*
▓ *Christian Library Journal*
▓ *County Families Magazine*
▓ *Equality Today*
▓ *Health & You*
▓ *Hullabaloo*
▓ *Northern Nevada Family*
▓ *Northern Virginia Parent*
▓ *Pet Life*
▓ *Rainy Day Corner*
▓ *Soccer Junior*
▓ *The Whyvillian*
▓ *Youth Update*

$8.4 billion to $13.8 billion—a 64 percent increase.

The number of markets has generally remained stable, but are editors buying more manuscripts in the children's, teen, and parenting markets? According to an unscientific poll done by Gaynor, the glass is either half-empty or half-full, depending on your degree of optimism. "It's split about 50/50. Some publications only use freelancers and that's it," she says. "Others have said because last year was a particularly tight time that they went to more in-house articles."

With magazines trying to carve out their own niches, and establish their own identities, you may find that the days of circulating the general interest article to a number of potential markets are fading fast. Carefully targeting your article to a specific magazine or age group is the wave of the future as readers seek magazines that meet their individual needs, and editors seek articles that meet their readers' individual needs.

Profile

Karen Bokram: Meeting Girls' Needs

By Mark Haverstock

Karen Bokram has always been a magazine person. "I was fascinated by magazines. I read a lot of them." She began her magazine career at age 16 as an intern with the *Detroit Monthly*, thanks to a reference from an unlikely source. "I was the only babysitter the managing editor's kid liked," she says. From there, she went to college for a couple of years and interned at *Rolling Stone*. A brief hiatus from college led to a stint at *Seventeen*. Later, she went back to school and graduated in 1990 with a bachelor of arts degree in English from Ohio Wesleyan University.

Her next journey into the magazine world took her to a company that was managing the assets of the New American Magazine Company. "I was on a team that relaunched *Psychology Today* and *Mother Earth News*," says Bokram. "Once the company got going, I decided to go off on my own." Going off on her own meant talking to an overlooked audience in a new way.

Reinventing the Teen Magazine

When *Girls' Life* (now known as *GL*) started a decade ago, Bokram's goal was to make a fun magazine that celebrated being a girl. She chose to focus on young teens, she says, "Because when I was 11 to 16 years old, I was annoyed that every teen magazine focused on being 17 or older. I always thought to myself, 'What's wrong with being younger than 17? Don't I matter now?' There's so much to think about and deal with, so many changes to go through, and so much to figure out about yourself."

Bokram first pitched the idea of addressing the tween audience when she was working for *Seventeen* in 1988. "We had *Seventeen* readers who were way younger than 17, though we were never supposed to say that," she explains. "In all my infinite wisdom as a 19-year-old, I trotted into [Editor] Midge Richardson's office and said, 'We need to have a junior section for all of our younger readers whom we aren't serving.' We had wedding pages back in those days if you can believe it—articles with tips on how to plan your wedding. I told her we needed to service our younger readers, who didn't know anything about what to do when they got their period, how to buy bras, or resolve fights with their friends."

When Bokram started *GL*, she was 23, and looked about 16. "Trying to convince people to give you millions to start a business that 90 percent of people fail at is hard enough," she says. "Try doing it when you look like you should be interviewing to be their babysitter. Lucky for me, most of my first encounters with people in the magazine business were over the phone." She used her secret weapon—*the Voice*—a unique, low-pitched, gravel-sounding voice that gave no clue to her age. "I'd call people, lay on the Voice, and convince them I was a seasoned professional," Bokram says. "Since I often did business with companies located far away, it was usually months before they met me and discovered my dirty little secret: I was young enough to be their daughter." But, by then, Bokram had proven herself. She and her clients would later have a good laugh over the fact that they'd expected a middle-aged woman.

Bokram initially had a tough time convincing advertisers they were sitting on a gold mine of tween consumers. "That was a long battle. It's taken us 10 years of banging on the door to get certain accounts," she says. "It's not Mom doing the buying. The girls themselves are the consumers. I think that everyone now realizes there are 12- and 13-year-olds out there with plenty of money to spend."

In 1994, the dream became a reality. "I'll never forget holding the very first copy of *Girls' Life* in my hands. I was sitting on the front steps of a printing plant in Mendota, Illinois," she says. "When the first magazine rolled off, the press guy handed it to me. 'Here,' he said with a wink, 'save this. Maybe it will be a collector's item someday.' I still have that issue tucked away, though I doubt it's worth much to anyone besides me."

Keeping It Real

GL is number one in its market niche and has been serving the tween/young teen audience for a decade now. "Many other teen magazines have been all over the board. They've changed owners, they've changed editors, they've changed focus," says Bokram. "*GL* stands out by doing good quality, thoughtful work for this age group and our readers respond to that. And we all know that age 10 is the new age 13. Girls are maturing even more quickly. We inadvertently ended up cashing in on this fact."

Bokram and her staff don't try to confuse themselves by getting inside teens' heads. "We aren't obsessed with using all the latest terminology and trying to come off as 'hey, we're cool.' We write in plain English because our readers can always tell if someone's for real or not. Because we're always in contact with them, we have a very good idea of what they respond to and what they don't."

Another reason for *GL*'s success is that girls come first. The bimonthly isn't particularly advertiser- or celebrity-driven. "We don't live and die on advertising, but of course, we'd always love more," Bokram says. "We're focused more on the real girl. We're not a celebrity flavor-of-the-month publication." *GL* has always differentiated itself by focusing on real girls and their issues—what they like, not what they look like. They try to give readers more service pieces than the average magazine, articles that are going to actually help them.

It took nine years, but in 2002 *GL* did finally put a celebrity on the cover. "For the earlier 53 issues, we'd featured girls whose biggest claim to fame was probably scoring 98 on a trig test an hour before stepping in front of our camera," says Bokram. When they did decide to use a celebrity, she says, "We purposely chose Alexis Bledel for who she was—a real girl who happens to be a celebrity because she plays a real girl (Rory Gilmore) on a very cool TV show (*Gilmore Girls*). She also happens to be exactly like millions of girls out there today—smart, involved, confident, cool, and not about to sacrifice her ideals for her social life. In short, this is a cover of a girl a lot like our readers."

Putting It All Together

GL is very committed to helping bring up the next generation of magazine writers and editors. In fact, many of its former interns have gone on to high-ranking positions at other magazines or to publish articles and books.

"We're very committed to giving back to the industry by helping to nurture talented people and to help develop their careers," Bokram

says. "In fact, we have two former interns now on our regular staff." Editorial interns can be as young as their readership age, 12, up to age 22. Their term ranges from two weeks to an entire year. "We really take a look at the girls who have a talent and interest, who take it seriously and will work hard," says Bokram. "Many of them have school newspaper experience or have in some way or another impressed us with their abilities."

A successful writer for *GL* is one who has actually picked up the magazine. "I'm amazed how many writers have not read *GL* before they've pitched me," she says. "What a lot of mom-types do is write the article they want their daughter to read, not what their daughter wants to read. I get a lot of off-target pitches from moms, like 'This Is What My Daughter Should Know' or 'Ten Ways You Can Listen Better to Your Parents and Do More Chores.'" Clueless queries like these rate a standard rejection letter or email. Ideas and articles that show promise and knowledge of their audience—if you're a first-time writer for *GL*—are reviewed on speculation.

Getting Involved

When Bokram isn't at a photo shoot, editing, or checking out newsstand sales, she's involved in community service in the Baltimore area. She's president of the board of directors for a large nonprofit contemporary art space in the mid-Atlantic, Maryland Art Place. She's worked with numerous local charities that support girls and was the head of the Governor's Council on the Status of Girls, a policy advising organization for Maryland's governor.

Bokram has also published a book, *The* Girls' Life *Guide to Growing Up,* which covers the crucial areas of adolescent angst. "Basically, we've always gotten questions from girls like, 'I just got braces. What do I do?' or 'Someone in my family died. What do I do?' They are typically evergreen questions that would show up in our mail. We might have even done an article about the question in *GL* at one time, but often the reader wouldn't have that issue. This was a way for us to collect our best of the best and put it in one place. Girls can use it as an ongoing resource."

GL staffers and Bokram also did a 13-part book series for Scholastic that's available through their continuity club. The *Girls' Life* Club offers books on topics from parties to friends, accessory kits, and copies of the magazine.

Bokram believes she has the best job on earth. "I want to think that we reach some of the most important and influential people on the planet, which is girls 12 to 15," she says. "We've been able to put out a great magazine for 10 years and being able to do that is certainly a thrill."

But the world has changed considerably in those 10 years. "When I sat down to write my first editor's letter in July 1994, I didn't foresee *GL* would have to talk about things like 9/11," explains Bokram. "Or two wars. Or Oklahoma City. Or school shootings. I doubt if any of us did." But girls' basic problems haven't changed much. "For a fifth-grader 10 years ago, now, or in the future, the worst day they're ever going to have is when they're dumped by their best friend. And I don't think there's anyone alive who's single that thinks dating has gotten any easier. The situations aren't really that unique."

One comment from readers has made her efforts all worthwhile: "I hope *GL* is around when I have a daughter because I want her to have this magazine too."

Profile

Kent Brown, Jr.: Planting the Seeds

By Mark Haverstock

Whether it's raising market vegetables, nurturing the next generation of writers, or sowing the seeds of learning and literacy, Kent Brown, Jr., always has an interest in making things grow.

His interest in literacy and learning was encouraged by his grandparents, Dr. Gary Myers and Carolyn Clark Myers, who founded *Highlights for Children* in 1946. "They were interested in starting from where you were and moving you forward," says Brown. "So whether you started with a 13 percent average in school and got to 67 percent, or you started at an 87 percent and got to a 97 percent, they wanted to celebrate and encourage that growth."

The Myers's hallmark, a concept that's been used in connection with their publishing, is to celebrate your child's successes. Brown admittedly wasn't a strong student in his early days, but his grandparents always encouraged him. "Whenever I wrote something and sent it to them, they didn't tell me what

was wrong; instead they told me what was right," he says. "That was their philosophy: encourage learners, praise children's efforts, and motivate them." Brown once received a congratulatory telegram from them for making a marked improvement on a high school French midterm—though it was barely in the passing range.

Class Act

Brown was involved in his high school newspaper, but as a business manager, not a writer. His first job out of college was with Agway, a farm co-operative. "After a while on the job, I told them I wanted to work for their member magazine because I was interested in agriculture and writing," he says. "I thought maybe I'd have a future as an agriculture journalist." Instead, their answer was a transfer to the credit department. He soon left to become a seventh-grade teacher.

His teaching experience taught Brown two lessons that later helped him as an editor. "When you work in a classroom, you see the diverse interests and abilities in any grade level," he explains. "You see first-hand that interest level can have a direct effect on reading ability. Imagine a 16-year-old kid wants to get a driver's license. Even if he's a poor reader, he's got motivation to read the driver's test manual."

Brown also learned the difference between theory and practice. While taking education courses, teachers in training are often led to believe the current popular learning theory is the one true way. "But when you get to the class-room, you re-alize there is a need for a va-riety of ap-proaches to meet stu-dents' needs," he says. "If you're writing a magazine for a variety of kids, you also want to take a variety of approaches." To this day, *Highlights* continues to apply these two principles: Provide a variety of interesting stories and activities that appeal to a broad range of kids.

Spreading the Word

Brown started in the magazine business from the ground up and eventually became Editor in Chief. "I began at *Highlights* as a proof-reader and copy editor," he says.

"We were getting a thousand unso-licited manuscripts a month." He once figured that he'd read more than a quarter million manuscripts during his editorial career.

According to Brown, editors learn much about writing by reading the numerous submissions that come across their desks every month. Some pieces are obviously better than others. "But if you read enough manuscripts, you also begin to put yourself in the place of the child who's reading the magazine," he says. "You ask yourself, where has this missed the mark? How can we make it easier to understand? The editor's job is to take away all the barriers to the reader's understand-ing and enjoyment of the piece."

Brown wears another hat at the *Highlights* organization, as Publisher at the book division, Boyds Mills Press. "Boyds Mills Press is just a logical extension for somebody that's been publishing for kids," he says. "It broadens our base. Some of the people who have a long relation-ship with *Highlights* publish with Boyds Mills Press and some of the people who have written for Boyds Mills Press have become valued con-tributors to *Highlights*."

The house has two imprints, one in poetry, Wordsong, and the new history imprint, Calkins Creek. Brown rarely serves as a line editor on single books anymore, but he works closely with Editorial Direc-tor Larry Rosler on manuscript ac-quisitions. "I still read manuscripts, but I also spend much time on the business and marketing," Brown says. "The people who edit the books really ought to be dealing with ideas and excitement instead of the legal and commercial issues."

Boyds Mills is an anomaly in the publishing industry. "We're focused on the reader and that sometimes makes things tougher in the trade business," says Brown. "It may be that we would prosper more if we were market-oriented." Rather than seeking celebrity books or licensed characters, or promoting pop culture, Boyds Mills would rather publish books on topics it's passionate about, ones that fit the tradition of quality children's books with literary merit. "They're not always the things that tend to sell in huge quantities," says Brown, "but I think *one* is a big number. If a book can change one kid, that's a big number."

Boyds Mills also keeps a larger than average backlist. "We probably don't have the strongest start with many of our books when they're first published, but we tend to keep books in print for a long time," explains Brown. "There are still people who are discovering our books, though they were published five or six years ago. We tend to be longer-term thinkers than mass-market publishers."

Foundations of Writing

While Brown has handed over most of the day-to-day operation of *Highlights* and Boyds Mills to Editor Christine French Clark and Boyds Mills Editorial Director Larry Rosler respectively, he's become more in-

volved in the Highlights Foundation. Since 1985, the Foundation had been providing instruction and inspiration to children's writers and illustrators. Through high-quality workshops and faculty, they've been able to mentor writers at all levels of experience.

Brown says the Foundation "actually happened backwards. I spent time at Chautauqua as a kid and rediscovered it as an adult as a kind of Mecca to promote the arts and education. I was trying to figure out how to put together that wonderful inspiring place and work with writers and artists for children. That's how we started the conference at Chautauqua."

You don't have a magazine or book company without creative people contributing, and Brown realized that Chautauqua was a way of nurturing new writers and giving back to the profession. "We've been in business a long time and our success is based on the people who contribute to our magazine," he says. "We wanted to do a deluxe conference. It's one of the longest, most intense, and has the smallest ratio of faculty to students of any writers' conference."

Egos are checked at the door at

Chautauqua. The faculty, which includes editors, illustrators, and the occasional Newbery or Caldecott winner, routinely mingles with all the conferees at meals and conference activities. They make sure conferees have the opportunity to know professional writers on a personal level and recognize that they're real people. "Just because they're famous doesn't mean they're any smarter. They've just suffered more rejection and worked at it harder," says Brown. "Even Lois Lowry and Eve Bunting worry about rejection."

Brown notes that it takes a tremendous effort and money to sponsor the Chautauqua Conference, which is heavily subsidized by the Highlights Corporation and Highlights Foundation. "It's a big undertaking, so intially we decided only to do one great one," he says. "But three years ago, we saw we could also fill a need for writers by offering short two-, three-, or four-day workshops in my grandparents' home in the country near Honesdale, Pennsylvania." The Foundation now sponsors about 14 a year. They differ from the Chautauqua Conference because they're more targeted, each covering a single topic.

There's no question in Brown's mind that all the effort is worth it. "I find it rewarding when people come and get something they need to move forward. We've had a lot of people benefit and succeed from that conference, mostly because they gain self-confidence."

Encouraging Authors

Beginning writers, as well as more seasoned ones, sometimes link their self-esteem to the number of acceptances and rejections they receive. Brown suggests writers put themselves in the place of the editors to understand their perspectives. "You've got to realize that for the most part, editors don't reject authors, but they often have to say no to manuscripts," he explains. "Editors have limited space in their magazines or a limited number of books they can publish. As a result, they decide which ones fit them best and they are most enthusiastic about. It doesn't mean manuscripts not chosen are failures, nor does it mean that some other editor won't choose them."

Brown counsels authors to be persistent and have faith in themselves. They have to avoid being discouraged. "It's impossible to go to more than a couple of writers' conferences, weekends, or critique groups and not discover that there are a lot of people who have waited a very long time and worked on things very hard and revised pieces before they got accepted. Newbery winner Jerry Spinelli wrote novels for 20 years before he got published."

Over the years, *Highlights* editors have built a reputation for encouraging authors with a quick note or comment, even on form rejection letters. "It's the decent thing to do, but the facts are you can't give everyone the feedback you'd like," says Brown. "It's just a question of how much time we can spend. In a perfect world, anyone who sent a story to *Highlights* would get some kind of personal critique and encourage them." Brown looks at it this way: The great writers for magazines and books of the next 50 years haven't all published yet. "The joy is finding them when they're beginning their careers. So philosophically and theoretically, you do what you can do for writers to help them."

Right now, Brown is also President of the United States Board on Books for Young People (USBBY), a part of the International Board on Books for Young People (IBBY). "I've been interested for a long time in the whole idea that books can make a difference in the lives of kids and their beliefs about people in other lands," says Brown. He has also been active in EdPress (the Association of Educational Publishers) and regularly attends International Reading Association (IRA), American Library Association (ALA), and National Council of Teachers of English (NCTE) national meetings. "My favorite thing is to go to these for books. I'm not a serious collector, but I come home from conventions with bunches of signed books. There are so many great juvenile books I haven't read. I love Laurence Yep, Jerry Spinelli, and Boyds Mills Press books, of course."

Brown continues to plant seeds in many rows. "My wish is that I will spend more time with authors at conventions and less time being a paper shuffler and administrator." "Farmer Brown" is also interested in returning to one of his favorite pastimes—raising vegetables, sheep, and hogs. "Right now I'm not doing any of these, but I dream about going back to it. I like being outdoors, working with my hands and building—these activities are a refreshing diversion from editing and publishing." Or another form of learning and creativity in a life dedicated to them.

Profile

Mike Goldman: Hitting a Home Run in the Children's Market

By Mark Haverstock

Many kids pretend they're sports stars. Mike Goldman liked to pretend he was a sportswriter covering big-league stars. "From as early as I can remember, I was writing my own stories about the Cincinnati Reds," he says. "I never had any job aspirations other than to be just like my grandfather." His grandfather, the late Si Burick, was a longtime sports editor for the *Dayton Daily News* and is enshrined in the writers' wing of the Baseball Hall of Fame at Cooperstown, New York.

Goldman's interest in sports led to being sports editor of his high school newspaper, then his college paper. "I earned my B.A. in journalism from the University of Missouri, a school that gives every student extensive real-world journalism and creative writing experience," Goldman says. "You get a chance to work at city newspapers, radio or TV stations, depending on your program." He got his first newsroom experience at the *Columbia Missourian* while still a student, later serving as Assistant Sports Editor. After graduation, he moved to the *Dallas Times Herald* as its Assistant Sports Editor, spent two years running *Neil Sperry's Gardens,* a regional gardening magazine, and did lots of freelance work, especially for sports publications.

Serving Scouts

In 1994, Goldman joined the *Boys' Life* staff, where he's currently Senior Editor. Goldman admits one of his best qualifications for his job is that he never grew up. "I have the attention span of a 12-year-old, so if a writer can hold my attention, I know he or she can hold our readers' attention."

Boys' Life remains successful because it is what it is—a 90-plus-year-old magazine published by the Boy Scouts of America that offers boys what they want. "No marketing games or crazy stunts," Goldman says. "We treat our audience as interested, and interesting, readers, not children. We keep things fresh, exciting, and entertaining."

Most of all, the magazine listens to readers and gives them what they want. The magazine is for the boys, not parents or editorial staff.

There's one fact that's not widely known by writers or readers: *Boys' Life* actually publishes three versions every month. The first is targeted to Tiger Cubs through Bear Cubs—generally ages 7 to 9. The second targets ages 10 and 11, and the third covers older readers, ages 12 to 18. "The key is being age-appropriate," says Goldman. "We don't want to try to dumb down older kids' stuff and spoon feed it to the younger kids, nor do we want to take something too simple and try to give it an edge for the older kids."

If you picked up a copy of their youngest edition, you'd see more comics. "That's been what our readers have wanted," says Goldman. "You'll see more Cub Scout activities in the lower demo, such as very simple *let's look-ats*: We pull out a specific topic—like, let's look at fire engines. It would be a two-page spread on fire engines and their parts, and then a second spread with coloring sheets, puzzles, and mazes about fire engines. These are on very general topics that younger kids can grab onto and learn about."

The oldest demographic version offers edgier feature articles that specifically appeal to the teen audience. "In a recent issue, we did a piece on finances," says Goldman. "A kid who's 14, 15, or 16 who's looking toward getting his first job, or is getting a sizeable allowance, is interested in what he can do with his money, either save it or spend it wisely." Many of the product features are geared toward older readers—things such as pocket knives, hiking boots, and other items kids this age will likely use in Scouting.

Writing in the Market

The key to writing for *Boys' Life*, or any other magazine in the children's and teen market, is to understand and respect your readers. "Successful writers do not talk down to their audience, nor do they treat their audience like children," says Goldman. "They write simply, but there's a big difference between good, clear, simple writing and being preachy or 'dumbing-down' your writing."

Since Goldman has considerable experience as a freelancer, he knows what it means to be rejected and what it takes to succeed. "As an editor, I like to think that I give every prospective writer the same opportunity to succeed that I would want to be given," he says.

To succeed at *Boys' Life*, you really need to know the magazine and its policies. The first mistake many writers make is sending unsolicited manuscripts instead of queries. "I get about 30 unsolicited manuscripts a month and those are turned around right away with a rejection," says Goldman. "As for queries, we get about 100 to 150 per month. Quite honestly, what distinguishes a good query from one not so good comes down to feel. I've looked at queries for so long that I can tell pretty quickly what I like and what I don't like."

He also notes that *Boys' Life* is a very specific market with very specific needs. "Often the material we get is too general—the kind of stuff you'd find in a textbook, which isn't what we're looking for," he says. "Coming up with an idea for kids is not rocket science. We've all been kids, and many writers have kids." Articles on topics of boy interest or with a Scouting hook are a plus.

Occasionally, Goldman will get a query that's on target and will take a chance on the author because he or she has presented the idea well and more important, told him why they should be the person to write it. "Anybody can write to me and say I want to do a story about Alex Rodriguez. Fine, so do I. But why should *you* do it?" says Goldman. "I need to know why a writer is *the* writer to do the subject. What special insight or angle can this author come up with to make it a creative piece, and make it truly a *Boys' Life* piece?"

Changing Times

Not satisfied to maintain the status quo, *Boys' Life* has just undergone an extensive redesign to bring it more up-to-date and it will continue to be updated as needed. "Our basic audience and emphasis have not changed, nor will they," explains Goldman. "The mission is simple and timeless: to reach every level of reader through an entertaining and educating variety of general interest articles, fiction, and cartoons, while reinforcing Scouting's strong values and programs." The magazine "For All Boys," as its subtitle calls it, has positively influenced generations of readers and will continue to educate and entertain generations to come.

Its most recent redesign is both graphic and editorial. In the past, the front of book material consisted of one full page on a subject, such as science, history, or aviation, and occasionally up to three briefs on another page. Now there's much more material incorporated into those few pages—shorter but meatier content. "A kid can flip through that Heads-Up section and he's going to find something he wants to read in there. I can guarantee it," says Goldman. "Every kid's going to pick it up every month and find something that he wants to read because there's so much good material in there." The strategy, also used by other magazines and newspapers, is to present a variety of bite-sized nuggets up front to draw the reader in.

According to regular focus groups on subject matter, readers' wants and requests are remarkably similar year after year. "They still like reading about sports and cars; they still like our Think & Grin and Scouts in Action departments," says Goldman. "The same things that ranked high this year ranked high when I started here 10 years ago, which is really amazing when you think about the changes in the marketplace in general." *Boys' Life* also gets feedback from their mail, which gives them a handle on kids' thoughts and interests. "We'll know if there is a trend developing in the automotive or sports world the kids are following. If you're not in tune with your readership, you're failing them."

Scouting content in *Boys' Life* has remained much the same. "We'll always cover the outings; they're a staple. Without them, we're just another kids' magazine," says Goldman. "Kids still want to read about great trips they can take, so we still tell them how to do it. You can't take outing out of Scouting, and you can't take it out of *Boys' Life*."

Purpose and Values

Boys' Life reflects the beliefs and values of the Boy Scout organization, as well as the traditional values of middle America. "There are magazines, lots of them, that do not seem to place any value on values," says Goldman. "*Boys' Life* proves that it is possible, and highly desirable, to reach out to our youth through solid content, not trash."

According to Goldman, messages are not heavy-handed. "We don't hit them over the head by telling them what they should or shouldn't do. The principles are integrated into the Scouting program," he says. "We're successful because we are what we are. I say that seriously. *Boys' Life* has developed itself over the years. People expect a certain something out of our magazine and we try to give them that."

As a parent and editor, Goldman has a particular interest in literacy. "Our goal all along has been to get kids to read, whether it's *Boys' Life* or something else," says Goldman. "For instance, if a kid picks up our magazine and reads about a trek up Mount Rainier, he might think it's a really neat place and continue to find out more about it at the library or on the Internet. We want to pique their interest so they'll want to find out more."

Goldman's goal is to keep hitting those home runs with his audience and making *Boys' Life* the best possible magazine it can be. "As long as we keep giving our readers the solid content they want in a form they enjoy, we're going to succeed and we'll continue to grow."

Profile

Paula Morrow: In Touch with Writers & Writing

By Mark Haverstock

Paula Morrow has had a connection with stories and writing since her earliest days. She's currently Executive Editor of *Ladybug* and *Babybug*, both magazines in the Cricket Group, and Editor with Cricket Books. She is a published author of children's, adult, and professional materials and a regular columnist for *Once Upon a Time,* a writer's magazine.

In the Beginning

"I can't remember a time when I didn't know I was a writer," says Morrow. "Even before I could read and write by myself, it was just sort of in there. My mother read to me, but then after she turned out the light and went away, I'd lie awake in the dark making up stories."

Morrow was 14 when her first published piece appeared in the old Girl Scout magazine called *American Girl,* no relation to the current *American Girl* published by the Pleasant Company. "My dad was in the Army, and we had moved so I missed the issue of the magazine" in which the story was published, says Morrow. "I didn't even know it had been published until I received some fan mail." The fan letter was addressed with only her name and Camp Zama, Japan, but amazingly the Army postal clerks tracked her down and forwarded it.

Morrow used to write stories in a notebook she always carried with her, often practicing her creative writing talents instead of doing homework. "I had a faithful group of friends who'd follow me around and want to hear the latest chapter," she says. "That attention was reinforcing." She was also a natural at editing. "Way back in grade school and junior high, other kids would have me read their writing assignments, and I would correct them before they turned them in."

When she was in junior high, Morrow decided on a library career. "I discovered that, when my friends had to write papers, I loved finding books for them," she explains. Morrow graduated from college with no major but an eclectic liberal arts degree. "My three Rs were rhetoric, religion, and Russian," she jokes. Her broad variety of courses qualified her for graduate school, where she earned her library degree. After completing her master's degree, Morrow worked in a variety of libraries—government, medical, academic, and corporate.

At first she resisted when a friend asked her to apply for a children's librarian opening in a public library. "Much to my surprise, I was hooked. That's the library position where I was happiest. I stayed there for a long time."

Once she discovered the professional world of children's literature, Morrow set herself a goal. "I decided to aim for the [American Library Association] Newbery Committee," which selects the best children's book of the year. "I figured it would take five years. Two years later, I was on the Newbery Committee." This was a high point in her library career. Morrow also worked several years as a freelance librarian for a variety of individual, school, and corporate clients—until she heard from the Cricket Magazine Group.

Bit by the Bug

Actually, the Cricket connection originated with her husband. "Bob was foreman of a 1,200-acre cattle ranch in southwest Missouri," she says. "One day, I came home from town and found him sitting on the porch swing with a tablet in his lap, writing something. He said, 'I'm writing a children's story. I'm gonna sell it to *Cricket*.' I said, 'yeah, right.' Well, darned if he didn't sell them that story, and the next one and the next. The folks at *Cricket* all called him 'Farmer Bob.'" Somewhere during this time, he mentioned his wife Paula in a letter to his editor, telling of her library and literary background. Not long after, she received a call from the Carus personnel director asking if she would like to interview for an opening. The rest is history. She began as *Ladybug* editor in 1991, helped launch *Babybug* in 1994, and began editing books in 2001.

Being editor of two of the Cricket Group magazines would seem to be a daunting task, especially with the volume of manuscripts they receive—collectively averaging 1,500 a month. Morrow explains their system for dealing with the large number of submissions. "When the mail comes in every morning, the administrative assistant date-stamps every envelope and reads every cover letter. Unsolicited pieces are forwarded to a first reader. The first readers are instructed to be very generous. If there's any kind of spark in a manuscript, they write comments on the envelope and send it back to the office for a second reading. At that point, the manuscript goes to an in-house editor, who decides whether it gets a third reading."

According to Morrow, any of the readers can opt to form-reject. But once something goes to the second in-house reader (the third reading) a file is created. Each editor writes a reader report. The compiled comments go to the Editor in Chief of *Cricket* and *Cicada* or the Editorial Director of *Ladybug, Spider,* and *Babybug,* who then makes the accept or reject decision and sends it back to the issue editor. "We do have the option of arguing if we don't agree," Morrow says. "You can see why it takes so long for a submission to work its way through this route and why we appreciate writers' patience."

Staying on Target

So how do you get your writing past that third reader? "The most important thing is sensitivity to children," says Morrow. "It always amazes me when I meet writers who talk about how anxious they are to be published, yet as I listen, I get the feeling they don't really like children. Why would anyone write for an audience he or she doesn't like?"

Morrow also believes authors need to have a sensitivity to literature. You have to be able to write something that's worth reading. You have to be playful and not take yourself too seriously. Keep your sense of humor and your sense of wonder. "When my husband was a kid, he heard his dad tell his mom, 'That boy is like a goose. He wakes up to a new world every morning,'"

says Morrow. "I think that's a great compliment. In fact, he still looks at the world each day with a fresh perspective."

Since Morrow deals with magazines for the preschool set, she knows that targeting this age group can be a challenge for writers. "You really have to understand child development," says Morrow. "Writing a story and marketing it as being for ages 6 to 14 reveals that you really don't understand either the 6-year-old or the 14-year-old."

One of the most common manuscript problems she sees is authors underestimating children. "The tone should never be condescending or cutesy, especially with readaloud stories," Morrow explains. "Treat children with respect. Some manuscripts seem to be winking at the adult who is reading and not simply enjoying a good story with the child. The best manuscripts address both the child listener and the adult listener—especially if that adult has to read the story 50 times."

Rejections are a fact of life in the publishing industry, and sometimes Morrow finds herself in a bind when it comes to responding to authors. "I do respect people who send in manuscripts. If they can go to the trouble of sending them, I can certainly go to the trouble of responding with a positive comment," she says. "When I put a form rejection in an envelope, I know what it can mean to add a little personal note. It buoys the writer, and I like to do that if I can do it honestly. I like to take a minute to jot a note saying a particular aspect was well-done, or perhaps saying the manuscript is good, but we can't use it for a particular reason."

Sometimes these notes backfire. Writers start submitting unrequested revisions, and Morrow ends up reading the same manuscripts over and over. "When that happens, I get bummed out and I stop writing the notes," she says. "But after a while, I'll see something I can't resist mentioning, and then I start all over again."

Networking with the Writing Community

Part of Morrow's job description includes speaking at conferences and workshops. "I hadn't been at *Ladybug* very long before they handed me an airplane ticket and an itinerary," she says. "Fortunately, I'd had all those years in the library to get used to being in front of groups and planning literary programs; the two jobs are actually very compatible!" Over the years, Morrow has become a very popular speaker at these events.

Conferences and workshops are part of the growth process and a way to meet editors, agents, and other writers. "You're learning skills, finding out about the market, and picking up all kinds of valuable information," Morrow says. "Yes, you'll really have an opportunity to talk to the speakers at a conference. There's lots of elbow-rubbing at meal functions, break times, small group sessions." According to Morrow, the face-to-face time gives writers a chance to pick editors' brains, to find out what they're looking for, how they think, and what they like or don't like. It's also an opportunity to find out first-hand whether your own work is a good fit for a particular publisher, or whether you'd rather cross that house off your list and focus your efforts elsewhere.

Making connections with other writers at conferences and workshops is one of the most valuable things you can do. Don't hesitate to schmooze a little. Take a supply of business cards, including your e-mail address, for later communication and maybe participation in email manuscript critiques. "Pay attention to the questions other people ask in the sessions and the comments you hear at meals. Notice the other writers who seem to be on your wavelength or who write in your area of interest," says Morrow. "Then introduce yourself and ask if they'd like to stay in touch." Networking with other writers gives you the opportunity to share market tips, give each other suggestions, and support each other.

While it won't directly improve

your chances of acceptance, a conference will give you some of the tools to hone your skills. "Attending a conference will never get a bad manuscript accepted," says Morrow. "The bottom line is that your work has to be good. If it is, then publication is only a matter of time."

Take That Job & Love It

Morrow's tenure with the Cricket Group has been relatively long, considering the turnover in the publishing business. She credits this stability in large part to Marianne Carus, *Cricket*'s founder, Editor in Chief, and guiding spirit. "One reason I've been with them so long and have no intention of leaving is that Marianne and I share the same literary sensibilities," says Morrow. "We don't agree on every individual manuscript, but we have the same core values, the same appreciation for language and substance and literary quality. It's just a really good fit."

She does daydream about other possibilities. "When my kids were in college, it reminded me how much I loved that life," she says. "I think it would be cool to teach at the college level. I've got all the course work completed toward a Ph.D. in English, but I haven't gotten around to registering for the comps."

Asked whether she has any wish yet to be granted, Morrow hesitated only a moment. "I'd love to edit a Newbery or Caldecott book," she said. "Why don't you send me one?"

Book Publishing

A Peek at Packagers & Novelty Books

By Gail Minett Eltringham

If an award were given for the flashiest segment of book publishing, one of the contenders would have to be novelty books and the packagers who produce them.

I've been writing for packagers of children's books for almost 14 years, and I love it. Mostly, I've authored novelty books: the children's books with plush animals, toys, acetate see-through windows, flaps, split pages, holes, pop-ups, wheels, shaped books, books that make sounds, and all manner of interactive and innovative aspects that add dimension to a story. Novelty book packagers, because of the special physical needs of their projects, take their involvement in producing the books further than other publishers.

Book packaging is a part of publishing little known by people outside the industry. Also called *book producers* or *book developers,* packagers are responsible for many of the more complicated books found in stores. A majority of packagers specialize in one type of book, but whatever that type, the titles are almost always highly illustrated and elaborately designed or multi-authored. They may be for adults or children: how-to books, coffee-table books, reference books, textbooks, cookbooks, preschool arts and crafts activity books, children's storybooks, and many more categories. The products run the gamut of publishing markets, including trade, mass-market, educational, professional, reference, and juvenile.

An idea might begin with a packager, who takes it to a publisher or other possible customer, such as a museum. Or a publisher or other customer has a need and approaches the packager. The packager then pulls together a team of writers, editors, designers, illustrators, photographers, researchers, and other specialized talent to develop a book—finding the most creative, most knowledgeable people for a particular assignment.

Case Study One: Books or Toys?

World-renowned novelty book creator Stewart Cowley, Publishing

Director and cofounder of Cowley Hunter in Bath, in the U.K., says that a writer's skill in meeting specifications is essential to a packager: "The ability of a contributor to understand what we are looking for and accurately reflect the brief is paramount. The fact that we are talking to them means that we already like the way they work."

Cowley Hunter produces approximately 40 titles a year, handling all aspects of production and delivering finished books to the customer. "The nature of our books," says Cowley, "means that we have to work closely with printers and suppliers to ensure production quality, as they are often being called on to supply concepts that, by definition, have not been produced before."

Therein lies proof of packager genius. In lead times varying from six to nine months, depending on the nature of the novelty element, Cowley and his staff use their expertise in paper and board book concepts that often incorporate plush, plastics, or even wood to make books that perform physically. They prefer these various elements because they believe that they effectively preserve the tactile appeal of a book.

Where does Cowley get his ideas? "I'm not certain," he answers thoughtfully. "I'm not sure that I know. Never having really grown up

> "I don't believe children make clear distinctions between books and toys . . . so I try and find new ways of drawing both fields together. If successful, the result can be a particularly powerful tool for information and learning."

helps. I still get excited at finding new ways of making existing materials and technologies do something they were not intended to do. I don't believe young children make clear distinctions between books and toys and regard both as forms of entertainment, so I try and find new ways of drawing both fields together. If successful, the result can be a particularly powerful tool for information and learning."

The novelty book market really is a contest of new ideas. What will intrigue an age group? What will sell? It takes a lot of upfront time to produce just one original format. This research and design work is what makes the motor run at packaging houses like Cowley Hunter.

The company serves markets throughout the world, so they have to do a great deal of work on meeting and exceeding international safety standards. The safety of a new concept is an issue that looms over every decision. Once the format has been created, it is sold to publishers. This means researching markets, categories, and price points to ensure that their proposals are as commercially viable as possible.

Cowley explains, "Exceptions are primarily in the area of licensed character applications, where publishers advise us of new acquisitions

Soundly Growing

The fastest growing segment of the novelty book market consists of interactive books with electronic devices that work in conjunction with the text. Since LeapFrog Enterprises introduced its LeapPad in 1995, these electronic books have (excuse the pun) leapt over the competition, particularly with preschoolers. Preschoolers and early readers can learn to read as an electronic device speaks the words aloud.

These soundbooks are the wave of the future. As of this writing, most industry soundbook leaders have stayed with well-known children's titles and licensed characters. Sometimes, the authors of the original books are involved in the production. For example, Sam McBratney recorded *Guess How Much I Love You?* and Marc Brown recorded some new material for *Arthur Writes a Story*. However, with the larger demand for interactive readers, this could be yet another way for a writer to go. Whatever the book format, the story still has to hold up. Dependence on the interactivity will not keep a child's attention for the long haul.

Not every packager is heading in this direction, however. "Relying on electronics moves the product closer to the toy field than we are comfortable with and often addresses older age groups," says Stewart Cowley, Publishing Director and cofounder of the U.K.'s Cowley Hunter Ltd. But he acknowledges about the future of novelty books, "Preconceptions about what comprises a book are broadening all the time, and publishers are increasingly aware of steadily growing interest in original novelty formats. They are recognizing the entertainment and educational appeal provided by truly interactive book forms."

and brief us on target age groups, price points, and the nature of the license. We then adapt or devise suitable formats accordingly."

To find the most receptive markets, Cowley says, "We study markets and inform ourselves of their lists, house styles, and market channels of the key players, so that when we come up with new formats, we have a sales strategy for each market."

Case Study 2: Into the Novelty Book Pool

Personal experience in publishing moved me from traditional books to packaging and ultimately to writing novelty books myself.

After five years of producing traditional 32-page children's books for a small publishing company, I changed jobs and found myself thrown head first into the deep end of the novelty book pool at Reader's

Working for a Packager

If you are interested in writing for a packager, make sure you research each company before you send samples. Your skills must match their needs. In some cases, the characters and setting are already developed. In the case of more experienced writers, they may be given an idea and asked to come up with characters and plot.

Once you are hired to write a book or part of a book (some reference books have multiple authors), you are sent an outline to work from. If you are inexperienced, the packager may need to receive a chapter or two from you—written based on the packager's directives and an outline—before you are formally hired. You may be asked to write in a very specific style in keeping with the rest of the book or a series of books.

Writing for a packager is on a work-for-hire basis. Packagers do not pay an advance or royalties. You receive a flat fee negotiated in advance. The amount of the fee depends on the packager and the assignment. All rights to your work automatically transfer to the packager. It depends on the project, but generally, the pay is modest. As the writer, you will have your name printed on the cover or copyright page as the author or one of the authors. This helps beginning writers to accumulate experience.

Prospective freelance writers should send a cover letter with a strong pitch. Include information about current and past writing credits, editing

Digest Children's Books. Suddenly, I was managing editor for more than 90 novelty titles a year, produced in the U.K. and the U.S. Everything squeaked or clicked or moved or had pages you could see through. On top of the editorial overload of titles running through my office (both British and American), I worked for the creative director of the company, an exceptionally gifted perfectionist whose deep voice could be heard on the floor below when he was unhappy. I figured I'd better learn the novelty book business fast.

First, I strolled down to production (even though I'd been a production director before) and set up an interview with the head of that department. You see, there are extra steps in producing a novelty book. The plush reindeer must look like a cute little Rudolph. In China, where many of the plush animals for these books are made, they had no clue as to how a reindeer should look and didn't believe our illustrations. So, they found a picture of one in an encyclopedia.

Working for a Packager

or other publishing experience, and other relevant background. Indicate how much time you can give to freelance work, and your computer and other technological knowledge and capabilities. The package should include a list of writing credits, and several samples of your writing, preferably showing some variety but also targeted to the kind of materials the packager produces. Don't forget to say why this particular packager is of interest to you as a writer, and include all contact information.

One of the challenges of writing for novelty formats is that you have to meet deadlines much faster than a publisher allows for a traditional title. This is particularly true of books based on licensed names.

Everything works backward from the time the book is due to be displayed at the stores. When you're dealing with a new Disney movie, the books have to be available on or before the movie opens. Any delay in production (a sound module doesn't work properly; die-cut pages line up incorrectly) can cost precious time. The text, especially for a series, may have to be written and revised in a matter of days. Sometimes, the client takes a long time approving the text, leaving the packager with a very small time window to revise. Hopefully, the original text is close to publishable. Again, follow the criteria of the packager's editor. Awareness of style and approach is extremely important.

Real reindeer are not all that cute. It took months before we had a cuddly, usable sample. The scenes behind the acetate "windows" of a book would have to fit exactly, as would the text. I needed to know how all these situations were handled before I could perform my job competently.

My first experience writing stories for novelty books came when I was asked to rewrite two story lines from the U.K., which turned out to be *The Big Yellow Bus* and *The Big Blue Plane*. In these oversized books shaped to look like their titles, animal characters were getting on and off at different places. Although large formats, these books were actually for preschoolers. I had never written for ages three and four before. Ages eight and above were my earlier territory. It took days, but I finally got all the animals to and from their destinations using words that were age-appropriate.

Once I got the hang of creating and writing for a packager of novelty books, I decided it was much more challenging and fun than writing for the traditional kind. We did everything in-house. The ideas were created there. Some of the books we kept under the Reader's Digest logo, and some ideas we sold to companies like Fisher-Price, Disney, and Mattel, the maker of Barbie. There were three divisions, with an art director for each one in the U.S. and one art director in the U.K. The art directors would hire the artists, who had to be well-versed in the peculiar intricacies of each format. There was one managing editor for the U.S., and I handled the U.S. editions of the U.K. titles.

The world of novelty children's book packagers can be intense for everyone involved, including the authors. For writers, mostly you have to do your homework. Know what will be expected of you, and give it to them. Once the company knows you can follow instructions for a certain type of project, and once they like your work, packagers will return to you, a known source of talent.

Children's Novelty Book Packagers

Cowley Hunter Publishing: 8 Belmont Bath, United Kingdom BA1 5DZ. www.cowleyhunter. com. Stewart Cowley, Publishing Director.

Dreamland: 3 Morgan Ave., Norwalk, CT 06851. Michael Morris, President.

Emma Treehouse: Little Orchard House, Mill Lane, Beckington, Somerset, United Kingdom BA11 6SN. www.emmatreehouse.com Contact: Hilary Allom, Sales.

Innovative Kids: 18 Ann St., Norwalk, CT 06854. www.innovativekids.com Shari Kaufman, President.

Parragon: 1250 Broadway, 24th floor, New York, NY 10001. www.parragon.com. Contact: Creative Director.

Reader's Digest Children's Publishing: Reader's Digest Road, Pleasantville, NY 10570. www.rd.com. Rosanne McManus, Associate Publisher.

Book Agents

To Have & to Hold, 'Til out of Print We Do Part

By Judy Bradbury

In the life of an author, there are those who support, those who cheer, and those who aid and abet. (We won't mention distracting detractors.) These good souls include spouses or partners, children, pets, relatives, friends, critique groups, editors, and possibly an agent. And while you may think the editor is the single most important person you interact with on a professional level, think again. An editor is with you as you work to produce one book, maybe two books, maybe a series of books. Your agent, on the other hand, if you choose to hire one, and if the union is a match made in heaven, is with you from when you send your manuscripts out into the world until your books have permanently disappeared from the shelves. That could mean beyond your life-span! It's a marriage. Hopefully, a solid one.

The question is how to get to a proposal when you can't even find an eligible date.

Much like finding an editor who seems like a good match, finding an agent requires work on the author's part. Follow the advice you got from Mom when you began dating: Take your time. Don't be hasty. By attending conferences, reading writer publications, and visiting online sites, an author can vicariously get to know who's out there, who's open to submissions, and most of all, what specific agents are looking for. Are you and a prospective agent a good match?

Getting to Know You

With this in mind, welcome to a panel in print. Gathered here are selected agents who work primarily in the children's field. Like a live panel, they all answered the same questions. Unlike an actual panel, they didn't have the benefit of hearing each other's responses. Good news, bad news. They didn't have the opportunity to add to each other's responses, make pithy remarks, interject a one-liner, or vociferously interrupt each other. The audience doesn't get a sense of the agents' personalities by way of their tone of voice, facial expressions, impromptu comments, or reactions to the questions. Nevertheless, we've invited them—and you—in. So come get acquainted!

Sit back and relax. Think of this as a virtual first date. Read the responses and reflect on the advice these agents offer. Then when you're ready, wash your hair, put on your best duds, smile, and head out into the world. In other words, when your work is the best it can be, start looking. Choose an agent carefully, and when marriage seems the next best step, propose!

Your Dance Card: The Panel

Andrea Cascardi: "I worked as an editor and publisher of children's books for 20 years, with various houses, starting at Houghton Mifflin. I was part of the start-up team at Hyperion Books for Children, and was the Associate Publishing Director for Knopf and Crown Books for Young Readers before my current role as a U.S. agent affiliated with Canada's Transatlantic Literary Agency."

Steven Chudney: "My very first job in publishing was selling paperbacks for Dell Publishing in their telemarketing department. Since then I have held various sales and marketing positions at Viking Penguin; Farrar, Straus & Giroux; Simon & Schuster; and Winslow Press, where I held the position of Senior Director of Marketing, Sales & Subsidiary Rights. After over 15 years in book publishing I decided in 2002 to become an agent. I opened the Chudney Agency, specializing in the wonderful world of children's books and other kid-related properties."

Jennie Dunham: "I have been a literary agent in New York, New York, since May 1992. Before starting my own agency, I worked at Russell & Volkening, which has a quality list of literary writers. In August 2000, I founded Dunham Literary. I have been a member of AAR (Association of Authors' Representatives) since 1993. I have been on the Program Committee since 1993 and served several of those years as Program Committee Director. Dunham Literary represents authors of quality fiction and nonfiction books for adults and children. We also represent some illustrators for children's books."

Barry Goldblatt: "I began my publishing career as a lowly but energetic rights assistant at Dutton Children's Books, and proceeded to assiduously climb the corporate ladder, moving first to the Putnam & Grosset Group, then finally to Orchard Books as Rights and Contracts Director. In September 2000, I decided it was time to switch to the other side of the desk, and so I opened my own literary agency. Barry Goldblatt Literary Agency represents everything from very young picture books up through high YA fiction. I do not handle nonfiction (unless, of course, someone decides to write the YA equivalent of *Midnight in the Garden of Good and Evil*)."

Karen Grencik: "I am a part-time literary agent and a full-time court reporter. I love my day job, but I tackled the book business because of my love of books and desire to help people succeed. My clients have won numerous awards, including the Golden Kite for best picture book text, the Parents' Choice Gold Award for nonfiction, and the Benjamin Franklin Award for best first fiction. Unfortunately, as much as I'd like to assist more writers in achieving their dreams, in an effort to lead a balanced life, I am not able to accept submissions at this time."

The Lowdown: Questions and Answers

■ *In your opinion, what is the advantage of having the services of an agent?*

AC: "An agent is your partner. You can discuss things with your agent, whether about what you're working on, or something to do with the business side of writing, such as contracts, or marketing, that authors without an agent must handle on their own. Your agent is not only your advocate to the publisher; he also wants the best for you because that's in his best interest, too."

SC: "There are several advantages: An agent is someone who understands the intricacies of the business, knows the editors and their tastes, has the ability to move things forward, helps you develop your career as an author, and most important, allows you the time to write, write, write."

BG: "Most important, it allows a writer to focus on writing. No need to spend hours researching editors,

negotiating contracts, trying to stay on top of all the paperwork that is involved in any deal, etc. It's also great to have a partner as you head out into the big, bad world of publishing."

KG: "There are people who need an agent and those who don't. Some people are very organized and do an excellent job of keeping their manuscripts circulating. Others have a difficult time staying on top of it, and that's where an agent can really help. It's also nice to have someone to call when you have a question or a concern, knowing that person is in your court. We're good at negotiating, know what to look for in your contracts, and hopefully can alleviate a lot of the pressure from the business aspect of writing."

JD: "There are many advantages. Writers and illustrators can concentrate more on the creative process if they have someone to handle the noncreative part of the business. Also, the writer can have someone else play bad cop when necessary. And it's helpful to a writer to have an expert on top of contacts and contracts."

■ *In your opinion, at what point in his/her career should an author begin to think about looking for an agent?*

BG: "There's no right or wrong answer here. For some, an agent from the get-go is a great idea. For others, an agent isn't needed until mid-career. It's all about what the writer feels most comfortable doing. The caveat is that, of course, it is easier to get read by editors if you have a good, reputable agent."

AC: "I think it can happen at any time in a writer's career. This depends on the writer and their goal in obtaining an agent: whether to get a first foot in the door or to handle more complicated aspects of a growing career."

JD: "This is different for every author. Some like an agent to help them break into the business. Some don't want an agent until they need to manage schedules and organize money."

SC: "Different authors have different needs. I have taken on unpublished authors and have started mapping out their careers, and then I have taken on an author who had written 10 previous books, and I've successfully jump-started her career. So it really all depends on the individual client."

KG: "After they've done a whole lot of homework, attended many conferences, worked on dozens of manuscripts, and received lots of positive feedback from professionals in the industry. I am so tired of hearing people say, 'I wrote a picture book for my granddaughter last week and everyone thinks I should get it published!'"

■ *How should an author go about choosing an agent?*

JD: "This process is different for every author. Some ask author friends about their agents. Some people look in books to read about agents. Some people go to conferences to meet agents. The agent should be enthusiastic about the author and his or her work and know how to pitch it."

SC: "I always recommend that they do so just as they would when going about looking for a new doctor or lawyer. The best way is word of mouth: a glowing recommendation by a fellow writer would be ideal. If not, try looking into the various list-servs and chatrooms, and ask for help from others. The SCBWI (Society of Children's Book Writers and Illustrators) is also a good source, as are the many books about how to get published."

AC: "Research and word-of-mouth. Ask writer friends who have an agent what the benefits are, what they like about their arrangement with their agent, and what they would change if they could. Ask for recommendations if at all possible. Find an agency and an agent whose philosophy and style of working seems best suited to your own."

KG: "The easiest way is through the SCBWI's list of agents or the *Children's Writer's & Illustrator's Market* list, where you can see what each agent is looking for. There's also the Association of Authors' Representatives (AAR) list, which you can get off the Internet. Some agents (like me) don't want the exposure of being on a list, so when you meet an unlisted, independent agent at an SCBWI conference, it doesn't mean they aren't good. It simply means they're trying to regulate the amount of mail and phone calls they receive."

BG: "The same way an author would go about choosing which editor to submit a manuscript to. Research, research, research. Online, in books, talking to other writers—that's how you find out all you can about a particular agent. If you then feel you'd make a good fit, find out the agent's submission guidelines and go for it."

If you were an author, what types of questions would you ask an agent whom you were considering working with?

SC: "How long have you been an agent? What is your background, and how did you decide to become an agent? What is your work style? Do you charge any fees?"

KG: "Do you return your phone calls and emails? How long is the term of your contract? Do you keep your authors apprised of what you're doing for them? Is it possible for me to speak with one of your clients? Since agents are so busy, it's best if you can get this information before you approach them. It's somewhat off-putting to be approached by someone who asks for your help, then grills you to see what you can do for him or her."

AC: "I would ask what the agent's expectations were, and I would ask what would happen if the agent and the author disagree on whether or not a manuscript is ready for submission. In other words, how will you deal with any conflict in the relationship? An agent/client relationship is in many ways a partnership

Spruce up for the First Date

Ask friends and colleagues who represents them and how the relationship is going.

Consult resources that provide information on agents.

Follow submission guidelines.

Be professional in all interactions.

Be ready to "interview" your prospective agent if he or she is interested in representing you.

Is the agent a member of the Association of Authors' Representatives (AAR)? This is a professional, not-for-profit organization that sets standards, has strict requirements for membership, and requires members to subscribe to its Canon of Ethics.

Never pay for the *date:* Don't sign with an agent who asks for reading or similar fees.

and you have to be prepared for disagreements. If your style and method of communicating is too different, if your expectations are too different, the relationship will have little chance of being a successful one in the long run."

BG: "Aside from all the obvious things (commission rate/submission style/turnaround time), I'd really focus on the personality and character of the agent. Not that you should go poking and prying with personal questions per se, but just have a good long conversation with him or her and see if you are compatible."

Meeting Places

▨ Conferences
▨ Personal introductions from colleagues
▨ Through resources such as:
   – Association of Authors' Representatives, Inc., P.O. Box 237201, Ansonia Station, New York, NY 10003; www.aar-online.org
   – Authors Guild, 31 East 28th Street, 10th Floor, New York, NY 10016; www.authorsguild.org
   – Harold Underdown's website: www.underdown.org
   – *Literary Market Place:* annual publication; often available in the reference section of libraries.

JD: "I'd ask about the terms of doing business with that agent. I'd ask how they see the manuscript and how they'd pitch me as a writer. I'd be clear about what's important to me and ask if the agent could be behind me to support those issues."

▨ *Do you have caveats for a writer looking for an agent?*

KG: "It's best if you can talk to someone the agent represents in order to find out how they conduct business. You don't want to be locked into a long-term contract when things aren't working out between the two of you. Although it's very exciting to hear that someone is interested in your work, you must research that person before you sign. People from many industries prey on authors desperate to be published and unscrupulous agents abound."

BG: "Never sign with an agent who charges you fees. Any agent who asks you for a check is not legit, and should be avoided at all costs. Also, don't think getting an agent is a guarantee of publication; it certainly can help, but sometimes, we're wrong. Finally, never forget that an agent is an author's employee, working on his or her behalf; just like a lawyer, an agent can advise, but the author calls the shots."

AC: "Make sure that your goals in having an agent are realistic. Be prepared to hear negative as well as enthusiastic comments from your agent from time to time. Be prepared to write and revise and write again. An agent can't change the fact that writing is still hard work and that getting published is largely the by-product of that hard work, the same as it is for writers without an agent."

JD: "Having an agent means having someone to help you with the business. It doesn't mean an immediate sale."

SC: "Make sure that your agent doesn't charge any fees, and make certain that you both have the right chemistry—which is as important as it would be in any relationship."

▨ *What types of work do you represent?*

KG: "Trade picture books, middle-grade, and young adult, both fiction and nonfiction. No specialty markets, easy readers, or board books, and very few chapter books. I like emotion. I like to learn something new. I like beautiful language. I like beautiful images."

AC: "I represent all types of work for all ages through young adult, though not much science fiction or fantasy because it's not a personal passion of mine despite its popularity right now."

JD: "I represent authors and illustrators who create work from high-end novelty (birth to 3) to young adult (13 to 16 and 17 to 22). I also represent adult book writers."

SC: "I represent everything from young picture books all the way up to edgy teen novels. And I do have a couple of adult clients as well. Although due to the current marketplace, I am not looking for any new picture book clients (or poetry or nonfiction), I am looking for older fiction, particularly teen novels."

GB: "I'm mostly focused on YA right now, but middle-grade is also appealing to me. I don't have any particular genre needs, because I don't make decisions based on genre. I make it based on quality of the work, and sometimes that quality will turn out to be a gothic horror novel, or a girls-go-shopping tell-all. I do tend to gravitate towards edgier work, but I'm always eagerly searching for great comic writing as well. I prefer character-driven work, and also lean towards the quirky, edgy, and offbeat. What matters most is the writing; if it's brilliantly written, I'm interested."

What piques your interest in a prospective client?

SC: "It really all comes down to their writing. Nothing else: not that they are a parent or grandparent, that they taught kids for 15 years, that a whole bunch of people just love their stories. Wonderful writing by an author who understands what kids love to read is key."

BG: "Great writing. I know it's a cop out of an answer, but it really is the only thing that matters. After I'm hooked by the writing, however, there are lots of other factors, the most important being how well we connect when I call to discuss possible representation."

AC: "Always, I have to be passionate about the writer's work. I like to see as much from the prospective client as possible before deciding whether to represent someone because while I may be excited about the first manuscript they send me, I might not be as excited about the next five things, and then our relationship wouldn't work. Also, I look to balance my client list as much as possible, so depending on my current client list, I may be looking for new writers who work in different areas."

JD: "I like a compelling story and a fresh, strong voice."

KG: "A serious author who attends conferences, works with a strong critique group, and has a delightful disposition! Also, because I do this for reasons different from most, I want my clients to care as much about my well-being as I do theirs. I like to work with nice, pleasant, talented people. I don't have time for aggressive, complaining, self-centered people."

■ *How do you work with your clients?*

GB: "I'm pretty hands-on in just about every facet of my clients' careers. I do a lot of editorial work with each of my clients, when it's necessary, to get a manuscript into the best shape possible. Obviously I negotiate deals, sell foreign, film, TV and other subsidiary rights, and I also advise on marketing issues when possible."

JD: "The writing is up to the client, but I often respond with comments about the manuscript in order to have it as strong as possible when submitting."

SC: "I am very hands-on when it comes to editing: If I feel a piece isn't quite ready to go out, I wouldn't submit it, and I work with the author on revisions. I like to be involved editorially, and then because of my background, I can also work with my client and the publisher with some sales and marketing issues further on in the process."

AC: "Since I was an editor for 20 years, I do tend to give editorial input to my clients, but only up to a point. I wouldn't take on a client if I didn't feel that the core of their work had value that was perceivable by an editor other than myself. However, I would never send out something without making sure it represented the author's best capabilities."

KG: "I do some copy editing, but mostly I offer a lot of support during the stressful periods. The waiting game is very hard on most authors. Again, since I do this for different reasons, my priority is that my authors lead fulfilling and happy lives, so I'm not one to push an author. I'm here for whatever they decide they need. I negotiate their contracts, keep track of their submissions, apprise them of their rejections, and help them navigate the rough waters of the publishing industry."

■ *Care to share the names of a few of your clients?*

AC: "Nancy Van Laan, Mary Casanova, John Coy, Roger Roth. I had either direct editorial relationships or indirect publishing relationships with many of my clients prior to becoming an agent."

KG: "I found my first client, Becky White, while searching for an author to put into publishable form some verbatim notes I had taken of the life story of a Chinese man. I'd chased unwilling authors all over conference grounds before I finally found Becky. We sold the book to Holiday House within four months of her completing it.

"My second and third clients I picked up from the Asilomar Writer's Conference, where I'd gone to hear Steven Malk speak. He had an ear infection and was unable to make it, so the conference coordinator asked me to take over his appointments. It was there I had the

Chatting up Your Date

Questions you may want to ask in addition to those asked of the panel, include:

▨ Does the agent specialize in children's books? The type(s) of material you write? Has s/he been successful?
▨ What are the financial arrangements? Do these seem to be in line with those of other agencies?
▨ How long has the agency been in existence?
▨ Where is the agency based?
▨ Does the agent give editorial assistance, or does the agent prefer to concentrate only on aspects of negotiation of the contract? Which do you prefer?
▨ Must you sign a contract?
▨ How will the agent keep you informed of submissions and their outcome?
▨ Who does the marketing of your work? How is this accomplished?
▨ Ask yourself: Does the agent's personality and work style seem to be a good fit for me?

good fortune to meet Margaret O'Hair and Susan Taylor Brown. I sold Margaret's first two books and one book for Susan, who has now moved on to a big agency that can handle both her adult and children's material.

"My fourth client, Lana Bloch, I picked up after attending just one day at an SCBWI annual conference.

I sat next to her and fell in love with the colorful plush toy that sat in her lap. I just had to have the toy, and she agreed to sell it to me at the end of the day. She's gone on to publish an award-winning picture book to accompany the toy, and now has an animated DVD and licensed products in the works with an independent production company.

"So, as you can see, each meeting has been rather serendipitous, leading me to believe that I was following the path I was meant to take."

GB: "Some of my best-known clients are Angela Johnson, Holly Black, Libba Bray, and Lauren Myracle. Of course, there are lots of other talented folks on my list, but too many to list them all here."

SC: "Gaby Triana, Susan Heyboer O'Keefe, Dia Calhoun, Marlene Perez."

Down the Aisle, Into the Sunset
Finding a good agent can be as challenging as finding a good mate. Someone who seems perfect for your friend may not be right for you. So if happily ever after is your goal, do your homework. Attend conferences where agents speak, read industry news, and most of all, hone your work to make it the best it possibly can be. And then step out in those three-inch heels. Your prince(ss) awaits.

Magazine Publishing

Our Town: Writing for Regional Magazines

By Kristi Collier

Wherever you go, there is a story waiting to be told. That is never truer than in the field of regional magazines. Regional magazines, the majority of which are geared toward parents of children from birth to age 14, focus on the events, activities, people, and trends in a particular geographic area.

Many regional magazines are available free of charge at various locations throughout the city in which they are published. Their funding comes almost entirely from advertising. The national statistic for this type of magazine is 2.1 readers per copy, which means that a magazine with a circulation of 60,000 has more than 120,000 readers.

The market directory *Magazine Markets for Children's Writers* lists almost 90 regional magazines looking for submissions. They can be found in nearly every major city or geographic region in the United States. Many areas boast more than one magazine. For example, the New York metropolitan area hosts both *Big Apple Parent* and *New York Family*.

So whether you live in Chicago or Charlotte, Birmingham or Boise, chances are there is a regional magazine near you.

Will It Play in Peoria?

Regional magazines serve the parents in their community by providing informational articles and topics that focus on local resources and events. Many have columns and departments that highlight local people, places, and activities. It is often necessary for writers who are interested in writing for a regional press to go on location.

Editors are looking for writers who know the area and who have access to the local resources that readers find invaluable. "Our mission is to be a local parenting news magazine, which means we want to be the one-stop shopping source for Chicago-area parents who have children ages birth to 14," says Susy Schultz, Editor of *Chicago Parent*. "So, we want writers to use local sources and local parents for any story appearing in our magazine. But our Chicago parents are also interested in the latest parenting news not covered by other outlets, so we look to our reporters to also use top experts in the field to break national parenting news stories."

For this reason, Schultz prefers to assign stories to local writers. "I've been a freelance writer and I don't think it is cost-effective for someone outside the Chicago area to write for *Chicago Parent*."

Living in the area is one way to capture the nuances of the region for which you want to write. Not every regional magazine insists on using local writers, but to most, it is imperative that the story reflects the magazine's locale. "It is important to us, and our audience, that as much as possible there is some connection to the Boise area, Idaho, or even to the Northwest in general that our readers can identify with," says Liz Buckingham, Publisher of *Boise Family Magazine*.

Buckingham looks for a writing style that reflects the tone and profiles of the area and the demographics. She suggests that writers can capture this local flavor through quotes, associations, or statewide websites.

If you don't live full-time in the area for which you wish to write, there are other ways to discover the particular qualities that make one city different from another.

Vacationing in an area or visiting tourist sites may offer story ideas. "Go to tourism sites and see what attractions are here. That's important," says Amy Dusek, Managing Editor at *Atlanta Parent*. She reiterates the importance of writing about topics that relate to the community she serves. She insists that writers know what is going on in the community, and she gives suggestions for capturing the local flavor of Atlanta. "Definitely read our magazine. Read other Atlanta magazines and newspapers. Thanks to the Internet, you can do that."

Individual cities have individual personalities. Although Cincinnati, Ohio, and Indianapolis, Indiana, are both Midwestern cities, each with a population of close to one million people, they have different perceptions of themselves. Tom Wynne, Editor of both *Indy's Child,* out of Indianapolis, and *All About Kids,* out of Cincinnati, states that Indianapolis is viewed as a more urban city while Cincinnati is more like many small towns tied together with the same name. "It's just a difference of perception," he says.

Stories that would work in one part of the country wouldn't get a second glace somewhere else.

Elaine Heitman, Executive Editor of *Charlotte Parent,* gives an example of the need to consider one's audience when tailoring stories for the regional press. "Charlotte is a vital, fast-growing banking city. But the conservative element is very strong here. We are very careful about nudity, etc. For example, breast-feeding is a topic we cover often, but we have to be careful that the picture is discreet because of our conservative readership."

Buckingham agrees. "To write about families, you'd need to have a sense of the local make-up and the history of the area and its growth," she says. "How our state ranks on certain issues may provide you with information that may change a theme or idea."

National News

While the regional stories may get first priority, stories with national appeal also appeal to editors, but with a twist.

Dusek says that it's important for writers to know what is being featured in the national parenting magazines. Regional writers then need to figure out how to cover the topic in relation to their audience. "We do cover national topics, but it's always a better story when it covers our region. We don't want to give them the same material they've been seeing elsewhere."

A subject that has gotten national media attention may fit into a regional magazine, but the writer needs to add local sources and local voices to the story. Occasionally, if the writer doesn't live in the area, the editorial staff may track down the local sources themselves.

"Recently we used a story about working teens that was written by a Kentucky-based freelance writer. She is very knowledgeable about the subject," says Heitman. To localize it to the Charlotte area, Heitman found four local teens and interviewed them about why they work and what it means for their school grades and participation.

"We'd love it if national writers could localize stories," continues Heitman, "but sometimes it's more appropriate for us to do it ourselves."

"The strengths of our publications are the regional content," agrees Wynne. "We are very cognizant of what our strengths are, but on the other side of the coin, if I find a story that is just plain good, I will run it. But I may localize it with a sidebar."

A New Spin

Most regional magazines operate on theme lists, which can be found on their websites or in their writers' guidelines. Heitman says that it is easiest to break into *Charlotte Parent* with a themed feature, and that she always needs stories that offer a new look at the topics that are written about each year.

Many regional magazines have contractual agreements with their advertisers stating that they will cover certain themes during certain times of the year, each and every year.

Indy's Child is under contract to run four camp stories a year. "I have done every possible camp story that can be done," says Wynne. "I'm always looking for a fresh perspective on this. The writer who can give me a new spin on camps has a sweet gig with me."

Atlanta Parent always runs a big education edition in January that  covers public schools, private schools, and home-schooling. Dusek says that it takes a creative mind to give a new spin to the same stories. "It has to be covered, but we have to do it in a fresh way." Dusek cites the need for innovation, using the analogy of Solo cups. "These cups have been around forever, but this year they added the gripper. It's the same cup, but with a new feature. That's what editors and writers need to cover these tried-and-true topics."

Heitman agrees. "I could make you a whole list of topics that are overdone, like homemade Valentines, etc. I'd like to see an old topic that is updated, or with a twist. For example, Valentine etiquette: Does a child have to give a Valentine to *every* kid in the class?"

Right & Responsible

Not only do stories for regional magazines have to be local and in-novative, they also have to be right. The readership of regional parenting magazines tends to be primarily women, the majority of whom have graduated from college and live in households earning more than $50,000 a year. They tend to be a well-read, vocal group. Regional magazines take their responsibility to their readers seriously, and editors depend on their writers to get it right.

"Some dismiss us as just a regional parenting magazine," says Schultz. "But we think of ourselves as responsible to 250,000 readers in a six-county area for the best and most accurate parenting information we can bring them. Our readers are an educated and vocal group. They demand we get it right. In all we do, we strive to get it right and write it well."

Chicago Parent is the rule, rather than the exception. They expect their writers to cite reliable sources and credible research. Editors of regional parenting magazines bring experience and high standards to their editing, copyediting, and fact-checking process, and they demand the same from the writers with whom they work.

"For locally assigned stories, we require writers to provide us with the names, interview dates, and contact information for sources. This shows them we're really serious about accuracy and provides a backup for the files if we ever need it," says Heitman. "We prefer that experts (preferably local) be quoted in every story."

The parents who are reading these magazines often put the stories to use by utilizing the recommendations, contacting the local sources, or trying the activities with their children.

"We put a lot of stock in the facts, resources, and research that we see when reviewing a piece," says Buckingham. "We prefer features that have some sources for our own readers to act upon or follow-up with. As parents, our readers are looking and trusting us for credible information."

Community Connection

Because their stories are so readily applicable, regional magazines offer more than parenting news and ideas. For many parents, these magazines become a community resource. "We try to be a solid voice on parenting, on dealing with issues that affect parents today. We are very involved in the community," says Wynne.

Heitman says that *Charlotte Parent* benefits the community by strengthening the family bond. "We give our readers tons of information to help them resolve childhood problems, to anticipate stages, and to know how to handle them, and to know where resources are if they need them." *Charlotte Parent,* like many of the regional magazines, also offers a number of activities for the family to do together.

Dusek says her readers know that they can turn to *Atlanta Parent* for sound guidance and well-researched parenting information.

Because parents call her so frequently for advice, she jokes that she has to be more than a magazine editor, she also has to be a community concierge. "Parents call me and ask, 'Who can I turn to for help?' We build a community of parents."

Regional magazines take seriously their mission to serve as a resource to the parents and the children in their community. "We give stressed-out parents who have too much to juggle a source for one-stop shopping on parenting news and information," says Schultz.

Writing for the Grownups

Because regional magazines are written for the parents, the children's writer interested in this market will find themselves writing for the grownups rather than the children. But the editors of regional magazines don't see this as a problem. "I think a good writer and reporter can translate their skills to

Regional Magazines

Numbers indicate circulation and the percentage of freelance.

■ **Arizona Parenting:** Suite 100, 4041 North Central Ave., Phoenix, AZ 85012. www.azparenting.com. Monthly. 80,000. 50%.

■ **Atlanta Parent:** Suite 101, 2346 Perimeter Park, Atlanta, GA 30341. www.atlantaparent.com. Monthly. 100,000. 25%.

■ **Austin Family:** P.O. Box 7559, Round Rock, TX 78684. www.austinfamily.com. Monthly. 35,000. 70%.

■ **Bay Area Baby:** Suite 120, 2280 Vehicle Dr., Rancho Cordova, CA 95670. www.bayareaparent.com. 3x/year. 80,000. 50%.

■ **Bay State Parent:** P.O. Box 617, Holden, MA 01520. Monthly. 44,000. 80%.

■ **Big Apple Parent:** 4th floor, 9 East 38th St., New York, NY 10016. www.parentsknow.com. Monthly. 70,000. 95%.

■ **Birmingham Christian Family:** P.O. Box 382724, Birmingham, AL 35238. www.birminghamchristian.com. Monthly. 35,000. 50%.

■ **The Boston Parents' Paper:** 370 Centre St., Jamaica Plain, MA 02130. www.bostonparentspaper.com. Monthly. 70,000. 75%.

■ **Central Penn Parent:** 101 North Second St., 2nd floor, Harrisburg, PA 17101. www.centralpennparent.com. Monthly. 35,000. 50%.

■ **Charlotte Parent:** Suite 201, 1100 South Mint St., Charlotte, NC 28230. www.charlotteparent.com. Monthly. 55,000. 40%.

■ **Chesapeake Family:** Suite 100, 102 West St., Annapolis, MD 21401. www.chesapeakefamily.com. Monthly. 40,000. 85%.

■ **Chicago Parent:** 141 South Oak Park Ave., Chicago, IL 60302. www.chicagoparent.com. Monthly. 138,000. 85%.

■ **City Parent:** 467 Speers Road, Oakville, Ontario L6K 3S4 Canada. www.cityparent.com. Monthly. 285,000. 100%.

■ **Cleveland/Akron Family:** Suite 224, 35475 Vine St., Eastlake, OH 44095. www.clevelandakronfamily.com. Monthly. 65,000. 75%.

■ **Connecticut Parent:** Suite 18, 420 East Main St., Branford, CT 06405. www.ctparent.com. Monthly. 50,000, 20%.

■ **Dallas Child:** Suite 146, 4275 Kellway Circle, Addison, TX 75001. www.dallaschild.com. Monthly. 120,000. 50%.

■ **Dane County Kids:** P.O. Box 45050, Madison, WI 53744. www.ericksonpublishing.com. Monthly. 28,000. 80%.

■ **Genesee Valley Parent:** Suite 204, 1 Grove St., Pittsford, NY 14534. www.gvparent.com. Monthly. 37,000. 75%.

■ **Georgia Family:** 523 Sioux Dr., Macon, GA 31210. www.georgiafamily.com. Monthly. 23,000. 50%.

■ **Great Lakes Family:** P.O. Box 714, Kalamazoo, MI 49004. www.glfamily.com. 6x/year. 47,000. 90%.

■ **Hudson Valley & Capital District Parent:** 174 South St., Newburgh, NY 12550. www.excitingread.com. Monthly. 70,000. 90%.

■ **Imperial Valley Family:** P.O. Box 1397, El Centro, CA 92243. www.imperialvalleyfamily.org. Monthly. 40,000. 40%.

Regional Magazines

Indy's Child: 1901 Broad Ripple Ave., Indianapolis, IN 46220.
www.indyschild.com. Monthly. 144,000. 98%.

Iowa Parent: P.O. Box 957, Des Moines, IA 50304. www.iowaparent. com.
Monthly. 26,000. 20%.

Kids VT: 10 1/2 Alfred St., Burlington, VT 05401. www.kidsvt.com.
10x/year. 22,000. 75%.

Lexington Family: 3529 Cornwall Dr., Lexington, KY 40503.
www.lexingtonfamily.com. Monthly. 30,000. 40%.

Los Angeles Family: Suite 312, 17522 Ventura Blvd., Encino, CA 91316.
www.lafamily.com. Monthly. 150,000. 85%.

Lowcountry Parent: 1277 Stiles Bee Ave., Charleston, SC 29412.
www.lowcountryparent.com. 10x/year. 38,000. 90%.

Mahoning Valley Parent: Suite 210, 100 DeBartolo Place, Youngstown, OH
44512. www.forparentsonline.com. Monthly. 50,000. 85%.

Maryland Family: 10750 Little Patuxent Pkwy., Columbia, MD 21044.
www.marylandfamilymagazine.com. Monthly. 50,000. 40%.

Metro Parent: Suite 150, 24567 Northwestern Hwy., Southfield, MI 48075.
www.metroparent.com. Monthly. 80,000. 66%.

Monterey County Family: P.O. Box 2354, Salinas, CA 93902.
www.family-mc.com. Monthly. 40,000. 40%.

Nashville Parent: 2228 Metro Center Blvd., Nashville, TN 37228.
www. parentworld.com. Monthly. 73,000. 60%.

New York Family: Suite 302, 141 Halstead Ave., Mamaroneck, NY 10543.
www.parenthood.com. 11x/year. 50,000. 80%.

Northwest Family News: Suite 204, 16 West Harrison St., Seattle, WA
98119. www.nwfamily.com. Monthly. 56,200. 80%.

OC Family: Suite 201, 1451 Quail St., Newport Beach, CA 92660.
www.ocfamily.com. Monthly. 80,000. 82%.

Parenting New Hampshire: P.O. Box 1291, Nashua, NH 03061.
www.parentingnh.com. Monthly. 27,500. 70%.

Piedmont Parent: P.O. Box 11740, Winston-Salem, NC 27116.
www.piedmontparent.com. Monthly. 33,000. 75%.

Pikes Peak Parent: 30 South Prospect St., Colorado Springs, CO 80903.
www.pikespeakparent.net. Monthly. 35,000. 23%.

Pittsburgh Parent: P.O. Box 374, Bakerstown, PA 15007.
www

Richmond Parents: 5511 Staples Mill RD #103, Richmond, VA 23228.
www.richmondparents.com. Monthly. 30,000. 100%.

South Florida Parenting: 5555 Nob Hill Road, Sunrise Hill, FL 33151.
www.sfparenting.com. Monthly. 110,000. 90%.

Toledo Area Parent News: 4120 Adams St., Toledo, OH 46624.
www.toledoparent.com. Monthly. 81,000. 75%.

Tulsa Kids: Suite 100, 1820 South Boulder Ave., Tulsa, OK 74119.
www.tulsakids.com. Monthly. 20,000. 99%.

many areas. If you are writing for children, you are writing with honesty and directness. Children require it. It's also what we require," says Schultz. "So the markets are not that far apart."

Children's writers know children, so they also know the issues that affect children and the topics with which they are dealing. These issues and topics are also of interest to parents. "For our best and most consistent writers, we tell them to write thinking as a parent," says Buckingham. "Put on the hat and think, 'Is this of interest to me, or of concern to me as a parent?' It's usually a winning combination, then."

Writers who know and enjoy the city and state in which they live, and who can write with clarity and freshness, may find a home with a regional magazine.

Magazine Publishing

Writing for Children about Careers

By Jan Goldberg

Talking about what they want to be when they grow up is a familiar pastime for children. It's also a common topic that adults ask youngsters about. Regardless of who brings it up, this is one topic that children love to converse about, contemplate, and change their minds about hundreds of times from the minute they are old enough to know what a career is!

"I want to fly planes."
"I want to arrest people who break laws."
"I want to make people feel better."
"I want to be with animals."
"I want to sing and dance."
"I want to help others."

So, while it's true that informing children about careers is an important topic for writers to offer, it's not one that can be approached the same way for children of varying ages.

Writing for primary students requires a different focus than when writing for intermediate levels, or when writing for young adults (teens). So, age level is at the very heart of what authors need to consider when preparing to write for children about careers.

Gauge by Age: Elementary

No matter what the content, early readers (generally about five to eight years old and in kindergarten to grade three) require text that includes short sentences, simple language (with a limited number of words per page), and word repetition. Pictures and other visuals are of critical importance to their understanding and enjoyment. It's wise to include a word list, to minimize misunderstanding of any ideas in the text because a reader doesn't know the meaning of a word. This can be of particular concern when talking about jobs and careers, which may have equipment and tasks that children won't know from their usual experiences.

"At this stage of development, children are most interested in the uniform or clothing people wear on the job, the tools people use on the

Sage Advice from the Experts

What is the proper starting point for embarking on a career project? "The topic list of questions that your editor provides is a great place to begin your research or to prepare questions for interviewees," says Mary Pitchford, Editor in Chief of *American Careers*. "That list reflects content that needs to be included in every story. Other interesting information is a plus."

Experienced career author Blythe Camenson says, "As far as sources go, I use the same ones regardless of my audience. The information the sources provide is the same. However, your audience determines how you present and organize the material."

Kay Olson, Editorial Director of Capstone Press, advises writers, "Follow writers' guidelines faithfully. Perform solid research using reliable sources. Document facts in the text. Write in a concise expository style. Create well-organized paragraphs with clear topic sentences every time. Utilize solid grammar and mechanics."

"I look for a good command of the English language—the basics, the right choice of words," says Pitchford. "I also like to see an organizational framework linked with appropriate transitions. On top of that, I like word pictures, interesting phrases, plays on words, and sound devices."

Make sure that you present "an on-time, thorough job," says Monica Stoll, Associate Editor at McGraw-Hill. "This is the most important thing a writer can do to impress me. Also, don't be afraid to ask questions. I would prefer a writer to ask for direction so that the end result is the best possible work. Paying attention to seemingly minor details like formatting is important, too. If you're given a sample manuscript to follow, don't disregard it. The more time an editor has to spend on formatting, the less time he or she can spend on content."

job, and job functions, particularly those involving reading and math skills," says Kay Olson, Editorial Director of Capstone Press, a publishing company that is responsible for book series that include Women in . . . Careers without College; Getting Ready for Careers; High/ Low Careers; Looking at Careers; Community Helpers; and A Day in the Life of . . . .

An article or book on teachers written for an elementary audience, for example, might cover what teachers *do*, with the most basic focus: Teachers work, they work during the school day, they help children. Alternatively, it might focus on *tools* and functions: Teachers use books, blackboards, computers, charts, maps, slide projectors, pencils, pens, and paper to help them teach. They grade papers and tests. They take students on field trips. Or, the direction might be more conceptual: Teachers are in charge. They show children how to get along with others. They are helpers—helping children learn, helping the community, helping children feel good about themselves.

Younger children are most interested in the careers of the people with whom they might come in contact, those who are familiar to them in their communities and their daily lives. Think firefighters, police officers, cashiers, child-care workers, doctors, dentists, garbage collectors, librarians, mail carriers, nurses, pilots, school bus drivers, school crossing guards, school principals, school secretaries, teachers, truck drivers, and veterinarians.

Ups & Downs: Middle Grades

When writing for the middle-grades, ages 8 to 12, Olson says that writers should answer the following questions: (1) what functions do people perform on the job; (2) what requirements must people in this occupation meet; (3) what education/experience is involved; (4) what are the potential hazards; and (5) what are the unique or unusual aspects of the job?

For that article or book on teachers, the focus might turn to facts such as that teachers must graduate from an accredited college and

pass a test for certification; teacher candidates must student-teach under the tutelage of a master teacher; they are charged with assessing students and administering standardized tests; and they spend considerable amounts of time outside of the classroom in preparing and record keeping tasks.

At Capstone Press, where middle-graders are the specialty, Olson says, "Children in this category use career books primarily to complete

homework assignments. Many of these readers are looking for answers, instead of reading the book from beginning to end. All information must be accessible and easy-to-understand." She reminds writers, "Children do not have the prior knowledge that adult authors possess. Authors cannot assume that child readers will understand anything that is not presented in the text. Writing must be clear, concise, and written with age-appropriate vocabulary."

Writer Blythe Camenson says, "One of the most important things to remember is to write for the appropriate reading level, but at the same time be careful not to write down to them." Camenson is the author of 50 career books, among them *Careers for Aquatic Types and Others Who Want to Make a Splash, Nursing, Firefighting, Writing,* and *Careers in Foreign Languages.*

"Children want to know what the day-to-day life would be like in any given career," says Camenson. "Young readers are not too concerned with salaries or training or job outlook statistics. They want a feel for the ups and downs and the realities of the job."

As children face their ever expanding world during the middle grades, a wider variety of careers becomes of interest. These might include auto mechanics, bank tellers, carpenters, chefs and cooks, flight attendants, coaches, construction workers, dental hygienists, electricians, machinists, farmers, food service workers, lifeguards, emergency medical technicians, park rangers, pharmacists, photographers, plumbers, security guards, supermarket managers, and TV reporters.

Mary Pitchford is Editor in Chief of *American Careers,* a magazine that appears in middle and high school versions. She says, "Remember the word *active* when writing for students of any age. Use active voice, and choose words and scenarios that paint a picture of on-the-job activities. Also address how academics relate to job needs when writing for publications that are used in schools, like ours. Then teachers can relate topics to lessons. Adjust sentence structure, and when possible, word choice for the age group of the audience."

Pitchford points to author Joan Rhine, who "has a lot of fun playing with words from start to finish in her article on David Hupman, a landscape technician." Here's Rhine's opening, from the middle school edition of the *2003-2004 American Careers Planner:*

> Certified landscape technician David Hupman dreams in vivid colors: flowering pastels of yellow, pink and blue, rolling green lawns and stately pines, bubbling blue pools and silvery waterfalls. And that's just in the daytime. 'I get to do the fun stuff, and I love doing the whole package,' explained David, whose dream job takes a project from paper drawing to outdoor completion. David is a production supervisor.

Lines of books by the same publishing house reveal the age and focus variations possible when writing about occupations. Lucent Books publishes career titles in series for middle-graders and young adults. Chandra Howard, Senior Acquisitions Editor at Lucent, describes three career series under different imprints at parent company Thomson Gale. "Lucent Books publishes a Careers for the Twenty-first Century series, focusing on careers that are thematically linked by a subject, such as Art or Military. Each chapter then discusses a specific career within that genre. KidHaven Press's series is called

Career & Industry Clusters

American Careers breaks occupations into 16 clusters, a good starting point for those interested in writing for children about jobs:

- Agriculture, Food & Natural Resources
- Architecture & Construction
- Arts, AV Technology & Communications
- Business, Management & Administration
- Education & Training
- Finance
- Government & Public Administration
- Health Science
- Hospitality & Tourism
- Human Services
- Information Technology
- Law, Public Safety & Security
- Manufacturing
- Marketing, Sales & Service
- Science, Technology, Engineering & Mathematics
- Transportation, Distribution & Logistics

Exploring Careers, and focuses on a day in the life of a particular career. Blackbirch Press has the How Do I Become a . . . series, which discusses the talent, education, and training needed to become a particular professional."

Young Adults: Real World

Career writing for teenagers takes on a new dimension as young readers move closer to long-term choices for their lives.

"When writing for high school readers, it's important to address ways that the reader can gauge his or her interest in a career, and the preparation necessary for it," says Monica Stoll, Associate Editor at McGraw-Hill, one of the largest publishers of career books for junior high and up. "Information about educational requirements or classes that would expose the reader to aspects of the career are very useful. These kinds of details help readers understand the concrete steps necessary in order to pursue a given career."

At the teen level, readers are often involved in serious contemplation of what career they might pursue. It's important that they are provided with as much practical infor-

111

Additional Sources for Career Writing

▓ **Career Journal:**
www.careerjournal.com/index.html.
A *Wall Street Journal* site.
▓ **Jobweb:** www.jobweb.com.
National Association of Colleges
and Employers (NACE)
▓ **My Future:**
www.myfuture.com/t2_ctoolbox.html
Military careers.
▓ **The Princeton Review:**
www.princetonreview.com/cte/
default.asp
▓ **O*Net Online:**
http://online.onetcenter.org. Occupational Information Network,
United States Department of Labor
▓ **Occupational Outlook Hand-
book:** www.bls.gov/oco. United
States Department of Labor, Bureau
of Labor Statistics
▓ **UniXL:** www.unixl.com/dir. An
international education resource
portal for education and industry.

of job duties; (2) educational/expe-
rience requirements and the general cost of gaining this education/
experience; (3) potential earning
power and information about how
one is paid; (4) a typical work
schedule; (5) benefits and hazards;
(6) a history of the profession; (7)
the future outlook for this career as
well as advancement opportunities.

That article or book on teaching,
for instance, could cover a typical
day in the life of a teacher; varia-
tions in work settings; working conditions; the current employment
market for teaching or finding
teaching jobs, and the outlook; education and training needed and
other qualifications; possible titles
for teachers, advancement potential, and career paths; earnings;
and related occupations.

For young adults, it is wise to
add a wide variety of firsthand interviews with individuals who are
already on the job, information on
résumés, interviewing, the positives
and negatives of the job, possible
job locations, and want ads that reveal information about what it is
like to do that job.

Careers that could be added at
this stage of development are almost limitless, but consider the possibilities: actors, correction officers,
crime lab technicians, customer service representatives, food service
managers, hazardous waste technicians, heating-and-air-conditioning
servicers, home health aides,
makeup artists, medical assistants,
medical record technicians, nurse
assistants, occupational therapy

mation as possible, but in a way
that depicts the realities—the challenges, the mundane, the appealing.
What is it really like to be doing
that job on a daily basis? What is a
typical day like? What hours are you
likely to be working? What is the
work environment like? Who are
you likely to be working with? Will
you be part of a team or work as an
individual most of the time?

Career writing for teens, says
Olson, may look at (1) the specifics

aides, paralegals, physical therapist assistants, radio announcers, real estate sales agents, surgical technicians, television production assistants, athletic trainers, computer programmers, graphic designers, construction carpenters, directors, marine biologists, mechanical drafters, park naturalists, pediatricians, U.S. Special Forces members, and controllers.

As practical and real world as writing about careers may be, editors want interesting presentations, solid writing, and appeal for their young readers. From the *American Careers* high school edition, Pitchford points to another example of the type of career writing she sees as exemplary. "Wildlife Manager for the New Millennium" was written by Bill Haggerty for the fall 2003 *American Careers*.

> Headlights from the Ford four-wheel drive truck bobbed across the mountainside as Terry Mathieson traversed the steep, icy slope of Baxter Pass. . . .
>
> She'd been on this road a hundred times but tonight, travel was difficult. It snowed hard that day. Earlier, Mathieson had crawled under the truck and put chains on all four tires. Her fingers were still numb, it was getting late, and she'd been up since 4 A.M.
>
> Suddenly, a spotlight ripped through the coal black night. That's a poacher, Mathieson thought. She picked up

her radio, called the Colorado State Patrol to notify them of the situation, turned off her headlights, and waited. She was in for a long night.

Perhaps more than with many other nonfiction categories, writers about careers—especially for young adults entering the employment or collegiate environment—need to stay up-to-date about changes in the field.

"We cover 16 career and industry clusters in our annual high school publication," explains Pitchford, of *American Careers*. She advises that writers know which occupations are of most interest now, for this or any career writing. "We like writers who work to understand our needs. We get dozens of queries related to employability skills, such as how to handle interview questions, how to dress for an interview, how to write a résumé, etc. What we really need are story proposals related to career clusters such as agriculture and natural resources, architecture and construction, and arts and communications."

Then some young readers may say in their imaginings, "I want to be a crop consultant when I grow up . . . or a writer."

Publishers of Career Materials

<u>BOOK PUBLISHERS</u>

▓ **Bebop Books:** 95 Madison Ave., New York, NY 10016. www.bebopbooks.com

▓ **Capstone Press:** 15 Good Council Dr., Mankato, MN 56001. www.capstonepress.com

▓ **Marshall Cavendish, Benchmark Books:** 99 White Plains Road, Tarrytown, NY 10591. www.edureference.com/mc.htm

▓ **Charlesbridge Publishing:** 85 Main St., Watertown, MA 02472. www.charlesbridge.com

▓ **Dorling Kindersley:** 375 Hudson St., New York, NY 10014. www.dk.com

▓ **Enslow Publishers:** Box 398, 40 Industrial Road, Berkeley Heights, NJ 07922. www.enslow.com

▓ **Facts on File:** 17th floor, 132 West 31st St., New York, NY 10001. www.factsonfile.com

▓ **Houghton Mifflin:** 222 Berkeley St., Boston, MA 02116. www.houghtonmifflinbooks.com

▓ **Kaeden Books:** P.O. Box 16190, Rocky River, OH 44116. www.kaeden.com

▓ **Lucent Books:** Suite C, 15822 Bernardo Center Dr., San Diego, CA 92127. www.gale.com/lucent

▓ **McGraw-Hill Publishing, Wright Group:** Suite 400, 1 Prudential Plaza, 130 East Randolph St., Chicago, IL 60601. www.mcgraw-hill.com

▓ **Perfection Learning Corporation:** 10520 New York Ave., Des Moines, IA 50322. www.perfectionlearning.com

▓ **Rosen Publishing, PowerKids Press:** 29 East 21st St., New York, NY 10010. www.rosenpublishing.com

▓ **Tricycle Press, Ten Speed Press:** P.O. Box 7123, Berkeley, CA 94707. www.tenspeed.com

▓ **World Book:** Suite 2000, 233 North Michigan Ave., Chicago, IL 60601. www.worldbook.com

Publishers of Career Materials

MAGAZINE PUBLISHERS

American Careers: Careers Communications, Inc., 6701 West 64th St., Overland Park, KS 66202. www.carcom. com

The Black Collegian: 34th floor, 909 Poydras St., New Orleans, LA 70112. www.black-collegian.com

Campus Life: Christianity Today, 465 Gunderson Dr., Carol Stream, IL 60188. www.campuslife.com

Careers & College: P.O. Box 22, Keyport, NJ 07735. www.careersandcolleges.com

Career World: Weekly Reader Corporation, 200 First Stamford Place, P.O. Box 120023, Stamford, CT 06912. www.weeklyreader.com

Circle K: Circle K International, 3636 Woodview Trace, Indianapolis, IN 46268. www.circlek.org

CollegeBound Teen: Suite 202, 1200 South Ave., Staten Island, NY 10314. www.collegebound.net

College Outlook: 20 East Gregory Blvd., Kansas City, MO 64114. www.townsend-outlook.com

Keynoter: Key Club International, 3636 Woodview Trace, Indianapolis, IN 46268. www.keyclub.org

Tech Directions: Prakken Publications, 832 Phoenix Dr., P.O. Box 8623, Ann Arbor, MI 48107.

The Publishing Industry

News of the Year

By Janine Mangiamele

Anniversaries

Random House Children's Books honored the hundredth anniversary of the birth of Dr. Seuss, born Theodor Seuss Geisel, with a *Seussentennial* 100 days of celebrations and events. The tour spanned 40 cities and featured interactive workshops, readings, and theatrical perfor-

mances. In addition, two new titles based on the life of Dr. Seuss were released by Random House: a picture book biography of Geisel's childhood, *The Boy on Fairfield Street,* by Kathleen Krull, illustrated by Lou Fancher and Steve Johnson, and a history of Seuss's life, *The Seuss, The Whole Seuss and Nothing but the Seuss: A Visual Biography of Theodor Seuss Geisel,* by Charles D. Cohen. A Theodor Seuss Geisel stamp was released by the United States Postal Service in March, and in June, Audrey Geisel was presented with a star on the Hollywood Walk of Fame, in honor of her husband's film accomplishments.

In celebration of Nancy Drew's seventy-fifth anniversary, Simon & Schuster expanded its licensing programs to offer merchandise to Nancy Drew fans and collectors. It includes apparel, home decor, stationery, a new line of graphic novels, audiobooks, and mini-books.

Awards

Judy Blume was named the annual recipient of the National Book Foundation Medal for Distinguished Contributions to American Literature. Among the titles cited in the announcement of the award were the young people's books *Are You There God? It's Me, Margaret; Super-*

fudge; Blubber; Just As Long As We're Together; and *Forever.*

The winner of the National Book Award for Young People's Literature was Pete Hautman, for *Godless* (Simon & Schuster). The other nominees were Deb Caletti, for *Honey, Baby, Sweetheart* (Simon & Schuster); Laban Carrick Hill, for *Harlem Stomp!: A Cultural History of the Harlem Renaissance* (Megan Tingley Books/Little, Brown); Shelia P. Moses, for *The Legend of Buddy Bush* (Margaret K. McElderry Books/ Simon & Schuster); and Julie Anne Peters, *Luna: A Novel* (Megan Tingley Books/Little, Brown).

Winners of the Golden Kite Awards from the Society of Children's Book Writers and Illustrators (SCBWI) were: *Milkweed,* by Jerry Spinelli (Knopf), for fiction; Robert Byrd, *Leonardo: Beautiful Dreamer* (Dutton), for nonfiction; *The Dirty Cowboy* (Farrar, Straus & Giroux), by Amy Timberlake and illustrated by Adam Rex, for picture book text; and *I Dream of Trains* (Simon & Schuster), by Angela Johnson and illustrated by Loren Long, for best picture book illustration. The SCBWI's Sid Fleischman Humor Award went to *Millicent Min,* by Lisa Yee (Random House).

The Tale of Despereaux, by Kate DiCamillo (Candlewick), won the American Library Association (ALA) John Newbery Medal. Her first novel, *Because of Winn-Dixie,* was a 2001 Newbery Honor winner.

An American Plague: The True and Terrifying Story of the Yellow Fever Epidemic of 1793, by Jim Murphy (Clarion), and *Olive's Ocean,* by Kevin Henkes (HarperCollins/ Greenwillow), were the year's Newbery Honor winners.

Mordicai Gerstein won the ALA Caldecott Medal for *The Man Who Walked Between the Towers.* The book was published by Roaring Brook, whose *My Friend Rabbit,* by Eric Rohmann, won the Caldecott the preceding year. Roaring Brook was purchased by Henry Holt from the financially troubled Millbrook Press in April.

The Caldecott Honor winners were *Ella Sarah Gets Dressed,* by Margaret Chodos-Irvine (Harcourt); *Don't Let the Pigeon Drive the Bus!,* by Mo Willems (Hyperion); *What Do You Do with a Tail Like This?,* written by Robin Page and illustrated by Steve Jenkins (Houghton).

The winner of the ALA Michael L. Printz Award in recognition of excellence in literature for young adults was *The First Part Last* by Angela Johnson (Simon & Schuster). This follows Johnson's win the preceding year for the MacArthur "genius" award.

The Printz Honor winners were *Fat Kid Rules the World,* by K. L. Going (Putnam); *The Earth, My Butt, and Other Big Round Things,* by Carolyn Mackler (Candlewick); *A Northern Light,* by Jennifer Donnelly (Harcourt); and *Keesha's House,* by Helen Frost (Farrar, Straus & Giroux/ Frances Foster Books).

The ALA Coretta Scott King Author Award went to Angela Johnson for *The First Part Last* (Simon & Schuster). Author Honors were received by Patricia C. and Fredrick McKissack for *Days of Jubilee: The End of Slavery in the United States* (Scholastic); Sharon Draper for *The Battle of Jericho* (Simon & Schuster/Atheneum); and Jacqueline Woodson for *Locomotion* (Putnam).

Ashley Bryan was presented with the ALA Coretta Scott King Illustrator Award for *Beautiful Blackbird* (Simon & Schuster/Atheneum). Illustrator Honors were given to Colin Bootman for *Almost to Freedom,* written by Vaunda Micheaux Nelson (Carolrhoda); and to Kadir Nelson for *Thunder Rose,* written by Jerdine Nolen (Harcourt/Silver Whistle).

Recipients of the ALA Coretta Scott King/John Steptoe New Talent Awards were Hope Anita Smith, author of *The Way a Door Closes,* illustrated by Shane Evans (Holt); and illustrator Elbrite Brown, for *My Family Plays Music,* written by Judy Cox (Holiday House).

Run, Boy, Run, by Uri Orlev and translated from the Hebrew by Hillel Halkin (Houghton/Walter Lorraine Books), won the ALA Mildred L. Batchelder Award for best work of translation. A Batchelder Honor went to *The Man Who Went to the Far Side of the Moon,* by Bea Uusma Schyuger, translated from the Swedish by Emi Guner (Chronicle).

Jim Murphy, author of *An American Plague: The True and Terrifying Story of the Yellow Fever Epidemic of 1793* (Clarion), won the ALA Robert F. Sibert Award for the most distinguished informational book for children. *I Face the Wind* (HarperCollins), by Vicki Cobb and illustrated by Julia Gorton, won the Sibert Honor.

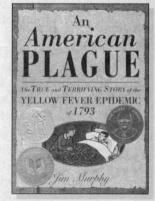

Ursula K. Le Guin was presented with the ALA Margaret A. Edwards Award for lifetime contribution in writing for young adults.

Giggle, Giggle, Quack (Weston Woods) was the ALA Andrew Carnegie Medal winner for outstanding video production for children.

Editor in Chief and Publisher of Scholastic Books Jean Feiwel was the recipient of the Curtis Benjamin Award from the Association of American Publishers in recognition of her contributions to Scholastic's success in trade publishing.

Mergers, Acquisitions, & Reorganizations

Books

Front Street Books was acquired by Boyds Mills Press, and is now an imprint of the Honesdale, Pennsylvania-based publisher. Stephen Roxburgh continues as Front Street's Publisher and President, in addition to his new title of Associate Publisher at Boyds Mills. Front Street publishes 12 books a year and has a backlist of approximately 100 titles.

Earlier last year, Front Street allied with picture book publisher Handprint Books to form a catalogue, share trade show space and costs, and share other sales and marketing resources and expenses. Front Street also shares Handprint's distributor, Chronicle Books. Its titles will continue to be distributed by Chronicle.

▨ After months of financial difficulties, the Connecticut-based Millbrook Press filed for Chapter 11 bankruptcy in February 2004. The company put its Twenty-First Century, Millbrook, and Roaring Brook Press imprints up for sale. Holtzbrinck Publishers acquired Roaring Brook and made the trade imprint a division of its subsidiary, Henry Holt. Roaring Brook brought two consecutive Caldecott winners—*The Man Who Walked Between the Towers* and *My Friend Rabbit*—and approximately $3 million in sales to Holtzbrinck.

Millbrook and Twenty-First Century were sold to the educational company Lerner Publishing Group, located in Minneapolis, Minnesota. Most of Millbrook and Twenty-First Century's titles target the school library market; their backlist has more than 1,000 titles. Lerner kept an editorial office in Connecticut and continued to use Millbrook and Twenty-First Century's names. It projects publishing approximately 100 new titles in 2005.

▨ McGraw-Hill sold its supplementary educational materials division, M-H Children's Publishing, to School Specialty, Inc. School Specialty deals in direct market sales of elementary through high school supplemental materials to schools and teachers. It is headquartered in Greenville, Wisconsin. The acquisition expands School Specialty's sales in warehouse clubs, bookstores, teacher stores, and other retail channels.

▨ DIC Entertainment selected Scholastic as its publisher for graphic novels, chapter books, and activity books related to its Trollz brand. Despite the renaming from Trolls to Trollz, these are the same popular troll dolls launched more than 50 years ago. DIC's relaunch includes new licensing, television, books, and videos. Trollz books for preteens debut in the fall.

▨ Founded in 1981, Saxon Publishers was acquired by the supplemental publishing branch of Harcourt Inc., Harcourt Achieve. Saxon is the third division at Harcourt Achieve, along with Rigby and Steck-Vaughn. Saxon offers instructional materials on early childhood development, phonics, and math for prekindergarten through grade

12, and has estimated sales of more than $70 million.

▨ Penguin Group USA and publisher Digital Manga have a three-year contract to publish a series of adult and young adult graphic novels. California-based DMI is an importer and publisher of Japanese manga graphic novels, animation, and related merchandise. Penguin anticipates offering about 8 graphic novels the first year and up to 15 titles in subsequent years.

A new division, Puffin Graphics, is working with Byron Preiss Visuals to develop a graphic series of classic works, such as *Macbeth, Frankenstein, Red Badge of Courage,* and *Black Beauty.* The target audience is young adults.

▨ Dominie Press was acquired by New Jersey-based Pearson Education. Pearson imprints include Pearson Early Learning, Pearson Prentice Hall, and Celebration Press. Dominie Press titles include reading and writing assessment materials, leveled readers, and Spanish-language materials, and a catalogue of more than 2,000 titles for the kindergarten to grade eight supplemental market.

Launches & Ventures

Books

▨ The worldwide English language publishing rights for the first three novels of P. B. Kerr's scheduled book series Children of the Lamp were bought by Scholastic US and Scholastic UK. The first novel in the series is *The Akhenaten Adventure.* Publication of the hardcover titles was planned for three consecutive autumns. Best known for his adult thrillers, these are Kerr's first children's books.

▨ Simon & Schuster's David Gale purchased two young adult titles in the Deaf Child Crossing series developed by Academy Award-winning actress Marlee Matlin. Lin Oliver, author and TV writer/producer, will co-author *Leading Ladies* and *Nobody's Perfect* with Matlin.

▨ Amulet Books is the new imprint of Abrams Books for Young Readers. Targeting middle-grade and young adults, the line includes fiction and nonfiction by new and well-known

authors. Amulet Books plans to publish between 8 and 12 titles a year. Its first hardcover releases included two middle-grade fiction titles: *TruckDogs,* a novel by Graeme Base, who is known for his picture books; and Maiya Williams's *The Golden Hour.* The nonfiction line, Sunscreen, offers advice books.

Anne Schwartz edited James Carville's debut children's book for her imprint at Simon & Schuster Children's Books. The picture book *Lu and the Swamp Thing* was based on his mother's childhood experiences and was co-authored with Patricia McKissack and illustrated by David Catrow.

Houghton Mifflin Children's Books launched Graphia, a paperback imprint for teens. It publishes original paperbacks and reprints from hardcover titles from Houghton Mifflin, Clarion Books, and Walter Lorraine Books. The first list offered six titles. Graphia features contemporary and classic fiction, nonfiction, graphic novels, and poetry.

Razorbill is Penguin's new YA imprint, publishing fiction and nonfiction for ages 12 and up. Eloise Flood is Senior Vice President and Publisher. Razorbill primarily publishes teen novels—single title hardcovers and paperback series—as well as some older middle-grade titles. It will also publish some nonfiction, celebrity biographies, and media tie-in titles. Among its first titles were a thriller, a contemporary novel of friendship, and first installments of a series of suspense stories told in diary form.

Electronic publisher Ibooks established a new line of picture books, Milk & Cookies Press. One of its goals was to revive picture book classics in visually exciting new editions. Contributions from several Caldecott winners, as well as from film and music celebrities, are anticipated. Simon & Schuster will distribute its titles.

Bloomsbury Paperbacks is the new imprint of two-year old Bloomsbury USA Children's Books. The debut list consists of reprints and two original YA novels. Victoria Wells Arms is Editorial Director of Bloomsbury Children's Books.

Targeting readers 14 and up, Weston, Connecticut-based Brown Barn Books is a new YA trade paperback line. It is a division of Pictures of Record. Nancy Hammerslough is owner and Editor in Chief. Brown Barn is focusing on fiction and launched with five novels. The list is expected to grow eventually to 10 titles a year.

Adult publisher Red Rock Press began its Red Pebble children's imprint with a first picture book, *Where Do the Balloons Go?* It will look for similarly "magical" titles and to grow to publishing about six children's titles a year. Approximately half of Red Pebbles' books will target the gift market, continuing the marketing direction of Red Rock Press's adult titles. Creative Director Ilene Barth also expects to publish fiction for older children.

Calkins Creek Books is the new history imprint from Boyds Mills Press. Targeting the school and library markets, it focuses on historical fiction and nonfiction for ages

8 to 14, including picture books, with an emphasis on the events, people, and places in U.S. history. It will enhance and expand upon some of the American history titles previously published by Boyds Mills. Headed by Carolyn Yoder, Calkins Creek plans to publish eight titles a year.

Mirrorstone is the new mass-market paperback imprint of Wizards of the Coast. Inspired by Dungeons & Dragons, Mirrorstone targets ages 8 to 14 with two fantasy series, Knights of the Silver Dragon and Dragonlance: The New Adventures. Each series plans to release one title a month.

Trafalgar Square is a North Pomfret, Vermont-based book distributor specializing in U.K. companies. It took on its first children's publisher in Egmont Books, one of Britain's largest. Its list includes licensed characters such as Winnie-the-Pooh, Thomas the Tank Engine, as well as Lemony Snicket's A Series of Unfortunate Events.

Meredith Books, part of the corporation that publishes *Better Homes & Gardens* and other magazines, entered the children's book market with the release of more than 15 children's titles last year. It signed several licensing deals that produced titles based on *Spiderman II* and Strawberry Shortcake. Books will be fiction and nonfiction and some will be based on its magazine content.

Houghton Mifflin Children's Books signed a two-book deal with Venus and Serena Williams. The first title, *Venus and Serena: Serving from the Hip*, is a mix of advice on tennis and offers game stories for readers 10 and up. The second book will offer insights into their values at home and on the court. The sisters also wrote *How to Play Tennis* for DK Publishing, targeting children 8 and up.

The hugely successful teen magical thriller *Shadowmancer*, written by English author G. P. Taylor, was followed by *Wormwood*, another suspense title. Taylor signed for two more books with his English publisher, Faber & Faber, and Penguin Young Readers Group in the U.S., in  addition to the three that he had previously committed to. A new hardcover will be published yearly in both countries.

Hyperion Books for Children published nine paperbacks based on a popular girls' comics magazine, *W.I.T.C.H.*, an acronym of the first letter in each of the character's names. Hyperion is joining with *Disney Adventures* to publish a graphic novel/magazine format using the same characters. Stories focus on the girls' adventures and friendships, each having the power to control a natural element. Future plans for *W.I.T.C.H.* include 20 more titles, a television show, and consumer products.

■ Simon & Schuster published talk show host Jay Leno's children's book debut *If Roast Beef Could Fly,* illustrated by S. B. Whitehead.

■ Billy Crystal's picture book from HarperCollins, *I Already Know I Love You,* describes being a grandfather for the first time. Elizabeth Sayles is illustrator.

■ Scholastic offered *Promises to Keep: How Jackie Robinson Changed America,* by Sharon Robinson, daughter of Jackie Robinson. The picture book explores his life as one of the greats in baseball and as a civil rights pioneer.

■ BBC Children's Books is a new imprint created by BBC Worldwide and Penguin Group. The large Penguin licensing list increases dramatically with BBC Worldwide titles, such as *Tweenies* and *Teletubbies.* BBC Children's Books will offer approximately 60 titles a year.

■ A new line from Barron's Educational Series targets the parents of students in kindergarten through sixth grade. Making the Grade offers advice, lesson plans, and manuals to reach its goal of helping students meet the new standards in education set by the government.

■ Located in East Orange, New Jersey, Sankofa Books is a new imprint from Just Us Books, an African American children's publisher. Sankofa features classic African American reprints for young adults and children.

■ Marvel Comics started a book imprint based on its Marvel characters. Marvel Press is headed by Ruwan Jayatilleke, formerly of Scholastic, and offers three new lines for adults, young adults, and children. Three titles were published last year, and plans are for 12 in the coming year.

Marvel Enterprises also extended a relationship with Meredith Books to publish titles featuring classic Marvel characters such as the X-Men, Spider-Man, and the Incredible Hulk. The new line includes picture books, sound storybooks, and coloring books. Meredith also has the rights to offer tie-ins to upcoming Marvel-based movies.

■ Dark Horse Comics is launching two book imprints: M Press, featuring novels, and DH Press, focusing on pop culture art books. Among the books from M Press will be *Mary Jane II,* a Spider-Man title. It expects to publish 12 books this year.

■ Scholastic is debuting a book line based on a new construction set line from LEGO Company, Knights' Kingdom. It was the first of several upcoming launches based on a new publishing deal between LEGO and Scholastic. The new books, activity, and sticker books, will all be based on new lines of LEGO Duplo preschool products, construction, and adventure toys.

The latest from Berenstain Bears authors Stan and Jan Berenstain is their new guide, *The Bear Essentials, Everything Today's Hard-Pressed Parent Needs to Know About Bringing Up Happy, Healthy Kids*. It offers practical wisdom for parents from more than 25 best-selling Berenstain Bears titles. Random House Children's Books acquired publication rights for the book from Sterling Lord Literistic, Inc.

Scholastic Publisher and Editor in Chief Jean Feiwel and Creative Director David Saylor will direct the launch of Graphix, its new graphic-novel imprint. Targeting the younger reader and teen markets, Graphix will publish up to four projects a year. The first title was the fantasy adventure story *Bone*, by author Jeff Smith, followed by the Baby-Sitters Club series by Ann M. Martin.

Three months after being acquired by Henry Holt, Roaring Brook announced its new graphic novels and comics imprint. The new unnamed imprint will launch its book-format comics in early 2006 and target the young readers and teen market. The new imprint expects to release up to 15 titles a year.

The picture book *Eddie: Harold's Little Brother* is published by Putnam and written by former New York City mayor Ed Koch and his sister, Pat Koch Thaler. James Warhola is illustrator. The two will also collaborate on a second children's title for Putnam.

Controversial news talk-show host Bill O'Reilly targets teen issues in *The O'Reilly Factor for Kids: A Survival Guide for America's Families*. Published by HarperEntertainment, it addresses topics that include bullies, friends, sex, alcohol, and politics.

Author Mike Davis signed on for three young adult novels for Perceval Press. PGW signed on as its new distributor, and plans to relaunch some of Perceval's previous titles. The small press was launched in 2002 by actor Viggo Mortensen, star of *The Lord of the Rings*. Mortensen has also written several titles for Perceval.

Based in Lexington, Massachusetts, B*tween Productions, Inc. is a new company that features merchandise and books targeted for girls ages 9 to 13. Created as a safe and fun choice for tweens, the Beacon Street Girls series follows Charlotte, Katani, Maeve, and Avery, who reside in a multicultural community near Boston. B*tween Productions was launched in spring last year, and is offering three titles in the Beacon Street series this year.

The parent company of North-South Books, publisher NordSud Verlag, was acquired by a German and Swiss private investors' group in September 2004. North-South sold its SeaStar imprint to Chronicle Books in 2003. The American office will be run by Managing Director Matthew Navarro and Publisher Mary Chris Bradley.

Smithsonian Books launched its new line of children's books for middle school children, Smithsonian Kids. Its debut list included the Story of Science series and the Smithsonian Answer Book series, as well as plans for an upcoming version of the Answer Book for younger readers. The new children's line is produced and edited by its Smithsonian Books staff, and will feature up to 30 titles a year.

Targeting children ages two to ten, MacAdam/Cage has a new Children's Books imprint. Finding a need for out-of-print and foreign language children's books, Chandler Crawford joined with her literary agency client to form MacAdam/Cage Children's Books. The company will publish eight titles a year, and primarily feature out-of-print books and titles translated from other languages. Crawford is Editor in Chief.

New publisher Tanglewood Press was founded by Peggy Tierney and provides picture books, early readers, and chapter books for middle readers. Its debut list included the picture book *It All Began with a Bean,* by Katie McKy and illustrated by Tracy Hill, and the middle-grade novel *Mystery at Blackbeard's Cove,* by Audrey Penn, and illustrated by Philip Howard and Josh Miller.

Launches & Ventures

Magazines

Offering "hip and wholesome" reading for girls 14 to 21, *Justine* provides inspirational role models, real teen fashions and beauty, tools to accomplish life's goals, and uplifting stories.

A new quarterly magazine about music and the hip-hop lifestyle, *Rap-Up* aims at readers ages 12 to 24. Devin Lazerine is the Editor in Chief and Publisher. Its online edition is at www.rap-up.com.

Targeting parents with children up to age 14, *Time Out New York Kids* was launched by *Time Out New York,* an arts and entertainment publication. Barbara Aria is the Editor. The magazine is published quarterly and also has a subscriber-only online edition.

Healthy Family offers a wide variety of features geared toward family issues: health, home and pet care, travel. Richard Bulman is the founder and Publisher.

Targeting wrestlers ages 5 to 14, their families, and their coaches, new publication *American Adrenaline* also provides information on health and fitness.

Star Publishers launched *Yin Magazine* for young Asian women. A vehicle for the multi-ethnic voice of Asian women, it features articles on topics that include lifestyle, fashion, beauty, travel, culture, and careers.

Published quarterly, *Boutique* specializes in fashion, home decor, gifts, and related items for infants and young children.

Tween boys, ages 8 to 13, are the audience for the new magazine *Riot*. It features editorial on electronic games, sports gear, clothing, bicycles, snowboards, and technology. Irreverent humor is a large component. Robert Edelstein is the Editor.

Launches & Ventures

Multimedia

A new line of novels based on EverQuest, Sony Online Entertainment's interactive game, is being published by CDS Books. All of its books will be written by well-known fantasy and science fiction writers.

Wee Sing Productions is a new company launched by Susan Nipp and Pam Beall, the two music educators who created the Wee Sing line in the 1970s. They bough back the rights to the videos and DVDs from MCA/Universal. Penguin Young Readers Group continues to publish the Wee Sing line of CDs and books.

Closings

The following magazines have closed:

- *Baby Years*
- *Beautiful Girl*
- *Best of Dragon Ball Z*
- *Black Parenting Today*
- *Boy Crazy!*
- *Child Care Business*
- *Christian Library Journal*
- *College*
- *County Families*
- *Dallas Family*
- *Dream/Girl*
- *Equality Today*
- *Just Weird Enough*
- *Health & You*
- *Hullabaloo*
- *Northern Nevada Family*
- *Northern Virginia Parent*
- *Our Kids Atlanta*
- *Pet Life*
- *Rainy Day Corner*
- *r*w*t*
- *Soccer Junior*
- *Team NYI*
- *Teenpreneur*
- *Writes of Passage*
- *The Whyvillian*
- *YM*
- *Youth Update*

People

Books

Brenda Bowen was appointed Vice President and Editor in Chief at Hyperion Books for Children, responsible for Hyperion, Volo, Jump at the Sun, and Miramax Books imprints.

Houghton Mifflin Children's Books named Margaret Raymo to Executive Editor.

Tracy Tang stepped down from her position as President and Publisher of Puffin Books. Eileen Bishop Kreit was named as the replacement.

After six years as the head of Scholastic's trade publishing unit, Michael Jacobs stepped down from his position. Jacobs directed the publication of all of the Harry Potter books.

Jacobs became President and Chief Executive Officer of Abrams Books, replacing Steven Parr.

Laura Godwin was promoted to Vice President and Publisher at Henry Holt Books for Young Readers.

Simon Spotlight hired Melissa Torres as Associate Editor.

Little, Brown for Young Readers hired Liza Baker in the newly created position of Executive Editor and Director of Special Projects.

Suzanne Harper became Senior Vice President and Publisher at Simon & Schuster Children's Publishing. She oversees Simon & Schuster Books for Young Readers, Margaret K. McElderry Books, and Atheneum Books for Young Readers.

Formerly Executive Editor at Henry Holt Books for Young Readers, Marc Aronson was hired at Candlewick Press to edit books and acquire young adult novels.

Yolanda LeRoy was promoted to Editorial Director at Charlesbridge Publishing.

Judy O'Malley joined and then left Houghton Mifflin Children's Books. She was hired for the position of Executive Editor at Charlesbridge.

Lerner Publishing Group appointed Jean Reynolds to the position of Associate Publisher. Reynolds was Publisher and Co-founder of the Millbrook Press, which was acquired by Lerner along with its imprint, Twenty-First Century Books. Reynolds remains in Lerner's Connecticut-based office and oversees Twenty-First Century and Millbrook projects generated from that location. Lerner anticipates offering 100 new books under the two imprints.

Philip Lee resigned from Lee and Low and the position of Publisher was filled by Jason Low. Louise May became Editor in Chief.

Magazines

Elaine Cipriano is the new Managing Editor at *Women's Day* Special Interest Publications.

The new Managing Editor of *Child* is Iris Sutcliffe.

Good Housekeeping has promoted Sarah Felix to Associate Editor.

The new West Coast Editor of *Teen People* is Lauren Tabach-Bank.

Michelle Lee Ribeiro has been named Senior Editor at *CosmoGirl!*

The new features editor at *Parents* is Debra Immergut. She was also appointed the new Editor in Chief at *Parents Baby*.

Susan Lapinski was appointed Editor in Chief at *Working Mother*.

The new Executive Editor at *Working Mother* is Betty Wong. She had stepped down from her position as Editor in Chief of *Parents Baby*.

Executive Editor Gillian Fassel has stepped down from her position at *ELLEgirl*. Deborah Burns was named the Vice President and Publisher of *ELLEgirl*. She was the former Vice President of Global Advertising at ELLE Group.
   ELLEgirl promoted Melissa Walker to Senior Editor.

Lisa Chudnofsky is the new Senior Editor at TeenPeople.com.

Jennifer Barnett was named the new Managing Editor at *Teen Vogue*.

The new Editor in Chief at *Twist* is Betsy Fast. Two new Associate Editors are Maria Zukin and Caroline Stanley.

The new Deputy Editor at *Seventeen* is Joanna Saltz and its new Senior Associate Editor is Whitney Joiner.

Dawn Roode was named Managing Editor at *Child*.

Formerly the Senior Health Editor at *Baby Talk*, Lisa Singer Moran was promoted to the position of Executive Editor.

Deaths

Joan Aiken, author of 92 novels, 65 of them for children, died last year at age 79. She was well known for her children's series, Wolves Chronicles. The third book in the series, *Whispering Mountain*, was the recipient of the 1968 Guardian's Children's Book Prize. Her children's mystery, *Night Fall*, won the 1972 Edgar Award. Aiken's last book, *The Witch of Clattering Shaws*, was published posthumously.

Children's illustrator and author Syd Hoff died at age 91. His first book, *Danny and the Dinosaur*, has sold more than 10 million copies since it was published in 1958. Hoff illustrated and wrote more than 60 children's books.

Roger W. Straus, founder of Farrar, Straus & Giroux, died at age 87. He had a degree in journalism from the University of Missouri and was a newspaper reporter and editor before serving in World War II. He joined with John Farrar in 1946 to found the literary publishing company. In 1994, Farrar, Straus & Giroux joined the Von Holtzbrinck Group. Straus served on several boards, including the National Endowment for the Arts, University of Missouri Press, PEN, and the John Simon Guggenheim Foundation. He received the Curtis Benjamin Award for Creative Publishing from the Association of American Publishers (AAP), as well as the 2001 Authors Guild Award for Distinguished Service to the Literary Community.

James Rice, author and illustrator of books in the Night Before Christmas series, died at age 70. The Pelican Books children's division was launched by his *Cajun Night Before Christmas.* Rice's last two titles, *The Principal's Night Before Christmas* and *Ozark Night Before Christmas,* were released posthumously.

Author of the well-known *The Cat Ate My Gymsuit,* children's author Paula Danziger died at age 59. Danziger published more than 30 children's titles for beginning and older readers, including her best-selling novel co-written with Ann M. Martin, *P.S. Longer Letter Later,* and her popular Amber Brown series.

Lilian Moore, poet and children's author, died at age 95. She published her first children's book in 1952, *Old Rosie, the Horse Nobody Understood.* Many of her children's titles were written under her pseudonym, Sara Asherton. Moore's final book, *Mural on Second Avenue and Other City Poems,* was published posthumously by Candlewick Press.

Children's author Bill Martin, Jr., died at age 88. Martin wrote more than 300 children's books, including *Brown Bear, Brown Bear, What Do You See?,* illustrated by Eric Carle. Martin published his first book, *The Little Squeegy Bug,* in 1945.

Illustrator Martin Matje died at the age of 42. Some of his work included *Stuart's Cape* and *Stuart Goes to School,* by Sara Pennypacker, and *Celeste: A Day in the Park.* In addition to illustrating children's books, Matje's work also appeared in many newspapers and magazines, including *Time,* the *New York Times,* and the *Washington Post.*

Picture Books

Page by Page

By Nancy Markham Alberts

Open a skinny-spined picture book and begin to read. Packed within its pages you'll find gifts—not ribbony, wrapped gifts, but intangible gifts like humor, surprise, suspense, and the perfect placement of words, as well as the feast of illustration. "If the words are carefully chosen," says Dutton Editor Michele Coppola, "and the pictures give that added dimension to the text, then there should be magic on every spread."

The 32-page limit of most picture books translates into about 14 *spreads*. A spread consists of the two pages you see with each page turn, so 14 spreads use 28 pages. The title page, copyright, and dedication page gobble up three more pages. A wordless picture, an author's note, or other supplementary material often fills the final page. The value of each spread increases when you realize that picture book texts are becoming more and more spare for very young children. Sometimes no more than a line or two graces each spread.

This can pose a challenge for the writer, who has only 14 opportunities to wow the reader with words. Pictures offer another dimension of *wow-power*.

Emma D. Dryden, Vice President and Editorial Director of Margaret K. McElderry Books, an imprint of Simon & Schuster Children's Publishing Division, emphasizes that "pictures in a picture book really ought not to be seen as separate from the text. The two work together in seamless tandem to form a picture book, in the truest sense of the phrase."

Author-illustrators have the advantage of visualizing a picture book as this seamless tandem from the start and presenting it as such to the editor. Writers who are not illustrators must depend on words alone to grab and keep editorial and young reader attention.

Sometimes a text depends on a picture to deliver an idea. Should writers include illustrator notes? Candlewick Press Editor Monica Perez believes, "It's okay for the writer to communicate their artistic vision for the book. I'd prefer a summary in the cover letter or limited commentary in parentheses within the text."

Coppola cautions that notes should be added only "when the text is so reliant on the art that it won't be understood without illustration notes." She prefers the notes be "in the margins of the manuscript so that they don't interfere with the text." Dryden accepts "a few illustration notes on a separate page," but only "if a text is extremely minimal—or if the story necessitates some sort of visual joke or twist that's not indicated by the text itself."

First the Story

In *Cowboy Sam and Those Confounded Secrets* (Clarion Books), an illustration inspired a different birth process than what happens with most picture books. Coppola, a Clarion editor at the time, showed writer Kitty Griffin a picture of a cowboy with a Texas-sized hat, drawn by the book's illustrator, Mike Wohnoutka, and asked Griffin if she could write a book to go along with the picture. Griffin agreed to try, a task she figured would be easier after she lassoed her Texan friend and co-author, Kathy Combs.

"Now that we had an image of a cowboy with a great big hat, we knew right away it would be a hat that didn't stay on his head," says Griffin. She and Combs decided that Cowboy Sam had one big secret, which he kept in his hat, but because he really wanted to tell someone, his hat kept flying off. The important secret was that "his wife was going to have a baby."

Dinah Stevenson, Vice President and Associate Publisher of Clarion, liked the basic idea, but found Sam's conflict of keeping mum about his wife's pregnancy "unkid-like." So Griffin and Combs brainstormed about plot possibilities and came up with the notion that Sam would keep secrets from all the townsfolk under his hat. The plot was working better, but the ending still eluded them. If Cowboy Sam's hat couldn't hold so many secrets, what could? After testing several scenarios with Coppola, they finally hit upon a simplistic but satisfying conclusion—that Sam could hold an unlimited number of secrets in his heart—which added just the right emotional touch to the book.

Marjorie Dennis Murray similarly struggled with the ending of *Little Wolf and the Moon* (Marshall Cavendish). The beginning came easier. "First of all, I have to know what I want to convey to the reader," says Murray, "and I have to know the title. I knew I wanted to write something that would connect children to the natural world." Because Murray's work in preschool puts her in daily contact with children, whose environment is increasingly dominated by technology, she wanted her story to bring them closer to nature by showing a little wolf who is captivated by the mystery of the moon. Her theme clearly directed her initial drafts.

Even so, she says, "It took several years and several revisions for the story to evolve into the final text." The story's first three-quarters stayed pretty much the same, showing Little Wolf looking up at the moon night after night, in awe of its beauty, wondering where it gets its light, how it climbs over the stars, and how it shines at night.

One editor, who loved the story's beginning, rejected the "overused" dream sequence ending. Murray rethought the conclusion and came up with a twist—the moon looking down on and wondering about the sleeping Little Wolf—that won her a contract and critical acclaim after the book was published.

The Magic of Language

Reviewers also praised the "gentle, poetic narrative" (*School Library Journal*) of *Little Wolf and the Moon*, as in this line: "At night he watched the harvest moon. It loomed heavy in the sky and Little Wolf caught the scent of winter."

Murray's fourth book, *Don't Wake Up the Bear!* (Marshall Cavendish), also received accolades for language: "The pitch-perfect text is skillfully told with repeated phrases and a polished rhythm . . . "

(*Kirkus Reviews*). Murray stresses that getting the language to flow smoothly takes much time and thought.

Margery Cuyler, Editorial Director of Marshall Cavendish, helped Murray pare down the ending of *Don't Wake Up the Bear!* by suggesting she remove some dialogue and rely more on simply stated action. While cutting words can be painful for any writer, particularly when working with an already spare picture book text, Murray acted on the sound advice, and a simpler, smoother, well-paced ending resulted.

Many more words populate the pages of *Cowboy Sam,* but the language is hardly cluttered. Its "passel of colorful descriptions" and "rhythmic phrases" (*Publishers Weekly*) serve the outlandish telling well. Combs, a Texan, set the tone for the rollicking lingo. While Griffin had Cowboy Sam's hat merely popping off his head, Combs went further, making the hat pop "higher than a jackrabbit jumping over a prickly pear cactus." Now, both writers began to play with language, as shown in the first lines of the book:

Might could be Cowboy Sam was the most favorite man in the whole town of Dry Gulch.

It wasn't just 'cause Cowboy

Sam was smart. Whoa, dog-
gies, that Sam was smart—
smart as an armadillo rootin'
up insects in the dark.

The duo continued their joint
verbal high jinks in *The Foot-Stomp-
ing Adventures of Clementine Sweet*
(Clarion) with such harmony that
even when Griffin and Combs contributed lines back and forth "like a
tennis match," the resulting paragraphs meshed like magic.

Magic takes time to happen,
though. Mem Fox admits to taking
one and a half to two years getting
the language right in her award-
winning books. In "Visitors from My
Childhood" from *Worlds of Childhood,* Maurice Sendak discusses how
he works on the text before the pictures: "With me, everything begins
with writing," he says. "I've never
spent less than two years on the text
of one of my picture books, even
though each of them is approximately 380 words long."

What about Rhyme?

Scan the listings of a recent market guide and you may find several
publisher listings that discourage
rhyming manuscripts. Then visit
your local bookstore and you'll
find scores of new picture book
texts in rhyme.

So should you write your picture book manuscript in rhyme?
Perez says, "Don't do it. Ninety-
nine out of a hundred people have
no talent for rhyme. One in a
hundred have some, but it will
usually need lots of development if

the writer isn't an experienced
poet. Writers should only consider
it if their minds won't work any
other way."

Dryden is also wary of rhyme
even though it's "a splendid way in
which to tell certain kinds of stories. Authors need to be very careful that their rhymes don't sound
too forced. In addition, authors
must read their rhyming texts out
loud over and over again in order
to make sure the rhymes and
rhythms of the text work."

Reading aloud benefits the revision of any picture book manuscript; having someone else read it
aloud reaps even more advantages,
especially for rhyming texts. An objective reading aloud can highlight
the language glitches—forced
rhymes, inconsistent meter, and in-
correct syllable stresses—that the
writer often glosses over.

No glossed-over glitches mar
the text of *A Frog in the Bog*
(McElderry), by Karma Wilson.
The book sings with rhythm and
rhyme as a frog gobbles:

> ONE tick, TWO fleas, THREE
> flies (Oh my!),
> FOUR slugs, (Ew, ugh!), and FIVE
>   slimy snails
> in the belly of the frog
> on a half-sunk log in the middle
>   of the bog.
> What a hog, that frog!

Then the catapulting rhythm takes
a pace-slowing, suspense-building
break with the line: "And the frog
grows a little bit bigger!!!"

Get Smart: Make a Dummy

"I absolutely visualize the layout of the story as I read a picture book manuscript," says Emma D. Dryden, Vice President and Editorial Director of Margaret K. McElderry Books. "Writers need not provide extra space between blocks of text to indicate page breaks. However, before writers submit their picture book manuscripts to me, I suggest they break the text into a 32-page dummy to understand the pacing of the text and how it might lay out in a picture book."

Experienced writers often believe they can skip the dummy step, thinking they can visualize the blocks of text without cutting apart their manuscripts. But the hands-on activity of making a dummy can highlight pages that suddenly cry out: "Revise me!" Besides, what do you have to lose besides a little extra time and paper? What you have to gain is a stronger, tighter manuscript, and a possible future sale.

Dummy Directions

■ Staple together 16 blank sheets of paper and number the pages 1 to 32.

■ On page 1, write the title. On page 2, write "copyright information." Make page 3 the dedication (pages 2 and 3 can be combined, if you wish).

■ Literally—with scissors—cut your manuscript into 14 blocks of text. Paper clip one block on one side of each of your 14 two-page spreads.

■ Read the manuscript aloud, as you turn the pages. It should now feel like a real book.

■ Now ask yourself:

– Does each page spread provide distinct picture possibilities?

– Do I have too much text on some spreads? What words, phrases, sentences, or even scenes are not essential and should be cut?

– Is each page turn necessary?

– What *gift(s)* do I give the reader on each page spread?

Editor Picks

Monica Perez, Editor, Candlewick Press

Perez wants picture books with "universality (truth in a common experience), readability (smooth, effortless prose), strong emotional content, and originality." Some of her favorites include:

- *Owl Babies,* Martin Waddell (Candlewick Press)
- *Guess How Much I Love You?* Sam McBratney (Candlewick Press)
- *Olivia,* Ian Falconer (Anne Schwartz/Atheneum Books)
- *Martin's Big Words,* Doreen Rappaport (Hyperion)
- *Where the Wild Things Are,* Maurice Sendak (HarperCollins)

Michele Coppola, Editor, Dutton's Children's Books

Coppola looks for "emotional resonance; well-crafted language; characters that jump off the page; stories that have a strong beginning, middle, and ending." Classic picks include titles such as:

- The George and Martha books, James Marshall (Houghton Mifflin)
- *The Runaway Bunny,* Margaret Wise Brown (HarperCollins)
- *Alexander and the Terrible, Horrible, No Good, Very Bad Day,* Judith Viorst (Atheneum)

Emma D. Dryden, Vice President and Editorial Director, Margaret K. McElderry Books

Dryden likes "believable and memorable characters; a lyrical, rhythmic text that is pleasing to the ear; a story with a beginning that asks a question, a middle that sets up some roadblocks, but keeps the end in sight, and an ending that answers those questions and resolves the story completely; a story that raises some emotions." Favorites include all the following Margaret K. McElderry Books:

- *The Bear Snores On,* Karma Wilson
- *A Frog in the Bog,* Karma Wilson
- *I Am NOT Going to School Today,* Robie H. Harris
- *We're Going on a Bear Hunt,* Michael Rosen

Gifts Galore

Plenty of "picture books don't rely on rhyme," says Coppola, "but still have rhythm and musicality that is fun for a child to read." With or without rhyme, Dryden feels that "the best picture book texts *sing*, inasmuch as they have a rhythm and cadence that sounds good when heard, that feels good when said, and that feels right all over when experienced by a child. Just as a good song makes you tap your foot and sing along, a picture book text can do almost the same."

Click, Clack, Moo: Cows That Type (Simon & Schuster), by Doreen Cronin, has foot-tapping cadence. "Click, clack, moo. Click, clack, moo. Clickety, clack, moo," rattles the alliterative refrain that punctuates the hilarious narration. Each page spread offers lively language as well as other gifts to the reader. When the farmer refuses to give into the cows' typed demands for electric blankets, he issues an ultimatum.

> The cows held an emergency meeting. All the animals gathered around the barn to snoop, but none of them could understand Moo.

Here we have multiple gifts on one page spread—obviously humor, but also surprise (the notion of needing to understand Moo) and suspense (what will happen?). The darkened picture, by illustrator Betsy Lewin, showing the animals gathering at the padlocked barn door, heightens the tension.

Suspense rules the page spreads of the nonfiction Caldecott winner, *The Man Who Walked Between the Towers,* by author-illustrator Mordicai Gerstein. Phillipe, a French tightrope artist, surreptitiously strings a heavy wire between the World Trade Center towers while they're being built in 1974 and then walks from one building to  the other. His preparations for this illegal act provide page-turning tension, especially when he comes perilously close to falling as he and his friends struggle with setting up the cable. Perez emphasizes that "a page turn should be necessary." *The Man Who Walked Between the Towers* does indeed compel the reader to turn pages. As we read, we silently wonder: How will Phillipe sneak his supplies to the top? Will he string the heavy cable between the buildings before dawn? Will the police stop him from walking the wire? Will he fall?

Dryden looks for such progression from each page spread to the next. "I am looking for some sort of physical or emotional journey that plays out to a satisfying conclusion," she explains. "Each spread should encourage the reader ever

137

Recent Books to Study

- *And Here's to You*, David Elliot (Candlewick)
- *Don't Forget to Come Back*, Robie H. Harris (Candlewick)
- *Flower Girl Butterflies*, Elizabeth Fitzgerald Howard (Greenwillow)
- *Gator Gumbo*, Candace Fleming (Farrar, Straus & Giroux)
- *The Lighthouse Cat*, Sue Stainton (HarperCollins)
- *Matthew's Truck*, Katherine Ayres (Candlewick)
- *Slithery Jake*, Rose-Marie Provencher (HarperCollins)
- *Too Big to Dance*, Doug Anderson (Handprint)
- *What's That Awful Smell?*, Heather Tekavec (Dial)

books? They look easy to write!"

Anyone who has ever struggled with the right turn of phrase, the perfect page-turning point, or an ending that satisfies the reader without preaching knows that writing picture books is a challenging art form.

Besides failing to appreciate the genre's demands, what other mistakes do picture book writers make? "Writing down their personal stories," says Perez. "An author has to think big. Is an idea worth being shared with thousands of parents and children? Is the message that important or the story that good? The author should also ask: Has this idea been done before, and if so, can I add something special or unique?"

Fellow Candlewick Editor Sarah Ketchersid notes that she sees "a lot of picture book stories that are well written, well constructed, but don't have enough kid-appeal." Coppola likes to quote Charlotte Zolotow's view of adult-oriented texts: "Many fine writers can write about children, but are unable to write for them . . . the writers writing about children are looking back. The writers writing for children are feeling back into childhood."

So feel back into your childhood as you write your picture book text. You, too, can make magic happen—page by page.

forward so that the reader wants to turn the page—has to turn the page—to experience the complete story." Coppola has the same vision for a picture book manuscript. Optimally, "the reader becomes more emotionally invested with each page turn so that they are sorry when the book comes to an end."

Perez looks for another quality in nonfiction: "clarity of narrative." She loves lyrical language, "but with younger picture books or nonfiction, being comprehensible is more important."

Clear narrative in picture books often results in deceptively simple language that sometimes causes the uninitiated to proclaim, "Picture

Fiction

Scene by Scene

By Kristi Collier

Imagine yourself in a movie theater, a bag of popcorn on your lap, a soda within easy reach. The house lights go down, the soundtrack blares, and on the screen the opening scene flashes before your eyes. You are transported into another world.

Movies are comprised of scenes. Series of them, brief episodes, are linked to make a complete production. Books, too, are created scene by scene by scene. It is often helpful for authors to think in terms of movie scenes while writing because children today expect the same immediacy and visibility from books that they get from videos and television. They want to see the action unfold before their eyes while they read. The most enjoyable books are those with scenes that are visible to the reader, and especially those that involve two or more characters who engage in dialogue and action in a single setting.

Paul Ingram, an Associate Editor at Kregel Publications, uses J. K. Rowling as an example of an author who creates this type of immediate, filmable scene. "Her progression of vivid, interlocking scenes engages children (and their parents) through seven hundred pages of plot. She doesn't overdress, overdescribe, or overdialogue."

A Pivotal Point

While scene structure varies from book to book, and even within a particular book, a common definition of a scene is that it contains an important occurrence with a beginning and an end, but that it is not in and of itself a complete story.

In a novel, a chapter may be comprised of one or more scenes. "There's a difference between a scene and a chapter," says Nancy Butts, author of *The Door in the Lake* and *Cheshire Moon,* both published by Front Street Books. "A chapter, just like a story or a novel, needs a dramatic beginning, a well-developed middle, and an intriguing end to lure you into reading the next chapter. But a scene doesn't have to tell the reader everything.

Think of it as one course in a meal, one verse of a song, or better yet, a snapshot. That's what a scene should do, illustrate a pivotal point in your story, whether it's a plot event, a vital bit of characterization, or an emotional revelation."

A scene, at its basic level, is necessary to move the reader through the book—though not necessarily in a linear direction, since some of the best novels are filled with twists and turns.

Shannon Barefield, Editorial Director of Carolrhoda Books, a division of Lerner Publishing Group, defines a scene as "a piece of writing that carries the reader from point A in the story to point B, or B to C, and so on."

Individual scenes are the cogs in the wheel that operate, often without fanfare or notice, to keep a story moving. "Every scene must either advance character or plot. There's no room for deadwood," says Kristin Wolden Nitz, author of *Defending Irene* (Peachtree Publishers). "As I write, I try to pass off many things that will become important later, in casual conversations or observations."

While a scene may be looked at on an individual basis, it does not occur in isolation. Its purpose is in contributing to the work as a whole.

"Scenes have to advance character and plot, but I also look at how a scene fits into the entire picture, the progression of scenes," says Lisa Banim, Senior Editor of Acquisitions and Development at Peachtree Publishers.

"You want the key scenes to take the main character, and the reader, to the next place, the next level, whether that is on a plot or a character level," says Karen Wojtyla, Senior Editor at Margaret K. McElderry Books. "Then you want to leave the reader expectant for what will happen next, whether that's the next plot twist or, in a more introspective book, the next level of understanding or realization for the character and therefore the reader."

As in architecture, where individual building blocks don't demand attention for themselves but contribute to the structure as a whole, a powerful scene has a sort of invisibility about it.

"If scenes are working well and advancing the characterization and the plot, the structure of the book is unlikely to call attention to itself," says Barefield. "There's a seamlessness in effective scene construction; if the storytelling is strong, I'm not aware that I'm reading individual scenes."

Planning

Hard work and planning are needed to achieve that level of seamlessness and readability. But no hard and fast rules dictate how to go about creating effective scenes. There are as many ways to construct a scene as there are writers.

Many authors don't even think in terms of scene construction as such, preferring to concentrate on a bigger picture. "I think in terms of the arc of the novel and the main character first, and then I break that down into chapters," writes Elaine Marie Alphin, author of many award-winning novels, including *Counterfeit Son* (Harcourt), *Simon Says* (Harcourt), and *Picture Perfect* (Lerner/Carolrhoda). "After this thinking, I outline the novel in detail before I start writing."

LeAnne Hardy, author of *Between Two Worlds* and *The Wooden Ox*, (both published by Kregel), also begins her planning with an outline. "I work from a story outline, so when I begin a scene I know what needs to happen to move the story forward. I also have a clear idea of the mood I want to convey, but I don't normally outline the scene so I can be free to go where the characters take me."

While many authors find that working from a story outline enables them to lay out clues and determine what happens when, other authors find this device constraining. "I never, never outline," says Kimberly Brubaker Bradley, author of several award-winning novels, including *Weaver's Daughter* (Delacorte), *Halfway to the Sky* (Delacorte), *For Freedom: The Story of a French Spy* (Delacorte), and *The President's Daughter* (Delacorte). "It completely kills my creativity, since in essence I've already written down the book. It also tends to make me package things too neatly—and therefore too dully—right from the start. I'm better off writing a messy first draft, and later tightening the plot."

Still other writers use both an outline and a messy first draft. "I know what the point of each scene is going to be, and I know what I want it to accomplish in a reader's mind," says Nitz. "At the same time, I'm not afraid to go off in an unexpected direction if inspiration strikes."

On her first pass through a scene, Nitz writes fast, concentrating on action and dialogue. On her second pass, she adds descriptions and details that help the reader to visualize the scene. On the final few passes, she checks for grammar, punctuation, smoothness, and coherency.

While the methods that authors use to plan a scene vary widely, all agree that planning is essential to effective scene construction.

Who, What, When, Where, Why

Setting is often the first element that comes to mind when thinking about a scene, and rightly so.

"Setting is important to my books, and you can't write a scene without it," says Bradley. "I write a lot of historical fiction, and I've learned that getting the details completely right is essential."

Wojtyla, Bradley's editor for *Weaver's Daughter, Halfway to the Sky,* and *For Freedom,* agrees on the need for authenticity when setting the scene in a historical novel. "Getting the details right—the costume, the feel of the wood in the girl's hand, the strings of dried apples in the cabin—those kinds of details bring the reader firmly into the historical setting. To get that right, the author has to research."

Bradley's modern-day novel, *Halfway to the Sky,* is set along the Appalachian Trail, and the setting was crucial, its construction nitpicking. Bradley began each chapter with a heading that included location, miles hiked that day, miles hiked thus far, and weather. "To create these headings, I had to *walk* the trail with Dani," explains Bradley. "I got a calendar, marked her start date, then started marking out how far she should get each day, where she would sleep, when she would take a rest day, where she would buy groceries."

The Wooden Ox is set in the midst of an African civil war, an experience the majority of Hardy's readers will never have. "Since I often work in settings that are unfamiliar to the typical reader, I may need to begin a scene by conveying the right details to paint a picture," says Hardy. "In chapter five, the Anderson family is captured by rebels, but I wanted to contrast this violence with normal African life, so I begin with dinner."

The late afternoon light was turning to gold as they entered the large rondavel to enjoy the chief's hospitality. Keri giggled when she noticed the bright plastic toothbrushes stuck conveniently in the thatch over the door. A slender girl, so dark she almost disappeared in the shadows, held out a basin and pitcher for them to wash their hands. (page 51)

While setting details are crucial, an effective scene must convey more than location. It must also illuminate *who* (character), *what* (action and plot), and *why* (motivation).

Ingram says that Hardy is adept at painting the "right details" around her characters. "She almost always introduces a scene with a reference to one of the people who will be central to that scene. It may be a jungle setting, but LeAnne doesn't give us a travelogue. She tells us how the heat or ropes binding the captive's hands relate the character to the physical context."

Nancy Butts uses the initial scene in *The Door in the Lake* to capture a crucial moment in the life of her main character, the day he mysteriously reappears after he's been missing for two years. She used description, dialogue, and action to show Joey's disorientation. "Every detail is important, down to the color of the leaves that blow in the door. Even the dialogue between the storekeeper and the trucker gives hints. They think he looks 11 or 12, when he's actually 14. The way Joey moves, how his sweatpants sag, the sunburn that is just beginning to peel, his unwashed hair, his extreme thirst—all are essential details in this scene whose entire point is to show how Joey has been completely dislocated."

The path a character takes through the course of a story or book is an important consideration when constructing each scene. Each individual scene must track the character's progress, whatever the pace of the piece. "For character development, you have to talk about more than one scene," says Wojtyla. "Characters, especially the main ones, have to grow over the course of the novel. They have to be shaped by the events of the novel."

An individual scene often illuminates the stage of the voyage the character inhabits at a particular moment, and why. "I plan the character's journey," says Alphin. "I want the reader to be caught up in the character's journey and travel along with him. So I'm planning where I want each chapter to take the protagonist."

Transitioning

Transitioning from one scene to the next contains many pitfalls that successful authors avoid to keep reader attention and interest.

"When I think about scenes, I think primarily about how to segue

---

Play Cards

Nancy Butts uses index cards to determine how the scenes she has written fit into the overall pace of her book.

"I write one scene per card, and then rate it on a scale of 1 to 4 in terms of how dramatic I think it is, or how important the emotion is in that scene. I do this for each scene in the book, and then I make sure the numbers on the cards follow a pattern of rising and falling action, going from 1 to 4, and then dropping down to 1 or 2 again before rising to 4. If need be, I shuffle scenes to get this rollercoaster effect, writing new scenes or deleting others."

---

from the previous scene into this one, without spending too much time doing so, which would invite the reader to insert a bookmark and take a break," says Alphin.

Alphin's editor at Lerner, Shannon Barefield, agrees, and says that when editing a novel she looks for an effortlessness in scene transitions. She looks for "a sense that I've been led somewhere without even noticing. A poor transition creates a jarring feeling, either through overwork or underwork. If there's no link at all to the previous scene, readers will feel a *bump* as they try to orient themselves to where they are in the new one. On the other hand, if the author has overworked the transition—laboring to force it to link to the last passage in an intricate, wordy way—chances are it won't be effective either."

When transitioning from scene to scene, authors must be cognizant of where their characters were in the last scene, what they were doing and saying, and tie all to the next scene in a relevant yet subtle way. It is the lack of such connections that often causes awkward structure, and reader confusion or loss of interest.

Banim uses a theatrical analogy to help authors understand the process of transitioning. "Often authors don't watch their *staging*," she says. "Many times, at least part of a transition that's missing is that staging. If a character exited stage right three scenes ago, and suddenly pops up with dialogue, the reader becomes confused about where he came from and when." To move effectively from scene to scene, understand where the characters are in relation to the stage at all times.

Breaking It Down

After scenes are constructed, then tied together into a story or novel, it is often the editor's job to determine which scenes are working to advance the book and which are not.

"In the early stages of revision, I find it most helpful to look at the big picture," says Barefield. "Is the book accomplishing what the author hopes it will, and am I intrigued by it, as a reader? Usually the answer is *yes*, in some ways, and *not quite yet* in others. I try to identify the *not quite yets* and the reasons behind them."

Some of those reasons may have to do with scene construction and transition. Perhaps a scene isn't contributing to the purpose of the novel or is confusing or slows the pace of the book. Other reasons may have more to do with the arc of the entire work.

After the big picture issues are addressed, Barefield looks carefully at specifics, which include scene construction. "This is the time to ask the hard questions about each scene," she says. "Is it earning its space, do transitions need help, etc.? I'd also be looking within the scene to see if dialogue, interior thought, and action are working well to accomplish the scene's goals."

Banim also edits on a big picture scale, allowing scenes to work as building blocks. "I don't break things down into scenes as much as I edit as a whole," she says. "I'm looking at how a scene fits into the entire picture. I'm not the type of editor who says 'this scene must go.' Sometimes the author has a destination in mind but was in either too much of a hurry or took too long to get there in the first draft. Limping scenes (that aren't working) often disappear magically when the author rewrites."

In addition to determining whether a scene contributes to the whole of a book and whether the scenes goals are being met, editors also look at the length and influence of an individual scene. "I try to help the writer to shape scenes so that they have an impact, but are manageable for the reader. You don't want too much happening so that it becomes too hard to follow or the reader gets too distracted. Nor do you want so little happening that the reader yawns and puts the book down," says Wojtyla.

Reworking scenes often calls for care and diligence in the author-editor relationship. Editors are able to take a more objective look at what needs to be reworked, and they must then communicate this to the writer. "Sometimes it means prying the author's fingers from around the lifeless form of a scene that made perfect sense in the first draft," says Ingram. "The writer has lived in and bled over these scenes, and such an emotional investment can poison the entire project."

It isn't always necessary to cut a scene when reworking an aspect of a book that isn't quite right. "I'm more into adding or fixing scenes than deleting them," says Banim. "Often there's something missing, and an additional scene may be needed to further the character or plot."

The scene is the building block of the novel. Scenes are often immediate and visible, and they transport the reader throughout the book. But when building a book, the scenes are not static, nor are they set in stone. The writer must be open to inspiration. "If you try too hard to construct or deconstruct each individual scene, it becomes an academic exercise and you take all the heart out of your writing," says Alphin.

"Really, the way I plan a scene is to not plan it," says Bradley. "I just jump in, go next where I think my character needs to go. I try to limit the navel-gazing and just rush from adventure to adventure."

Capturing that adventure is the nucleus of creating a powerful scene.

Fiction

Classic Storytelling

By Ellen Macaulay

Many of us and many of the children in our lives are huge fans of retellings—those classic folktales, fairy tales, legends, and stories that have been passed down, told and retold, beloved throughout the years. They are loved because they have universal qualities that appeal to our minds, hearts, desire for action and excitement, for symmetry and resolution, and for all they reveal about the human condition.

Retellings are everywhere: in books, plays, movies, television. Sometimes, a retelling is easy to spot because a story plays off the original, as in Jon Scieszka's *The True Story of the Three Little Pigs*. At other times, a classic story is so modernized or altered, it's harder to recognize. The quirky movie *Oh Brother, Where Art Thou?* follows the classic tale of Homer's *Odyssey*. The teen hit of a few years ago, *Clueless*, is a thinly disguised version of Jane Austen's *Emma*.

When you think about all the retellings out there, you begin to realize that there really is nothing new under the sun, especially in Hollywood. Yet, with retellings, the creative possibilities are endless.

Tales upon Tales

The very basis of retelling classical stories is to relate a story in a new and contemporary way. It worked for Mark Twain. His first published work was a retelling of an oral tale about a local frog, "The Celebrated Jumping Frog of Calaveras County."

Retelling is virtually prehistoric. It is the stories, handed down from generation to generation, that define a culture. Start investigating, and you'll see retellings everywhere. Could *Highlights for Children*'s ongoing pair, Goofus and Gallant, really be a variation of the Bible's bad brother/good brother, Cain and Abel? Could the latest movie hits—all those teen girl stories—really be preceded by tales out of the Brothers Grimm?

Cinderella may be the most popular retelling of them all. The mind boggles with the vast number of

Sources for Retellings

▨ **Religious works:** the Bible, Koran, the Vedas, Kojiki, Nihon shoki, Buddhist texts.

▨ **Mythology:** Egyptian, Greek, Roman, Norse, Persian, Hindu, Shinto.

▨ **Fairy tales:** the Brothers Grimm, Hans Christian Andersen.

▨ **Folktales:** Native American; other American (Paul Bunyan, etc.); Eastern European: Baltic, Slavic, Russian; Scandinavian: Icelandic, Finnish, etc.; Germanic; Australian aboriginal.

▨ **Legends:** Native American; African; Arthurian; Celtic; medieval romances; fables; saints' legends; Asian: Indian, Chinese, Indonesian.

▨ **Literary works:** Boccaccio; Chaucer; Shakespeare; epics such as *Beowulf,* the *Odyssey*, the *Aeneid*.

▨ **Geography:** stories from the various regions of the United States; historical legends, such as how different places got names.

▨ **Personal heritage:** oral traditions in your own family.

▨ **Other:** Even old songs, riddles, nursery rhymes have stories behind them.

renditions, among them, *Cinderella Skeleton,* by a master of storytelling, Robert D. San Souci,

Ah, San Souci! He was a huge hit in my household when my kids were young (their favorites included *Young Guinevere* and *The Talking Eggs*) and he's still going strong. If anyone can make clear the art of retellings—and

The Well at the End of the World

By Robert D. San Souci • Illustrated by Rebecca Walsh

through them, the classic qualities of storytelling that still resound today— it was the man himself. I contacted him and he graciously agreed to share his knowledge.

A Success Story

Robert D. San Souci is the award-winning author of more than 80 books, primarily children's and adult fantasy novels. His first, published in 1978, was a retelling, the acclaimed *The Legend of Scarface.* His 1998 book, *Fa Mulan,* inspired the production of the Disney movie *Mulan.* San Souci went on to create the animation story for the highly successful movie.

Elements of a Successful Retelling

Reworked story lines: Aim at children with stories originally written for adults. Perhaps take great, classic novels and rethink and retell the stories—always respecting copyright issues.

Or focus on the contemporary and add a twist. For example, vary the original story of the Little Mermaid so she doesn't marry the prince. She may die, or better yet, she finds definition of her own beauty and intelligence and heart in another way. She finds a way of bridging worlds and doesn't need to give up either.

Enduring themes. Look in your storytelling for human conditions, struggles, joys, conflicts, responsibilities, delights—the qualities of living that don't change with the times.

Humor. Make 'em laugh. Humor, irreverence, if it suits the material, is always welcome in children's literature. Jon Scieszka and Lane Smith's fractured fairy tales—*The Stinky Cheese Man and Other Fairly Stupid Tales*—are examples.

San Souci's books are a perpetual favorite with kids. Many, like *Fa Mulan*, feature strong girl characters and/or scary or amusing monsters. He has built his career primarily on retellings. Even his original stories contain an element of folklore, legend, trailing through them. He simply loves them and always has: "I have such a love of these stories. As a boy, I was fascinated by knights, dragons, and the Arthurian legends. I continue to mine the wealth of myths, legends, and folktales from around the world in dramatic retellings for today's children."

In an *AppleSeeds* issue on becoming a writer (January 2001), San Souci spoke to children about this early interest in retellings: "I retell folktales or myths or legends in new, exciting (I hope!), but sensible ways. Before I learned to write, I listened carefully to stories read to me then I retold them to my friends. But I left out things I didn't like, and added my own ideas. (I also added plenty of monsters to make things more interesting.)"

Fluid Art, Moral Wisdom

Granted, retellings provide exciting reading that kids love. That's a great incentive for delving into this genre. But there's more to it than just entertainment. Retellings provide additional benefits to children, and to their teachers. These stories often draw the reader into an unfamiliar part of the world, carry on cultural traditions that might otherwise be lost, and, perhaps, most important of all, impart lessons to be learned.

San Souci explains: "Folktales as such were originally designed to carry a variety of practical and moral wisdom in them. I love sharing a story that also has that little inner value, that something else, to share." He continues: "Storytelling is a fluid art. It goes on and on and on. The best of the old stories survive simply because storytellers, before stories were ever written down, were finding new and fresh ways to tell a story that had meaning for a new audience."

Having done many school visits, San Souci knows firsthand of the significance of these types of stories. Here is what he has heard again and again from teachers: "They are getting kids from every background who aren't being read to, who haven't been exposed to fairy tales. We use so much of the imagery of folktales, fairy tales, and even nursery rhymes in everyday reference. Children who aren't exposed to it don't have that commonality. As a result, the new generation almost loses a large cultural language. It becomes meaningless to say: 'Oh, that's a Cinderella story, or, he thinks he's a Prince Charming.'"

Retellings may also be a major factor in children's behavior, in the classroom and out. San Souci certainly believes this to be true. "Even nursery rhymes, which may seem silly to adults, actually begin to teach kids basic lessons. Folktales do the same. If you act well and appropriately, good things will happen. If you act foolishly and do things that have risks or treat people badly, there can be very bad consequences. It's a start of a whole learning program in a sense. By retelling these timeless stories, I like to feel I'm doing a little bit to keep them alive and also keeping the lesson moving forward."

Attaining Authenticity
Every retelling starts with research —finding original sources, investigating the culture and history, time, and the place of the story. San Souci admits to being a total perfectionist when it comes to research. He wants every fact, every nuance to be exact. That's why he's so good at what he does. His books radiate authenticity. He conducts his extensive research primarily in the library — San Francisco's, as well as his own. He has more than 6,000 books in his personal collection.

Selected Works of Robert D. San Souci

The Birds of Killingworth, based on the poem by Henry Wadsworth Longfellow (Dial, 2002).

The Boy and the Ghost: A Folktale from the American South (Simon & Schuster, 1989).

The Brave Little Tailor, Retold from the Brothers Grimm (Bantam, 1994).

Brave Margaret, An Irish Adventure (Simon & Schuster, 1999).

Callie Ann and Mistah Bear, based on a Georgia folktale (Dial, 2000).

Cinderella Skeleton: A Fractured Fairy Tale in Rhyme (Silver Whistle, 2000).

Cendrillion: A Caribbean Cinderella (Simon & Schuster, 1998).

Cut from the Same Cloth: American Women of Myth, Legend, and Tall Tale (Philomel, 1993).

The Faithful Friend: A Story from the Caribbean (Simon & Schuster, 1995).

Fa Mulan: The Story of a Woman Warrior (Hyperion, 1998).

The Hired Hand: An African-American Folktale (Dial, 1997).

The Hobyahs, adapted from British folklore (Bantam, 1994).

Kate Shelley: Bound for Legend (Dial, 1995).

Little Gold Star: A Spanish American Cinderella Story (HarperCollins, 2000).

Little Pierre, A Cajun Story from Louisiana (Silver Whistle, 2003).

Nicholas Pipe: The Legend of a Merman (Dial, 1997).

Peter and the Blue Witch Baby: A Russian Folktale (Doubleday, 2000).

The Reluctant Dragon, retold from the classic tale by Kenneth Grahame (Orchard, 2004).

The Samurai's Daughter: A Japanese Legend Retold (Dial, 1992).

The Secret of the Stones: An African American Folktale (Phyllis Fogelman Books, 2000).

Short & Shivery: Thirty Ghostly Stories Retold from World Folk Literature (Bantam, 1987).

The Silver Charm: A Folktale from Japan (Knopf Delacorte Dell, 2002).

Six Foolish Fishermen: A Cajun Story from Louisiana (Hyperion, 2000).

Sootface: An Ojibwa Cinderella Story (Bantam, 1994).

Sukey and the Mermaid: An African American Folktale (Simon & Schuster, 1992).

The Talking Eggs, adapted from a Louisiana Creole Folktale (Dial, 1989).

The Twins and the Bird of Darkness: A Hero Tale from the Caribbean (Simon & Schuster, 2002).

Two Bear Cubs: A Miwok Legend from California's Yosemite Valley (Yosemite Association, 1997).

A Weave of Words: An Armenian Tale Retold (Orchard, 1998).

The Well at the End of the World (Chronicle, 2004).

White Cat: An Old French Fairy Tale (Orchard, 1990).

Young Arthur (Bantam, 1997).

Young Guinevere (Bantam, 1993).

Young Merlin (Bantam, 1990).

San Souci loves the research as much as the writing. "Researching the culture, traditions, and background for folktales is an enjoyable and important aspect of my writing. I delve deep into journals, diaries, histories of the times, so the adaptation of the folktales rings true. I consult people who grew up in the various regions. I listen to tapes of narratives and music from the area. In short, I steep myself in a time and place.

"Research is largely where it begins. I'm constantly reading. I feel it is important to immerse myself in the culture and know the reason behind images and phrases used in the legend. I may read 250 pages of a book to find a description of a breeze at a certain time of night, so I can weave this impression into the story."

Needless to say, research as intense as this can take a tremendous amount of time. But, occasionally, he does just luck out. "Sometimes inspiration can happen by accident. In reading a large collection of Russian folktales, I wound up finding a story from Armenia, a place I knew nothing about. It just popped. It had all those elements—a wonderful message about literacy, a highly dramatic situation, a very strong woman at the heart of things, a wonderful monster, which gives instant kid-appeal. So it had action, adventure, romance, and an important message about courage and creativity." The result was *A Weave of Words: An Armenian Tale* (Orchard Books).

Folklore or Fakelore

When searching for tales to retell, a writer must use some caution. You can only retell true folklore, not someone else's original story, which may be under copyright. The way to tell if something is true folklore is to look for variants—different, rewritten versions of an original tale. In other words, you don't want to be the second person to tell this story, you want to be the fourth, tenth, even hundredth.

San Souci elaborates on how this works: "When I find a story that I want to retell, I look for every variant that I can find. Unless they can find at least one substantial variant, and preferably many variants, writers shouldn't assume they have a real folktale in hand. In the 1930s through probably the 1960s, books were often put forward as an authentic folktale, but, what they really meant was it is an original story in a folkloric vein. Most of those are still under copyright and they're not authentic. Most publishers will insist that you have at least two variant sources to eliminate this risk of copyright infringement."

Writers can get into trouble for copyright infringement if they lift language, phrasing, even distinctive restructuring, of a copyrighted retelling. (It is generally safe if the original source is 80 to 100 years old.) Getting permission to use or adapt a story can also be a headache, according to San Souci. Now he only works with variants. More variants will be at your disposal if you can read other languages. If not, translations are often available.

But, no matter what form of variant is used, San Souci says: "The earliest version is the purest inspiration. Your retelling will be more authentic if you go back to the original source."

"So, finding a variant is important. Once I find a tale, I find the variant. Then I begin the process, usually simultaneously, of working with the material, seeing how best to shape it for child appeal in a way that's fresh and appealing, but still honors the source material. Folk material often has a lot of redundancy. Repeat, repeat, repeat, and repeat worked well in the original oral tellings, but on the page, endless repetition can sometimes become a little dulling. So I shape it for the best appeal but still try to keep the inner truth there. And then, simultaneously, the research and the rewriting usually go hand in hand."

As San Souci pores over any and all writings of the time and place in which he's interested (even though only a fraction of this information will appear in the actual retelling), he's constantly on the lookout for deeper cultural references: "I think there's a feeling in the book hopefully that this person knows the people and place he's talking about. It's when I get all those details in place that I feel that I'm really moving ahead and able to retell the story and capture the flavor of the time and place. I like these stories to be not only the retellings but also, when possible, to give chil-dren a real feel for corners of the world that they might not otherwise be exposed to."

To write a retelling, San Souci believes it is vital to understand the particular culture thoroughly first. Then he takes his research a step further by having his manuscript reviewed by someone knowledgeable in the culture, in an effort to catch the tiniest cultural faux pas or inaccuracy. "The research doesn't stop all through the process of rewriting, I try to make sure I have everything down and checked and rechecked. Wherever possible, I take the manuscript and have it looked over by somebody who is either an expert in the history of the times or better yet someone from the area I'm writing about. Small details are crucial."

Key Ingredients

When asked for his advice on how a potential author can make a familiar story their own, San Souci offers: "The most important thing to remember is that with a folktale you have a wonderful source of raw material. No matter where the tale originally came from, there's a universal relevance there for today's children."

At the same time, he says, "You will find the originals tend to be very generic. That's how they were. Often the characters aren't even named. ('Once there was a little boy who lived on his farm with his mother. One day she said, "Go to market." And when he went into the woods . . . ') In working with those

An Editor's Perspective:
A Q&A with Abigail Samoun,
Editor, Tricycle Press

How popular are retellings to editors in the market today?

"Well, like everything, it all depends on how they're done. Retellings of classic stories are fun because these are stories we're all familiar with and we know how they're *supposed* to go. So there's an anticipation created when readers ask themselves, 'what's the twist going to be?'

"Also, to a certain degree, there's already a built-in readership of fans of the original work. Since the classic stories are so familiar to us, there's an openness towards retellings; people know these stories and have affection for them. There's a reason why these old stories have stayed in our collective consciousness for so long. If a writer is able to use whatever it is about the story that's fascinated us and present it from a different perspective, in a different setting, from a different point of view, it can make for a truly powerful story."

Which, if any, types of retellings would you personally be interested in?

"We see a lot of the obvious retellings: "Frog and Princess," "Princess and the Pea" (I came across no less than three retellings of this one on my last reading day), the "Three Bears." I think it would be refreshing to read a retelling of more unexplored works: classics of literature, like *Great Expectations* or *Moby Dick*. The fairy tale territory is well-trodden at this point."

What would a writer have to do to get an editor's attention on a retelling?

"Fresh and unexpected pairings always get my attention. For example, setting the story of *Cinderella* in Africa; or taking one of Aesop's fables and using it to teach science and math. Retellings should delight and surprise the reader, helping them see something familiar with fresh eyes."

What are some retellings that Tricycle Press has published?

"A few years ago, we published a classic retelling of the Indian sacred text, the Ramayana, which told the story of Hanuman, the monkey king. Nowadays, though, we're more likely to do more

An Editor's Perspective:
A Q&A with Abigail Samoun,
Editor, Tricycle Press

unusual, less straightforward retellings. For example, we took the classic Aesop fable, "The Crow and the Pitcher" and turned it into a lesson on the scientific method: Crow develops a hypothesis about how he can get water from the pitcher, then tests out the hypothesis and shares his results.

"We also published a book that took the classic fairy tale about a prince's search for a princess to marry and gave it a twist. The prince discovers that his perfect match isn't a princess but rather another prince. *King & King* (by Linda De Haan and Stern Nijland) played with readers' expectations about a classic love story.

"Reviewers said that the story 'firmly challenges the assumptions established and perpetuated by the entire canon of children's picture books.' (*Kirkus Reviews*) It brought a modern, and humane, perspective to the classic fairy tale love story."

Why do you think the rewriting of classic stories endures? What is the overall appeal?

"We grow up hearing stories that have endured for generations. Classics are classics necessarily because they have elements that transcend the times in which they were written. I think at some point we have to ask ourselves what these stories mean to us now, at this time in history."

Any other tidbits you'd like writers to know about submitting retellings to a publisher?

"Be familiar with the publishers to whom you submit your work. Have a good sense of their style and sensibilities. Stay away from the obvious twists and be sure that your story can withstand repeated readings. It also helps to know what's already out there by doing an Internet search. If your story idea has been done, a publisher probably won't want to publish it."

early sources, you have the raw material: the basic characters, the basic story line, the basic lesson if you want one. Then, it's up to the writer to begin fleshing out the details."

Characterization in folktales is somewhat unique. "One of the most crucial things is naming the characters. Make the characters three-dimensional," San Souci advises. "Bring the culture, setting, and history alive. I always like to give enough visual details so children can picture the story in their minds without actually looking at the pictures on the page. That's where research comes in very handy. Often, things happen in the story and you say: 'Why did he act that way?' Your research will validate that he acted that way because the people who lived in that place at that time would act that way."

Next comes voice. "Then, find the appropriate voice. Is it going to be a very dramatic story? Or, is it more humorous (which I highly recommend, by the way)? Also, a lot of the time folktales are just narrative. ('Then the boy went there and met a man. The man offered him three beans . . . .') What I recommend is to find out how much of the story you can recap in dialogue. The more dialogue you can put in a story, the better it works. It breaks up the text, makes it more appealing on the page. Even when children are read to, they love the dialogue. It helps them get a flavor of time and place and character."

Whenever a retelling appears, inevitably a reviewer or a reader suggests it may be time to hang up some of these stories. San Souci invites these folks to think again: "Popular stories (such as *Cinderella*) can be retold in an infinite number of ways. They survive because they work as stories. And if you bring something fresh and interesting to the story, either a particular cultural retelling or a silly spin (i.e., skeletons go to the ball in *Cinderella Skeleton*), the stories go on and on and on. There's always that challenge for the writer to come up with a fresh spin on a familiar tale and make it new and exciting in a very different way. And, there's always that balance that needs to be maintained between being true to original and the newness of the retelling. But, vibrant and dynamic retelling can make everyone sit up and take notice."

Retellings are a wonderful, fun source of material for writers—an instant cure for writer's block if you will. So, the next time you read or recall an interesting classic story, tell yourself: "Let's hear it again one more time, only this time as written by me." Because Robert San Souci always says, with retellings: "The sky's the limit."

Fiction

The Teen Voice: What Makes YA Literature Different

By Kelly Easton

A girl follows a rabbit down a hole, changes sizes numerous times, almost drowns in a pool of tears, meets a grinning invisible cat. . . .

A girl's house is lifted in a tornado, depositing her in a land of munchkins, a talking scarecrow, flying monkeys, witches, and wizards . . . .

A boy with a lightning bolt on his head receives an invitation to a school where he will study magic, learn to fly a broom, and battle with villains. . . .

A boy discovers a tollbooth in his room. . . .

An unhappy boy enters a giant peach. . . .

Imagine trying to synopsize what happens next in these books.

Children's literature is a wonderland of imagination, a universe where story is everything—turning the writing teacher's adage, "write what you know," on its stodgy head.

In the inner landscape of childhood, clouds can become sheep, brooms can morph into vehicles of flight, and a blanket on the floor can transform into a creeping monster in the dark. For a few slight years, the mind is filled with the fantastic.

Yet when children move into their teen years, the capacity for wild leaps of imagination decreases. At the same time, the ability to understand psychological, social, and political issues increases. So while children's literature is notable for its flights of fancy and turns of plot, young adult literature is notable for its focus on theme, and on the primacy of voice.

Theme

A quick survey of a few respected novels that appeal to teens reflects the importance of theme in YA literature: Harper Lee's *To Kill a Mockingbird* (racism and justice); J. D. Salinger's *Catcher in the Rye* (alienation); S. E. Hinton's *The Outsiders* (gangs); *You Don't Know Me*, by David Klass (child abuse); *Speak*, by Laurie Halse Anderson (date rape); *Lost in the War*, by Nancy Antle (the Vietnam war).

ALA Best YA Books

Each year the Young Adult Library Services Association (YALSA) division of the American Library Association (ALA) names the year's best teen books. Here is a sampling taken from recent nominations and final top ten lists.

▪ Brooks, Martha. *True Confessions of a Heartless Girl* (Farrar, Straus & Giroux/Melanie Kroupa Books, 2003).
▪ Burgess, Melvin. *Doing It* (Henry Holt, 2004).
▪ Donnelly, Jennifer. *A Northern Light* (Harcourt, 2003).
▪ Flinn, Alex. *Nothing to Lose* (HarperCollins/Avon Tempest, 2004).
▪ Haddon, Mark. *The Curious Incident of the Dog in the Night-Time: A Novel* (Random House/Doubleday, 2003).
▪ Hinton, S. E. *Hawkes Harbor* (St. Martin's Press/Tor Books, 2004).
▪ Johnson, Angela. *The First Part Last* (Simon & Schuster, 2003).
▪ Lawrence, Iain. *B for Buster* (Random House/Delacorte, 2004).
▪ Levithan, David. *The Realm of Possibility* (Random House/Knopf, 2004).
▪ Maynard, Joyce. *The Usual Rules* (St. Martin's Press, 2003).
▪ Pattou, Edith. *East* (Harcourt, 2003).
▪ Rapp, Adam. *33 Snowfish* (Candlewick Press, 2003).
▪ Stroud, Jonathan. *The Amulet of Samarkand: Bartimaeus Trilogy, Book One* (Hyperion Books, 2003).
▪ Thompson, Craig. *Blankets: An Illustrated Novel* (Top Shelf, 2003).

Authors who write for a variety of ages know that the topics change markedly for teens. Antle, the author of YA books, picture books, and early and middle readers, says it clearly: "In YA fiction, I write about psychological issues that I might not write about for younger kids." My own YA novels, *The Life History of a Star,* and *Walking on Air,* respectively, address the horrors of war, and the use of religion to control and abuse, in contrast to my novels for younger children about a boy who solves mysteries from his pet store.

Discovering a theme for your book is as easy as looking inside of yourself and finding what disturbs you or inspires you. Mark Twain once wrote, "Man is the only animal who blushes, or needs to." Those of us who take theme seriously tend to write about those aspects for which humanity must blush: war, religious intolerance, racism, bullying, poverty, injustice, sexual abuse, political corruption, domestic violence, drug abuse. The list goes on.

Filter any theme through the voice of a teenage character and the focus becomes more crystallized, the details and emotions crisper. It is the emotional intensity that draws many of us into writing for teens, just as it is the imaginative possibilities that lead us to write for children.

Teens are acutely aware of the most dramatic and painful aspects of their world, as they strive to find a way of being within it. They also can be trapped in familial, social, or economic structures that do not allow them to act upon reality or change it.

This sense of powerlessness is well-illustrated in *Holes*, by Louis Sachar, about a boy who is imprisoned in a Texas prison, digging holes. The main character, Stanley Yelnats, is humane and ethical, but utterly powerless to alter the absurd condition in which he finds himself.

The world acts upon teens, but they are not yet equal players in it. In other words, literature offers voice to teens' strivings, their sense of entrapment, their understanding of justice, their fears and joys, their longing, and their intensity.

Voice

The second primary difference between children's and young adult literature is just that: voice. The voice is the soul of the character expressed through narrative. It is informed by the multitude of elements that go into shaping all of us. In essence, the same complex ingredients that make us who we are, create voice.

Most teen novels are written in the first person, with the voice of the character as a primary force of the piece. Imagine *Catcher in the Rye* without Holden Caulfield's wry perceptions, or *To Kill a Mockingbird* without Scout's Southern dialect.

Voice itself is often a central or secondary theme in YA books. In *Speak*, the main character, Melinda, the victim of both rape and shunning by her peers, finds her voice through art, and is eventually able to bear witness against her attacker, freeing herself and others from the trauma of being raped.

In *Holes*, Stanley begins to access his power by teaching another prisoner, Zero, to read. The act itself allows Stanley to maintain his humanity in a situation that threatens to strip him of it. Zero has been without identity (as his name implies), but by giving Zero voice the boys regain the power to act, and escape.

In *Tending to Grace*, by Kimberly Newton Fusco, a girl, Cornelia, is trapped by her stuttering, so that the people in her world are "lookaways" whose inability to see past her speech negates her existence. The book chronicles Cornelia's struggle to speak, to articulate the beauty of her internal vision. In the beginning of the book, Cornelia describes herself as "a shadow." Like Stanley, Cornelia strengthens her own sense of self by teaching

another to read. By the end of the
book, having asserted herself, she
assesses that "Most of my life I have
been a bird tethered to the ground,
my speech the leather strap that
binds me to earth." But, as she sits
in a church she feels "the tethers
loosen, and I can almost fly."

The literal finding of voice becomes a potent metaphor for identity and power.

The Main Artery

How do writers find this voice, the
central artery of our books for young
adults? Take a look at these lines from
a variety of teen novels to get a feeling for how distinctive a voice can be:

> Maycomb was an old town,
> but it was a tired old town
> when I first knew it. In rainy
> weather the streets turned to
> red slop; grass grew on the
> sidewalks, the courthouse
> sagged in the square.
> *To Kill a Mockingbird,*
> Harper Lee

> When I stepped out into
> the bright sunlight from the
> darkness of the movie house,
> I had only two things on my
> mind: Paul Newman and a
> ride home. I was wishing I
> looked like Paul Newman—he
> looks tough and I don't.
> *The Outsiders,*
> S. E. Hinton

> If you really want to hear
> about it, the first thing you'll
> probably want to know is

> where I was born, and what
> my lousy childhood was like,
> and how my parents were oc-
> cupied and all before they had
> me, and all that David Cop-
> perfield kind of crap, but I
> don't feel like going into it, if
> you want to know the truth.
> *Catcher in the Rye,*
> J. D. Salinger

> Dr. Alger was going on and
> on about the Big Bang Theory,
> much to everyone's boredom.
> I believe in the Small Fry The-
> ory. I think the universe
> started not with a big bang,
> but with some tiny organism
> who was enough of a fighter
> to continue against the odds.
> *The Life History of a Star,*
> Kelly Easton

> We went to the moon to
> have fun, but the moon turned
> out to completely suck.
> *feed,*
> M. T. Anderson

The key is to know your character implicitly. Characters are defined by their gender, geography,
genetics, level of education, religion, race, appearance, habits, secrets, traumas, idiosyncrasies, desires, ethics, and tastes. Not everything you know about your character will be visible in the novel, but
the more you know, the richer the
character will be drawn.

Be as informed as possible.
Know what she would do if there
were people trapped in a burning

building, what he would order from the menu, how she would respond to a politician, what books he would read, what music she loves, what traumatic event has occurred, what she doesn't want anyone else to know, what kind of animal would charge into his dreams. In addition to all of the basics, the following elements are particularly helpful in drawing a teen character.

History: Your character's past may not be a prominent part of the plot but it informs their identity. Memories, anecdotes, and secrets give your character depth. A recollection of a joyful Ferris wheel ride with an abusive father deepens the sense of longing and tragedy. A secret about a friend committing a crime adds tension. An anecdote of a crazed uncle brightens dialogue.

Interests: Teens are passionate about their hobbies and interests. A character's obsession with the cello, Jim Morrison, or the mating habits of tree frogs can offer potent metaphors to articulate theme, as well as adding layers to the character.

Desires: Longing is a hallmark of the adolescent years. Most interesting characters desperately want something, although they may not overtly express it, or even know it themselves.

Defenses: While we all have our defenses, the teenage years are marked by them. Drugs, alcohol, behavioral issues, sarcasm, silence, posing, playacting, and repression, allow the character to block strong emotions and/or a need to act.

Melinda (*Speak*) and Cornelia's (*Tending to Grace*) defenses are silence. Kristin's (*The Life History of a Star*) is sarcasm. Similarly, a character can be undefended or defenseless. Stanley Yelnats, in *Holes*, has no advocate and is therefore defenseless. His good-heartedness also leaves him undefended.

Language: Language is the gauge of the character's intellect and emotional life. In *The Life History of a Star,* Kristin's prime emotional fuel is anger (also her defense). She is intelligent enough to note the hypocrisy and wastefulness of the Vietnam War, and her anger gives her perceptions bite. It is only at the end of the novel that the love she feels for her family softens her satiric stance to poetic imagery. The shift in language is the sign of the character's transformation. Imagining her dead brother who had loved astronomy, she says, "I could see our bodies in the sky. No space stations. Or rockets. Or cities on the moon. Just our bodies, like birds, soaring through those galaxies."

Language is vital. As Fusco says about her process: "I get into voice by writing poetry. Before I write a chapter of prose I often write the chapter as a poem. This helps me fall deeply into the character."

"Deeply" is just where we want to fall when we're writing for this unusual and emotional audience, a population who has only just managed to have their own small section of the bookstore, but who has a larger share of some of the most innovative fiction being written today.

Nonfiction

Fiction Techniques to Make Nonfiction Sparkle

By Jan Goldberg

Crack! crack! crack!

"What in the world is that?" Michelle cried out as she leapt from her bed.

With sleep in her eyes, she tried to focus on the clock beside her. 3:30 AM!

Crack! Crack!

Though it was velvety dark, Michelle could see the perfect zigzag outline of a bolt of lightning high in the sky. Oh, it's just a storm, she thought.

But then, almost imperceptibly, her bedroom door creaked opened and a dark figure moved slowly towards her. As it swayed dangerously close, she heard a "whirring" sound that reminded her of a swarm of bees.

Can you tell if the opening above is fiction or nonfiction? It could very well be either. Fiction and nonfiction are not the completely different entities they are sometimes thought to be.

Smart writers know that they can make their nonfiction more interesting and appealing by using many of the fiction techniques that pique readers' interest and make them want to read more.

"Other than the theoretical insistence on factual information in nonfiction titles," says John Kemmerer, Senior Editor at the Rosen Publishing Group, "there really should not be any distinction between good fiction writing and good nonfiction writing. Good writing is good writing, and the techniques and strategies are more or less universal."

Experienced nonfiction writers are familiar with the positives derived from using fiction techniques in their nonfiction works. "I try to use language that is both snappy and informal," says Carolyn Crimi, author of children's books for Harcourt, Simon & Schuster, Random House, Orchard Books, Candlewick Press, Marshall Cavendish, and others. "I don't want readers to be intimidated by the information, so I keep my style as conversational as I can to avoid what I call *encyclopedia-*

itis, or that dull, dry tone that some authors use when writing nonfiction. I always advise new writers to make their nonfiction exciting to read. I advise them to avoid getting so caught up in the facts that they lose sight of the fun of the story."

Allison Payne, Associate Editor of the teen magazine *Guideposts Sweet 16*, says, "Using fiction techniques makes all the difference in the world. It puts readers right there with the narrator in the middle of the action. The same elements that make fiction fun are what make our true stories compelling."

Novelistic Strategies

"Great nonfiction, like the work of John McPhee or Rosemary Mahoney or Barbara Tuchman," says Kemmerer, "features a keen ear for dialogue and speech patterns, vivid physical descriptions, highly tactile prose, and the delivery of substantial amounts of information in subtle, entertaining, and sometimes indirect ways. Nonfiction writers like these can perhaps be described as novelistic, but in fact they are just good writers, period. They seek to entertain at least as much as they inform, and they infuse their work with a sense of both artistry and craft. So, depending on the nature and desired tone of the project, feel free to employ any writing methods or strategies in your nonfiction work that have worked on you as a reader, even if these are more traditionally associated with the realm of fiction."

Here then, is an overview of some of the plethora of fictional techniques that also strengthen nonfiction writing.

Leads

Whether they are introducing fiction or nonfiction, beginnings must capture the reader's interest, introduce the subject or problem, and move smoothly into the body of the piece. Several categories of leads are typically used in fiction. Using them for nonfiction pieces can substantially enrich them.

■ *Anecdote:* a short, revealing, or humorous narrative that falls within the central idea of the article or book.

■ *Analogy:* comparing your subject to something unrelated, but common, to reveal some aspect of the subject.

■ *Description:* using vivid details to seize the reader's attention.

■ *Provocative Assertion:* challenging your reader's thinking with an interesting fact or statistic, or a provocative assertion.

Dialogue or Quotations:

Leading with dialogue in fiction, or quotations in nonfiction, is a strong way to draw readers in, but it is also an important component of entire pieces of writing. Dialogue and quotes also move the plot or text along, add interest; make the reader feel closer to the story or subject, provide information, and personalize your work.

"Many of our projects require quotes to illustrate ideas," says Chandra Howard, Senior Acquisitions Editor at Greenhaven Press. "Pertinent anecdotes and vivid examples that show why a topic is important are very effective. Though our publications are exclusively nonfiction, we do seek out a high level of engagement in the narrative."

"Nearly all of our books feature the real voices of young people," says Douglas Fehlen, Acquisitions Editor at Free Spirit Publishing. "Quotes and essays are used to complement self-help material and maintain readers' interest. Kids and teens love reading about others' experiences, particularly when they're facing similar challenges and can glean insight from them. A few of our titles are anthologies of first-person stories from youth. Dialogue and a conversational tone make the profiles fun to read and easy to relate to. A number of our books, too, have featured the results of surveys supplied by students from across the nation. It is very important to us that kids and teens find people like themselves in our books. They keep reading and discover insight that doesn't seem force-fed, but captured from the experience of a peer."

Details

■ *Sensory description:* Using the five senses (touch, smell, hearing, taste, and sight) as we do in all of these activities is just one more way to help readers identify with your work.

Use details to create a picture, a setting, and an atmosphere. Everyone knows what pain feels like, or heat or cold. We all recognize the odor of garbage or fragrant flowers. We know what it's like to hear the twittering of the robins and to see a rainbow. We know what a hot fudge banana split tastes like.

Sensory details are critical to powerful nonfiction writing because they can set a mood, and evoke a huge array of feelings, and therefore convey an understanding simple declarations cannot. Sensory details can add real power, zest, life, and energy to your work.

"When reading nonfiction," says Howard, "students are faced with a lot of information and sometimes so many facts, it's hard to remember all of them. When an author energizes the text with anecdotes or sensory details, he or she helps in grounding all those facts (and the importance of those facts) in the reader's memory."

Authors who handle this well

COCAINE AND YOUR NOSE
The Incredibly Disgusting Story
Melanie Apel

include Jennifer Owings Dewey in her *Poison Dart Frogs* (Boyds Mills Press) and Meredith Hooper in her *Antarctic Adventure* (Dorling Kindersley Book).

■ *Specific words*: Getting a point across means using words that are quite specific. Readers can then create a mental image of what the author is trying to describe. General terms are just not enough. Readers want to be provided with words that give no doubt about the images the mind should be receiving.

Readers are dissatisfied with general statements. They want to know more. They want descriptive details that will bring that situation to life.

It is easy to create a mental picture of the scene when Dewey writes in *Family Ties* (Marshall Cavendish), "A disk of stiff, densely packed feathers covered the owl's face. The shape and size of these helped funnel noises from the outside world to the owl's ears, two holes hidden beneath layers of feathers on the sides of her skull." Another author who uses this technique well is Gary Paulsen.

Active & Vivid

■ *Show/Don't Tell*: This concept represents one of the most basic rules of writing strong fiction, and it holds true for nonfiction. *Tell* means you dictate to the reader what is or has happened. *Show* means you demonstrate, with dialogue or action, what has happened. Showing requires more words than telling.

Let readers come to their own conclusions. Show them what they need to consider and then let them make up their own minds. To catch and keep the reader's attention, you must continually show what's going on in word pictures. Compare the following, telling and showing:

- Steve's room was a mess.
- The desk was strewn with a variety of semi-eaten food and a pile of papers that reached far above eye level. Books, clothes, and games lay on the floor in various parts of the room.

Showing may involve creating what amounts to a character, even if you are writing nonfiction.

Melanie Ann Apel has authored children's books for Rosen Publishing, Arcadia Publishing, Scarecrow Press, and Kidhaven Press. She endorses this transplanted fiction technique. "I like to use scenarios in which children or teens are doing something that the reader can relate to," she says. "In other words, instead of just giving the information outright, I like to put a character into a scenario similar to that which the reader is himself experiencing—and reading the book to learn more about. I also like to give the reader examples of things to consider by asking questions within the text."

■ *Active voice:* Writing in the active voice keeps the focus on the important place—the subject of the sentence. It creates a more vivid visual or place to direct understanding. In a sentence in the passive voice, the subject is acted upon instead of taking the action himself or herself. An active verb is more powerful than a passive verb because it shows the subject of a sentence doing or experiencing something.

For instance, in *Behind the Blue and Gray* (Lodestar Books), author Delia Ray writes, "The blast of cannon often jolted the soldiers out of their quiet reflections." Now, she could have written: "The soldiers were jolted out of their quiet reflections by the blast of cannon." She wanted to keep the focus on the cannon blast, however, so that is the subject of the sentence and it is kept in the active voice.

■ *Strong Verbs:* Strong verbs can fill your writing with zest because the action of your story or article is in the verbs. Conversely, using weak verbs can make even a well-written piece seem slow and tedious. Always attempt to select verbs that are filled with action.

Meredith Hooper, in her book, *Antarctic Adventure, Exploring the Frozen Continent,* begins with the following: "Lumps of ice the size of refrigerators bump and roll against the ship's sides." Can't you just feel the movement?

■ *Poetic Devices:* Poetic devices are definitely not just for poetry. They are typically used in fiction, but are definitely worth transferring to nonfiction. These devices include:

– *alliteration:* repetition of initial consonant sounds.
– *assonance:* repetition of vowel sounds.
– *hyperbole:* exaggeration.
– *metaphor:* comparison of one thing to another, without the use of *as* or *like.*
– *onomatopoeia:* words that sound like what they are.
– *personification:* giving human traits to animals or things.
– *puns:* words with double meanings.
– *simile:* comparison of one thing to another using the words *like* or *as.*

In *Tibet Through the Red Box* (Farrar, Straus & Giroux), when the story's narrator unlocks a special box, Peter Sis tells readers, "It's like an ancient anthill or a grave of memories buried in the sweet smell of honey, rosin, and sandalwood . . ."

In the End
Writers of nonfiction also give the same essential advice as writers of

Writing Opportunities

■ Douglas Fehlen, Acquisitions Editor, Free Spirit Publishing
www.freespirit.com

"Yes, we are always looking to work with new authors," says Fehlen. "We publish books and creative learning tools in three main areas: (1) self-help for kids and teens, (2) enrichment activities for classroom teachers and youth workers, and (3) successful parenting and teaching strategies. Our award-winning books are recognized and respected for their creative, practical, jargon-free, and solution-based focus. We're looking for strong proposals in topic areas that include kids' and teens' mental, social, and emotional health, bullying, conflict resolution, social skills, school's success, creative teaching and learning, gifted and talented youth, LD (learning differences), family issues, social activism, violence prevention, healthy youth development, character development, and service learning."

"When submitting a proposal," continues Fehlen, "closely follow our submission guidelines (located on the website). Generally, we require a summary, a description of your intended audience, an annotated table of contents, a market analysis (including how your book is different from others available), your bio, and at least two sample chapters (or the full manuscript if your project is a picture book)."

■ Chandra Howard, Senior Acquisitions Editor, Greenhaven Press
www.gale.com/greenhaven

"Title assignments for our company are ongoing" explains Howard. "The best way to contact me is by sending a query letter with a résumé attached by email to chandra.howard@thomson.com. If you seem like a match for what we do, I will send you our writing guidelines. Current publications can be viewed at the website address above."

Writing Opportunities

John Kemmerer, Senior Editor, Rosen Publishing Group
www.RosenPublishing.com

"We are always looking for talented and responsible writers," says Kemmerer, "as are most publishers of children's and young adult books. The best way to start is to update your résumé and writing history and send it (via email or conventional mail), along with any relevant writing samples, to the editorial director of the publishing house. He or she will review the materials you send and distribute them to the relevant editors."

Allison Payne, Associate Editor, *Guideposts Sweet 16*
www.guidepostssweet16mag.com

Guideposts Sweet 16 is a new general interest magazine for girls 11 to 17; it replaces *Guideposts for Teens*. *Sweet 16* is a bimonthly, four-color publication that contains a number of publication possibilities for both teens and adults. The departments include: Mysterious Moments, Positive Thinker, My (True!) Bad Day, My Own Thing, TGTBT (about boys), DIHY (crafts), Fashion/Beauty/Self-Help, and Quizzes. In addition, five True Stories that each focus on a teen are published in each issue. Check the website for additional information and more specific guidelines.

"Voice is the most important element of the stories and articles we publish," says Payne. "Our first-person, true stories are either written by teens or ghostwritten for them by adult writers. It is critical that these stories sound like a teen girl sitting down across the table from another teen girl and saying, 'Guess what happened to me the other day.' In our third-person features, the important things are not to sound preachy and to give teens the valuable information that they both need and want to know in a way that doesn't taste like medicine."

nonfiction: "Read as many current children's books as you can. I can't stress this enough. *Read, read read.* I know everyone says that, but there is a reason why they do," says Crimi. "The best education you can get is through the books themselves. If you find a book you love, type out part of it (or the whole thing, if it's a picture book). That will help you get inside the piece and see how it's crafted. Keep a journal of all the books you read and record what you like and don't like about each one. Just trust me on this and try it!"

Apel says, "I think it's important to remember that children are interested in the topic they are reading about. Children are capable of understanding more than we often give them credit for. I think it's important to be honest with them. Tell the truth (without being gory). They are reading our books because they either need or want information on a specific topic. If we are not totally honest as authors, the children will find the complete truth elsewhere and our books will lose credibility. Try hard to remember what it was to *be* a child! Remember what you liked to read about and why? Remember your favorite author and why she or he was your favorite? Then, go read lots of children's books in the genre you wish to write. If you find yourself too short on time for reading, check out books on tape at the library and listen to them. Get the tone, the feel, the nuance of children's writing. Then test out your manuscript on real children. Ask them if they understand what you're trying to say with your writing."

Nonfiction articles and books are indeed made up of facts, but the organizing and shaping of those facts into appealing text requires all the skills of a storyteller. Anyone can perform research, find facts, do interviews. How you put them together, what you add to them, is how you make the piece your own as a writer. So, whether you are writing fiction or nonfiction, you are still, in essence, telling a story.

Nonfiction

Putting in the Extra Effort: Sidebars, Photos, & More

By Jennifer Reed

The opportunity to sell nonfiction has never been greater. The doors of magazines are wide open to nonfiction writers. But with an increase in opportunity comes an increase in competition. Writers who never felt they would want to write nonfiction are now trying. They are finding that nonfiction writing can be as creative as fiction, as personally rewarding, and often more practically rewarding. Established writers realize that the nonfiction potential for sales has continued to increase in a trend that is valuable both to the writer and the reader.

Children love to read nonfiction. Like sponges, they are eager to learn about the world around them and they easily absorb information. Writers who discover how to package that information in forms that pull in young readers are likely (always given a solid, well-written article) to make more sales. Still, much is to be said for adding a little *extra*—sidebars.

Sidebars take many forms, but editors welcome them for their content, visual interest, and punch. Undoubtedly, the article itself is the substance of a submission. If it can't stand up to the competition or to the editor's standards, it won't sell no matter how good the extras—sidebars, photos, reading lists. As Rosanne Tolin, Editor of *Guideposts for Kids Online,* puts it, "The bottom line is still the quality of the writing." But the care and extra effort that a writer puts into the addition of sidebars often catch an editor's attention and move the manuscript out of the slush pile.

Making It Better

Let's assume that you have written a thorough article, with style. You did the research and documented it with a solid bibliography. The article is tight, to the point, and just what an editor wants. Many writers would assume that their work is done and it is time to submit the article to a publisher. Think again! Before you seal that envelope, ask yourself how you can make it even better.

If you look through any given magazine that publishes nonfiction for children, you will see how ubiquitous sidebars and other visuals have become. Sidebars pop out on the page, photos and illustrations capture the subject, an activity or how-to further demonstrates what the article is about, and reading lists and websites encourage readers to learn more about the subject.

Where did this extra stuff come from? Sometimes the editor finds or creates it, but often it is the author who supplies the extra information. Deborah Vetter, Executive Editor of *Cricket*, likes to see authors include *extras*, though the article must first of all be carefully researched, in-depth, and use primary sources and interviews with experts. "Extras do make an article stand out if they are substantive and creative," she says. "For example, if you're writing about Mesopotamian cultures and include an ancient recipe or game, that's a plus."

Marilyn Edwards, Editor of *Hopscotch, Boys' Quest,* and *Fun For Kidz,* agrees. She looks not only for an unusual article that fits an issue's designated theme, but also for good photo support and additional information like sidebars and reading lists.

It is particularly true with ezines such as *Guideposts for Kids Online* (www.gp4k.com) and my own publication, *Wee Ones Magazine* (www.weeonesmag.com), that catching the child's attention is vitally important. After all, what child really wants to sit at a computer and sift through long pieces of text? At *Guideposts for Kids Online,* Tolin points out the importance of breaking up an article with extras like an interactive quiz, a sidebar, craft, or activity. "This makes it much more enticing to the online reader."

Since research must be thorough, you are bound to come across interesting ideas along the way that won't work within the body of the article—ideas that could be used as extras and complement the piece. These extras also make the article truly complete, and thus easier for an editor to place. Edwards, for example, has a small staff and often doesn't have the time to research for more material to fill out an issue. If your article is well written, fits the theme, has supporting photos, and *extras*, the chance of it being accepted greatly increases.

Sidebars

These boxes of additional information or things to do are virtual requirements in many publications for children and adults. They catch the eye and serve the dual function of drawing readers even more into the article, and they contain additional information that is relevant to the article but not part of it. Sidebars are a good place to define words, insert an interesting fact or anecdote, or put a timeline. Often, a sidebar tells a new story about the subject you are writing about. Other forms of sidebar include puzzles, crafts, and activities.

For a *Boys' Quest* article on Benjamin Bannaker, Edwards and her editorial team made my "author's notes" into a sidebar. This was information that I didn't mention in the article but that was pertinent to Benjamin Bannaker—when he lived, the town he lived in, and how he helped design the city of Washington, D.C.

The *Guideposts for Kids Online* website emphasizes making submissions interactive. Sidebars are a perfect means to do that: Whether for features or secondary articles, sidebars might contain links to even more sites.

In print or online, puzzles, crafts, and activities can stand by themselves as articles, but more and more, editors seek them out as accompaniment. Provide a craft idea, or an activity or puzzle that ties well to a strong article, and the likelihood is that an editor will scoop it up quickly.

These, like all sidebars, should serve to support the article and take the concept, theme, or theory a step further. Sidebars can teach in a wonderfully fun way. Children love hands-on activities. If a child can actually make something, play a game, try a puzzle, the subject of the concept in the article will be easier for the child to understand.

Puzzles can include anything from a word search to a math word problem. Software is available that allows you to create your own puzzles and a popular site, www.puzzlemaker.com, offers both the software and ways to create puzzles like word searches and mazes. Do not rely solely on these simple tools, however. Be creative and original and create your own puzzle ideas. Although word searches are fun, many are submitted and editors often develop them in-house.

Crafts also work very well as accompaniment. If your subject is, say, bluebirds, tie in a craft on how to build a bluebird birdhouse or a bird feeder. An article in *Guideposts for Kids Online* on toads included a craft that showed children how to make a toad house. Crafts should be relatively simple to do with easy to find materials. If it requires little adult supervision that is even better. If children read an article that captures their imaginations, then many will want to experience it in some hands-on way, too. By providing a craft, children can learn by doing, not just by reading!

Activities also get children involved in an article or story. With an article on pantomime I included photos, but also an activity showing children how they could mime being a chair, an elephant, a dog. The sidebar showed them how to use their bodies to express emotions and show action.

Science articles offer many opportunities for activities. This is a great idea because if you are going to talk about volcanoes, it would be fun for a child to create his or her own mini volcano right at home! An article on health or the body might have a recipe. An article on genealogy might show kids how to create their own family tree. The possibilities seem endless but again, it is these little extras that enhance and hopefully sell an article!

What's Further

Children are naturally inquisitive and so are the parents and teachers who want to encourage learning. To serve this audience, many editors like to publish a list of books and websites with articles or books where readers can go to find out more information on a particular subject. Keep track of the many resources you use as you research. By providing a list of further reading material and websites, you show the editor that you have done additional research and you provide the reader with an extra service. Vetter says she loves to pass on this kind of information to *Cricket*'s readers.

Bibliographies are not strictly *extras,* but many writers neglect to include them. Editors agree they are a must-have with any nonfiction. Tolin says she questions the validity of an article if a bibliography does not accompany it. Vetter will not accept an article without a bibliography. "We like to see articles that have been carefully researched, in depth, using primary sources and interviews with experts." Edwards wants to see a bibliography with all nonfiction submissions. "I think that is pretty standard."

Photos

Photographs are another extra that always gain attention. Many magazines and ezines work with professional photographers, but you don't need to be a professional to submit photos. When I am out and about, I bring a typical 35 mm camera. If I am visiting a landmark, museum, or event I take pictures and lots of them. Often they have come in handy to remind me of what was happening that day, but also to accompany articles.

If you can, carry a camera with you at all times. Once I worked on an article about a small wooden building in my town that dated to the mid-1800s. I saw it week after week and kept telling myself that I needed to get a photo of it so I could accurately portray it. When I finally went to take the picture, the building had been torn down. Sad at the loss, I traipsed over to the historical society and did find some photos of the building. But, it meant more work.

Many editors appreciate the author also providing photos. Vetter thinks photos help editors edit a manuscript intelligently. Even if the photos are not of publishable quality, the editor and illustrator can use them as guides.

If you can't actually provide the pictures, you can often include leads to good photos. That makes the editor's job that much easier, and increases the chance of a sale. Edwards says, "If an article comes in that has some problems, that can be fixed or edited. But if a photo comes in that isn't very clear, there isn't much we can do. If a good article comes in without the photo support, we have to take it

Photo Searches

Many photos, free and not, are available through online sources. Some are in the public domain, and some are not. Some are found on subscription websites, some are not. A handful of websites follows, to illustrate the range of possibilities. Don't forget news organizations, museums, historical societies, professional organizations, and many other sources.

American Memory: http://memory.loc.gov/ammem/amhome.html. A Library of Congress source.

Gimp-Savvy: http://www.gimp-savvy.com/PHOTO-ARCHIVE/index.html. An independently maintained archival site leading to a variety of sources for free images.

Images of American Political History: http://teachpol.tcnj.edu/amer_pol_hist/index.htm. Images related to American history, from 1750 to the present day. (The site indicates it was to close; but at presstime for *Children's Writer Guide* it continued to be accessible.)

NOAA Photo Library: http://www.photolib.noaa.gov/index.html. Collections of photos from the National Ocean Service, National Marine Fisheries Service, National Weather Service, Office of Oceanic and Atmospheric Research, the National Environmental Satellite, Data, and Information Service.

PD Photo: http://pdphoto.org/index.php. This independently maintained site calls itself a repository for public domain photos, but reminds users to check into copyrights if necessary.

Picture Quest: www.picturequest.com. Royalty free stock house.

Time & Life Pictures: www.timelifepictures.com. Photographs from *Life, Time,* and other Time, Inc. publications.

U.S. Fish and Wildlife Service: www.fws.gov. The National Image Library includes links to sources around the U.S.

upon ourselves to find photos for the article." That means time and money.

Many authors are intimidated about asking to use photos or obtaining permission. There is a very easy and cost-effective way to obtain quality photos that will support your article. There are millions of websites on every subject and many websites contain valuable photos. Some are taken by experts but others are taken by amateurs, who are often quite willing to let authors use them. Sometimes they are free of charge. As long as the website owner, photographer, or owner of the photos gets a byline in the article, most are eager and willing to help.

That article I wrote about pantomime, for *Fun For Kidz*, really needed photos. But I didn't know any mimes or even where I could find one. Internet research led to the Marcel Marceau Foundation. The article spoke of this world-famous mime, so I contacted the foundation and they provided two photos of Marceau for me to use.

You can also do a keyword search online for public domain photos and images. This will bring up many websites to investigate.

Guideposts for Kids Online likes to see clear, colorful photos sent to them in jpeg format. At *Wee Ones* we also prefer to see articles come in with quality photos. If two articles come in on the same topic, both equally well written but one has photos, that will be the one that is most often accepted.

"A good nonfiction article is always kid-friendly, and includes pertinent quotes, snappy subheads, and vibrant writing," says Tolin. Without a solid, well-developed article, most editors won't look beyond. The extras won't sell the article first. They will enhance it. Vetter feels that the extras are just that. "If the article isn't substantive, then extras don't matter." The bottom line is to put your passion and love for writing and research solidly into the article. Make it the best you can. Then make it better by adding a little extra.

The Art of Book Production

Journey of the Written Word

By Gail Minett Eltringham

You submit your manuscript to a book publisher and wait to receive a rejection letter or—miracles do happen!—to hear from an editor that your story has been accepted. An assistant editor at the publishing house was assigned to wade through the piles of unsolicited manuscripts to see if any of them fit its future editorial needs. This person scrutinized your story line and style of writing. It was checked to be sure it's age-appropriate. Would this material mix well with the list of upcoming titles?

Turns out, yours would! Of course, you don't know this until you get the letter or call from an editor telling you the good news. The letter comes, and you call your spouse, your children, your parents, the rest of your family, friends, and members of your writing group. All that research, rewriting, and your belief in your talent has paid off. You have risen to the top of the slush pile, and your writing career has gotten the boost you've been dreaming about.

Now, where do your words go? What is the process that turns your text into the reality of a bound book? How do you, as a writer, contribute to making this process a smooth road, or deal with speed bumps along the way?

Seasons & Decisions

The editorial and production processes can be handled differently according to the type of publisher. Book publishers come in all sizes and shapes. Giant houses employ hundreds of people. Small houses may employ fewer than 20. Some companies perform most of the production work in-house, while others farm out art and production work to specialists.

These and other pertinent facts are mostly unknown to writers. But the way a publisher goes about producing a book can mean the difference between your title getting out on time or having to wait until the following list. Spring and fall are the major publishing seasons, with winter coming in a distant third.

Writers should not let their work go into an abyss as it enters the production process, trusting that all is going well because "no news is good news." Writers *should* be in touch with their editors to check on the status of their book. This does not mean, however, that they should be asking questions or giving opinions every week. An occasional call or email is appropriate.

Of course, at the very beginning of the journey, you and your editor will review your manuscript, make necessary changes, and generally polish and make your book more marketable. This leads into production since how the book presents your text helps make it work. Writers must be open-minded and cooperative, however, as the production process progresses, and at the same time remain true to their work.

Melanie McMahon Ives, Production Manager at Peachtree Publishers, recalls an incident when an author wanted the word *Christmas* in the title even though the story had only one brief mention of the holiday. The author was adamant, although her editor pointed out that including the holiday would turn her book into a seasonal one with a shorter shelf life. Omitting *Christmas* from the title would mean that the book would have year-round shelf life and therefore, more sales. After much discussion, the author wisely relented. Writers need to be flexible with editors. As Ives puts it, "Writers can be very, very sensitive. They need to be open to change. Editors only want to improve sales

by making each title as good as possible."

Candlewick Press staffs nine editors, headed by Elizabeth Bicknell, Editorial Director and Associate Publisher. Bicknell is proud of the fact that Candlewick is known for its editorial expertise. "We really do *edit* books here," she says. At a recent American Library Association awards conference, a librarian who serves on the Newbery Committee said that in the process of reading books from many publishers, she can see which books have been edited carefully and which have not. It shows in every part of the final product.

Candlewick is also known as "an author's publisher." With an author they've never worked with before, Candlewick is unlikely to sign a contract for a picture book text until it is very close to ready. The reason is that the author may never get the ending right. With one of their middle-grade or young adult fiction titles, there is more room to maneuver editorially. "When we see that the author is talented with a definite voice, then we are more likely to sign the novel even though we may still need two or three rounds of revisions," explains Bicknell.

Artful

What are most children's books without art—a major component in the production process?

Christina A. Tugeau, a nationally known artist's agent, says: "Some of the best, most conceptually creative art out there is found in

Raw Manuscript to Bound Book

1. An author submits a manuscript in electronic (disk) and printed form, already having worked with the in-house editor on revisions and rewrites.

2. The manuscript is reviewed by an in-house editor once again and is sent to a copy editor.

3. Copyedited manuscript is sent to the author for review and comments.

4. The art director, designer, or in-house editor designs the book's interior, resulting in design specifications or specs (i.e., the placement of illustrations, type and size of type, etc.).

5. The manuscript is typeset in-house (if the text is relatively short) or by a typesetter.

6. Galley proofs are produced.

7. The in-house editor sends a set of galley proofs to the author for review.

8. Corrected text is combined with the art to produce second or page proofs.

9. The editor or proofreader checks proof for errors.

10. Corrected proofs are sent to the printer in an electronic version or in the form of film negatives.

11. The printer uses the disk or film to create a complete set of proofs called bluelines or ozalids.

12. The editor carefully reviews the bluelines and returns them to the printer. Corrections now can be very costly.

13. The printer makes any corrections, creates printing plates, and starts the printrun, in a designated number of copies. Folded and gathered sheets (F & G's) are sent to the editor at the very beginning of the run so any major flaws can be recognized and the run potentially stopped.

14. The signatures (sheets) go to the bindery.

Who's Who in the Production Line

In-house editor: Has overall responsibility for getting the manuscript in printed form and, often, for developing the project.

Copy editor: Frequently a specialist in the subject or genre; turns the manuscript into a thoroughly cohesive text. The copy editor imposes consistency and correctness, including stylistic changes (often working with a style sheet provided by the publisher); rewriting where the point is unclear but not altering the author's message; rearranging content as needed; verifying data as appropriate; checking headings; verifying cross-references; reviewing sequences, bibliographic style, tables, artwork; and checking for copyright violations, plagiarism, or other potential legal problems.

Proofreader: Compares manuscript copy with proofs for typographical errors, obvious style errors missed by copy editor, grammar, punctuation, etc.

Art director: The person in the publishing house who is responsible for obtaining and tracking photographs, transparencies, illustrations, etc. for books in progress. The art director may be a book designer, and hires illustrators.

Designer: Designs the book's interior. Today, the role of a designer is to use a computer program, such as Quark XPress, to transpose text and art into complete layouts in disk format for the printer. In many instances, this role is supervised by the art director.

Production manager: Responsible for each title coming through the publishing house from approved disk or film to bound books. The production manager keeps the books on schedule and works with all outside sources providing technical expertise to the finished product.

children's books. The United States is the most healthy illustrative market around today. Artists have to be very, very, very good at what they do, know who they are, be unique, professional in attitude, and team players. It may sound simplistic, but they have to be good at drawing, have good color, and good composition. I hear the same thing from the editors. Editors are also looking for a good sense of humor and an individual *stroke* or *voice*."

Tugeau continues: "Whenever I am speaking in front of new writers, they are always shocked to learn that, more likely than not, they have no choice regarding an illustrator for their books. The editors are going to give the book their vision based on their experience and the market. The best case scenario, which is rare, is when an editor shows three choices to an author. However, most authors have no way of knowing what is going on in the market today, so almost always the choices are left to the experts, the editors."

Candlewick offers this best-case scenario. After a brainstorming meeting about illustration with the design department, editors come up with a short list of the three top artist choices, then inform the author and send samples of the illustrators' work. When an author disagrees with the editor's and art director's vision, Candlewick repeats their efforts with three more illustrator choices. "It slows down the process," admits Bicknell, "but it means a happy author 99 percent of the time."

Naturally, the art director at the publishing house has much to say about who will illustrate which book, and determining timing for the artist's work. The art director will need to keep on schedule and is often pushed to do so by the production director who, in turn, is on a tight deadline to get the book to the printer. Art directors are therefore often pushing the artist/illustrator to meet a deadline. "Books can be late due to last-minute editorial changes," according to Peachtree's Ives, "but mostly, it's due to the illustrators not making their deadlines."

Candlewick Press shows a patience unheard of at most other publishing houses: They often let illustrators take as long as they need to, virtually dictating the schedule. If an artist can't start right away or the project is interrupted for personal reasons, the author is informed, and everyone decides if they want to wait for the illustrator or go back to the selection process.

The designer will *page* the manuscript for the illustrator, or an experienced illustrator will do the page breaks personally. After the illustrator's character sketches and sketch dummy are approved by Candlewick and the author, the artist goes to final art.

Novelty Books

Since Reader's Digest Children's Books specializes in novelty books—which have very high production requirements—there is considerable

Production Terminology

▓ **On-screen editing:** Word processing programs now include editing functions whereby substituted text appears underlined and in color next to the deleted text. The editor or author can then accept or reject the change readily. Queries and comments can be written in *windows* that pop up. Using a special electronic *pen*, editors and authors can write on the screen itself.

▓ **Galley proofs:** These first proofs of the text (and only text) are set the width of the type page, leaving room for art.

▓ **Page proofs:** Second set of proofs. The galleys and camera-ready artwork are sent to an in-house designer, who works on a computer to complete the master disk, or to a typesetter. The disk or proofs of the il-lustrations, which have been photographed from camera-ready artwork, are combined. A proofreader compares the marked-up galleys with the new second proofs to confirm that all corrections have been made. Sometimes, computer typesetting causes character spacing, end-of-line breaks, or paragraph problems.

▓ **Repro (Reproduction) proofs:** High-quality, camera-ready positive prints on specially coated paper that are photographed to make nega-tives, from which the book plates are created. Whether repro or film, these are sent directly to the printer. With today's new technology, a printer may receive only an electronic version.

▓ **Bluelines/ozalids:** In one to four weeks, the printer sends the pub-lisher proofs printed in blue ink only. They are folded into signatures matching the signatures in the book. Now, the editor carefully inspects everything, usually on the same day they arrive or shortly thereafter. Printer's schedules are tight, and their deadlines have to be met. If not, they will move on to another job.

▓ **Signatures:** Large sheets showing the pages of the book.

teamwork and back and forth be-tween the editors and art directors. "A writer's manuscript frequently turns into a first draft, as we try to work it in with the art and format of the books," says Editorial Man-ager Sherry Gerstein. Often, the editors do the revising. The writers wind up providing us with the germ of an idea, or we provide them with one and wait to receive their text."

Gerstein reports that she uses tried-and-true authors most often, but also likes to find new talent. "Recently, I was impressed with a cover letter and sample, so I gave the writer a shot. She did a fabu-

Production Terminology

Folded and gathered sheets: The very last form the editor sees. Known as F & G's, they are a complete set of the actual signatures that will be bound—the actual ink colors on the same paper stock. F & G's are sent immediately to the publisher when the printrun begins. If all the previous stages have been properly checked, the bound books should be perfect (unless the bindery makes a mistake).

Folios: Page numbers.

Halftones: Black-and-white art that contains shades of gray. The art is transformed into a mass of dots of pure black and white for reproduction in the book.

Color separations: Original art must be separated into four colors: cyan (blue) yellow, magenta (red), and black, and the page printed on a four-color printing press. The art is attached to a small, whirling cylinder and beams of light (lasers) pass through colored filters and cross over the art. The results are then fed directly to the computer, which produces separations. Preset controls permit the operator to manipulate the color as needed. Publishers receive proofs that are commonly produced as an acetate overlay of four proofs/colors called a color key. The separations are reviewed by the art director and editor.

Platemaking: Printing plates are large sheets of very thin and flexible aluminum, plastic, or even paper that are imprinted with the images of several pages, attached to cylinders on the printing press, and inked to transfer the images to paper sheets, and passed over a cylinder's surface. Today, plates are produced directly from the digital file in a direct computer-to-plate process. Computer-driven lasers engrave the images onto the plate.

lous job!" Reader's Digest Children's Books produces many novelty books for licensed clients like Barbie, Fisher-Price, Disney, and most recently, NASCAR.

Writing to fit the particular specifications of novelty books can be difficult: It means dealing with die-cut pages or pages with acetate see-through windows or plush animals imbedded on the page. Writers need to be flexible and willing to let the art director and format dictate how their words appear on the pages. The text could be wrapped around a fluffy bear or overlaid on a working part of the book.

As Gerstein says, "In nonfiction, the information is more important. In a storybook, the interactive element must be logical, with the art and the editorial working together to create a whole. Readers will always be aware of a bad story line; but if the story line is good, it will be invisible."

What is the most common cause of oversights and mistakes in the production of a book? The answer is tight schedules. "With improved technology, everyone expects the process to move quickly. I am always amazed at the stupid mistakes that can occur due to tight schedules," says Gerstein. "However, schedules have to be tight so we can be timely, particularly with our licensed products. You never know when a character will lose its appeal! If a schedule isn't timely, we risk losing the market. As well, a lot of mass-market books are seasonal. It's tough when we have a 24-hour turnaround back to the production department, and we have to get client approval!"

Ives agrees. "When editors have been rushing, mistakes have been introduced into the electronic files. Once, an entire chapter was missing, which went unnoticed until it was time to input it for the printer. However, I put a lot of leeway into the editorial schedule, usually a couple of weeks. Editors don't get the absolute drop dead date. As well, there are no changes on ozalids (final proofs) unless it's a glaring, bad mistake. If it's a minor one, we have to just let it go." At

Reader's Digest Children's Books, "There are no changes on ozalids unless ordered by the client," concurs Gerstein.

Living Color

Now the final text is in place and the illustrator has made that drop dead date. We have the basic making of a book. Where do we go from here? Nowadays, we go to the computer, of course. Text and art are brought together digitally using a publishing program, most often Quark XPress. This is a versatile interface software that lets publishers combine writing, editing, and typography with color and pictures to produce professional, finished pages. Among the processes is the placement of pictures, which are scanned in FPO (for position only), and the original art is provided in separate files as well.

Then, the disks containing the text in layout and the art are sent to the printer. Many children's book publishers print their titles in the Far East—Hong Kong, China, and Singapore, especially. It is far less expensive, and the quality is excellent. Ives at Peachtree remarks that "The color separations are amazing! They are so close to the original art! Working with the Far East has been a great experience for me."

Candlewick Press does their color work in the Far East and Europe. Some of their more text-driven books are printed in the United States.

Michael Braunschweiger, Director of Production and Product Development at Reader's Digest Children's Books, says, "Printing in the Far East is great. We print solely in China. China also supplies 99 percent of our plush and other novelty items [toys accompanying the books]. Communications have improved over the years. The language barriers have come down. They are extremely fast with timely deliveries. Looking at the whole package, I would rate Chinese printers in the top bracket."

Advances in the field have been rapid. Braunschweiger says, "Technology has hugely changed my job and book production in general. Email changed everything. No more multiple faxes. I can email everyone involved with a project so we are all informed at the same time. This is also much cheaper. Of course, we have CTP (computer to plate), which gives us a better quality printout."

At Reader's Digest, everything is done in-house: layout, scanning, typesetting, etc. Usually, there is only one set of proofs to read, then it goes right to ozalids. Candlewick, allows as many proofs as needed, usually two or three.

Worldwide

Braunschweiger heads a department of ten, counting six in the U.S., two in the Far East, and two in Bath, England, where the reprints are handled. Reprints are where the pressure comes in. "We have a huge amount of printing on-demand (reprints) internationally, and they want them faster, faster,

faster. I have to hold out until we have a run that will be profitable before I 'press the button.'"

Even on a first run, international editions are increasingly more important to the bottom line. Candlewick Press has sister companies in England and Australia, called Walker Books. "Walker Books U.K. has an excellent foreign sales department that represents a huge part of the company's overall profit," reports Bicknell. International editions in all publishing houses, particularly on a first run, present editorial decisions that go beyond U.S. boundaries. The text and art must translate easily into the different cultures. Every change on four-color artwork is expensive. Since text is usually in black ink, the cost is considerably less for changes.

At Peachtree, Candlewick, and Reader's Digest, good teamwork is a must. "Teamwork between editorial and production is very important for the success of the company," says Braunschweiger. "Also, leadership and how the company is run are vital. In my department, we have weekly worldwide meetings via phone conferences. These are essential. Email doesn't take away the need for personal conversations."

At Reader's Digest, hold-ups in production are usually about the relationship between licenses and art: "The development of licensed material creates the most delays because the new artwork may not be available in time for us to produce the book when we need to,"

Braunschweiger explains. "If we have to wait, we could miss the cut-off dates to get on the racks for club sales," at warehouse stores like Sam's and Costco.

At Candlewick Press, according to Bicknell, "The bumpiest part of the process is before the book goes into copyediting. The production part is not a problem. It is really rare that we have a delay. Out of the 200 new titles we publish per year, only one or two get postponed. We have a financial forecast that we want to meet."

New Journeys

New technology also allows for many possibilities in children's books. For authors, illustrators, and the production/product development editors, creating a new work can be a journey of discovery. The question always is, "How can we adapt these new technological ideas to our books?"

There is always a competition among publishers in the novelty field to be the first to come out with something totally new and vastly appealing to the children's market. Reader's Digest Children's Books has a winner of a very new kind with its Disney Princess Movie Theater, which comes with a removable projector so children can show slides on the wall. This idea and many like it "make our jobs interesting and challenging," says Braunschweiger.

So, whether your manuscript is bought by a publisher of traditional books or novelty books, the production process is basically the same. The technological advances in computer software and good teamwork combine to bring about a smooth journey through all areas of the creative and production processes. Can there be obstacles? Absolutely! The goal is always to create the best book possible, including writing that will engage children, art that will excite them, and a format that will be easy to read and pleasing to the eye. Would a timetable that is too tight allow for something to fall through the cracks? Sure, it would. Would artwork that isn't available or ready on time prevent publishing the book when the catalog says it will be published? It can happen. In the end, the most important part of the process are the professionals who guide the book at each crossroads to create a quality product that everyone will take pride in. Isn't that what every writer wants?

Online Publishing

Making the Most of Writing for the Web

By Jan Goldberg

Sherri is a fledgling writer with a lot of enthusiasm for writing for children but no writing credits.

Deborah has had a few pieces published in anthologies and her local newspaper.

Larry is an experienced author who has published articles and books for children.

Could any of these three set their sights on writing for children on the Web? Into which of these three categories do you fit? It doesn't matter. Individuals in all three of these categories could and should pursue online writing as one of their goals.

Though it is true that the Web has experienced some shifts in the last years, it undoubtedly will continue to have a strong presence in all our lives. It is an unparalleled means of communication that informs, entertains, and persuades readers in ways unlike any other. It allows millions of people to make connections never before imagined. In addition, it offers a universe of diverse worlds for every possible age group, walk of life, and personality. For those of us who are established authors, not-so-established writers, and brand-new writers, the Web offers huge potential.

Publishing on the Web

The joy of writing and becoming published on the Web is undoubtedly much the same as that of seeing your work published in any other form: in print markets, through performances, or via audio or video formats. Is the process of writing for the Web the same as writing for print markets, or different?

As far as quality of writing and the rules to follow, writing for the Web and print publication is the same. In both, editors have high expectations for writers' work and professionalism:

- Write effective sentences.
- Use strong wording.
- Avoid needless words and phrases.
- Avoid overly long sentences.
- Avoid awkward syntax and stilted language.

Selected Online Children's Publications

▨ **Connect:** www.synergylearning.org/connect/index.html

▨ **Devo'Zine:** Upper Room Ministries, www.upperroom.org/devozine

▨ **Guideposts for Kids Online:** www.gp4k.com

▨ **KidVisions:** Sam's Dot Publishing, www.samsdotpublishing.com/kids/main.htm

▨ **Story Station:** www.viatouch.com/learn/Storystation/Storystation_main.jsp

▨ **Teenage Christian:** www.teenagechristian.net

▨ **Teenwire.com:** www.teenwire.com

▨ **VegetarianTeen.com:** www.vegetarianteen.com

▨ **Wee Ones:** www.weeonesmag.com

▨ **Young Bucks Outdoors:** www.youngbucksoutdoors.com

▨ Organize your paragraphs.

▨ Spell correctly.

▨ Display strong grammar skills.

▨ Begin the story or article by getting the reader's attention with an effective hook.

▨ End your story or article with a satisfying conclusion.

▨ Show that you know how to target your work to the appropriate audience.

▨ Be careful about choosing your words.

▨ Use the active rather than the passive voice.

▨ Always have a beginning, a middle, and an ending.

▨ Show, rather than tell. Showing allows readers to experience what the writer is trying to convey through seeing, hearing, touching, tasting, smelling.

Jennifer Reed, Editor and Publisher of the ezine *Wee Ones* (www.weeonesmag.com), for ages 3 to 10, says, "For fiction, solid writing means a strong main character, a strong problem that is relevant to children today, and a resolution that is both believable and has a twist. Solid nonfiction pieces mean that the writer has done the research and documents it accordingly, has chosen a topic that children are interested in, and made it fun to read and learn from."

"A writer needs to keep in mind that writing for the Web is different than writing for a print publication," says Rosanne Tolin, Editor of *Guideposts for Kids Online* (www.gp4k.com). "Any opportunity for interactive sidebars, subheads, fun links, and the like are elements that need to be present."

While the following is relevant to

Finding Online Markets

Print Publications

■ Allen, Moira Anderson. *Writing.com: Creative Internet Strategies to Advance Your Writing Career*. Revised. New York: Allworth Press, 2003.

■ *Best of the Magazine Markets*. Annual. West Redding, CT: Institute of Children's Literature, 2005.

■ *Book Markets for Children's Writers*. Annual. West Redding, CT: Institute of Children's Literature, 2005.

■ *Children's Writer, Newsletter of Writing and Publishing Trends*. Monthly. West Redding, CT: Institute of Children's Literature.

■ *Children's Writer's and Illustrator's Market*. Annual. Cincinnati, Ohio: Writer's Digest Books, F&W Publications, 2005.

■ *Magazine Markets for Children's Writers*. Annual. West Redding, CT: Institute of Children's Literature, 2005.

■ Shapiro, Ellen R. *Writer's and Illustrator's Guide to Children's Book Publishers and Agents*. New York: Three Rivers Press, 2003.

■ *The Writer*. Monthly. Waukesha, WI: Kalmbach Publishing.

■ *Writers Digest*. Annual. Cincinnati, Ohio: F&W Publications.

■ *Writer's Market*. Annual. Cincinnati, Ohio: Writer's Digest Books, F&W Publications, 2005.

On the Web

Remember that if you want to write for the Web, you need to be familiar with the Web. Surf whenever you can. Use some of the better search engines: google.com, dogpile.com, goto.com, and askjeeves.com.

Look also at websites of children's writers, and at newsletters, listservs, and writing groups online.

The same rules that apply to targeting your print markets apply to online writing. Study the publication, then find out whatever you can via guidelines (which you can usually find online but may need to request by mail), information bases (like www.writersdigest.com), and the editorial department of your targeted market.

other media, for online writing in particular:

- Keep the tone fast-paced.
- Keep it brief—short bites (or is that bytes?). Unless writers' guidelines suggest otherwise, small paragraphs of around eight lines are best.
- Always include good sub-heads.
- Write clearly and concisely—straightforward and tight.
- Use the first person.
- Think about how the piece will look on the screen.

Research Resources

One of the most important uses of the Web is in research. The Internet as a whole has brought associations, companies, government agencies, educational institutions, and all the arts and sciences to our fingertips as never before. The amount of information available is staggering. Yet it must be used with caution.

"It's most important for writers to remember that not all research is reliable," says Tolin. "Therefore, it's best to gather a variety of information. The Internet is a wonderful tool, but be sure to include reputable books from the library as well. Personal interviews with those in the know are key, too. Make sure your bibliography is a diverse list of sources."

"I advise you to be thorough and double and triple check your facts," says Reed. "Don't always rely on the Internet for information. I do not like to see articles that have

only websites listed in their bibliographies. I like to know that an author has gone the extra step and searched out other resources on the subject. Use primary resources whenever possible."

"Not every fact you uncover must be used," says Mark Justice, Editor of *Story Station* (located at www.preschoolexpress.com/story_station.shtml). "I read too many stories that are so loaded down with fact, they virtually scream, 'Look! I've done research!' Research should serve your story, not the other way around."

Thrills & Dreams & Practicalities

Editors of online publications reinforce the essentials of writing well for children, whatever the medium.

Don't preach: "Writers need to understand that they can't preach to children," says Tolin. Kids "immediately lose interest in a piece that sermonizes. Particularly because of *Guidepost for Kids*'s inspirational basis, some authors have a tendency to submit stories that have heavy-handed moral take-aways. If you're trying to teach a lesson, make sure it's handled subtly. Also, writers often mistakenly let adults do the teaching in these instances. Make sure the child protagonist makes his own mistakes and then the right decisions, without the obvious intrusion of a grown-up."

Stay kid-friendly: "It's imperative to know how to write in a kid-friendly way," says Tolin. "This is not as easy as one might think, so

Conducting Online Interviews

Many writers prefer performing their interviews online and a considerable number of interviewees do also. For writers, there is little cost involved and they can compose, send their questions in a convenient and timely way, and there is no tape to transcribe. For the interviewees, they can complete the interview questions at their leisure, look over what they've written, and adjust anything they wish.

What is lost, however, is the give and take of a "live" interview process—the dialogue that may develop and the spontaneous questions and answers that may arise. When conducting interviews online, the traditional rules of interviewing still apply.

Allow enough time to do your homework. Research your subject and pertinent matters thoroughly beforehand.

Set your deadlines carefully. Build in some extra time.

First approach the potential interviewee via email, introduce yourself, and tell him or her the purpose of your note.

When making up your list of questions, try to avoid anything that you could easily answer through your own research. Focus on questions that will add depth and breadth or a personal touch to your topic and the piece you are writing.

If you receive a positive response, send your questions. Include the date by which you need the responses.

After you send the questions, ask the interviewee to email you to confirm receipt.

Always conclude with a request for a follow-up if needed.

Don't forget to thank your interviewees for their time and effort.

do your homework first and read plenty of children's literature before attempting to do so."

Target your readers: "Writing appropriate material for age and reading levels is very important," says Reed. "Often, writers just write without giving age or reading levels any consideration. Know your readers and know them well. Once you understand who your target audience is, then understand what this age level is interested in."

Remember being a child: "Remember what it was like to be a kid," says Justice. "Try to recall the excitement you felt when you read or heard a thrilling story. There is magic in words. Try to capture that when you write. And never write down to your audience. They always know when you do."

Make sure children can relate: "It's most important that the elements of the story or poem contain something that younger readers can relate to," says Tyree Campbell, Managing Editor of *KidVisions*, published by Sam's Dot Publishing (www.samsdotpublishing.com/kids/main.htm). "For those of us who write and publish in the genres, it's equally important that these elements relate in some way to dreams or fantasies that younger readers have. I suspect, deep down inside, we would each like to be something that we are, in fact, not. That's the appeal of science fiction, fantasy, and, to some extent, horror, for younger readers of all ages. Appeal to their dreams, their thoughts, their images of what they might want to be or to do."

How to Impress an Editor

Just how can you make a positive impression on an online editor?

"Most impressive to me is a thorough, well-written cover letter that displays good writing style and knowledge of the gp4k.com ezine, and a writer who has obviously studied the website," says Tolin. "Certain departments have particular kinds of stories written in distinct styles. Submissions must reflect that."

"Even though I accept submissions via email, I like to receive a cover letter with each submission," says Reed. "Being professional makes a great first impression, but, of course, the content of the story or article matters the most. If a writer writes well, knows his or her target audience, and has an understanding of what we publish, then I am impressed."

Justice says, "You can impress me by following the guidelines and by not sending me something that I would consider a first draft. Spelling and grammar are very important but nothing is more important than a good story. Show me you believe in your characters. Make them real. Then, when they are in peril, the reader will care."

At *KidVisions,* Campbell says, "Initially, correct spelling, grammar, and word usage impress me very much. These tell me that the writer knows what she or he is doing, and has actually taken the time to learn the tools of the craft."

She continues, "I like to see consistency in the narrative. Establish your point-of-view person and stick with it. Have reasons for what your protagonist says, does, and thinks. Most of all, infuse tension and conflict into the narrative. Make me wonder or dread what's going to happen next."

Perhaps these comments from Reed are most helpful: "Make sure that writing for children is a passion and not some fleeting fancy. It's a difficult business and your passion for children and literature must be strong. Read children's literature daily, either magazines or books, and write every day. Set realistic goals and work hard to meet them. This may mean you have to make some sacrifices, but believe me, it is well worth it."

Kid Magazine Writers

Author Jan Fields recently established an important website for children's writers called *Kid Magazine Writers* (www.kidmagwriters.com). Serving as editor, Fields has included a wide array of important information for children's writers of both online and print publications and for writers at all levels.

"We're looking for very specific material, so a writer who can go beyond generalities or basics impresses me," says Fields. "Some of the submissions I am getting are very good, but I have to find specific examples to back up points or specific markets to bolster suggestions. So, to me, a writer who reads our emagazine and sees what we're trying to do will impress me.

"I like to see a well-organized piece and I like practicality," she says. "Clarity is essential to passing on the knowledge you have to our readers. We're a very practical article market. Also, since we're online, our readers are looking for information they can consume and use easily.

"Read. There is nothing more important that you can do. Read the kind of writing you want to sell. As a teacher, I see so many writers who read consistently in one area but want to write in a different area. The structure, voice, pacing, and style of what you read gets absorbed into your head and it comes out through your keyboard. If you're feeding your brain adult romance novels, it's not going to turn out really good children's magazine stories. It simply doesn't work that way."

Submissions

Pitch Your Work & Open Doors

By Sue Bradford Edwards

You've written a young adult novel and polished it until it shines, but when the time comes to market your work, you get an unpleasant surprise. The first publisher on your list is closed to unsolicited manuscripts. The second publisher accepts only query letters. The third publisher is open but warns that it will take six months to hear back from them. Should you find an agent?

You could, but finding an agent is no easier than finding a publisher.

Well-equipped writers have tools to have their work read at publishers like the first two described above. Most publishers who are closed to unsolicited manuscripts will read a query letter or perhaps a synopsis and sample chapters. If the editor then asks to read your manuscript, it is no longer unsolicited. Other authors pitch their work through rare face-to-face meetings. For the prepared writer, the query letter, the synopsis, and the face-to-face meeting are the keys to opening the door into the publishing world. To use these keys, authors need to understand what each is and then learn what about them hooks busy editors.

Query: May I Send You This Manuscript?

A query letter is a one-page pitch in which an author asks permission to send a particular manuscript to an editor. Some publishers specifically request queries while others state they are closed to unsolicited manuscripts. Unless they state that they are also closed to unsolicited queries, they will usually read them.

The first paragraph of a query letter needs to hook the editor. "To put it crudely," says Emma D. Dryden, Vice President and Editorial Director of Margaret K. McElderry Books, "the query can be likened to a 30-second commercial that pitches a product in such a way as to make people want to buy it. This means it needs to appeal to the editor on some emotional level." This is most often done through a well-crafted introduction to the manuscript in question. "A query letter should include three or four concise sentences that describe the essence of the manuscript. The query letter should address in the simplest possible way the who, what, where, when, and why of the story. The query should not include every detail of the story," Dryden says.

Often this opening paragraph is followed by a nuts-and-bolts paragraph about the manuscript that includes title, length, manuscript type (YA novel versus early reader). The drier information in this paragraph can be preceded by something succinct and appealing. "I look for a sentence that encapsulates the theme of the book," says G. P. Putnam's Sons Senior Editor Susan Kochan.

In addition to introducing the work, the query should also briefly introduce the author. "For me, the most successful query letters include a succinct synopsis of the project," says Abrams Books and Amulet Books Senior Editor Susan Van Metre, and "a work *bio* of the author—what she does for a living, where she's been published, etc." Anything that relates to the manuscript can be listed, including the author's day job. Kochan offers the example of "an engineer writing about building bridges."

The very best query letters also demonstrate knowledge about the publisher. Van Metre looks for "an awareness of how the project might fit into the Abrams or Amulet programs. The project might be compared to a book on our lists." Let the publisher know why you chose them and they will know you studied the market and didn't simply pull their name from an article or a marketing directory.

Finally, conclude with a paragraph that states that you will submit the work as soon as you receive their request, which may be sent in the self-addressed stamped envelope (SASE) you have provided.

Synopsis: One Page Says It All

A synopsis is a one-page, present tense summary of a novel. If requested by the publisher, a synopsis should accompany a query letter and/or sample chapters so that an editor can see the full scope of the story.

A synopsis takes the information most often found in a query letter's first two paragraphs and expands on it. "The author should include an introduction of the main characters and events," says Front Street Editor Joy Neaves, providing "enough information to give an editor a sense of the story, but not so much that their eyes glaze over." Boredom sets in when the author gives each and every plot point in the book. "Avoid the approach of 'first this happened and then this and then that,'" Neaves says. "Think instead of providing a condensed version of the story, one that includes the most important, defining moments of the narrative. A synopsis reveals how the story logically progresses, what happens, and why it's important that it happened."

Most often, the synopsis should reveal how the story ends. "It should provide a revelation," Neaves says, "as to how the the internal/external conflicts, plot, and subplots, are resolved." And all this in one brief page.

What Else Do You Have? The Face-to-Face Meeting

Briefer still is the rare face-to-face pitch. Why so rare? Because writers who want to make a good impression do not waylay unsuspecting editors in conference restrooms, corner them in elevators, or otherwise pursue them with the sole intention of telling them about a manuscript.

When, then, is a face-to-face pitch acceptable? "The only time that I'd like to have a writer have a pitch ready at a conference," explains agent Erin Murphy, "would be in a one-on-one critique setting. If we were finished talking about the work they'd submitted and we had some more time, or if I was interested in their writing and wanted to know more about them, I might ask them to tell me what else they've written."

When this happens, the author needs to have something prepared. "Definitely include format and genre: 'It's a historical middle-grade novel,'" says Murphy. "Then, give me the hook. What makes it compelling? What is it that makes it different than other, similar books?" A good impression can result in a request to send the manuscript after the conference, even if the pub-

lisher or agency is closed to unagented submissions.

"They'll be better writers if they can conquer this demon," says Murphy of the brief face-to-face pitch. "Much like writing a synopsis. Knowing they can do it can lend tremendous confidence, and is extremely validating of the manuscript."

Baiting the Hook

Any of these pitches can be enough to open the door, but to stand out, writers need to know what grabs an editor's attention *fast*. "Aim to hook your reader as quickly as possible," says Philomel Associate Publisher and Editorial Director Michael Green. "You never know what may be competing for an editor's time and attention." Because of editors' busy schedules, brevity is key. Speaking about the query letter, Van Metre says, "I would suggest writing several drafts, working always toward brevity." Neaves also lists conciseness and brevity as the most important features of a synopsis.

The best pitches provide information both in what they say and how they say it. "First and foremost, I want to gain insight into the feel of the manuscript," says Green. "Be it through voice or through that one sentence that gets right to the heart of the story, I need something that will make me want to turn the page and begin reading."

Dryden says, "A well-written, imaginative query letter hooks me, because that gives me a sense of the kind of writing in which the story will be told." The writing and voice of the pitch should echo the manuscript. The synopsis for a humorous novel should make the reader laugh. A query for a mystery should project a sense of intrigue. Match the writing, tone, and voice with that of the manuscript itself and do it without going too far.

It doesn't take bells or neon to show editors what is vital and important about a particular manuscript or the writer who created it. "This is personal taste," says Van Metre, "but I tend to favor query letters that are to the point and not strenuously promotional, with lots of exclamation points and grand claims."

Be enthusiastic but realistic and professional. "Remember, you are also introducing yourself as someone the editor might, or might not, like to work with for a long period of time," says Van Metre. "I'm attracted to the calm, sensible, gracious writer."

Last but not least in hooking an editor, do not offer what isn't available. Explains Dryden, "Authors should not send query letters until their manuscript is completely written and ready to be submitted upon request."

1, 2, 3: Steps in Writing a Pitch

Even knowing the basic query components and what hooks an editor, pitches take both practice and study to create. Prepare yourself by researching how the editors pitch their books.

"Study book jackets and catalogues for books you've read and you feel were marketed effectively," Murphy says. "Get the *Publishers Weekly* spring and fall children's announcement issues and skim through the one-sentence descriptions of all those books. Which descriptions stand out? Which are disappointing? Keep those issues in mind, then go back and reread the descriptions after you've read some of that season's books. That can help you to hone in on what you need to do to sell your own work."

Green recommends that you go beyond reading and studying book jackets. "Pretend you are writing jacket flap copy for your book. Editors write that copy," he says, "and we aim to hook a reader's interest instantly." Go through your shelves. Which book jackets sent you straight to the cash register, book in one hand and credit card in the other? What about these descriptions hooked you? Can you use a similar technique in pitching your manuscript?

Study the market to know what makes your manuscript unique. "Ask yourself what is most interesting about your manuscript, and what makes it different," says Murphy. This could be your setting, characters, or a plot twist. "Then work on crafting a single sentence that distills that information and makes the listener *get* it. Makes them want more. Intrigues them."

Creating one key sentence stumping you? "Start by writing one paragraph about your manuscript," says Dryden, "then cut that down to three sentences, and

Rx: What Pitch Problems May Indicate

Have a well-written pitch that isn't generating any interest?

It might mean, warns Susan Kochan, G. P. Putnam's Senior Editor, "that the manuscript isn't covering new ground or treating a topic in a unique way." Recheck the markets. Are there already numerous books on this topic? If so, your story needs to have a twist absent from the others.

A manuscript may also be unique without being urgent. "It may be that the author is not clear enough as to what a manuscript is really about and why it needs to be read by an editor or published as a book," says Emma D. Dryden, Vice President and Editorial Director of Margaret K. McElderry Books. "If an author can't get a strong enough handle on their own work and isn't able to pitch it in a compelling way, it is likely that an editor will not find the manuscript itself to be compelling enough to publish."

Inability to generate a strong pitch can be equally revealing. Can't zero in on the main character's goal? Or why that goal is vital? These elements may then be lacking in the manuscript.

An overly long pitch can indicate a lack of focus. "The most common mistake is not having a strong sense of the work, going on too long, explaining backstory and secondary characters, and generally rambling." says agent Erin Murphy. "I always worry the writing rambles that way, as well. It is likely too sprawling and scattered. It needs to have themes, characters, and plot centralized into a tight package."

A strong work paired with a strong pitch form an unbeatable team.

finally cut it down to one key sentence. Forcing an author to think in this concise way about a manuscript helps them prepare good, strong query letters." After all, this is the kind of writing editors do every day for catalogue copy.

You can also start with your synopsis and then whittle that down to query or face-to-face length. Even writing a single page can be daunting with the plot, characters, setting, and intrigue fresh in your mind. This makes it hard to tell what to leave out.

"Think of the content of a synopsis as the highlights edition of a sporting event. If you're telling someone about a soccer game," Neaves says, "you're not going to give a second by second summary. Instead, you'll think back to the beginning of the game, the first defining moment, the awesome pass, or the miracle save. Then you follow with other significant defining moments—a great shot on goal or a penalty kick—until finally you reach the conclusion of what happened and why. I think this helps authors find the defining moments in their stories, the significant elements to be included in the synopsis and the not so significant elements that need not be included." Start long and then work your way down. Tough as it is, it pays off.

Technology

Writers' Office Technology

By Mark Haverstock

In 2005, writers have a wider than ever variety of technology at their fingertips to help them be more productive and professional. Word processors and printers make copy easy to produce and easier to read. Wireless connections make it more practical to work on the move. New storage devices help us keep the equivalent of several file boxes in a technical tool that's not much bigger than a pack of gum.

Though we still can't crank out manuscripts at the speed of light, at least we can send them with blazing speed across the Internet to meet those last-minute deadlines.

Computers: Your Key Tool

A few writers still stubbornly cling to their manual or electric typewriters, but most have now joined the electronic age and rely on computers as a more time and cost-efficient way to create manuscripts. More important, computers make it easy to transfer files electronically, which many editors now prefer.

Just about any computer can perform the basic chores from word processing to email. Today, there's really no reason to spend a bundle, either, for a suitable computer. Even a reliable used Power Mac or PC with a Pentium II or III will do the job for just a few hundred dollars. If you have a desire to purchase a new computer, you'll find desktop and notebook PC models generally available for less than $1,000 with just about all the bells and whistles you'll need. Macintosh units tend to run a bit higher; a G4 costs around $1,300 and a G5, $1,600.

Illustrators and graphic artists generally prefer Macintosh computers. However, if most of your work involves just writing and research, you'll probably be happier with PC compatible computers from manufacturers such as Dell, Gateway, HP, and Sony. You'll find a wider variety of software and accessories readily available, since PC compatibles are more widely used in homes and businesses.

Desktop or laptop? That is the

big question for most writers. Generally, desktop models cost about half the price of a comparable laptop, or notebook. If you don't mind working in the same old office or corner of the room, a desktop should suit you just fine. But if you crave the flexibility of working on the go or typing notes in the library, a laptop is the preferable choice.

Whichever you choose, a new purchase should have the following features as a minimum:

- An effective processor speed of 2.0 GHz or higher–AMD or Intel Pentium
- RAM memory of 256 MB
- CD-RW drive
- 40GB hard disk (30GB for laptops)

For desktop units, a 17-inch or larger screen is easier on the eyes—especially LCD (liquid crystal displays)—and are well worth the difference in price. If you plan to buy a notebook, think about buying one with a high-capacity battery or consider buying a spare. There's nothing worse than having your computer die while you're putting the finishing touches on that perfect paragraph. Also look for built-in wireless capabilities or consider buying a plug-in wireless card, especially if you travel or frequent areas that have wireless service.

Productivity Software

Once you've got the computer, it's time to get serious about the software. Many computers come with limited or trial versions of office productivity packages. Some offer starter software such as Microsoft Works Suite, which is great for home use but lacks some of the sophisticated features writers need. Make sure to get the full versions.

Retailers generally sell productivity packages at or near full retail price, sometimes with a rebate to sweeten the deal. But with Microsoft Office Standard weighing in at almost $400, you may want to consider some other options.

Academic Software. Academic products are for use by students, faculty, or staff of an educational facility and are sold at discounted prices. These products are identical to the standard (nonacademic) versions except the license is labeled *academic.* Customers usually need to provide some kind of proof with the order, such as a copy of a student ID, or a letter of verification from a supervisor.

OEM Packages. OEM, or Original Equipment Manufacturer, products are different from retail versions in both licensing and packaging. OEM products usually consist of a CD, COA (Certificate of Authenticity), and a quick start guide—no box or paper manuals. The full manual is accessible on the CD itself. Technically, OEM software is to be sold with computer equipment, but vendors have found loopholes to get around this requirement.

Upgrade Packages/Competitive Upgrades, Older Versions, and Other Marketing Methods. Sometimes marketing methods can make a price difference. Microsoft Standard Office for Students and Teachers gives you the full versions of four popular programs: Microsoft Word 2002, Microsoft Excel 2002, Microsoft Outlook 2002, and Microsoft PowerPoint 2002, for $129.99. This version is marketed for students and teachers at less than half the price of the same product sold to business customers and is sold over the counter. You really don't need a student ID to get one.

Yet another marketing strategy is to sell software upgrades at lower prices. The assumption is that you have an earlier version of the same product or a similar competitor's product and you want to update the software. Often, the upgrade is no more than a repackaged version of the retail version of the software and you don't actually need the older software or proof of purchase. Corel WordPerfect Office is one such example. However, be careful to read the packaging and ask about any upgrade requirements before you buy. Most software is not returnable.

Finally, you may find older versions of the same software packages at bargain prices. A quick search on the Web turned up copies of last year's Corel WordPerfect Office 11 for less than $20. The current version 12 sells for $149.99.

Go with the Underdog

Though Microsoft is the big dog in the industry, several other alternatives are easier on your wallet and will save files in Microsoft format to keep your editors happy. Sun Microsystem's Star Office Suite 7 is one example of inexpensive professional grade software, available for $79.95.

Plugging into the Internet

Library visits are becoming less frequent for writers as they continue to discover the broad range of information available on the Web. More and more information that traditionally appeared in print form is becoming available online. If you write nonfiction or research frequently, having an Internet connection is essential.

Online services have improved considerably from their humble beginnings, with data originally crawling through the phone lines at a pokey 300 baud. Though telephone dial-up connections still constitute a majority of home and home office connections, the tide is shifting to faster cable and DSL connections. Price, speed, and availability are the general criteria for making your choice.

A typical 56K dial-up phone connection is still the least expensive alternative, with monthly prices ranging from NetZero's $9.95 to America Online's $23.95. These dial-up connections are perfect for writers on budgets who do minimal research on the Internet and need a way to send occasional email and manuscripts. The downside is that you'll tie up your phone line while you're logged on, though you can sign up for a service similar to caller ID that will let you interrupt your online session to take calls.

Broadband connections, such as DSL and cable, are becoming more universally available and affordable. Promotional pricing in many areas starts at about $27 and gives you connection speeds from two to more than ten times that of dial-up, a necessity for those who need to find information in a hurry. Another advantage is that both cable and DSL free up your phone line. A relatively new option with potential, broadband over power lines (BPL) is being tested in cities like Manassas, Virginia. The advantage to BPL is that it can serve anyone who has electricity, including those in remote rural areas, by simply plugging into the wall socket.

Want to take your work to go? Wireless Internet (Wi-Fi) hot-spots are becoming popular in hotels, airports, coffee shops, and restaurants. If you own a laptop with wireless capabilities, you can log onto the Internet at speeds similar to home broadband connections if you're within the coverage area, usually inside the establishment or immediately adjacent to it. Some are free for patrons, others require pay-as-you-go or monthly fees. Another emerging wireless technology, WiMax promises to serve urban areas on a larger scale—up to a ten-mile radius. Whichever service brand or type you choose, be sure that it includes readily accessible technical support by phone. It's hard to get help online if you can't get online.

Guarding the Back Door

One of the hazards of connecting to the Internet or sharing files is the possibility of picking up malicious viruses, worms, Trojan horses, and other threats that can cripple your computer. Installing any good security program is a good means of avoiding infection and short-circuiting hacker attacks.

Your best bet for protection is to purchase a program that has both virus protection and a built-in software firewall. Good examples include Trend Micro's PC-cillin Internet Security and Symantec's Norton Internet Security. In addition to installing these programs, it's important that you regularly update your virus definitions at the program's website. These websites are also real goldmines for virus information. Check them to find out about hoaxes and real threats, and what to do about them.

If you have a DSL or cable connection to the Internet, installing a router adds an extra level of defense and also provides additional computer connections and/or wireless capability. Routers "hide" your computer from outside connections, which only see the router itself.

Archiving Your Work

Backing up your work is essential, especially with rampant computer viruses and unexplained computer glitches that vaporize your important files when you least expect it. Making back ups used to mean periodically dragging out a box of disks and copying files. Over the last few years, however, disk drives have become an option rather than standard equipment on laptop and desktop computers. Unless you have a fondness for floppy disks, it's time to move to more spacious storage quarters.

Flash drive storage media is deceptively tiny. It easily fits on your keychain yet holds considerably more information than a drawer full of disks. It's a bit like Dr. Who's Tardis, a fictional time travel machine disguised as a police call box. Outside, it looks barely big enough to hold one person. Inside, it's roomy enough to hold an entire spaceship crew, their quarters, and a few Klingon warriors for good measure. Flash drives plug into the Universal Serial Bus (USB) port of your computer. Prices start at about $40 for 128MB of storage (about the equivalent of 90 disks).

Almost all new computers come standard with a CD-RW (read-write) drive built in or as an inexpensive add-on. You've probably seen CD-ROM media in the form of software programs, but you can also buy blank CD-ROMs to back up your word processor files inexpensively. CD-RW blanks, which cost about $1 each, can be reused and updated every time you back up your files. CD-R media, typically less than 25¢, lets you make single permanent copies of your work—great for archiving your writing. A typical CD holds the equivalent of about 485 disks.

Other options include tape drives and Zip drives, but neither match the portability or cost effectiveness of flash drives and CD-ROMs.

Putting It to Paper

You'll find a whole range of printers, from inkjet to laser, color to monochrome. Some double as scanners, faxes, and will even print photos directly from a digital camera. So which one is best for the writer's home office?

Considering space, functionality, and cost of supplies, a multifunction laser printer gives writers the most bang for the buck. You can find suitable units from Brother, Hewlett Packard (HP), and Samsung in the $300 to $500 range, sometimes considerably less, with rebates. Typically, these multifunction units print, scan pictures, and copy documents; some even send faxes. They take up minimal desk space and are cheaper than buying each component separately.

If you don't need the multiple features, a basic laser printer will give you crisp black-and-white copy. Though small office laser printers are initially more expensive than their inkjet counterparts, typically $130 to $400 from makers like Brother, HP, Samsung, and Minolta, they're actually cheaper to operate over the long run, especially if you print several hundred pages a month. Color lasers are creeping below the $1,000 mark, but toner and other supplies for them are still prohibitively expensive.

Inkjet printers are best for those who may only print a few pages on an infrequent basis or don't want to make a large initial investment. They're a good choice if it's a printer you'll be sharing with the kids for an occasional school project or dabble in digital photography. Inkjet printers are also available as multifunction units, so you can have a convenient copier, scanner, and fax as well. The downside is that ink costs are high. For some low-end printers, a set of replacement cartridges actually costs more than the printer. Basic inkjet printers from manufacturers like Canon, HP, Lexmark, and Epson cost from $50 to $300. Multifunction units typically run $100 to $300.

On Call

First impressions count. What will an editor's or client's first impression be when they call you, and your three-year-old answers the house phone? Getting a second line allows you to help keep your professional image by keeping your business calls separate from the family. Consider getting voice mail—usually just a few dollars more a month—especially if you plan to use your computer or fax on the second line. Though voice mail is a bit more expensive over the long run than an answering machine, you'll never miss a call.

Consider your cell phone as a second line alternative. Wireless plans have become more affordable recently, with most plans including free long distance and voice mail services. Even low-tech cell phones will let you identify callers or even set distinct rings so you know when to put on your business voice.

VoIP (voice over IP) is a fairly new service that utilizes your cable Internet service as a phone. Many VoIP providers charge a flat rate for unlimited local and long distance, which might make this a good choice if you make frequent calls. Cable companies often package multiple services at a discount, such as Internet, VoIP, and cable—another reason it could be a cost-effective solution for an additional line.

Nice If You Can Get Them

Hundreds of cool gadgets are available online or at your local office supply and computer stores. Though you could spend a big chunk of next year's writing profits on them, here are a few you should seriously consider, or at least put on your wish list.

If you're frequently a victim of Murphy's Law (anything that can go wrong will go wrong), consider buying an uninterruptible power supply (UPS). In the event of a blackout, a UPS instantly switches your computer to emergency battery backup power and lets you work through brief power outages without losing data and protects your computer against power surges. Choose a unit with a rating of at least 500VA or higher, and you'll have sufficient time to finish that paragraph and save your work. Cost: $50 to $150 at most computer stores.

Personal digital assistants (PDAs) such as Palm or Ipaq are the electronic equivalent of the Swiss Army Knife. Use them to keep appointments, addresses, and remind you of important events. Keep notes; most will now let you record audio

Resources for the Writer's Home Office

Software

▥ *Microsoft Office:* office.microsoft.com/home/
▥ *Star Office:* wwws.sun.com/software/star/staroffice
▥ *WordPerfect:* www.corel.com
▥ *Trend Micro PC-cillin Internet Security:* www.trendmicro.com
▥ *Symantec Norton Internet Security:* www.symantec.com/product

Sources for OEM Software:
▥ www.thesoftwareguy.com
▥ www.softwarehousestore.com
▥ www.ebay.com

Sources for Academic Software:
▥ www.academicsuperstore.com
▥ www.journeyed.com
▥ www.studentdiscounts.com

Links to writer specific software:
▥ *Smatterings: Choosing the Right Tool:* smatterings.topcities.com/
rightjob.html
▥ *Writer Resources, Software:* dmoz.org/Arts/Writers_Resources/Software

Hardware

▥ *Brother Printers:* www.brother.com/usa/usalocal.html
▥ *Dell Computers:* www.dell.com
▥ *Gateway Computers:* www.gateway.com
▥ *Hewlett-Packard/Compaq Computers, Ipaq, and Printers:* www.hp.com
▥ *Minolta Printers:* printer.konicaminolta.net/usa
▥ *Palm:* www.palm.com
▥ *Samsung Printers:* www.samsung.com/Products/index.htm
▥ *Sony Computers:* www.sonystyle.com

Phone & Internet

▥ *1AND1 Web Hosting:* www.1and1.com
▥ *AOL:* www.aol.com
▥ *Earthlink:* www.earthlink.com
▥ *Vonage Internet broadband phones:* www.vonage.com
▥ *Yahoo's Geocities:* http://geocities.yahoo.com

Miscellaneous

▥ *Aaaagh, It's Not Working! Tips and solutions to common computer
problems:* smatterings.topcities.com/problems.html
▥ *Trojan, Virus and Worm Information:* www.ircbeginner.com/opvinfo/
trojan-virus.html

or written messages. You can also use them to entertain yourself during downtime, with music, books on tape, or video games. If money is no object, you might consider cell phones or Blackberry wireless messaging systems with built-in PDAs. Price range: $99 to $500.

Cut the cord. Go wireless and create your own Wi-Fi hot spot at home. For about $150, you can get a wireless router and a plug-in card for your laptop. Typically you can expect most wireless systems to work reliably within a 100- to 300-foot range.

Finally, having a personal website gives you some credibility as a professional and is yet another way to sell yourself. You can post published clips, publicize your next book, or advertise your availability for class visits and speaking engagements. I was able to set up www.markhaverstock.com at web host 1AND1.com in an afternoon and keep it online for about $5 a month. Your current Internet provider, such as Earthlink and AOL, may offer you free web page space as a subscriber. Sites like Yahoo's Geocities will provide you with a basic personal website for free.

Contracts

To Negotiate Yourself or Not, That Is the Question

By Kelly Easton

Hooray! You've sold your first children's book. An editor has called you and expressed delight, then told you they'll be offering you a contract.

You (a) fall to your knees and thank your favorite higher power; (b) call every person in your Rolodex and brag shamelessly; (c) think of a list of demands to be sure you are treated fairly by the publisher.

Not (c)? Change Your Psyche

To write a book is a wonderful achievement. To have created something original, funny, or beautiful enough to sell to a publisher, is monumental. The odds of being published are daunting. Depending on their size, publishing houses receive far more submissions than they can publish. At Margaret K. McElderry Books of Simon & Schuster, Editor Sarah Nielsen says that of the approximately 3,000 manuscripts it receives annually, McElderry is able to publish only 20 to 25.

It's no wonder that when our book is chosen, most of us feel like we've won the lottery. Still, no matter how much of your heart and your life has been poured onto the page, the world of children's books remains a *business*. If you need to be convinced of that, consider the fact that most publishers are owned by massive conglomerates whose origins as companies may have been as stereo or automobile manufacturers, cereal companies, or radio stations.

You only need to walk into a chain bookstore to see the business side (rather than the literary side) at work. The children's sections of bookstores are increasingly filled with commodities disguised as literature: TV show and movie books with cleverly attached products that attract children like chocolate chip cookies on a plate. A recent visit to my local chain turned up more than 20 *Shrek* products, from the movie, having very little connection with William Steig's marvelous original.

According to the Association of American Publishers, children's and young adult literature account for 10 percent of the sector, and grew by 19 percent in one year alone. Young adult literature, after years of being an orphan on a floating island, has become a literary commodity to be reckoned with in the world of publishing. Because of the success of the Harry Potter books, children's and young adult books have even garnered their own section in the *New York Times Book Review.*

As the business of writing for children has grown more profitable, so have the number of writers. The Society of Children's Book Writers and Illustrators (SCWBI) has more than 19,000 members who are either working or aspiring writers and illustrators.

It's no wonder that many of us just feel so grateful that we are also scared to make demands of editors or publishers, lest it all disappear in a puff of fairy tale smoke. The world also validates the idea that artists are so lucky to have any success that they really don't need much financial gain. Ask any published writer how many times they've been asked to review a book, make a speech, or edit someone's work for free. Yet no one would ask a dentist to pull a tooth without pay, or expect a lawyer to represent them at trial pro bono. And let's face it; it takes about as long to master the art of writing as it does to get an M.D.

Logical? Yes. But can this logic take hold in your psyche so that you feel capable of stating your case in contract negotiations? Can you make the distinction between your work as art and your work as a commodity?

If you were writing for adults, the question probably would not arise because in the adult market, you *must* have an agent to sell your work. Children's publishers, however, are aware that the next great thing in children's literature may come from a librarian, a teacher, or a single mother sitting on a train imagining a boy with a lightning bolt on his forehead. As Editor Hannah Rogers of Houghton Mifflin puts it: "An unagented submission from an informed writer carries just as much weight, if not more, than a submission from an agent—especially if that agent isn't experienced in the children's market or hasn't taken the time to handpick a project specifically for us."

In fact, I turned my novel, *The Life History of a Star,* into a YA project after many agents rejected it as an adult novel because of its diary form. It was a friend who told me that there was an "open door" policy at many publishers for the children's market. Within weeks, I had a contract. On that, my first book, I used an agent to negotiate my deal.

Agents, Pro & Con

So what is the benefit of using an agent to negotiate your contract? The obvious one is that agents have more experience, and may also be acquainted with the policies (and difficulties) of various publishers. The agent can push the publisher to promote your book, something that is uncomfortable for most authors. Using an agent also leaves your relationship with editors pure and focused on the art and craft of your book rather than money. If contractual problems arise, the agent will handle them, leaving you free to work on the next masterpiece.

The simplest reason not to use an agent is that they will receive 15 percent of your advance and royalties on a book, for the rest of your life. Should your book remain in print, this will also extend to the life of your children.

Second, the agent becomes a go-between for you and the editor, which could feel like a game of telephone, with comments translated before reaching your ear. Lastly, the agent's need to maintain a relationship with publishers may hinder his willingness to go past the "standard" in publishing contracts, although many standard points are innately unfair to authors. For example, most agents I've spoken with insist that the clause giving publishers an option on your next book is a matter of fact. If you are developing and marketing numerous projects, however, this could put you in a weaker position to negotiate with other publishers. In my own negotiations, I have requested an omission of this point, and the publisher offered a two-book deal as an alternative.

Agents

In negotiating for yourself, you need an understanding of the terms and issues of contracts. Once acquired, you then need to ask yourself if you have the confidence to ask for what you want without apology. Can you take the same assurance with which you wrote the book, and apply that to negotiations? If you make the decision to work on your own, keep in mind the following advice.

■ *Be prepared.* Know, in advance, your bottom line. Consider whether you are willing to walk away from an offer that doesn't fall within your expectations. Consider your arguments in advance. Know the numbers on your book sales and be ready with the prizes you've received, the reasons why you deserve more money.

■ *Be educated.* Read up on contract law, and/or contact your local organization for guidelines. Most offer free assistance with contracts. The National Writers Union, for example, has volunteers who are trained in contract law (although they are not lawyers) and who will advise members for free. SCBWI offers a pamphlet on contracts called "Answers to Some Questions about Contracts." Members need only send an SASE to receive it. The Authors Guild also offers a guide to contracts, by their legal staff. The more knowledgeable you are, the more confident you will feel.

■ *Be direct.* If possible, negotiate your requests by email so that you can edit your negotiations and refine language. This will also give you a written record. Use language that is precise and unemotional. Ask for what you want.

Resources

▓ **Society of Children's Book Writers and Illustrators:** 8271 Beverly Boulevard, Los Angeles, CA 90048. www.scbwi.org
▓ **The Authors Guild:** 31 E. 28th St., 10th Floor, New York, NY 10016. www.authorsguild.org
▓ **National Writers Union:** 113 University Place, 6th Floor, New York, NY 10003. www.nwu.org

Books:
▓ *Kirsch's Guide to the Book Contract: For Authors, Publishers, Editors, and Agents,* Jonathan Kirsch (Acrobat Books, 1998).
▓ *Negotiating a Book Contract: A Guide for Authors, Agents, and Lawyers,* Mark L. Levine (Moyer Bell Ltd., 1988).

▓ *Be polite.* Use the most courteous language possible.

▓ *Be calm.* Take your time to respond at each point in negotiations. The offer will not disappear if you wait to answer. It's perfectly acceptable to say, "Let me consider that and get back to you."

▓ *Be professional.* Leave out the personal details. If you need a higher advance because your boyfriend is a loafer, your dog needs surgery, or you want a Caribbean cruise for your nerves, the editor doesn't need to know. What she does need to know is that you are stable and capable of completing this work on the deadline.

When in doubt, consult an entertainment lawyer. While you'll have to pay the lawyer a fee to review the contract, you won't be beholden for 15 percent of your royalties in perpetuity as you would with an agent. And while most initial conversations on contracts relate to advances, royalties, and schedules, there are other issues to consider relating to potential legal problems.

At the time I'm writing this, I have just finished negotiating three contracts for myself. But it took me years to make the psychological transition from artist to artist/businesswoman, and only time will tell how I've done. I was reminded of the difficulty of making a living as a writer only last week. I was in the YMCA swimming laps when a nun I often see asked me about my profession. "I write children's books," I proudly offered.

"Wonderful," she said. "How much do you get paid?"

I told her.

"Oh, dear. You don't make much as an author, do you?"

"Well, you don't make much as a nun, either," I joked, my foot firmly placed in my mouth.

"No," she frowned, "but I knew that going into it."

That pretty much says it all.

Finances

Payment Issues for the Writer

By Ellen Macaulay

We write; we get paid. Of course, it doesn't always work out that way. Many a writer writes for free just to get a foot in the door, to publicize a book or a larger body of work. That's often a smart thing to do. After all, it's your publication credits that future editors will look at, not how much money you made.

Exceptions aside, most of us are in this business to make money, in addition to our urge to create. Many aspiring writers and students have informed me that they're taking an introductory writing course so they can quit their day job, put their kids through college, or simply become fabulously wealthy.

The fact is there aren't many rich writers, especially children's writers. The exceptions are well known: J. K. Rowling, author of the Harry Potter series, immediately leaps to mind. The hard, cold truth is that the bulk of writers are not only not well known, they are not well paid either according to most standards. I once looked up a statis-tical study on the best and worst-paying jobs. Guess which list we were on? That's right. That survey put it all in perspective for me—for every Rowling, there are thousands of struggling writers barely eking out a living.

So why does anyone bother at all? Well, because we writers are a notoriously scrappy and persistent bunch, that's why. Most professional writers supplement their meager incomes by teaching, taking editing or contract jobs, doing lectures/conferences/school visits, or just keeping their miscellaneous day jobs to pay the bills.

That brings us to the point of this article: payment issues. You write. You get paid something, sometimes. Why not optimize it?

Writing As a Hobby

One day, early in my career, I brought one of my kids to the pediatrician for a check-up. There, in the bustling waiting room, was a children's magazine with my article in it. I was so excited, I brought it in and waved it at the doctor. The next time we visited this pediatrician's office again, he said to me, "So, Ellen, how's that little hobby of yours going?" Harumph! was my reaction.

Hobby is such an unfortunate word. It makes it sound like what we do as writers is somewhat frivolous, a lark. All play and no work. I don't even have to qualify why writing is work: We all know all that's involved. But until we come up with a better word, it pains me to say that it turns out Dr. Pompous Boob was right. My writing at that time was a hobby. (But it was never little!)

The magic number is $600. According to the federal government, if you make less than $600 a year, it's a hobby, not a business. Also, if an employer, a publisher in our case, issues payment for any amount less than $600, they don't have to send you a 1099 at year-end. (The 1099 tax form is used to report income paid to independent contractors for services rendered.) That doesn't mean they won't. It just means they don't have to. If you do receive a 1099 (and I've gotten them for payments as low as $10), you are required to claim the payment as income on your tax return. If you don't receive a 1099, then, you know the drill: You're supposed to claim it anyway and you need to take care of Social Security payments.

Much is to be said for working as a hobbyist. Maybe you have another job, and writing is a sideline. Maybe you can't be bothered with fancy recordkeeping. Maybe you don't want to concern yourself with making a living with your writing, you just like the occasional lift you get when it's pay day at Hip National Bank (i.e., money that goes directly into your hip pocket). Your payments are made out to you. There are no taxes taken out of your checks. No employees to pay, few expenses to take care of, and, often, minimal taxes to pay outside of normal income tax.

After many years as a hobbyist, I started making more money. I also became involved in several writing offshoots. My writing was becoming more of a business and less of a "little hobby." It became time to handle my finances differently.

Professional Hobbyist

When I was growing up, swimming lessons were offered every summer at the local park. If it was your very first class, you were automatically classified a beginner. From there was advanced beginner, intermediate, and advanced. I was an advanced beginner every single summer. That suited me just fine. I wasn't planning on entering any races or joining a swim team. I never had to set foot on the dreaded diving board. I simply learned to swim.

That's basically how it is with a writing career. Everyone starts off as a beginner (hobbyist) and then you may move up to advanced beginner (professional hobbyist?). Again, lacking a good word to describe this financial level, I guess we're stuck with professional hobbyist, or professional amateur, for now.

Health Insurance

A major issue in supporting yourself as a writer is affordable health insurance. Peter Tabet with the Northwestern Mutual Financial Network offers writers this advice:

If you're not covered under an employer or spouse's health insurance, you will need to submit a medical statement to obtain an individual health insurance policy. These policies are costly and often difficult to obtain. Insurers have the option of rejecting an individual's request.

To qualify for a less expensive group rate and increase your underwriting chances, look into associations that accept individual members (e.g., chambers of commerce, writers organizations such as the Society of Children's Book Writers and Illustrators, Authors Guild). As with an individual policy, you will need to submit a health statement before being approved and allowed to join the group.

If you own your own corporation, you may qualify for a group rate as long as you have at least two employees in addition to yourself. Even though you will still submit a health statement, you usually can't be denied coverage.

Hobbyists may not deduct their health insurance costs. Self-proprietors, filing a Schedule C with their tax return, may deduct some portion (up to half the cost). A corporation's health premium is fully deductible.

If you're leaving a job to write full-time, consider keeping your current health benefits. C.O.B.R.A. Consolidated Omnibus Budget Reconciliation Act) permits you to continue health insurance benefits for up to one and a half years after you terminate your employment. Look elsewhere for coverage while still on the C.O.B.R.A. plan as it will not last indefinitely.

It is important to obtain disability insurance, which pays you in case you are no longer able to work as a writer. You will need a two-year track record of earnings to qualify for this coverage. Disability insurance is not available to hobbyists.

Health insurance regulations vary widely from state to state. Individuals should always verify the laws of their particular state as they pertain to obtaining health coverage.

Compare & Contrast Three Levels

Hobbyists: use their Social Security number, do not pay operating taxes, maintain only personal banking accounts, recordkeeping is easy to set up and maintain, will utilize some write-offs, don't have to use an accountant, least professional approach.

Self-Employed: use their Social Security number, pay self-employment taxes, can maintain separate personal and business banking accounts, recordkeeping is more difficult to set up and maintain, will utilize more write-offs, more likely to need an accountant, more professional approach.

Corporations: use a Corporate ID number, pay corporate taxes, must maintain separate corporate banking accounts, recordkeeping is most difficult to set up and maintain, will utilize many write-offs, most likely to need an accountant, most professional approach.

The qualifications for professional hobbyist are straightforward: You make more than $600 a year from your writing, more than a hobbyist. But you still make less than several thousand dollars a year, not enough to move on to the intermediate level of self-employed.

Most likely, professional hobbyists still handle their writing income as the hobbyist does. The only difference is more money means more recordkeeping. You will probably want to utilize some expenses as write-offs from your income. You will most likely be receiving more 1099s (definitely if your payment is $600 or more). More 1099s means more income to claim and more to pay taxes on.

Basically, you're running a part-time business with your writing. And, as with any business, part-time or not, you will need to keep records. Record your income— every payment you receive, the date you received it, and the source the payment was received from. Track your expenses—computer, paper, pens, phone calls, etc. Then, at the end of the year, deduct your expenses from your income for a true accounting of what you made. How are you doing?

I Hate My Boss

If you start making good, steady money from your writing (or writing outlets), say in the $5,000 to $10,000-plus a year range, you could consider the self-employed route. What's involved with self-employment? Basically, you work for you. You become your own boss, a sole proprietor. You're a business consisting of one employee—you!

Now how is that any different from the two levels of hobbyists we discussed? Hobbyists also work for themselves. After all, there's no one handing over writing assignments, collecting their money, finding appropriate markets for their work. But when you're a hobbyist, you pretty much accept what is offered you. Admit it. If an editor likes your story or article and offers you 20 bucks for it, chances are you snatch it up, deposit it in Hip National Bank, and do a celebratory dance. When you're self-employed, you don't act quite so fast.

That's because, when you're self-employed, you're running a full-time business. It doesn't matter that you're a business of one, you're still a business. As such, you have to determine your own rates. Consider your expenses when determining your rates. If an article pays $35, and your expenses (phone, paper, time, travel) eat up $30, you're only netting $5. Maybe seeing your writing in that publication is worth it to you, even for $5; maybe it isn't. You have to decide upfront, before doing the work.

Your writing is your livelihood; if you don't set your own rates, you could be losing money. Remember, you're not a nonprofit organization. Profit is what constitutes a business. If you don't make a profit, you won't be in business long.

So, tell the editor what you need. Every businessperson does this. When was the last time you hired someone and you got to set the rate? Never! You see, it's up to you to determine what to charge or what to accept in payment. It may

help to set a per word amount for your work. Or determine your hourly or weekly rate before you tackle a project. Use whatever method works for you, as long as you end up with enough money to continue running your business.

Writers typically have problems asking for more money. Knowing how much competition we face, we're meek and mild around editors. We constantly seek their approval. We often figure if we're cheap, we'll get the job. That's not the case at all. Editors appreciate professionalism. As long as you present a reasonable rate for the desired assignment (and have the writing chops to validate this rate), chances are the editor will consider your proposal. But, for some people, being assertive about money is like stepping out on that dreaded diving board. If you're one of these people, it'd probably be best if you stay a perennial advanced beginner, as I did with my swimming.

Okay, you've set your rates, generated some business for yourself, and started bringing in some money. Good for you! But you can't stop there the way a hobbyist can. As a self-employed businessperson, you have many more things that need your attention. Self-employment tax to cover your Social Security and Medicare benefits will run about 15 percent of your gross income. Your federal/state taxes will now be due and paid quarterly. And, while not required, it is more professional to maintain bank accounts for your business that are

Possible Tax Write-Offs for Writers

Possible tax write-offs include: phones, Internet, travel, office supplies (paper, pens, paper clips), seminars/conferences, books/educational materials (i.e., this book you're reading right now, any classes you take this year), computer equipment, and so on.

Any write-offs must be in proportion to your writing income (e.g., you can't write off a $1,500 laptop if you only made $50 in writing income that year).

Verify any write-offs with your tax attorney or accountant before filing your tax returns.

kept separate from your personal affairs. That way, if you're ever audited, your worlds don't collide.

Me, Inc.

Even though I never made it past advanced beginner in swimming, I did manage to reach the advanced level elsewhere. I started as a hobbyist, moved up to self-employed, and I am now an official corporation. I operate as any other corporation would. I am in business to sell a product. The product? My writing services.

It was my husband's idea to incorporate. As a business owner for 20-plus years, he knows all the ins and outs of establishing your own corporation, which is helpful to say the least. He pointed out that there are certain financial benefits to being incorporated. Of course, to receive these benefits, you have to go through quite a bit of rigmarole: hire an attorney to set up your corporation, pay set-up fees, file paperwork, and so on

My writing services constitute just one of the departments of our family corporation. We also operate other businesses out of the corporation. That's the beauty of being incorporated—we can diversify. It doesn't have to be writing related. It could be real estate, selling on eBay, any number of other ventures. Our corporation is planning on developing some self-publishing projects at some point.

It's important that your corporation, no matter how small, operates like a corporation. Ours has officers like any other corporation. (Not surprisingly, my husband and I are huge bigwigs in our corporation.) We hold annual meetings. We can hire employees. (Darn! Haven't quite gotten to that point yet.) We can reimburse ourselves for any corporate expense such as conferences, books, and meetings. But, keep it in check: You can reimburse only for legitimate business expenses. Plus, your expenses need to be proportional to your income.

Your corporate entity is totally separate from your individual identity. It's not your name and social security number that go on the documentation, it's your corporate name and corporate identification number. It's not your home address, it's a separate corporate address. You keep separate bank accounts for the corporation. You file separate tax returns: Your personal tax return is due annually, your corporate tax return is due quarterly.

The advantages to operating a corporation are many. All expenses associated with my business come out of this corporate account, not my personal account. It doesn't matter if you work out of your own home; you can still write off certain expenses.

The disadvantage is that it can be costly to run a corporation. Corporate business tax varies according to state and some states are more business-friendly than others. You also pay a number of financial and legal fees. But the fees are there to protect you. When you're incorporated, no one can sue you personally (and take your home, your firstborn child, etc.). They can only sue the corporation. The corporation acts as a separate entity; it stands alone. You, as a writer, work for the corporation.

Now, whenever I do a writing or teaching job, I simply inform the company paying me to send the check care of me, but payable to the corporate name at the corporate address. (I will have provided them with my corporate ID number.) While it takes a tad more effort to fill in the information on my contracts, no one has ever batted an eyelash at this financial arrangement.

The bottom line is I am taxed as a corporation, not as an individual. Taxwise, this is beneficial. The government wants to encourage new business and overall economic growth. As such, it allows corporations to deduct expenses first, then pay tax on what's left. It's the other way around for individuals (hobbyists and sole proprietors). They pay taxes first, and then deduct expenses.

Although it's much more work to set up and maintain your own corporation (and consult a good attorney and other professionals to do so), the opportunities it provides have certainly been worth it for me. It also forces me to look to the future and ask the important questions: How can I make more money with my writing? What other cool operations can I run out of my corporation?

No matter if you're happy at the financial level you're at or if you're interested in moving to a new level, it's important to consult with a tax advisor or accountant before you do anything. (And hey, the money you pay them is deductible!) Taxes

Helpful IRS Websites

- *Starting a business and keeping records:* www.irs.gov/pub/irs-pdf/ p583.pdf
- *Tax Guide for Small Business:* www.irs.gov/pub/irs-pdf/p334.pdf

are the big stickler in any payment issue. There's no getting around taxes. They are our biggest expense over our lifetime. But, if you set up a clean, efficient, financial organization system, save all your receipts, and strictly follow your financial professional's advice, you should be in good shape.

Examine your options as a professional writer and figure out the financial plan that works best for you. Once your payment issues are in order, you'll have more time, peace of mind, and, hopefully, money, to concentrate on what you do best—your writing.

Publicity

Promoting Your Book to the Children's Market

What You Need to Know, What You Need to Do, and If Your Mother-in-law Is Queen of England, Don't Forget to Mention It

By Stephen Roos

You've just had your first manuscript accepted for publication. What could be more exciting? What a thrill it is to see your gorgeous manuscript morph into a gorgeous book! Savor it all. You'll write dozens more, but the first time is special.

Well in advance of the actual publication date, you'll receive a questionnaire from the publicity department asking all about you and how you came to write your soon-to-be book. This should be a snap, shouldn't it? Haven't you dreamed of moments when you could tell your adoring public just how you came to write your masterpiece? This could be just the practice you need for the lifestyle you hope to become accustomed to in the very near future.

Well, yes and no. When I worked in publicity and promotion at Harper Junior Books, I was constantly surprised that so many authors who wrote so well about other people wrote so dully about themselves. All too often, they seemed to be rushing through the questions as quickly and as minimally as they could. The truth, as I found out eventually, is that writers, no matter how colossal their egos, tend to be horribly shy. Now that I write too, I see how our work lives tend to be dry, introspective, downright sedentary. Is it any wonder that most of us grit our teeth when the opportunity to talk about ourselves arises?

Even though I knew better, I have to admit that on more than one occasion I handled the questionnaires in too perfunctory a manner. If I had it to do all again I would devote more time, more energy to that simple questionnaire. I would work harder to create a memorable, marketable image of myself on paper. Remember, it's true what they say about first impressions. They're the ones that stick. Since you're probably not going to meet the publisher's sales, publicity, and promotion crew in person, the questionnaire may be the only impression you make. Don't miss out on your big chance to impress them with your viability as a promotable, publicizable literary persona.

> *Advertising* is the media time and space you pay for. *Publicity* is the media time and space you don't pay for. *Promotion* is everything in between—mailers, catalogues, bookmarks, author bios, conventions, etc.

Raised by Wolves

If you don't have a literary persona yet, you better get cracking! If you've already published a best seller, if you've already won a Newbery, you're pre-sold. You don't need to sell you. Your sales records and awards will do it for you. If you've never published before, however, and you're eager for success, it's time to pull your persona together.

The trick is to be thoroughly thrilling, of course. If you were born in Madagascar, mention it. If you were raised by wolves, that can only help. If you've recently discovered a cure for cancer, that's worth mention though a cure for acne will probably get you the most attention in this market. Celebrity helps. Julie Andrews, Sarah Ferguson, and Barbara Bush all jump-started their writing careers by getting famous before they sat down to write.

But what if you just haven't got around to being a movie star, or marrying a prince, or being First Lady? What if you've truly never been anywhere or done anything? Then you absolutely have to make sure your answers on the forms are as entertaining as you can make them. Be funny. Be brilliant. Be provocative. If you like bringing your readers to tears, go for it. Treat that questionnaire like it's the next major art form!

Keep stressing the connection between you and your book. What if your story is set in some unusual place? What if it takes place during some special era? Play up your own personal connection and/or interest to that locale and that era. What if your story deals with some serious issues and themes? Racism? The environment? Drug abuse? By all means, let your publisher know how these issues came to touch your life.

(If the price of going public with some very personal matters is going to cause you and the people who love you grief, I don't recommend it. You do have every right to keep private matters private. But if you're game for going public, I urge you to do so. Not because it's therapeutic, although it may be, but because it's good for business.)

The Hustle

▪ **Writer:** "If we were born sales-men, then why the heck would we be writers?" one writer friend asked me, and I could tell she was only half-kidding. "Selling my manuscript took all the hustle out of me. I didn't know the hustle had just begun."

▪ **Editor:** "Maybe publishers were more parental to their authors in the good old days way back when," says one editor. "Nowa-days, it's a different story. We're here to make money for our stock-holders. That's our primary pur-pose. If a book looks like it isn't going to make it, we don't throw good money after bad."

Personal Appearance Dividends

If you're good with kids—and not all kids' authors are—say so. If you've seen Judy Blume gently re-assuring teenagers that they will survive adolescence, if you ever heard the late Paula Danziger wise-cracking with the kids, if you've seen Maurice Sendak drawing a miniature "wild thing" when he gives an autograph, you'll see how an author makes a personal ap-pearance memorable.

What would you like to do on the personal appearance trail? What could you say to kids? What activity could you do in a classroom? What-ever it is, let the publisher know. Your publicity department will be eager to volunteer you for book fairs, author days, and book chats.

By all means, consider getting yourself a website. If that's not for you, get yourself an email address just for letters from readers and ask your publisher to include that ad-dress on the author biography on the flap copy. That will show them you mean business.

Your hard work will pay divi-dends. When the folks in the public-ity and promotion departments read your questionnaire, they're going to know who you are, what you're about. They're going to know how to promote you. When they see that there is to be a panel dis-cussion on how to make dirt bikes out of papier-maché, they're going to volunteer you. When the National Council of Social Studies wants a speaker on how to alter kids' mis-perceptions about race, your pub-lisher is going to propose you for it.

Publication Day Cometh

A few months before your book is published, you'll probably receive a seasonal catalogue featuring your book. Come publication day, you may well get a call from your edi-tor. If you live nearby, you may even get lunch. This is when it gets very exciting. You're waiting for an avalanche of reviews. Well, most likely you'll receive a Xerox of the review in *Kirkus Reviews,* a book re-view magazine and website that is read by bookstore owners and li-brarians. You may well get a review in *Publishers Weekly*, which of course caters mostly to bookstores.

Then a few weeks later will come the review from *School Library Journal*; and later still a review from the American Library Association (ALA) *Booklist*, both of which, as you no doubt surmise, are for librarians; and maybe from *Horn Book*. (Mainstream papers and magazines do very little children's book reviewing.) Depending on how good or bad the reviews are, you'll be very depressed or very relieved that hardly anyone outside the trade reads them.

It may seem like a very modest flurry of attention, but that's about as intense as it gets. After that, you may feel a very definite sense of letdown. There are no more reviews. There's not even an ad. The three copies at your local bookstore have sold out (to your best friend and two aunts!) and they're awfully slow about ordering new copies. It may feel that nothing is going on, that no one cares, that no one is doing anything. Is your book dead? Is it all over?

Actually, a lot is going on; the problem is you just can't see it. At that very moment, library boards all over the country are receiving free copies of your book and are reviewing it, usually at monthly meetings. At school and library conventions all over the country, your book is being featured in displays. The school and library promotion people, moreover, are taking every opportunity to "talk it up"—not to the general public but to the wheelers and dealers within the institutional market. And while 90 percent of new hardcover children's books sell to the institutional market, sales representatives are getting orders, trying to arrange in-store promotions.

What about advertising? You won't see much, if any. Publishers are very down on the power of ads, unless they can do a real saturation campaign and that's way too expensive. Hardcover children's book publishers focus on the school and library market. If the book's a hit there, it'll be a hit in the stores when it comes out in paperback.

The marketing may seem very intangible, but that doesn't mean it's not real. It may take a year or so, but if your book receives favorable reviews, the libraries are going to start ordering it. If the book seems to be a hit with young readers, then you'll see the orders continuing.

Freelance Promoters

What happens if your book doesn't get decent reviews? What if the libraries don't buy it? Does that mean that it's over for your book? Not necessarily. There are books that are hits with kids and if there's some demand for them, the schools and libraries will keep them in stock. There are some successful children's books that hardly sold at all to schools and libraries but found a ready market elsewhere. Shel Silverstein's *The Giving Tree,* for example, was a major hit on college campuses for years and years before it became a hit with kids.

One author friend, disappointed by her publisher's performance with

Steps to Take

■ When answering your publisher's questionnaire, be brilliant, be funny, be provocative.
■ Get your own website. Make it interactive.
■ Establish yourself locally. Contact your local paper. Visit bookstores.
■ Introduce yourself. Sign copies of your book.
■ Make a brochure about yourself and your book or books, including publication dates and names of publishers. When the good reviews come in, add some quotes!

her book, hired her own freelance book promoter. It was the author's belief and hope that if she could get things rolling, maybe the publisher would do more promotion later on. The freelance promoter arranged an author tour that the author financed herself; she visited seven or eight bookstores on the West Coast and spoke to several groups of people and on radio once.

Did it help? Well, a little, but the royalties the author earned from the books she sold on the tour didn't begin to pay for the costs of the trip. Nor was the publisher impressed, alas. The additional advertising the author hoped for was not forthcoming. As far as I'm concerned, freelance promoters just don't help. I'd avoid them.

Local Focus, Long Haul

Does that mean you can't do anything? No way! There's plenty you can do—even if you have no budget. Moreover, the smart authors do it no matter what kind of reception their books seem to be getting. Do it yourself! That's the way! The secret is to focus locally and to do it consistently. But be prepared for the long haul. Word gets around, but it gets around slowly. Don't start this unless you're prepared to stick with it. Be consistent. Stay focused. There are very few overnight successes here.

What I do for my books is what I saw authors doing for their books when I was still at Harper Junior Books. I've also learned quite a bit more since from my own experience as well as other authors' experiences. In other words, it's tried and true. If it works for me—and many, many other authors—it can work for you too.

One is introduce yourself to the men and women on the book scene in your community. Even two years ago when I moved to Northwestern Connecticut, I visited the local libraries, introduced myself to the folks at the desk. If they had copies of my book, I autographed them. If they didn't, I donated an autographed copy or two. I also visited the local bookstores. It's awkward if they've never heard of me, but I do it anyway. I think it's part of my job.

I've made up a brochure about myself and my writing. It has a recent photo of me. It includes a letter to children in which I answer questions they ask—or ones I think they'd ask if they were as astute and curious about me as I think they should be. It includes a list of my books with dates of publication and the names of the publishers. When I visit a bookstore or library, I leave a copy of it. They may throw it away the moment I'm out of the building, but you never know.

I make a list of the names and addresses and phone numbers of every bookstore in the area. I send them each a letter saying I'm in the area, hope they'll stock my titles, and say I'm looking forward to meeting them. When I have a new title coming out, I send them the updated brochure, tell them about the new title, and tell them I'm available for autograph parties. That's how I got to spend a day at the Waldenbooks at the Danbury, Connecticut, mall autographing copies of *Love Me, Love My Werewolf*. Yes, you can approach national chains, but you need to do it on the local level.

When I have a new book coming out, I send a letter to the editors of all the local papers. I send the book —so they know I'm for real—and invite them to come for lunch and do an interview with me. I got a whole page in the *Litchfield County Times* two years ago when *The Gypsies Never Came* was published. Nice, big picture of me too, though I'm not sure anyone else but me actually framed it.

Introducing myself around is how I inadvertently started getting invited to local book fairs and other book- and education-oriented events. Of course, I went to all of them. Sometimes I had a great time.

Book types are my kind of folks. Sometimes it was an effort. But I've seen world-famous authors get through disastrous public appearances with big grins plastered on their mugs. Having a good time wasn't the point. Making myself a presence on the local book scene was.

I started getting invitations to speak to kids at schools and libraries. At first I did it for free. After a while, I realized other children's authors were making money at it. So why shouldn't I? Of course, I had to develop a classroom program. Mine's called "Let's Make a Story" and it's a highly interactive, totally noisy hour in which a class of third, fourth, or fifth graders and I put together a totally original (sometimes outrageously so!) outline for a story.

I went through the phone books and got the name of every elementary and middle school in my county and two others. I made up a packet containing a cover letter, a description of my program, and my basic brochure and sent it to every principal, PTA president, and media coordinator in every elementary and middle school in the area.

Just Like Us

As for that website, ask your editor if you can use some of the artwork from your book. Use the material from your brochure, of course. Make it interactive. Invite comments from kids, teachers, and librarians. Make sure you answer every single email, too. Word will get around that you're a live one.

You'll get more emails and that should help generate more sales!

There are the basics. Promotion is not what you probably thought it would be. It's not what we thought we'd ever like doing. But more often than not, promoting your books is a great way for us authors to get out of the house, get into our own communities, meet some fabulous people, and become generally more pro-active in our own destinies. Is it any wonder that movie stars, First Ladies, and even royalty want to be children's writers just like us?

Children at ~~Work~~ Play

By Lizann Flatt

If you're like most writers, you want to write every spare moment you have, because those spare moments aren't exactly bowling you over with their sheer numbers. So when you're spectating in the stands at the sports field or find yourself sitting supervising in the sandbox, you're not to blame for thinking you should be wearing a bumper sticker on your back: "I'd rather be writing."

But let me stop you there. You can work at your writing and play at the same time. Really! Just think of it: You can play but justify it as work. We all think that writing is the best job on the planet, but this proves it beyond any doubt. So how exactly does this work? It's easy; child's play as they say. You're getting inspiration.

I'll give you an example. A few years ago I found myself having to watch yet another hockey tournament at a local arena. I confess that I was rather bored because I'm not exactly what you'd call a hockey fan. I found myself daydreaming rather than watching my husband stickhandle the puck. What if a kid was playing and maybe getting knocked around by another player? What if the kid had to decide between retaliating or ignoring the aggressor? What if the player was a girl? What if she had something at stake—something to lose by losing it and striking back, getting caught by the ref? What if the score had no bearing on the plot whatsoever?

After that scenario ricocheted around in my brain for a while, I did write a story along those lines. I submitted it to the 2001 *Highlights for Children* fiction contest. The theme that year was sports, and I was one of the three winners! Was I ever glad my husband dragged me to the arena that day.

Whether it's organized sports or a spontaneous session of *Scrabble*, to children, play is work. Young children spend almost all day playing with blocks, cars, dolls, or that nicely folded stack of laundry and the dirty toilet bowl. Older kids join organized sports, organize themselves into playing a friendly game of pickup, or park themselves in front of the computer for sessions of online gaming. Kids of all ages learn basic developmental skills through play or sport or games. It's an essential part of their lives. As a writer, look at play the way a kid does.

Play with Your Plot

The next time your children mess up your living room (in five minutes flat, if yours are like mine) don't get mad. Instead, find the story in the situation. Jane Yolen's children used to pull the cushions off her sofa and make a house out of them. She used that scenario in her new picture book *Soft House* (Candlewick).

"The entire picture book is about two children, a sister and brother, who build a play house out of sofa cushions on a rainy day, and re-establish their friendship as well," says Yolen. "After a little tiff, the younger brother is able to be brave and go up the scary stairs to get the blankets, and his older sister recognizes how courageous that is."

Or consider Susan Taylor Brown's forthcoming book *Leroy's Must Do List* (Boyds Mills Press). "It features knock-knock jokes, sliding down the stairs on pillows, and all the same sorts of adventures my children and I used to have," she says. "It was nice to be able to use the sliding down the stairs on pillows in a positive way because it used to make me nuts when the kids would have everyone in the neighborhood over so they could slide."

But the book isn't just a descrip-

tion of a series of games the main character plays. "I think the book shows that you have to make time for play in your life," states Brown. Like Yolen's book, some conflict is involved in the playing. "Leroy tries playing several fun things on his own but they just don't work without a play partner," Brown explains. "And of course it's his mother he wants as a play partner, but playing isn't something his mother has time for. Leroy comes up with a solution: a to do list! That's something his mother will understand."

If you don't want to make playing your plot, try applying skills or knowledge from a play situation to come up with a solution for the world outside the game. Let's say your character is good at those shoot-the-aliens video games. Might he be able to shoot real aliens from an interstellar spacecraft if the screen and controls were similar?

In *Vikki Vanishes,* Edgar award-nominated author Peni R. Griffin used a make-believe game of shipwreck to enable her novel's young character to know something at a critical point in the plot that might otherwise have seemed suspiciously convenient. During the game Vikki, the older sister, shows Nikki how to signal SOS. Vikki is then abducted and abandoned by the book's villain.

"The knowledge gained in the game is crucial to the story's resolution," says Griffin. She describes the scene:

While the searchers mill around finding the evidence of

where Vikki used to be, Nikki is the only one who spots the flash, flash, flash as Vikki, who has (with much trepidation) climbed an electrical tower, is flashing SOS off her compact mirror.

The make-believe play is so natural when introduced early in the novel. "The game was a simple way to introduce the necessary concept of signaling SOS," says Griffin, "and it reinforced the central fact of character that, although cast by their mother into good girl/bad girl roles, Vikki and Nikki shared a basic sisterly bond from the beginning."

Play with Your Character

As a writer, you've probably heard of the exercise to describe your character's room to get a better sense of who he or she is as a person. Games, sports, or hobbies play a large part in that exercise.

But don't just list those games; be more specific. What game does your character have out on the floor, as if in readiness for the next game five minutes from now? Which are hidden under the bed, dusty and long since used? What piece of sports equipment is still in its shiny store wrappings, never having been used?

Or think about it from another angle: What sort of kid plays checkers? learns lacrosse? fences? trades hockey cards? Maybe there's tennis equipment in the corner and World Cup soccer hero posters on the wall. Does your character hate a game but continue to play it for an-

other reason? Is she just mediocre at the sport she plays?

Not everyone is good at all games, and Toni Buzzeo has used this in *Ready or Not, Dawdle Duckling,* her upcoming sequel to *Dawdle Duckling.* "It's about hide and seek, a favorite childhood game of mine because I was such a focused kid that I was very good at it," Buzzeo explains. "It was a great deal of fun to imagine how it would be to be a child/duckling very different from myself, one who 'dawdles and dreams, preens and plays' and consider how a game of hide and seek might have turned out differently."

As she thought about this, Buzzeo realized that the game would be a great way to highlight her character's essential nature. "Who is good at hide and go seek?" she asks. "It's the eager beaver, on-the-money kinds of players who rush right off to find a great hiding spot. The dawdler, I thought, would never win." And indeed he doesn't.

Dawdle longs to win, though, and it's through the game that Dawdle learns something about himself. "Dawdle actually learns that he has to depend on his friends to help him hide, because he just can't overcome his true nature. So the game teaches him a valuable lesson, but it's not the lesson one might expect!"

Play with the Setting

Many games are played at home, but what about those played elsewhere? Think of a town sports field or a city sports arena. There are karate gyms, bowling halls, baseball diamonds, dance schools, video arcades, school playgrounds, skateboard parks, and more. Aha! Settings by the dozen.

"The third book in my series, the Freaky Joe Club (Secret File Number 3: *The Mystery of the Morphing Hockey Stick*), is all about, yes, that's right, roller hockey," says author Patricia McMahon. "The book takes place at the Siege of the Alamo Roller Hockey Rink, and the mystery is intrinsic to the sport." Doesn't the name of that place conjure up some great images? How could you not write about it?

McMahon has also used sports settings with an entirely different tone. "*One Belfast Boy,* which is about a young boy in Northern Ireland, looks at his life largely through the lens of boxing, and the boxing club, which is such a safe place in his world."

From unusual sports venues to the most popular, you can also play with the time period of your setting because people have been playing games since the beginning. Carol Matas chose to write *Play Ball!,* a novel set on the baseball field. "I wrote it as the second of a three-part series about a particularly spunky character, Rosie," she explains. "The series is set in 1909 and goes until 1911. When I started researching the second book, I knew it would be set in Chicago and, as an ardent baseball fan, I immediately started researching the baseball teams of the time. The more I read, the more interested I became in the game then, realizing how very little it had changed over the years. But everything else has. I decided it would be the perfect time to write that book about baseball I've always wanted to write."

Keeping in mind historical accuracy, though, Matas had to get creative. "Rosie would not have been able to play ball then, as girls weren't allowed on any teams. So Rosie plays in disguise." Readers may not immediately understand what it's like to have to disguise your gender just to play a sport or what it was like to live 100 years ago, but most readers know quite quickly what it's like to play baseball.

Play Makes a Connection

If you can make an immediate connection between your character and the reader, that connection will motivate readers to imagine what the rest of that character's life might be like.

What if your characters are highly unusual? Some of Dian Curtis Regan's characters are monsters. In *Monsters in Cyberspace,* Rilla, the human girl, has to care for the monsters who arrive monthly and part of that care is supervising their playtime.

"The July monster, Sparkler, came with a deck of cards," Regan explains, "so Rilla is very pleased to see them all playing cards together—until she notices that they are playing 'betting games.' The August monster, Butterscotch, is good at the game and starts winning the other monsters' possessions, which isn't a problem until she wins Owl's glasses. Owl, the September monster, has the ability to do Rilla's homework by eating copies of pages from her textbooks, then filling in the right answers on her homework sheets. Without his glasses, Owl fills in 'good answers,' however they are the wrong answers, so Rilla orders him to play cards with Butterscotch to win back his glasses."

Winners and losers? Playing games your caregiver doesn't like? Sounds like something kids can relate to. Indeed, "The whole *playtime* theme is meant to show them being more like us than different," Regan muses. "When they play, they are shown to be more human in ways than monsterly, and they certainly aren't scary, just annoying at times, but also lovable."

Getting readers to identify with characters is something we writers know is critical to a successful story. But sometimes it's also necessary to get one character to identify with another character within a story. Or perhaps you might want to make readers connect with a character in a different country or culture. Games, because of their universality, can often be an effec-

tive vehicle for doing this.

"From the window of my apartment in Venezuela," Regan says, "I saw kids trying to play ball with sticks and rocks instead of a ball and bat, or *surf* in the ocean with a piece of discarded wood." She used this as inspiration for her short story "El Golpe de Estado," in the anthology *Shattered: Stories of Children and War.*

She describes the story this way: "Zach is an American teen, newly arrived in South America. His focus is on the major move for his family, leaving his school and friends, and leaving life as he knows it. Once in Caracas, he wakes up to the reality that the poverty is so all-consuming many children in Venezuela do not have the same conveniences, opportunities, and many other things we take for granted in the U.S." As the author did, Zach sees how important baseball is for one girl in that country.

"When Zach saw the girl trying to play ball with a stick and a rock, it touched him deeply. Every child should have the right to play, to own a ball and a bat, such basic toys in the U.S. At the end of the story, Zach takes a softball and the nice H&B aluminum bat he got for his fifteenth birthday, and leaves them behind the wall in front of the shack the girl lives in, knowing that she'll find them in the morning. Giving her the gift was his way of affecting change—making life a little easier for one child who was so desperate to simply play ball that she made her own toys, however inefficient."

While that game created a way for two characters to make an emotional connection, it is that same game that creates a connection with readers because it brings the contrast between the two countries down to terms young readers can understand in terms of their everyday lives.

Play Makes a Difference

But you don't have to go to a different country to see games played in different ways. Regional variations are everywhere.

"In *Brooklyn, Bugsy, and Me*, Sam and his mom move from West Virginia to Brooklyn in the 1950s," says author Lynea Bowdish. "There's a lot to get used to, including language, living in an apartment house, the noise, the traffic, and the games played."

Game play can highlight how different other things are. "Sam meets Tony, who introduces him to many of these things, and mentions stickball," Bowdish continues. "Sam played softball at school in West Virginia, but Tony tells him that stickball is different: It's played in the street with a stick, not a bat, and there's no pitcher. The bases are the fire hydrant, the manhole covers, and the sewer. When traffic's bad, lookouts are posted on the one-way street."

As the novel progresses, Sam becomes more familiar with his new home and begins to adjust to his new life. The book ends with a game of stickball.

"The game is important in pointing up the urban setting, and the differences between Sam's old life and his new one. At the end, this game is also important in signifying to the reader, and to Sam, that he has become part of things now."

Play with Information

If observing kids playing, and playing yourself, can lead you to inspire your plots, characters, and setting, it's not surprising that you can also use the idea of playing to enhance your nonfiction. Today's nonfiction books are vibrant and interesting. Nonfiction articles always need a new twist or different angle. What if you used card games to teach probability statistics? What if you wrote an article detailing the origin of basketball and snuck in some basic history along the way? Pull out that nonfiction book manuscript you couldn't sell and put it into a different format.

"I had wanted to write a fish book for some time," says author April Pulley Sayre. "In fact, I was writing a quiet fish book about ocean fish when *Trout, Trout, Trout: The Fish Chant* began."

Ironically, it wasn't watching kids playing that inspired her at first, but rather it was watching an adult at work that first set her on a different course. "I looked out my window and saw a scientist doing a fish survey in the creek that ran through my backyard. I donned my waders and helped him do the survey. He taught me that there were lots of amazing freshwater fish. So I went out and bought a guide to freshwater fish. As I read through the book, I started laughing at the deliciously silly common names." And she ran with that sense of fun and playfulness.

"Soon the names started gathering into rhythmic groups in my mind. I felt compelled to speak them out loud. All of a sudden I started writing these chants with the words." If an author enjoys writing the book so much, it's not surprising that readers love to read it—or hear it.

"The book is meant to be a playful piece. For me, the book celebrates the deliciousness of words and names and the joy of playing with them," says Sayre. "It also celebrates the diversity of fish that can be found right here, in North American freshwater rivers, lakes, and streams." In this way, the nonfiction content has more in common with poetry than with dry fact.

Play with Poetry

Poetry is the form of writing that is most often likened to playing with words. Kay Winters played with playing as a subject, and wrote *Did You See What I Saw? Poems about School*. In it there is a poem about the see saw, the slide, and the swings. Not only are the subjects about playing, but she's played with the poetry form so that the poem's language mirrors the form of play—the form of a seesaw or a swing.

About the inspiration for her poetry, Winters jokes, "I always tell the students when I do school visits that there was one thing I didn't like about teaching. And into the hushed silence, at such a dreadful confession, I say: 'playground duty!' But I did what writers do: I noticed, and wrote about what I saw."

So whether it's the school playground or the baseball park, the soccer field or the sandbox, spend time watching or participating with kids at play—and don't feel guilty! Let child's play inspire your writing. Play like a child, play with a child, and work like a writer.

Authors

Bowdish, Lynea. *Brooklyn, Bugsy, and Me* (Farrar, Straus & Giroux, 2000).

Brown, Susan Taylor. *Leroy's Must Do List,* illustrated by Mary Sullivan (Boyds Mills Press, forthcoming). www.susantaylorbrown.com

Buzzeo, Toni. *Dawdle Duckling,* Illustrated by Margaret Spengler. (Dial, 2003). *Ready or Not, Dawdle Duckling,* illustrated by Margaret Spengler (Dial, 2005). www.tonibuzzeo.com

Griffin, Peni R. *Vikki Vanishes* (Margaret K. McElderry, 1995). www.txdirect.net/~griffin

Matas, Carol. *Play Ball!* (Aladdin, 2003). www.carolmatas.com

McMahon, P. J. *The Mystery of the Morphing Hockey Stick,* Freaky Joe Club 3 (Aladdin Paperbacks, 2004). *One Belfast Boy,* photos by Alan O'Connor (Houghton Mifflin Company, 1999).

Regan, Dian Curtis. "El Golpe de Estado," *Shattered: Stories of Children and War,* edited by Jennifer Armstrong (Knopf, 2002). *Monsters in Cyberspace,* from the Monster of the Month Club series (Henry Holt, 1997). www.diancurtisregan.com

Sayre, April Pulley. *Trout, Trout, Trout: The Fish Chant,* illustrated by Trip Park. (Creative Publishing International, 2004). www.aprilsayre.com

Winters, Kay. *Did You See What I Saw? Poems about School,* illustrated by Martha Weston. (Penguin Puffin, 2001). www.kaywinters.com

Yolen, Jane. Illustrated by Wendy Halperin. *Soft House* (Candlewick, 2005). www.janeyolen.com

Extreme Themes
Finding Big Ideas in Editors' Want Lists

By Pamela Holtz Beres

I've heard that some writers paper their walls with rejection letters. While those letters might remind you on a regular basis that you are a working writer, you might want to consider replacing them with something more practical and inspirational: editors' theme lists.

Editors of many popular children's magazines state a theme for each issue and post them on their websites or make them available by mail. For editors, a theme list ensures a sense of unity and purpose for their magazine. For writers, a theme list ensures endless ideas for stories, articles, puzzles, and activities. For sales-minded writers, those ideas mean paychecks.

"A theme list is essentially an itemized editor's want list," says Fiona Bayrock, a regular contributor to numerous children's magazines, including *Odyssey* and *YES Mag: Canada's Science Magazine for Kids.* "The goal is to get the right idea or article to the right editor at the right time, and anything I can do to zero in on what an editor wants will im-prove my chances of hitting the bull's-eye and making a sale."

Sharon Hart Addy, whose work includes the picture books *Right Here On This Spot* and *When Wishes Were Horses,* as well as many magazine pieces, says theme lists work for her, too. "I've sold a couple of stories and an article that started with theme lists, but my favorite is writing quizzes and other activities." With theme lists in hand, and *Boys' Quest* and *Hopscotch* as her favorites, Addy surrounds herself with dictionaries, encyclopedias, and other resources and lets the ideas flow. These magazines "have taken almost every activity I've sent," she adds.

Heart, Soul, & Theme

Some writers balk at the thought of using theme lists, preferring to come up with their own ideas. Good stories, they say, come from the heart.

I couldn't agree more. How can we expect our stories to touch readers unless they've touched us first?

But theme lists work because themes are multidimensional. They can be poked and prodded and looked at from different angles until we find the angle that speaks just to us. Once we find it, the theme becomes our own, and we are ready to write.

When I accepted an offer from *Pockets'* editors to write a monthly fiction series, I wondered about coming up with stories that would match each issue's theme. But in three years, that was never a problem. Besides giving writers a general theme, such as "Making and Keeping Friends" or "Teach Us to Pray," the *Pockets* theme list includes questions and statements to suggest different angles within that theme.

Usually, one of those statements pops out and becomes my angle. For example, for an issue with the theme Honoring the Body, the words, ". . . the unhealthy steps some people take to correct [body] image" leaped out at me. Memories of a friend's battle with an eating disorder in high school linger, even though the friendship has long faded. Being overweight is not healthy, but neither are the extremes some kids might take to avoid excess weight. My story, "Rebecca's Secret," appeared in the July 2002 issue of *Pockets* as part of my Timber Lake Road series and showed the struggle between three friends when one discovers that another has been taking diet pills.

When Addy saw gentleness was the theme for an issue of *Touch* (now called *Shine Brightly*), she was intrigued by the idea of finding "the still small voice of God" as mentioned in the list. How do we connect with God in bad times, Addy wondered. For her, choir songs help her find that "still small voice." Addy's story took form. A winter storm causes a power outage and Addy's main character, a baby-sitter, must remain calm and soothe young Willy's fears. The two huddle on the couch, wrapped in an afghan and the main character croons "Kum Ba Ya—Be With Us" until the storm passes.

For *Odyssey* writer Vijaya Bodach, the process is similar. "As a former scientist," she says, "some of its themes appeal to me naturally, particularly the ones in life sciences." Bodach wrote four queries for a bioterrorism issue: on smallpox, Lady Mary Wortley Montague (who had smallpox and later promoted innoculation in England), how vaccines work, and Robert Koch (a German doctor and a founder of bacteriology). All the queries were accepted. In a later discussion with the editor, Bodach mentioned SARS and monkey pox and walked away with two more article assignments. "I continue to write for *Odyssey* on topics that excite me," she says.

Take the Idea and Run!

If you think an editor's theme list can only spark ideas for that particular magazine, think again. Maybe you've been wanting to try the teen market. Perhaps you even have a character—a spunky redhead with dimples that says she hasn't a care in the world. But that's your problem. Your character has no problem. Well, you know she does; you just haven't found it yet. So you browse theme lists, looking for ideas. You pay no attention to the market that created the list. You're simply looking for inspiration. Finally, you run across a theme that focuses on dealing with emotions.

Teens, even cheerful ones, have problems with emotions, right? Fear, sadness, helping friends with their struggles—something starts to jell. Your character taps you on the shoulder. Her eyes gloss over and she tells you she's concerned about her friend. Her friend has changed. She's withdrawn, her grades have dropped and even in the warm spring breezes, she keeps herself wrapped in dark, long-sleeved sweatshirts. Your character swallows hard and whispers, "I think I've seen scars on her arms." Now your character has a problem: too tough for the middle-grade magazine that suggested the emotions theme but one that might appeal to the editor of a teen magazine.

Bayrock likes to keep upcoming themes for the magazines she writes for in mind as she researches her articles. "If I trip over some really cool fact or connection that sparks an idea, I know which publication it might suit," she says. Sometimes, writing about one theme naturally leads to another. A math theme article Bayrock wrote on  numerical palindromes for *YES Mag* led her to write a themed article on word palindromes for *Hopscotch*'s "reading is fun" issue.

For Addy, a magazine editor's theme list has even lead to a picture book contract. While researching an article for *Cobblestone*'s issue on the Great Lakes, she found a phone number for a Great Lakes archaeological research organization. Digging in the dirt appealed to Addy and she wrote her article. When *Cobblestone* rejected the article, she was disappointed, but still fascinated with the topic. She looked at her information again, this time with a fiction writer's eye. A story emerged and *Right Here on This Spot* found a home at Houghton Mifflin.

Sometimes writing *for* children leads to writing *about* children, and fiction themes for children's magazines can spark ideas for that market as well. As I wrote a story on making friends for *Pockets*, my main character's struggle with shyness stuck with me even after the story was submitted. Why are some kids shy while others are not? I wondered. Can shyness be overcome? How? What can parents do to help a shy child? I posed these questions to an editor at *Lutheran Parent* and got an assignment.

Some months later, I had a phone conversation with this same editor. He asked if I had any ideas for new articles. I didn't, but being unwilling to let an opportunity slip by, I scanned the papers on my desk. I had just finished another *Pockets* story, this one with the theme of priorities. "How about an article giving parents practical guidelines for setting priorities?" I asked. My article, "I Want! They Want! We Want! God Wants?" appeared in *Lutheran Parent* in January 2003 while "Tumbling Priorities" appeared as a Timber Lake Road story in *Pockets*.

Of course, ideas for shyness and priorities haven't dried up yet. Now, how about self-help articles for teens or young adults on dealing with those issues?

New Life

Sometimes, perusing a theme list brings new life to a rejected manuscript or query. A rejected math activity finally garnered an acceptance when Bodach spotted "fun with numbers" on the theme list of *Fun For Kidz*. Addy's "Fishwater Mess" was rejected for *Shine*

Brightly's issue on attitude but later accepted for *My Friend*'s issue on "Turning to God in Tough Times."

Stories or queries written to theme but rejected can also find success at non-themed publications. My story "Fishin' in the Ditch" was turned down by *Pockets* for their issue on laughter but accepted by *Children's Digest* and used to highlight April Fool's Day.

Bayrock queried *Odyssey* on a piece about spiny lobsters making sounds like a violin for their music issue. *Odyssey* rejected the idea. Bayrock then submitted the idea to *YES Mag* as a news item, where it was accepted. Bayrock also took the research from that article and reworked it as a meet-the-scientist piece, which sold to *Highlights*.

While editors' theme lists are proven idea-generators, Addy finds another benefit to reading them. "Studying themes keeps you aware of the threads that hold stories and books together," she says. "If I can state what I want the story to show about life—the theme—my writing is automatically tighter and the revision process is much quicker."

Now, how about stripping those rejection letters from your walls and replacing them with theme lists?

Free for the Asking

Collect theme lists from these editors and let the ideas flow:

Boys' Quest, Hopscotch: Virginia Edwards, Associate Editor, P. O. Box 227, Bluffton, OH 45817-0227. www.boysquest.com, www.hopscotchmagazine.com

Cadet Quest: G. Richard Broene, Editor, Calvinist Cadet Corp., P. O. Box 7259, Grand Rapids, MI 49510. www.calvinistcadets.org (formerly *Crusader*)

Club Connection: Ranee Carter, Associate Editor, Assemblies of God, 1445 North Boonville Avenue, Springfield, MO 65802-1894. www.clubconnections.ag.org

Cobblestone Publishing: Suite C, 30 Grove St., Peterborough, NH 03458. www.cobblestonepub.com. *AppleSeeds*, Susan Buckley, Editor. *Cobblestone*, Meg Chorlian, Editor. *Calliope*, Rosalie F. Baker, Co-Editor. *Dig*, Rosalie F. Baker, Editor. *Faces*, Elizabeth Crooker Carpentiere, Editor. *Footsteps*, Rosalie F. Baker, Associate Editor. *Odyssey*, Elizabeth E. Lindstrom, Senior Editor.

Cricket Magazine Group: Suite 1100, 332 S. Michigan Ave., Chicago, IL 60604. www.cricketmag.com. *ASK, Click*.

Crinkles: Paula Montgomery, Publisher, 17 East Henrietta St., Baltimore, MD 21230-3910. www.crinkles.com

Discoveries: Julie Smith, Editorial Assistant, 2923 Troost Ave., Kansas City, MO 64109. www.nph.com

Fun for Kidz: Virginia Edwards, Associate Editor, P.O. Box 227, Bluffton, OH 45817. www.funforkidz.com

My Friend: Sister Maria Grace Dateno, FSP, Editor, 50 St. Paul's Ave., Boston, MA 02130-3491. www.myfriendmagazine.org

Pockets: Lynn W. Gilliam, Editor, P. O. Box 340004, Nashville, TN 37203-0004. www.pockets.org

Shine Brightly: Sara Lynne Hilton, Managing Editor, P. O. Box 7259, Grand Rapids, MI 49510. www.gemsgc.org

Three Leaping Frogs: Ellen Hopkins, Publisher, P. O. Box 2205, Carson City, NV 89702. www.junipercreekpubs.com

With: Carol Duerksen, Editor, P. O. Box 347, 722 Main St., Newton, KS 67114. www.withonline.org

YES Mag: Canada's Science Magazine for Kids: Jude Isabella, Managing Editor, 3968 Long Gun Place, Victoria, British Columbia, V8N 3A9, Canada. www.yesmag.ca

Young Salvationist: Laura Ezzell, Managing Editor, P. O. Box 269, Alexandria, VA 22313-0269. www.thewarcry.com

Writing a Seasonal Treasure

By Jane Landreth

Seasons come and seasons go, and writers have a great opportunity to captivate children with the seasonal treasures that each calendar month holds. It takes little prodding for children to be conscious of the seasonal wonders around them. Their senses unlock doors to delightful experiences that also open opportunities for writers.

We work to keep alive that wonderful quality children display: interest in everything around them. We can help them learn, observe, explore their world, and the wider world, in all times of the year.

What Is Seasonal Writing?

Much magazine material is written around seasons or a holiday. Writers have an excellent opportunity to incorporate into stories and articles the winter, spring, summer, and autumn settings. Within each of these seasons, they can find holidays, celebrations, and events that can be the focus, the background, the source of ideas for articles, stories, and books for children of every age.

Just writing about a season or holiday is not enough. Editors look for strong stories that happen to be seasonal. "It's important to note that the step-by-step details of celebrations of and didactic explanations of the meaning of a given holiday aren't usually going to make a strong story. A holiday should be an element of a story, not the whole story. As with any story element, the material should be well woven into the fabric of the tale," says Heather Delabre, Associate Editor of *Spider*.

Seasons and holidays can be rather complex events. The emphasis of any piece of writing should be on one particular aspect, but the celebrations generally incorporate many facets of children's lives: family, school, church, religion, secular culture, and so on.

Consider this brainstorming list for writing about Christmas, for example: sacred event, secular season, national holiday, family gatherings, parties, church community, school, city activities, choir and band performances, plays and programs, winter, decorations, history, foods, regional and international differences, and on and on.

Every season and holiday offers some variety of such interesting and fun traditions. It is the nature of holidays often, too, to generate warm feelings, memories, and insights into people and events that give children a chance to connect in a special way. It is because there are so many directions to explore with seasons and holidays that they are such fertile ground for writers and publishers. Occasions for creating your seasonal treasures present themselves 365 days a year and in the form of articles, stories, puzzles, games, activities, books, poems, songs, and plays.

Where Do I Find Ideas for the Seasons?

Seasonal pieces offer possibilities for writers of all genres and for readers of all ages. Where do you find a list of holidays, celebrations, and events for writing seasonal treasures?

▓ Begin to compile a list of holidays and events, from calendars and sources such as *Chase's Calendar of Events.*

▓ First of all, find the main holidays for the year. Editors are always in need of material for these days.

▓ Sometimes church and religious groups have special days that incorporate children's plays and programs.

▓ Listen for special days in your community or state. Research the events, people, places, and interests in your locality or state. What occurred a year ago? Five, ten, or a hundred years ago? Find something that offers you a good "anniversary" tag that relates to children.

▓ Look in local newspapers for seasonal ideas. Small town newspapers are excellent sources for ideas.

▓ Ask school teachers about special days for children.

▓ Librarians can also be helpful in targeting seasonal needs.

▓ Tap into your memories. What did you and your family do together each season or holiday?

▓ What is your (or your friend's or neighbor's) child's favorite memory of a season or holiday?

Get active to generate ideas as well. Look at the world around you.

▓ Take binoculars and explore your backyard or the park nearby. Try watching the same location in different seasons.

▓ Take a hike, perhaps on snowshoes during a freezing weekend.

▓ Consider everything you hear, see, smell, taste, or touch as a potential seasonal piece. Use a season or holiday and put down all your ideas.

Example, spring:
Listen to the birds twitting

in the treetops. Look at the green grass and the sparkling blue lake. Smell the rich brown soil, the flowers in bloom. Taste the red ripe strawberries. Touch the velvety buds of the rose.

As you consider the sensory details of the season, cultivate them into a story, a poem or an activity for children. Keep those senses alive!

Each season and each holiday is dressed in its own special colors. Think about the colors of the seasons. How can they make a difference in the stories that you write?

- *spring:* Pastels such as yellow, green, blue, pink
- *summer:* Red, white, blue, bright yellow, gold, sea green
- *autumn:* Orange, yellow, deep red, brown, gray
- *winter:* Red, green, white, silver, gold, black

For magazines that use theme lists, you'll need to tie your seasonal ideas to the themes themselves. Theme lists can help you decide the type of seasonal materials you may write for publications such as *Fun for Kidz, Boys' Quest,* and *Hopscotch.* Associate Editor Virginia Edwards says, "We look for unusual articles that are somewhat seasonal." She gives the example of an issue on the theme of mothers that ran a story about the woman responsible for the United States celebrating Mother's Day. "The best thing is for a writer to

Aids for Generating Seasonal Ideas

Books

Chase's Calendar of Events: A yearly book that tells about seasonal and holiday events, festivals, special days, historical anniversaries, celebrity birthdays throughout the world. Great source of ideas. (McGraw-Hill)

Encyclopedia of American Facts and Dates: Find out what was happening in any given year. (HarperCollins)

Famous First Facts: Need to know when the first American newspaper was printed? Need to know when the first McDonald's was opened? Find hundreds of facts. (H. W. Wilson)

Gale Encyclopedia of Multicultural America: The history and culture of many ethnic groups. (Gale)

20th Century Day By Day: Tells what was happening in each month of each year of the century. (Dorling Kindersley)

Websites

www.chases.com
www.education-world.com/holidays/
www.newsletterfillers.com
www.teachingideas.co.uk

send in an SASE to receive a copy of our open themes and then write a seasonal article that would go with a particular theme."

Ellen Hopkins, Editor of *Three Leaping Frogs,* says, "All of our issues are themed and include appropriate seasonal stories, including less usual holidays like Veteran's Day or even Election Day."

What Are Editors Looking For?

Christmas is perhaps the most popular of holidays, but Peter Carver, Editor at Red Deer Press, says, "Christmas is the most productive season to publish for, but it is also demanding." He suggests "trying to avoid the clichés of Christmas stories and finding an original way to deal with the theme."

Material for religious holidays such as Christmas, Easter, Thanksgiving, and other Christian holidays, such as Pentecost and All Saints' Day, are needed at *Pockets*, says Assistant Editor Patty McIntyre.

"We always need something for the main religious holidays of the three major faiths, as well as lesser-known celebrations," says Marileta Robinson, Senior Editor of *Highlights for Children.* She adds, "It is important to study the magazine to see what has been published previously" about the holidays.

To break into a magazine, writers might explore writing pieces about some of the lesser-known or less frequently covered holidays. Or, McIntyre says, find a new twist or angle when writing seasonal pieces. "We receive a lot of submissions for

the major holidays, but often the approaches are overused. Think creatively," she says. "If you can come up with a fresh approach to holiday subjects, you're well on the way to crafting a good piece."

Deborah Vetter, Editor of *Cricket,* would also like to see "fresh ideas, fresh spins on traditional or little-known seasonal celebrations throughout the world."

Writers with an interest in various cultures should explore the possibility of holiday and seasonal pieces with an international twist. Vetter would like to see material about seasonal celebrations from a variety of cultures and countries. "This might include the Japanese doll festival, the Chinese New Year, Muslim Ramadan, or Mexican Cinco de Mayo," Vetter says. She would also like to see some multicultural material from Central and South America and Africa.

At *Spider*, Delabre also sees very few multicultural stories involving holidays, and would like to see pieces about Chinese New Year, Diwali, and Eid al-Adha.

When thinking seasonal, don't forget sports themes and historical events. "We will be looking for summer sports and recreation, winter sports and recreation, interesting historical pieces revolving around major holidays, ways holidays are celebrated in other countries, and any seasonal pieces about the West in particular for the year 2005," says Hopkins. She likes stories that link modern holidays to ancient traditions and celebrations.

Not only do most magazines use short stories and articles, but seasonal poetry as well. All types of poetry—traditional rhyming or free verse—are found in magazines, but it must be first-rate. "We like poetry revolving around the four seasons," says Vetter, in particular Nativity poems with a fresh twist and real originality.

Another category of seasonal treasures is puzzles for magazines. They can be matching games, word searches, fill-in-the-blanks, but unusual puzzles are always welcome. Be on the lookout for something distinct that can be worked into a holiday or seasonal puzzle. Remember younger children need simple puzzles, whereas older children and teens need to be challenged. Craft activities and easy holiday recipes are also needed.

Teacher magazines also need activities to be done with children. *Instructor* Assistant Editor Hannah Trierweiler comments that the magazine needs back-to-school activities, and one-hundredth-day-of-school activities. "Seasonal activities must be appropriate for the classroom and acknowledge the many different cultures and backgrounds that can be found in today's schools," says Trierweiler.

As with all genres of writing, there are key factors in getting seasonal treasures published. Take a close look at what is out there. Read the competition, read reviews, browse in bookstores and libraries and look at displays before a holiday. Find something that has been untouched. Do something different; tell an old story in a new way. Find an unexpected twist. And you will be on your way to seeing your seasonal treasure in print.

When Do I Submit Seasonal Pieces?

The business of writing a seasonal treasure is a matter of marketing strategy. It can be very rewarding and can produce sale opportunities that writers might otherwise overlook. Editors need writers to think, look ahead, look back, plan, and offer them good, fresh slants on holiday and seasonal subjects. It is a way for the new writer to approach editors and break into print.

Holiday or seasonal pieces also have good potential for repeat sales. After first publication, start looking for the most appropriate second rights, or reprint, market for next season. In many cases, the second sale might be a reprint in a national market, since a number of larger magazines like to use good "pick ups" from smaller publications. Your second sale could conceivably net you more money than your first!

Editors like timely pieces and it is wise to remember that most editors idea of "timely" for seasons and holidays is usually some months before the actual event. Editors look for a good fresh slant on a special seasonal piece the day after the holiday. Writers too must start looking for that good fresh slant the day after the holiday.

Many editors prefer material at least one year ahead of the season, agree McIntyne and Robinson. So, if you receive a rejection for seasonal material with a note stating "received too late," resubmit it again in plenty of time for the editor to consider it for next season. Always reevaluate the material before resubmitting.

"I've been known to accept a piece a month before my print date," says Hopkins, "but prefer a three-month lead time." She also added that people who do not do their homework frustrate her. "*Three Leaping Frogs* is bimonthly," she says, "so, a November piece goes with an October piece, which means you have to submit three months prior to October, not November."

Timing is very important in the market strategy of getting most seasonal material published. Check the theme lists and guidelines of the magazines you have in mind for your seasonal treasure. Do you need a query? If so, that will take extra mailing time, so allow for that. If a manuscript is preferred, make sure to send that too within an appropriate time for the targeted publication. Even a few weeks ahead of what the magazine's guidelines say can be rewarding.

Not all magazine editors have such limitations, however. At *Cricket* and *Spider*, Vetter and Delabre note that they "are happy to view seasonal material at any time. If we accept a piece, it goes into our file to await assignment."

Timing is also not as important with book publishers. Most read manuscripts year-round. Red Deer's Carver notes, "If you want to have a strong Christmas title that will be in bookstores from September on, you need to be working on the book a year in advance—doubly so if you're going to have a strong visual component." He adds that writers need not worry so much when to submit, "because invariably there will be a delay in slotting a project into a program, doing the necessary editorial work, and getting the visual prepared."

From January to December, seasonal treasures fill the editorial needs of dozens of children's magazines and book publishers. Whether you choose the history of a holiday, a fictional or true story, a holiday puzzle or a seasonal project, it is important that you look at it from a unique perspective. As with all other magazine and book writing, use good writing and marketing skills and be cognizant of calendars and themes so that your pieces will be on time and on target.

Plotting: The Mix & Match Approach

By Catherine Welch

Do you cringe at the idea of plotting? I used to dread plotting until I developed a mix and match approach to the process. Now I welcome my plotting sessions.

I start with a menu of ideas, much like the menu you would find at a Chinese restaurant. Then I explore the possible combinations of ideas that might lead to a plot summary. You know the drill with the Chinese food menu: one from column A, one from column B. If I start with wonton soup and an egg roll, should I then treat my taste buds to shrimp and lobster sauce, or be daring and go for the crispy imported jellyfish?

My plotting menu includes four lists: characters, settings, events/topics, and themes. Of course, to create the menu of ideas, I need a source of ideas. Where do I get the ideas? I read endlessly.

Like many writers, I learned long ago that reading is one of the greatest sources of inspiration. The idea for my first book, *Danger at the Breaker* (Carolrhoda), came as I was reading *Pennsylvania's Historic Places,* by Ruth Hoover Seitz. At the time, I knew I wanted to write historical fiction. I had just read *Keep the Lights Burning Abbie,* by Peter and Connie Roop (Carolrhoda). My goal was to write a book that would fit Carolrhoda's On My Own History series. When I read in Seitz's book about the *breaker boys* who worked at the breaker—a building outside the coal mines, where coal was crushed, washed, and sorted—I knew I had an idea for a story. I decided to write about the first day an eight-year-old boy begins working at the breaker.

Searching for Characters

In my initial search for characters, I focus on books that will give me ideas about child or teen characters. The parenting shelf in the library is a good place to start. When searching, I think about personality traits, family background, and motives for characters' actions.

I select books about child development that speak to parents and other caregivers. I also choose self-help books that speak directly to children or teens.

The Everything Toddler Book, by Linda Sonna, has a section about "bathroom explorers." As toddlers, my sons never had any great desire to explore the bathrooms of the world. But apparently some potty-trained toddlers take up the hobby of exploring the bathrooms of each building they enter. Perhaps this bathroom explorer might be a fun character for a short story or a picture book. This is one character that makes my list.

Books about children's literature that contain annotated lists are also helpful. If you take a look at *More Books Kids Will Sit Still For,* by Judy Freeman, you will find that the index alone will give you ideas about potential characters. Child and adult characters might be wizards, spies, twins, thieves, soldiers, runaways, magicians, or inventors. For purposes of the plotting exercises that follow, let's use the character list below:

Characters

▨ *Bathroom explorer:* our potty-trained toddler!

▨ *Slacker:* the flaky kid who wastes time by watching too much TV or making endless phone calls.

▨ *Plodder:* the kid who can prioritize and get jobs done.

▨ *Squeaky wheel:* the kid who wants and gets all the attention.

▨ *Chronic liar:* the kid who lies to avoid the consequences of his actions.

▨ *Rescue me kid:* he or she waits for his parents to solve problems—such as homework not done.

▨ *Fair weather friend:* this kid can't be counted on to defend a friend.

▨ *Queen of the clique:* the girl who sets the rules for the clique.

▨ *Underdog:* readers will always root for this kid.

▨ *Snooper:* the curious kid who wants to know everything about everyone.

Searching for Settings

Ideas for settings can come from a variety of books and other sources, but it is fun to search through travel books for possible story settings. One of my favorites is *101 Great Choices—New Orleans,* by Martin Hintz. For a short book, this is a gold mine. One setting that makes my list is the Pelican Club Restaurant, which supposedly has a haunted elevator. And there's the Voodoo Museum, which contains displays of love potions, healing powders, and a voodoo altar.

You'll find more spooky settings if you look at *Haunted Holidays* (Discovery Travel Adventures), edited by Laura Foreman. You'll find information about Poogan's Porch, for example, a restaurant in downtown Charleston, South Carolina, that is supposedly haunted by a Yorkshire terrier that was passed from one restaurant owner to the next until he died.

I don't want my settings list to include only spooky sites, so my list might look something like this:

Settings

▨ Pelican Club Restaurant in New Orleans with its haunted elevator.

▨ Voodoo Museum in New Orleans.

▨ Mammoth Cave National Park, Kentucky—the world's longest cave system.

▨ An animal shelter.

▨ A ranch in New Mexico.

▨ Poogan's Porch, Charleston, with its Yorkshire terrier ghost.

▨ Rose Resnick Lighthouse for the Blind in San Francisco.

▨ Central Park, New York City, with its animal statues or near the Metropolitan Museum of Art, with the Temple of Dendur visibly lit at night.

▨ Habitat for Humanity site.

▨ Steamboat cruise.

Searching for Events/Topics

By the time I am ready to search out books for inspiration about events or topics, I already have stumbled upon some ideas from the parenting, self-help, and travel books. But I press on. There is still so much to read—so many ideas waiting to grab hold of me. I read books of lists, books about community service projects, and almanacs.

I recently discovered *The Essential 55: An Award-Winning Educator's Rules for Discovering the Suc-*

cessful Student in Every Child, by Ron Clark, who has taught in some difficult schools, including one in Harlem, in New York City. His Rule #26 encourages respect and kindness in the lunchroom. The rule prohibits children from saving seats in the lunchroom and encourages children to welcome all to their table. What a great idea! I hate the thought of a child eating alone. This rule makes the top of my events/topics list:

Events/Topics

▨ Teacher prohibits children from saving seats in lunchroom.

▨ Child decides to play in bathtub until skin wrinkles.

▨ Teen explores Indonesian culture.

▨ Teaching children manners.

▨ Being embarrassed by your family.

▨ Do chores around the house without being paid.

▨ Pet orangutan becomes too big and bossy for owners to handle.

▨ Restaurant survival with toddlers.

▨ Create a secret code with friends.

▨ Service Project: Honor cooks, custodians, mail carriers, trash collectors.

Searching for Themes

Although as the process advances through characters, settings, and events/topics, I usually unearth some themes, I like to get books that force me to think specifically about themes. In the young adult section of the library, you can often find some great books about master plots and book reports. They are usually easy to read. In a matter of minutes, I can complete a theme list, which may look something like this:

Themes
- Looks can be deceiving.
- A small mistake can cause great damage.
- The right decision is often a difficult one.
- It is better to deal with a problem immediately—when the problem is small.
- Don't live to please your parents.
- Sometimes it is good to get out of your comfort zone and try something new.
- The way you win is just as important as winning.
- An act of revenge will not right a wrong.
- At times, a sacrifice is worth making.
- Every child has a longing to belong.

The Mixture

Once I have my four lists, the mental gymnastics begin. As I review my lists, certain ideas leap out at me. Since I despise cliques, I keep thinking about *queen of the clique*. I am also drawn to *snooper*, as curious people usually "find" trouble. And my heart always goes out to the Underdog, so this character stays in my mind.

Why Mix & Match Works

You need only small chunks of time. One day you might have 20 minutes to stop at the library and get books. Other days you may have only 10 minutes to scan a book and make a list.

The mix-and-match activities are low-energy activities. You can do them at night and other times when you are tired. You only need to scan books. Choose books that have an easy-to-read format— books with subheads, bullets, sidebars, and lists. The variety of books ensure an element of suspense in the process, which will keep you excited about your plotting sessions.

When it comes to settings, the one that excites me the most is the Voodoo Museum. I am sure I can use this somehow.

Before you read my three plot summaries below, review the four lists above. Underline the ideas that seem to leap out at you. Make some connections. For example, what if you take the *bathroom explorer* and place him in the Mammoth Cave or Poogan's Porch? Can you see the *slacker* taking care of the pet orangutan? How might *chronic liar* learn that a small mistake (a small lie, perhaps) could have serious consequences?

Making connections will get your creative juices flowing. As you brainstorm connections, and play a what-if game, you will soon see a story structure (beginning, middle, and end) evolving. Below are three examples of plot summaries that evolved from the four lists I presented above.

Plot Summary 1
■ Audience: 11 to 14
■ Synopsis: Fourteen-year-old Snooper longs to belong to the popular clique in school because she thinks her life will be more exciting. (She craves excitement. This is why she snoops.) She spies on the clique to learn ways to become part of the clique. While doing this she discovers that the clique has created a secret code, and she learns that code. Then one day, Snooper Welch realizes that Queen of the Clique and the other clique members cheat on tests by using this secret code. Snooper has a decision to make. Should she use this knowledge as a bargaining chip to get into the clique or should she tell her teacher about the clique's cheating system? Snooper learns that the right decision is not always the easy decision.

Plot Summary 2
■ Audience: 6 to 9
■ Synopsis: Nine-year-old Plodder is also an underdog. He always gets chosen last for teams. When he does make a team, he's always on the losing team. He works hard, but never seems to win anything. Meanwhile, he sees other classmates who don't work hard win everything. But he doesn't give up. In the cafeteria there is a rule: Children cannot save seats in the lunchroom. One day, Plodder takes a seat (the only empty seat) at a table of slackers. That particular day, the cafeteria teacher makes an announcement about a contest. Each table of children will have a week to think of a way to honor the cafeteria cooks. The table that wins gets to go on a steamboat ride. Plodder is stuck with the table of slackers, but he is dying to take a steamboat ride. Plodder has the challenge of motivating the slackers. Can he do it? Plodder discovers that the slackers have a genuine concern for the cafeteria workers, and he excites them into thinking of a winning plan.

Plot Summary 3
■ Audience: 8 to 12
■ Synopsis: Twelve-year-old Squeaky Wheel is embarrassed by her parents because she thinks they are boring. Other kids in her class have parents who do exciting things like bungee jumping and scuba diving. These kids seem to be the most popular. Squeaky Wheel craves the attention these kids get. One day she learns that she has an aunt who works in the Voodoo Museum in New Orleans. Squeaky Wheel plans

Suggested Reading

Parenting Books / Self-Help Books

■ Covey, Sean. *The 7 Habits of Highly Effective Teens* (Fireside, 1998).

■ Erlbach, Arlene. *The Middle School Survival Guide* (Walker & Company, 2003).

■ Glennon, Will. *200 Ways to Raise a Girl's Self-Esteem* (Conari Press, 1999).

■ Mosatche, Harriet S. and Unger, Karen. *Too Old for This, Too Young for That! Your Survival Guide for the Middle-School Years* (Free Spirit Publishing, 2000).

■ Sonna, Linda. *The Everything Toddler Book.* (Adams Media Corporation, 2002).

Settings

■ Foreman, Laura, editor. *Haunted Holidays* (Discovery Communications, Inc., 1999).

■ Hintz, Martin. *101 Great Choices: New Orleans* (Passport Books, 1996).

■ Hughes, Holly. *Frommer's New York City with Kids* (IDG Books Worldwide, 2001).

■ Lederman, Ellen. *Vacations That Can Change Your Life* (Sourcebooks, Inc., 1996).

■ *National Geographic Guide to America's Historic Places* (The Book Division of the National Geographic Society, 1996).

■ Welborn, B. J. *America's Best Historic Sites: 101 Terrific Places to Take the Family* (Chicago Review Press, 1998).

---

to spend spring break at the Voodoo Museum so she can come back to school with some great stories. While she is there, she learns that being the center of attention is not always desirable.

From these plot summaries, you can see how the mix and match approach can move you forward in the creation of a story. Of course, there is still much work to be done. The plots need to be fleshed out with specific details about the action. But you have primed the pump, and the writing should begin to flow.

Suggested Reading

Events/Topics

Campbell, Susan and Heald, Bill. *Connecticut Curiosities: Quirky Characters, Roadside Oddities & Other Offbeat Stuff* (The Globe Pequot Press, 2002).

Devantier, Alecia T. *101 Things Every Kid Should Do Growing Up.* (Sourcebooks, Inc., 2002).

Lamm, Kathryn. *10,000 Ideas for Term Papers, Projects, Reports, and Speeches.* (Macmillan, 1998).

Landes, Michael. *The Back Door Guide to Short-Term Job Adventures.* (Ten Speed Press, 2002).

The New York Public Library Student's Desk Reference. (Prentice Hall General Reference, 1993).

Wallechinsky, David and Wallace, Amy. *The People's Almanac Presents The Book of Lists/90s Edition.* (Little, Brown, 1993).

Themes

Bodart, Joni Richards. *The World's Best Thin Books: What to Read When Your Book Report Is Due Tomorrow.* (The Scarecrow Press, 2000).

Tobias, Ronald B. *20 Master Plots and How to Build Them.* (Writer's Digest Books, 1993).

Children's Literature

Codell, Esmé Raji. *How to Get Your Child to Love Reading.* (Algonquin Books of Chapel Hill, 2003).

Freeman, Judy. *More Books Kids Will Sit Still For.* (R.R. Bowker, 1995).

Idea Prompts

Good Ideas: Inventions, Firsts, & Flights of Fancy from History

By Louanne Lang

Ideas for writers are as infinite as history and all its events, people, creations, beginnings, endings. This calendar is a launching pad for your own invention of story, true or imagined, and in whatever form can make your writing soar.

▨ **Stone Age** *ski* fragments indicate this type of transportation was used 8,000 years ago.

▨ Prehistoric cave paintings indicate that men have tried to stay personally tidy by *shaving* since at least **30,000 B.C.**

▨ At least as early as **20,000 B.C.** needles were used to sew custom-fitted garments of fur and animal skins.

▨ *Bracelets* of carved mammoth ivory date back to **20,000 B.C.**

▨ The oldest *boomerang*, found in southern Poland, dates to **19,000 B.C.** and was used as a hunting tool.

▨ *Flutes* are the oldest known instruments, discovered in Old Stone Age deposits in France, and date back 15,000 to 25,000 years. *Bull-roarers*, which make loud, ethereal sounds when whirled in the air, are considered the second oldest instrument. Bull-roarer artifacts have been found in Denmark and Germany dating back to about **12,000 B.C.**

▨ **Fifteenth century B.C.**: An extant kit belonging to a Minoan doctor contains *forceps, drills, scalpels, large dilator* for internal examination, and *grinders* for medicinal ingredients.

▨ The Egyptian ruler Pharaoh Thutmose III, who lived in the **fifteenth-century B.C.**, is thought to be the world's first known serious *botanical collector*, bringing back specimens from military expeditions.

A mammoth tusk from Mezhirich in the Ukraine dating back to between **12,000 and 11,000 B.C.** shows a *map* of dwellings along a river.

The earliest written musical notation in existence is inscribed on stone tablets found at Delphi, Greece. While the tablets date back to about **100 B.C.**, it is generally believed that the system of musical notation was first invented by Pythagoras in the late **sixth century B.C.**

In a poem by the Greek Antipater dated around **4000 B.C.** is the first reference to a *waterwheel*, used to drive a small handmill for women grinding grain.

2700 B.C.: Egyptians had *surgical instruments* to stitch up wounds. The Ancient Egyptians also used moldy bread as poultices to heal wounds, a forerunner of *antibiotics*.

The world's earliest *metal pipes*, circa **2450 B.C.**, were found in Abusir, Egypt.

Soap was produced by Babylonian chemists who boiled together oil and alkalis, **2000 B.C.**

Circa 2000 B.C. *glassmaking* began in the Near East. Glass beads, ornamental inlays, and seals were the first products.

Clay *envelopes* and letters in **2000 B.C.** Iraq predated our modern postal service. Pigeons were first trained domestically in Sumer, southern Iraq, around **2000 B.C.** The Egyptians later perfected this type of communication, developing it into the first airmail service to deliver messages. Early postmasters in the Moslem world became the eyes and ears of the caliphs.

1500 B.C. Amenemhet, an Egyptian court official, invented the *water clock*. These were useful to Egyptian priests who needed to know the time in order to carry out rituals and sacrifices correctly.

As early as **1400 B.C.** there was a *"censor of morals"* or *food inspector,* who ensured that the food offered on the streets of Egypt was up to standard and not adulterated.

The world's oldest inscription of a *song* is found on a stone tablet dating to around **1400 B.C.** It was found at Ugarit, in northern Syria, and is written in Hurrian, one of the country's ancient languages.

Pipes for tobacco were used in the Americas about **1000 B.C.** In the eastern United States, the Hopewell culture (**100 B.C.-700 A.D.**) created the platform pipe, a new form of pipe, with an elaborately carved bowl of rare stones centered on a rectangular tablet. These pipes were carved into panthers, beavers, birds, and frogs, or humans, including heads and nude females. Comparable skill was not achieved elsewhere until hundreds of years later.

Robots are foreshadowed in Homer's *Illiad*, composed in the **eighth or ninth century B.C.,** by the mechanical golden handmaids who were capable of speech and intelligence.

753 B.C. Rome was founded.

■ **700 B.C.** Etruscans were producing partial *dentures* or bridgework fine enough to wear during meals.

■ **700 B.C.** a Babylonian tablet set forth a method for a *pregnancy test*.

■ Zoroaster, **630-553 B.C.**, founded the Persian religion.

■ **581 B.C.** Philosopher and scientist, Pythagoras, is born on the Aegean island of Samos.

■ **550 B.C.** Buddha is born.

■ **536 B.C.** Legendary athlete Milo of Crotona is crowned six times at the Olympic Games.

■ **525 B.C.** Aeschylus was born. This "Father of Tragedy" was the author of the plays *Prometheus Bound*, *Oresteia*, and about 80 more plays. In **471 B.C.** Aeschylus introduced a second actor, in addition to the protagonist and the chorus, into Greek dramas.

■ **521 B.C.** Buddha preached his first sermon.

■ **Circa 500 B.C.** Pericles was born. Naburiannu, Babylonian astronomer, determines the length of a *lunar month*. *Cataract operations* were performed by the Indian surgeon Susrata. The *eustachian tubes* were discovered by the Greek physician Alcmaeon.

■ **496 B.C.** Sophocles was born. His plays included *Antigone*, *Oedipus Rex*, and more than 120 other plays. In **468 B.C.** Sophocles introduced a third actor into his plays and defeated Aeschylus for the prize in tragedy.

■ **484 B.C.** Euripides was born. Among his plays were *Medea*, *The Trojan Women*, and *Iphigenia in Aulis*.

■ **479 B.C.** Confucius was born.

■ **470 B.C.** Socrates was born.

■ **462 B.C.** Soldiers and judges in Athens were receiving regular salaries.

■ **460 B.C.** The Greek physician Hippocrates, who came to be known as the father of medicine, was born.

■ **450 B.C.** Aristophanes was born. His plays included *The Clouds, The Peace, The Birds,* and *The Frogs*.

■ **438 B.C.** The Parthenon was consecrated.

■ **427 B.C.** Plato was born.

■ **Fourth century B.C.**, the Chinese used *poison gas* against invaders.

■ *Catheters* were invented by the Greek doctor Erasistratus in the **third century B.C.**

■ **356 B.C.** Alexander the Great was born.

■ The gardens adjoining the Museum of Alexandria during the reign of Ptolemy II (**284-245 B.C.**) were thought to house the first *zoo*. This expanded on the existing practice of bringing exotic animals home from successful military campaigns.

■ **264 B.C.** The first public combats of Roman *gladiators* took place.

■ **239 B.C.** Egypt introduced *leap year* into its calendar.

■ **221 B.C.** China unified all *weights and measures*.

■ **218 B.C.** Hannibal crossed the Alps with elephants.

■ **215 B.C.** *The Great Wall of China* was constructed.

■ **Circa 200 B.C.** *The Rosetta Stone* was inscribed.

■ **Circa 270 B.C.** Ptolemy II commissioned the world's first *lighthouse* to be built on the island of Pharos. It was later recognized as one of the Seven Wonders of the Ancient World.

■ **189 B.C.** Upper Egypt experienced insurrections due to exorbitant taxes.

■ **Circa 170 B.C.** The earliest known *paved streets* were constructed in Rome.

■ **168 B.C.** The Temple in Jerusalem was destroyed.

■ **149 B.C.** China produced a *dictionary* with 10,000 characters.

■ **Circa 140 B.C.** The Venus de Milo was created.

■ *Paper money* was first introduced in China during the reign of Emperor Han Wu-ti (**140-87 B.C.**) to offset the exhaustion of empire funds from fighting the Huns. Because it was made from the skin of rare white stags, it was doomed to failure. In **800 A.D.**, the Chinese again tried paper money, called "flying money," due to its tendency to blow away.

■ **Circa 105 B.C.** The first *technological college* was founded by engineer and mathematician Heron of Alexandria.

■ In the **first century B.C.**, the Chinese had a primitive *compass* made from a ladle-shaped piece of lodestone, which is a naturally occurring magnetic iron ore, placed on a polished plate of bronze.

■ In the **first century B.C.**, the Roman architect Vitruvius described the *hodometer* (from Greek *hodos*, *way* and *metron*, *measure*), a device for measuring distances traveled.

■ The ancestor to the game of *badminton* was played in China two thousand years ago with a feather bird. Players determined the number of years they would live by the number of times they could hit the bird without it falling to the ground.

■ **62 B.C.** Florence, Italy, was founded.

■ **54 B.C.** Caesar invaded Britain. Ten years later he was assassinated.

■ **4 B.C.** Jesus was born. (The year 4 was determined as accurate after adjusting for the 365.25 days of the Julian calendar and the introduction of leap year.) The probable date of his crucifixion was **30 A.D.**

■ In the **first century A.D.** the inventor Heron created the world's first *slot machine* in Alexandria. He also designed *automatic doors* for temples.

■ **2 A.D.** Emperor Wang Mang set up a temporary *hospital* to deal with a combination of drought and locusts.

■ In **43**, London was founded.

■ The new Emperor of China, Ming-Ti, introduced Buddhism to the Chinese in **58**.

■ **64** saw the first persecution of Christians.

■ Jews revolted against Rome in **70** and Jerusalem was destroyed.

■ Rome's Pantheon was completed in **124**. Its construction had begun around **30 B.C.**

■ A Chinese court personage invented the first *seismograph* to detect earthquakes occurring as far away as 400 miles, in **132**.

Circa 250, the *first book on algebra* was produced in Greece.

Bowling was part of religious rituals of purification from sin, in German monasteries in the year **300**.

Foundation of Schola Cantorum in Rome for *church singing* occurred in **350**.

The Huns invaded Europe in **360**, and Russia in **376**. Attila became ruler of the Huns in **433**. Venice was founded by refugees from Atilla in **452**. And in **470**, the Huns withdrew from Europe.

Hymn singing, by the congregation, was introduced in the Catholic Church by Ambrose, Bishop of Milan, in **386**. The first Christian *alleluia* hymns followed in **390**.

The Visigoths invaded Italy in **401**.

Circa 410 saw the beginnings of alchemy's search for the *philosopher's stone* and the *elixir of life*.

St. Patrick began his mission to Ireland in **432**.

The last Romans left Britain in **436**.

Aryabhata, the Hindu astronomer, mathematician, and writer on the power and roots of numbers, was born in **476**.

The Roman Empire ceased to exist in **476**, when the Germanic general Odacer or Odovacar overthrew the last Roman Emperor, Augustulus Romulus. From then on, the western part of the Empire was ruled by Germanic chieftains.

In **478**, the first *Shinto shrine* appeared in Japan.

In **486** the Clovis established a Frankish kingdom and began the Merovingian dynasty, after defeating the last Roman governor of Gaul. The Merovingians united many Germanic tribes. Clovis converted to Christianity and allied with the pope. A century of ecclesiastical building began.

The use of *incense* for religious ceremonies was introduced into Christian churches around **500**.

Toledo became the capital of Spain's Visigoth kingdom in **534**.

The Empress Theodora begins *fashion trends* such as purple cloaks, pointed shoes, and gold embroidery, circa **540**.

Rats from Syria and Egypt introduce the plague to Constantinople in **542**. It soon spreads throughout Europe, reaching Britain five years later.

550 witnessed the beginnings of chess games in India

Emperor Shotoko Taishi introduced Buddhism into Japan in **552**. The same year, missionaries sent by Byzantium Emperor Justinian smuggled *silkworms* out of China and Ceylon.

Mohammed was born in **570**. He had his vision on Mount Hira in **610**, began dictating the *Koran* in **625**, and died in **632**. A year later began the rapid progress of Mohammedanism as the churches of Antioch, Alexandria, and Jerusalem go over to the Muslim faith.

Rome could claim the first *church bell* in **604**.

Burning water, or *petroleum*, was first used in Japan in **615**.

China produced *porcelain* for the first time around **620**.

Feudalism began its rise in Japan in **636**.

Moslem forces conquered Egypt, Syria, and Mesopotamia in **642**.

The oldest Islamic shrine, the Dome of the Rock in Jerusalem was started in **643**.

300,000 papyrus scrolls were rediscovered in the Greek library at Alexandria, Egypt, in **640**. The next year, invading Moslem forces tried to destroy the city's book-copying industry and the school at Alexandria came to an end, and with it a center of Western culture. Cairo was founded at this time. In **646**, Alexandria was recaptured by the fleet of the Byzantine empire.

The Chinese use of lamp-black for rubbings gave rise to *wood block printing*, around **650**.

Caliphs began the first organized *news service* in **650**.

Glass windows appeared in English churches in **674**.

In **697**, Arab forces destroyed Carthage.

Around **700**, *Easter eggs* make their appearance among Christians.

Sugar was planted in Egypt around **710**.

In **711**, after the Islamic invasion of Christian Spain, the Moors freed the Spanish Jews, who then begin a period of cultural development. Arabs conquered Seville in **712** and by **715**, the Muslim empire extended from China to the Pyrenees. Its capital was Damascus.

In **723**, I-Hsing, a Buddhist monk and mathematician, invented the first mechanical *clock* called the Water-Driven Spherical Bird's-Eye-View Map of the Heavens. Water was used to power the invention, but machinery determined the movements.

The largest city in the world in **725** was Ch'ang-an, and Constantinople the second. That year, St. Boniface cut down the Germanic Donar oak tree, a symbol of pagan beliefs.

Charlamagne was born in **742**, and crowned the first Holy Roman Emperor in **800**.

Peking became home to the first printed newspaper in **748**.

The 40,000 horses in the royal stables of China were used mostly for polo in **750**.

That same year, Granada was founded.

Beds became popular in some European countries.

Germany witnessed epidemics of St. Vitus Dance, a neurological disorder.

Four sects of Islam were defined in **751**: Shafites, Hafenites, Sunnites, and Malikites.

The *illuminated manuscript Book of Kells,* a depiction of the Latin Gospels, was produced in the late **eighth century**, probably in Iona, on the Scottish coast. At some point the volume moved to a monastery in Kells, Ireland.

The Viking era began in Britain around **792**. The Norseman attacked the English monastery on the island of Lindisfarne. Dating from around this time, the famous *Lindisfarne Gospels,* like the *Book of Kells,* was a glorious example of an art that combined Irish and Byzantine elements.

▓ **793**, Japan's Kyoto (Heian) was founded.

▓ The Emperor Constantine VI was overthrown by his mother, Irene, who had been co-ruler with him for a time. She was arrested and pardoned, and then turned around and finally had him blinded and deposed, in **797**.

▓ **Ninth century**: Muslims open the first *drugstores*. Rose water and perfumes made them palatable, and it was at this time that the pharmacist became separate from the doctor.

▓ Earliest records of literature and poetry in Persia date to around **800**.

▓ Rose trees were planted in Europe for the first time in **802**.

▓ The Arab conquest of Sicily and Sardinia began in **827**.

▓ **828**, St. Mark's in Venice was founded. Building of the church began in 976 and was completed in 1094.

▓ Islamic invaders sacked Marseille in **838** and settled in Southern Italy. The Muslims also defeated the Byzantium army in Asia Minor. In **846**, they sacked Rome, damaging the Vatican and destroying the Venetian fleet.

▓ A Tao emperor of China began persecutions of Buddhists in **845**. As a result, Islam made inroads in the region.

▓ **850**, Yiddish began to develop among Jewish settlers in Germany.

▓ The Norse discovered Iceland and began settling there between **870** and **930**.

▓ In England, *calibrated candles* were used to measure time in **870**.

▓ Paris was besieged by Northmen in **885**.

▓ Germany and France were separated once and for all, the aftermath of Charlemagne's reign, in **887**.

▓ **900** marked the beginning of the Christian reconquest of Spain.

Constantinople was the first city in the world, in commerce and culture.

Castles become seats of nobility in Europe.

Southwestern America had its second Pueblo period, marked by houses built entirely above ground

Vikings discovered Greenland.

▓ The Chinese used *gunpowder* for the first time in **919**.

▓ North Africa was freed from Egypt in **972**.

▓ The first authenticated earthquake in Britain was in **974**.

▓ **988**, Christianity reached Russia.

▓ The system for the *canonization* of saints began in **993**.

▓ *Grenades* were used by city defenders against the Crusaders, around **1000**.

▓ Omar Khayyam, Persian scientist and poet, author of *The Rubiat of Omar Khayyam,* was born in **1027** and died in **1123**.

▓ Macbeth killed his cousin, King Duncan I in **1040**, and Duncan's son, Malcolm Canmore, killed Macbeth in **1057** to become king himself.

   Gregorian chant was replaced by *polyphonic singing* around **1050**. Time values were given to musical notations.

   The building of Westminster Abbey began under Edward the Confessor in **1052**; the abbey was consecrated in **1065**.

   The papal chair was empty for one year, **1054**.

   Marrakesh was founded in **1062**.

   William of Normandy conquered England in **1066**. The following year, work began on the extraordinary *Bayeux Tapestry*, which commemorated the Battle of Hastings, in which William defeated Harold II of England.

   The last Byzantine possessions in Italy were conquered by the Normans in **1071**.

   Also that year, Greek medicine was first brought to medieval Europe via the Muslim world, and the translations of medical texts by Constantine the African.

   Married priests were excommunicated in **1074**.

   Building commenced on the Tower of London in **1078**.

   In **1085**, Alfonso VI took back Toledo from the Arabs.

   The *Domesday Book*, a survey of the status of the estates of England, was compiled in 1086, under William the Conqueror. It was an unprecedented administrative accomplishment in the Middle Ages.

   The first recorded mention of a gondola in Venice dates to **1094**.

   The First Crusade to the Holy Land took place in **1096**. In **1098**, the Crusaders defeated the Turks at Antioch. In **1099** they took Jerusalem, and in **1104**, Acre.

   Around **1100**, Middle English superseded Old English, or Anglo-Saxon, with the infusion of many French/Latinate words following on William of Normandy's rule of England. In France, the dialect of the Ile de France, or Paris, became the prevailing idiom.

   Islamic science began its decline.

   Colonization of eastern Germany, which ultimately became modern Austria, began in **1105**.

   1110 marks the earliest known reference to a *miracle play,* also called a *saint's play*. It took place in Dunstable, England.

   The Aztec Nation began a period of wandering around **1116**, searching for new lands in which to settle. The tribe's history told that the Aztecs had left the mythical Aztlan, or White Land.

   Bologna University was founded in **1119**. It is among the oldest of universities and served as a model for many that followed.

   Scotland made its first silver pennies in **1124**, under King David I, who worked to unify the country.

   In the twelfth century began the *troubadour* tradition of poetry and music. It took root primarily in Provençal and other regions of France, but also in northern Spain and northern Italy, and through the influence of Eleanor of Aquitaine, wife of Henry II, in England. The troubadours often sang of *courtly love,* a feudal dedication of the poet to his mistress.

▧ A purported Messiah appeared in Persia and in France in **1138**.

▧ In **1145**, the Second Crusade was proclaimed by Pope Eugene III. It failed: The crusaders perished in Asia Minor. The first reference to Moscow dates to this year.

▧ **Circa 1150** was the Golden Age of Buddhist art in Burma.

Explosives were used in warfare by the Chinese.

Iceland became the first country to have fire and plague insurance.

Chess arrived in England.

Europe saw the advent of new dance forms that reflected the division of society into different classes.

▧ The University of Paris was founded in **1150**.

▧ The Toltec Empire in Mexico came to an end in **1151**.

▧ Ma Yu Ching's Bucket Chicken House opened in **1153** in Kaifeng, China, and is the longest-running *restaurant* in the world still operating today.

▧ Henry II of England named Thomas à Becket as his chancellor in **1154**; Becket was named Archbishop of Canterbury in **1162**.

▧ *Geography* was written by Mohammed al-Idrisi, a geographer who advised the king of Sicily, Roger II. He wrote other important medieval works, including *The Pleasure Excursion of One Who Is Eager to Traverse the Regions of the World*, also called *The Book of Roger,* published at Palermo in **1154**.

▧ In **1158**, Munich is at the center of the salt trade.

▧ Milan was destroyed by Frederick Barbarossa in **1162**; the city was rebuilt in **1168**.

▧ The Cathedral of Notre Dame de Paris was built in **1163**.

▧ In **1166**, the Assize of Clarendon ordered the building of jails in all English counties and boroughs. Under Henry II and his barons, it also established the *grand jury system.*

▧ **1167**, Oxford University was founded.

▧ Pope Alexander III established rules for the canonization of saints, in **1170**. In England, Thomas à Becket was murdered in Canterbury Cathedral. Becket was canonized three years later and in **1174**, King Henry II did penance for the murder.

▧ Henry II arrived in Ireland in **1171**, the beginning of centuries of English domination.

▧ **1173** has the earliest authentication of an influenza epidemic.

▧ The campanile—tower—and baptistry were constructed at Pisa in **1174**. England held its first horse races the same year.

▧ The legends of King Arthur were organized in 1176 into their current form by Walter Map.

▧ Belfast was founded in **1177**.

▧ In **1178**, the bridge at Avignon was constructed, and was later immortalized in a French nursery song, *Sur le pont d'Avignon.*

▧ *Glass windows* began appearing in England's private residences in **1180**.

Francis of Assisi was born in **1182**; he died in **1226**.

France banished Jews in 1182.

Henry II died in **1189** and was succeeded by Richard I, the Lion-Hearted.

The Third Crusade began.

London had its first mayor, Henry Fitzailwin.

Tea arrived in Japan by way of China in **1191**.

Returning from the Third Crusade in **1193**, Richard I was captured by Leopold, the Duke of Austria, and imprisoned. He is released in **1194**. The story became central to the Robin Hood legend in years to come.

The two collections of Scandinavian mythology known as the *Prose Edda* and the *Elder Edda,* appear in Iceland around **1200**.

In Ireland, professional *bards* emerged.

Engagement rings were a new fashion.

Cymbals as musical instruments were introduced.

In **1202**, the fourth crusade began under Boniface of Montferrat. The Crusaders took Constantinople.

Amsterdam was founded in **1204**.

The first *court jesters* served at European courts early in the thirteenth century.

1206, Genghis Khan founded the Mongol Empire. In **1211**, he invaded China; Peking fell in **1214**. He conquered Persia in **1218**.

Wolfram von Eschenbach's *Parzival* dates to about **1210**. Relating stories of the search for the Holy Grail, it also includes a version of the *Lohengrin* legend.

The Children's Crusade took place in **1212**.

In London, houses replaced thatched and wooden roofs with *tiles*.

King John granted the Magna Carta at Runnymede in **1215**.

Giraffes made their first appearance in Europe in **1220**.

The sonnet developed in Italy around **1220**.

In **1221**, Vienna became a city.

The Mongols invaded Russia in **1223**.

Cotton was manufactured in Spain in **1225**.

Construction of the cathedral in Toledo, Spain, began in **1227**.

Porcelain manufacturing was brought to Japan by the potter Toshiro after he had traveled in China for four years.

Emperor Frederick II began the Sixth Crusade in **1228**. He was crowned King of Jerusalem.

The Inquisition forbade all Bible reading by the laity.

In **1230**, Berlin was founded on the site of former Slav settlements. The Crusaders brought leprosy to Europe.

The pope entrusted the Inquisition to the Dominican order in **1233**. The Inquisition began using torture in **1252**.

Work began on the Alhambra, in Granada, Spain, in **1248**.

In **1249**, University College at Oxford was founded.

The Easter Play of Muri, dated

1250, was the first religious play written in vernacular German.

▓ Also around **1250**, *hats* became an important fashion, particularly for men.

A new writing implement was introduced at this time—the *goose quill*.

▓ *Linen* was first manufactured in England in **1253**.

▓ Paris's School of Theology, later called the Sorbonne, was established in **1254**.

Marco Polo was born the same year; he traveled in China from **1271** to **1295** and in much of that time was in the service of Kublai Khan, grandson of Genghis Khan. Marco Polo returned to Italy, and began to dictate his memoirs from a Genoese jail in **1298**.

▓ The Mongols won Baghdad by overthrowing the caliphate, in **1258**.

In England, the House of Commons was established.

▓ Dante Alighieri was born in **1265**. He was exiled from Florence in **1302** in the midst of political battles he would depict in the *Divine Comedy (La divina commedia)* in **1307**. The great medieval poem is an allegory of the journey through this life and the next.

▓ In **1267**, the Aztecs arrived in the Valley of Mexico.

▓ The papacy was vacant for three years beginning in **1268**.

▓ England established its first toll roads in **1269**.

▓ Kublai Khan failed in his attempted conquest of Japan in **1274**. He founded the Yuan Dynasty in China, which lasted until **1368**. Kublai Khan died in **1294**.

▓ In **1282**, Florence was recognized as the leading European city in commerce and finance.

▓ *The Pied Piper of Hamelin* was written in **1284**.

Sequins first appeared in Venice about this time.

▓ In **1285**, *eyeglasses* were invented in Italy by Salvino d'Armate.

The anonymous Middle High German epic *Lohengrin* originated.

▓ The Crusades ended, **1291**.

▓ Urine begins to be used as a tool of *medical diagnosis* around **1300**.

Professional musical entertainers, *jongleurs*, emerged in France.

▓ **1305**, England standardized the *acre* and *yard* under Edward I.

▓ Philip IV of France expelled the Jews in **1306**, confiscating their property.

▓ One of the earliest indoor tennis courts in Paris was built by Philip IV in **1308**.

▓ The papal residence moved to Avignon, France, in **1309**, in the beginnings of the Great Schism. Construction began on the Palace of the Popes in **1334**.

▓ France adopted Salic Law in **1317**, forbidding women from succession to the throne.

▓ *Counterpoint* in church music was forbidden by the pope in **1322**.

▓ In **1325**, the Aztecs founded Mexico-Tenochtitlan, later Mexico City. In Europe, *organ pedals* were first used.

▓ The *sawmill* was invented in **1328**.

John Gower, English author of the *Confessio Amantis*, was born in 1330. With Geoffrey Chaucer, he had a large effect on the movement of Middle English into Modern English through his poetry.

The first record of *weaving*, from York, England, dated to 1331.

In 1332, the Bubonic plague broke out in India.

The same year was the first division of England's Parliament into two houses, Lords and Commons.

1337 marked the start of the Hundred Years' War between France and England.

Geoffrey Chaucer was born in 1340. Among his works were the *Book of the Duchess, The House of Fame, Parlement of Foules, Troilus and Criseyde,* and in 1387, his masterpiece, *The Canterbury Tales.*

Two of the great Florentine banking houses went bankrupt in 1345.

The Black Death, or plague, consumed Europe from 1347 to 1351. Approximately 75 million people died. In England, that added up to one third of the population.

1349 saw persecution of Jews in Germany.

The Great Wall of China, the first parts of which may date as far back as the seventh century B.C., was restored in 1368.

Paris's Bastille was built by Charles V in 1369 as a fortress against possible English attack. In following centuries it became a prison and played a central role in the French Revolution four centuries later.

Steel crossbows were introduced as weapons of war in 1370.

Robin Hood makes his earliest forays into England's popular literature around 1375.

In some games, *dice* were replaced by *playing cards* in Germany in 1377.

Rome had grown into a European center of music.

In 1385, the first *court ball* in France was held at the wedding of Charles VI to Isabella of Bavaria.

The last Byzantine possessions in Asia Minor were lost to the Turks in 1390.

Dutch painter Jan van Eyck was born.

England forbade anyone not English to retail goods, 1392.

Johann Gutenberg, inventor of the printing press, was born in 1396. By 1455, he had printed his most important book, the *Forty-two-Line Bible,* in partnership with a financial backer, Johannes Fust. Gutenberg used metal plates in a technology used nowhere else, even in Japan and China where printing had taken other forms for centuries. At other times, Gutenberg printed school grammars, and even *indulgences*, which the Church said could remit punishment required for sin.

Jan Hus lectured on theology at Prague University in 1398. He and his followers were excommunicated by the Archbishop of Prague in 1410, and Hus was excommunicated by Pope John XXIII in 1411 and burned at the stake for heresy in 1415.

Italian sculptor Luca della Robbia was born in **1399**.

Florence, Italy, and the Medici start their political ascent around **1400** until they became the center of the Italian Renaissance and humanism. They became bankers to the papacy in **1414**.

In about this period, alchemy—an early form of chemistry at its best—slid into an activity for swindlers.

1403 saw compilation of the 22,937-volume Chinese encyclopedia, *Yung Lo Ta Tien*.

In **1407**, St. Mary's of Bethlehem Hospital in London, which comes to be known as *Bedlam*, was turned into a facility for the insane.

Joan of Arc was born in **1412**. In **1428**, she led the French armies against the English; she raised the siege of Orleans in **1429**; was captured by the Burgundians in **1430**; and was burned at the stake at Rouen in **1431**.

Around **1430**, Middle English began to evolve into Modern English, with the London dialect taking priority, the Scottish becoming distinguished from other northern dialects, and changes in inflection.

Incan rule was established in Peru by Pachacutec in **1438**.

The slave trade was reinvigorated in **1441** when Portuguese navigators came upon Negroes near Cape Blanc in western Africa.

1445, Copenhagen became the capital of Denmark.

Lorenzo de Medici, the Magnificent, was born in Florence in **1449**.

Architect Leon Battista Alberti devised a mechanical instrument to measure wind speed, the *anenometer*, in **1450**. Others were later credited for its invention.

1451, Christopher Columbus was born. Amerigo Vespucci was born in the same year.

1452, Leonardo da Vinci was born. He began the *Last Supper* in **1495** and painted the *Mona Lisa* in **1503**.

In **1453**, Constantinople was captured by the Turks and Emperor Constantine XI was killed, putting an end to the Byzantine Empire. Santa Sophia Basilica in Constantinople was converted to a mosque.

The Hundred Years' War ended; England handed over its French possessions, but kept Calais.

The Wars of the Roses, English civil wars fought between the houses of Lancaster, represented by the red rose, and York, the white rose, began in **1455**.

Athens was conquered by the Turks in **1456**. The Acropolis was sacked two years later. Bosnia was conquered by the Turks in **1463**. The fall of Herzegovina followed in **1467**.

Louis XI established French *royal mail service* in **1464**.

Desiderius Erasmus was born in Rotterdam in **1465**. He was the most noted humanist of the Renaissance in northern Europe, a friend of Thomas More, and widely influential. Erasmus taught at Oxford in **1498**.

Printed music appeared in the mid-fifteenth century.

▓ *Hustling of stones* and other *bowling* activities were forbidden by Edward IV in England in **1465**.

▓ In **1466**, the first Bible in German was printed by Johann Mentel in Strasbourg.

▓ Scotland decreed that *golfe* and *fute-ball* were not to be played, in **1467**.

▓ Niccolò Machiavelli was born in **1469**. He created the first *national army* in Italy in **1506** and wrote *The Prince* in **1513**.

▓ The Sorbonne set up the first French printing press in **1470**.

▓ In **1473**, Polish astronomer Nicolaus Copernicus was born. In 1512, he published his theory that the Earth and other planets revolve around the sun.

▓ The first book in English was printed in Bruges by William Caxton in **1474**. Part of the English trade community on the continent, he became interested in literature, and translated and printed the *Recueil des histoires de Troye*.

▓ Michelangelo Buonarroti was born in **1475**. In **1508**, he began painting the ceiling of the Sistine Chapel ceiling, in Rome. And Michelangelo designed the dome of St. Peter's in **1546**. The Pieta dates to **1555**.

▓ In **1478**, Thomas More was born. He became chancellor of England under Henry VIII, but his refusal to recognize the king as head of the church leads to his execution in **1535**, and canonization by the Roman Catholic Church. An important humanist, More was friends with Erasmus, who wrote In Praise of Folly in More's home, and More himself wrote *Utopia*, in **1516**.

▓ Ivan III, called Ivan the Great, assumes the role of Czar of Russia in **1480**. Sophia, his second wife, was niece of the last emperor of Byzantium and introduced the customs and openness of the Byzantine court to Russia.

Ferdinand Magellan, Portugese navigator, was born in **1480**.

German alchemist and magician Georg Faust, prototype of the Faust legend, was born.

▓ Ferdinand and Isabella of Spain appointed inquisitors against heresy among converted Jews. **1481** was the beginning of the Spanish Inquisition involving both church and state

▓ Russia began exploration of Siberia in **1483**. Martin Luther was born.

▓ In **1489**, the *mathematical symbols* of - (minus) and + (plus) were first used.

▓ Titian, or Tiziano Vecellio, the greatest of the Venetian Renaissance painters, was born around **1490**. He painted many mythological and allegorical scenes, as well as purely religious works, among the most famous, the *Assumption*, from around **1516**.

▓ The beginnings of *ballet* formed at Italian courts in **1490**.

Orphanages opened in Holland and Italy.

▓ The Spanish conquer Granada in **1492** and put an end to the Moorish kingdom. Spain also financed a trip to new world, led by Christopher Columbus, who sailed from Palos, Spain, on August 3.

■ Suleiman the Magnificent was born in **1494**.

The satiric poem *Ship of Fools (Das Narrenschiff)* was written by Sebastian Brant. The genre of *fool's literature* continued for centuries, and included Erasmus's **In Praise of Folly** (**1592**) and even Katherine Anne Porter's *Ship of Fools* (**1962**).

■ Jews were expelled from Portugal in **1495**.

A syphilis epidemic spread throughout Europe by way of French soldiers.

■ *Tobacco* plants were first described in **1496** by the monk Romano Pane, who accompanied Columbus on his second voyage. Tobacco from America arrived for the first time in Spain in **1555**.

■ In **1498**, Tomás de Torquemada, Inquisitor General of Spain, and known for fanatic bigotry and cruelty, died.

Vasco da Gama discovered a sea route to India.

In Nuremberg, the concept of the *pawnshop* was introduced.

■ The first political cartoons appeared in **1499**. Mass conversions of Moors to Christianity were ordered by the Spanish inquisitor general, resulting in a huge revolt in Granada.

■ The first *black-lead pencils* were in use in England in **1500**.

German *meistersingers* began to sing about worldly subjects, and were no longer limited to sacred texts.

■ In **1501**, a papal bull ordered the burning of all books with writings against the authority of the Church.

Ferdinand I declared Granada a Christian kingdom, but the Moors resisted the Spanish army.

By this year, 10 million copies of books had been produced by more than 1,000 print shops.

■ **1503**: Canterbury Cathedral, started in 1070, was finished.

French astrologer Nostradamus was born. He issued his first predictions in **1547**.

Pocket handkerchiefs became popular.

■ A Suez Canal was proposed to the Turkish Sultan by Venetian ambassadors in **1504**.

■ In **1506**, spices are imported from the East Indies to Germany.

■ In **1509**, Henry VIII ascended to England's throne.

In Germany, Emperor Maximilian I ordered all Jewish books, including the *Talmud*, to be confiscated and destroyed.

The Roman Catholic bishop of Chiapas, Spain, proposed that each settler bring a number of slaves to the New World, initiating the slave trade.

■ North America's southeastern coast was discovered in **1510**.

Everyman, the English morality play, was performed.

■ Quacks were banned in Augsburg, Germany, in **1512**. Doctors were required to be licensed.

■ John Knox, the central figure in the Protestant Reformation in Scotland, was born in **1514**. He was one of the "fathers" of Puritanism.

Pineapples were introduced into

Europe in 1514.

▨ **1517** saw *coffee* arrive in Europe.

▨ German sales of *indulgences* in **1517** were offered to finance the rebuilding of St. Peter's, in Rome, but there were political "kickbacks" unknown to many as well. Caught up in politics in Wittenberg, these sales of forgiveness came to the attention of an Augustinian priest, Martin Luther, who posted his *Ninety-five Theses*, arguing the theological errors behind the indulgences.

▨ License was granted in **1518** to import 4,000 African slaves to the Spanish-American colonies.

▨ In **1521**, Ferdinand Magellan was killed by natives in the Philippines.

That year, France began the manufacture of *silk*.

▨ Florence issued the first *marine-insurance policies* in **1523**.

▨ South American *turkeys* were eaten for the first time at the English court in **1524**.

▨ French imperial troops overran and sacked Rome in **1527**, confining the Pope and his supporters to Castel Sant'Angelo. At least 4,000 Roman citizens were killed during the looting and pillaging.

Also in **1527**, Philip the Magnanimous of Hesse established the first Protestant university, Philips University of Marburg.

▨ Women *actresses* first performed on the stage for the first time in Italy in **1529**.

▨ Brazil was colonized by Portugal in **1530**.

▨ The sight of Halley's Comet in **1531** sparked wide superstition.

▨ In **1533**, the Spanish explorer Francisco Pizarro executed Peru's Incans. Pizarro founded Lima in **1535**.

▨ Construction on St. Basil's in Moscow began in **1534**; it was finished in **1541**.

▨ A **1543** English decree forbade farmers to own more than 2,000 sheep.

▨ In mid-century, England's Henry VII put together the first true navy meant for battle.

▨ Around **1535,** a German in the service of Emperor Charles V wrote of a *diving bell* he witnessed in Toledo, used by two Greek divers.

▨ Music *conservatories* arose in Italy around **1537**.

▨ Spain annexed Cuba in **1539**.

The first Christmas tree was erected in Strasbourg Cathedral.

▨ The Cretan-born, Spanish painter known as El Greco was born in **1541** as Doménikos Theotokópoulos. Since Crete was a territory owned by Venice at the time, he came under the influence of the Venetian Renaissance painters and studied with Titian. El Greco was also a widely read humanist.

▨ Bavaria imposed heavy taxes on drinks in **1542**.

▨ The earliest evidence of Italian *commedia dell'arte,* an ensemble troupe, dates to **1545**.

▨ Moscow was destroyed by a fire in **1547**.

▨ Dwarves and cripples functioned as *court jesters* in Europe around **1550**, and are painted in court portraits.

Billiards was played for the first time in Italy.

Sealing wax was used for the first time.

The first *refracting telescope* was made by Leonard Digges.

St. Andrew's Golf Club was founded in Scotland in **1552**. Mary, Queen of Scots most likely became the first woman golfer.

In **1553**, the modern form of *violin* began to take shape.

The Sack-Full of Newes was the first play to be censored in England, in **1557**.

Europe experienced an influenza epidemic.

In **1560**, the Uffizi Gallery opened in Florence.

Naples became the site of the first *scientific society*.

The plague came to Paris in 1562; the following year saw a general outbreak in Europe, including more than 20,000 deaths in London.

1564: The Spanish occupied the Philippines, who built Manila.

William Shakespeare was born. He traveled from Stratford-on-Avon to London in **1585**. The first time he is mentioned as an actor in existing sources was **1592**.

Christopher Marlowe was born.

Galileo Galilei was born in **1564**. He described his experiments with falling objects in **1589**; invented the thermometer in **1596**; observed the satellites of Jupiter in **1610**. Galileo was brought before the Inquisition for the first time in **1615**. The next year, he was prohibited from further scientific work. The Inquisition forced him to renounce Copernicus's theories in **1633**.

Sweet potatoes and *tobacco* were introduced in England in **1565**.

Japan centralized its government by deposing its shogunate in **1567**.

Bottled beer was invented in London in **1568**.

Japan opened up to overseas trade in **1570**.

The Moral Fables of Aesop were published.

Ben Jonson, Shakespeare's primary competitor, was born in **1572**. He wrote *The Alchemist, Bartholo-mew Fair, Every Man in His Humour,* and *Volpone*.

John Donne was born. He was the great figure of Metaphysical poetry, complex and often raw writing about love and faith both—the Songs and Sonnets, and the Holy Sonnets. He was a recusant, a Roman Catholic, but became an Anglican and ultimately Dean of St. Paul's. His sermons, gathered in such works as *Devotions upon Emergent Occasions,* are among the best in a century known for its sermons. The *Devotions* included the line, "No man is an island."

In **1573**, Francis Drake saw the Pacific Ocean for the first time. Four years later he embarked on his trip around the world by way of Cape Horn.

English Parliament members and their servants were granted freedom from arrest in **1575,** in the reign of Elizabeth I.

Spain went bankrupt.

The Flemish Baroque painter

Peter Paul Rubens was born in **1577**.

▓ Rome's catacombs were redis-covered in **1578**.

▓ In **1582**, the Roman Catholic Church adopted the Gregorian calendar. New Year's Day was changed from March 15, the Feast of the Annunciation, to January 1. It took some time for various countries to follow suit. Scotland made the change to January 1, in **1660**; around **1700**, Germany and Denmark did the same; then England, in **1752**; and Russia did not change until after the Revolution, in **1918**.

▓ England's first recognized *life insurance* was taken out on William Gibbons in **1583**.

▓ **1584**: Russia's Ivan the Terrible died, succeeded as czar by his son Fyodor, who soon gave up most of his powers to brother-in-law Boris Godunov.

Virginia was discovered by Sir Walter Raleigh, who promptly annexed it for England.

▓ The first English *traveling and standing clocks* were devised in **1585**.

▓ In **1586**, Kabuki theater originated in Japan.

▓ A first book of *madrigals* was composed by Claudio Monteverdi in **1587**. A pioneer in the development of opera, his *Orfeo* was staged in **1607**.

Venice's Rialto Bridge was built in **1587**.

▓ The Vatican Library in Rome opened in **1588**.

▓ In **1589**, *forks* were used for the first time at the French court.

The *knitting machine* was invented in Cambridge, England.

Coal mining began in the Ruhr valley, Germany.

▓ Elizabeth I of England established Dublin's Trinity College in **1591**.

▓ In **1592**, the ruins of Pompeii were discovered.

Mechanical saws were first driven by *windmills* in Holland.

▓ **1595** brought the first *shoes with heels*.

▓ *Tomatoes* were brought to England in **1596**.

The first *water closets* were developed.

French philosopher and mathematician René Descartes was born and became most famous for the phrase *cogito ergo sum,* or *I think, therefore I am,* published in a book in **1644**.

▓ An *iron-clad warship* was invented in **1598**.

▓ Oliver Cromwell was born in **1599**. He led the parliamentary forces against the crown in the English Civil War. He served as Lord Protector of the Commonwealth from **1653** to **1658**.

The first *chamber of commerce* was founded in Marseille in 1599.

▓ The *optical telescope* was invented by Dutch opticians in **1608**. Galileo advanced its use by studying astronomical bodies with one he built himself.

▓ *Monopolies* were banned in England in **1601**.

Peking admitted a Jesuit missionary.

▓ In **1603**, a *grammar book* was published that led to the development of Bohemian, or the modern Czech language.

Controversial religious philosopher Roger Williams was born.

The *valves* in human veins were discovered.

Part I of Cervántes' *Don Quixote* was published in **1605**. Part II was published ten years later.

Santa Fe, New Mexico, was founded.

The first of Rome's public libraries opened.

Dutch painter Rembrandt van Rijn was born in **1606**.

France began an extensive road construction program.

Jamestown, Virginia, the first English colony in America, was settled in **1607**.

John Milton was born in **1608**. He wrote Paradise Lost in **1655**.

The Netherlands issued the first *paper checks* in **1608**.

In **1609**, the Congregation of Female Jesuits was founded, but later was dissolved by Pope Urban VIII.

Bohemia granted *freedom of religion*.

The Blue Mosque in Constantinople (now Istanbul) was built.

England produced the first example of *engraved music*.

Chinese tea came to England for the first time through the Dutch East India Company. *Tea* debuted in Paris in **1636**.

Padua established the Academy of Poetry in **1610**.

Sunspots were discovered by Thomas Harriott.

Henry Hudson discovered Hudson's Bay.

Oxford's Bodleian Library began to collect every book printed.

1611 saw the founding of the University of Rome.

Rainbows were explained in scientific terms.

Japan permitted Dutch trade.

The last recorded burning of heretics in England was in **1612**.

German mathematician Bartholomew Pitiscus used the *decimal point* in trigonometrical tables.

Manhattan was the locale of *fur trading* for the first time by the Dutch.

Tobacco was planted for the first time in Virginia.

Russia's House of Romanov was founded in **1613** with the election of Michael Romanov as Czar.

London's Globe Theatre was destroyed by fire.

In **1614**, Pocahontas married John Rolfe.

Ben Johnson is made Poet Laureate in England in **1617**.

Sir Walter Raleigh was executed for treason on his return to England in **1618**.

The circulation of blood was discovered by William Harvey in London in **1619**.

Virginia saw the arrival of the first Negro slaves in North America.

The *Mayflower* left England in **1620** with Miles Standish and other Pilgrims, ultimately to establish Plymouth Colony in Massachusetts; John Carver was elected as its first governor.

London's Fortune Theatre

burned down in **1621**.

London published the first periodical with *international news* content.

Germany planted the first *potato* crops.

▨ Molière, the stage name of the actor and playwright named Jean-Baptiste Poquelin, was born in **1622**. In **1643** he founded the Illustre-thèatre, later known as la Comèdie Français. *Tartuffe* was first performed in **1664** and *Le Bourgeois Gentilhomme* in **1670**.

▨ In **1623**, England established *patent laws* to protect inventors.

▨ **1624**: The Dutch settled in New Amsterdam, later New York City.

▨ The first *fire engines* appeared in London in **1625**.

Full-bottomed wigs were introduced in Europe.

▨ In Rome, the façade of St. Peter's Basilica was finished in **1626**.

France issued a death edict for anyone who killed an opponent in a duel.

The Dutch purchased the island of Manhattan from native Indian chiefs, and established the colony of New Amsterdam on the Hudson River.

▨ In **1627**, China made Korea a tributary state.

Johann Kepler fixed the places of more than 1,000 *stars* in his Rudolphine Tables.

▨ In the early seventeenth century, Japan's kabuki theater developed from a female dancer's parodies of Buddhist prayers, though by **1629**, women were forbidden to perform.

Brackets and other mathematical abbreviations were first used in 1629.

The Peacock Throne was ordered by the Great Mogul Shah Jahan.

The colony of Massachusetts was founded.

▨ The high Baroque period began in Italy in **1630** and continued until **1680**.

The game of *cribbage* was invented.

Paris witnessed *public advertising*.

Pirates settled off the coast of Hispaniola.

▨ In **1631**, John Dryden was born. The late seventeenth century became known as the Age of Dryden. He was a poet, playwright, and critic.

x was proposed as a symbol for *multiplication*.

Mount Vesuvius erupted after an earthquake in Naples.

▨ London's first coffee shop opened in **1632**.

▨ In **1633**, Lancashire, England, held *witch trials*.

Colonization of Connecticut began in **1633** with moves from the Massachusetts Bay Colony to the Connecticut River Valley and then to the coast near New Haven and Saybrook.

▨ The first *passion play* was presented in Oberammergau, Germany, in **1634**. It started to fulfill a vow after an outbreak of the plague in Bavaria and has been performed every 10 years since.

The Wisconsin area was explored by Jean Nicolet.

A three mile-per-hour speed limit was imposed on London hackneys in **1635**.

France restricted the sale of tobacco to prescriptions only.

The route between London and Edinburgh became a first postal service.

Harvard College was founded in **1636**.

In **1637**, Japan eradicated Christianity and prohibited foreign contacts and books.

England issued a proclamation restricting emigration to America.

England abolished torture in **1638**.

The first French language *dictionary* was published in **1639**.

Cambridge, Massachusetts, was the site of the first printing press in North America.

In **1642**, the Puritans forced the closing of all theaters in England until **1660**. England introduced *income and property taxes.*

Isaac Newton was born in **1642**. He may have invented *differential calculus* in **1665**, in his experimentation with gravity, although some argue that calculus was invented by Gottfried Wilhelm Leibniz. Newton discovered the composition of white light, leading to modern optics; formulated the three laws of motion, the basis of modern physics; contributed to the understanding of planetary motion.

New Zealand and Tasmania were discovered by Abel Tasman.

Montreal was founded.

American Calvinist Roger Williams published *Key into the Language of America* in **1643**.

The *barometer* was invented.

Coffee became popular in Paris.

China's Ming Dynasty ended in **1644**. It was the last age of fine Chinese porcelain. It was followed by the Manchu dynasty, which stayed in power until **1912**.

William Penn was born.

John Milton argued for freedom of the press.

Roger Williams argued for separation of church and state.

Italian violin maker Antonio Stradivari was born. He marketed his first violin in **1666**.

The Bahamas were occupied by the English in **1645**.

Berlin planted first lime trees, originating its famous *Unter den Linden Boulevard.*

In **1648,** Germany's population dropped to 8 million, less than half of the population of 30 years earlier. Causes were plague, war, and famine.

The manufacture of *mirrors* and *chandeliers* began in Murano, an island near Venice.

Modern *harmony* had its beginnings in **1650**, along with the emergence of the *overture* as a musical form in France and Italy.

Vienna opened the first *comedy house* **1651**.

The Cape of Good Hope was settled by the Dutch.

A *lunar map* contained many of the names for lunar features still in modern use.

The separation of printer and publisher began.

History of Japan was published

in **1652**.

Vienna opened its first *opera house*.

The *minuet* was popular in the French court.

Composer Johann Pachelbel was born in **1653**.

The first *post boxes* appeared in Paris.

Johann Sebastian Bach was born in **1655**. He composed his first cantata in **1704**. Among his greatest works were the *Branden-berg Concertos, the Goldberg Varia-tions, the Mass in B Minor, the Well-Tempered Clavier,* and many hymns and fugues.

Berlin had its first standard *newspaper* in 1655.

The first clock pendulum was designed in the Netherlands in **1657**.

Chocolate drinking began in London.

Paris saw the manufacture of *fountain pens* and *stockings*.

In **1658**, *cremation* was supported by physicians in England.

Germany and England saw the first *actresses* on stage in **1660**.

The Dutch Boers settled in South Africa.

French *water closets* were introduced in England.

The Royal Society—its full name the Royal Society of London for the Promotion of Natural Knowledge—England's oldest scientific association, was founded in 1660.

London issued its last silver pennies in **1662**.

Cotton Mather, Massachusetts writer and prominent witch hunter,

was born in **1663**.

Hearth tax and *turnpike tolls* began in England.

The first American Indian received a degree from Harvard in **1665**.

The Great Plague of London, which eventually killed more than 68,000, began.

1666 was the year of the Great Fire of London.

Cheddar cheese first appeared.

Jonathan Swift was born in **1667**. He published *Gulliver's Travels* in **1726**.

Hand grenades were used by the French army in 1667.

Dutch microscopist Antonie von Leeuwenhoek accurately described *red corpuscles* for the first time.

In **1670**, the use of *artificial wings* for flying was attempted for the first time.

Minute hands appeared on watches.

The first Arabic Bible was printed in **1671**.

The Paris Opera opened with its first performance, *Pomone*.

Rob Roy (Red Rob) was born Robert MacGregor in Scotland. He was either a self-interested Highland highwayman, or a romantic Scottish hero, depending on the chronicler.

The *flexible fire hose* was used for first time in **1672**.

The French missionary Jacques Marquette explored the area that would later become Chicago.

England banned Roman Catholics from holding office with the **1673** Test Act. Scotland had done the same nearly a century before.

Zhitie (*Life*), by Archpriest Petrovich Avvakum, was the first biography in Russian.

Mississippi's headwaters were reached by explorers Jacques Marquette and Louis Joliet.

Italian composer and priest Antonio Vivaldi was born in 1675.

England's Greenwich Observatory established.

Differential and integral calculus were arguably invented by Gottfried Wilhelm Leibniz, though some attribute it to Isaac Newton.

The finite *velocity of light* was discovered.

In **1676**, England provided legal protection for Sabbath observances.

A famous French chef committed suicide after a state dinner did not meet the expectations of Louis XIV.

Paris residents made *ice cream* desserts popular, in **1677**.

Part I of the *Pilgrim's Progress,* Part I, by John Bunyan, was published in **1673**; Part II was published in **1684**.

In Hamburg, the first *German opera house* opened.

The Great Lakes were explored by Robert de La Salle. In **1682**, La Salle claimed the area of modern Louisiana for France.

The first *medical book* was published in America.

Japan received first *chrysanthemums* from Holland; mum growing gradually became a countrywide passion.

England prohibited all French imports.

Niagara Falls was discovered by Louis Hannepin in **1679**.

France outlawed dueling.

The *dodo bird* became extinct in **1680**.

Ballet arrived in Germany, from France.

London established the *penny post*.

The Paris Opera used female dancers for the first time in 1681.

France made Versailles the royal residence in **1682**.

China admitted Dutch traders to Canton in **1683**. In1685, China opened all ports to foreign trade.

The first German immigrants arrived in North America.

Vienna opened its first coffee houses.

In England, wild boars became extinct.

London witnessed first attempts at providing street lighting in **1684**.

France opens a *convent school* for girls of poor parents in **1686**.

1688 was the year of England's so-called Glorious Revolution, when James II was deposed and his daughter Mary and her husband William of Orange, of the Netherlands, became sovereigns. The political causes were often religious in basis.

Alexander Pope was born. He was deformed, a Roman Catholic in Protestant England, and a brilliant satirist and poet.

The year marked the first use of *plate glass*.

Lloyd's of London, the famous

insurance association, takes shape. It began in Edward Lloyd's coffeehouse, with informal business among merchants, bankers, mariners, and then underwriters.

In 1689, Peter the Great became Czar of Russia.

Holland organized the first modern *trade fair*.

Paris publishes the first directory of addresses in 1691.

1682 marked the founding of William and Mary College in Virginia.

Voltaire was born as François-Marie Arouet in 1694. His philosophical influence was enormous in the American and French revolutions. Voltaire's writings included the novel *Candide*, and his collection of thoughts, *Dictionnaire philosophique*.

The Bank of England was established in 1694.

England ended *press censorship* in 1695.

A window tax began in England, and lasted until 1851.

In 1697, the Spanish destroyed the remains of Mayan civilization in the Yucatan.

Russia set a *tax on beards* in 1698.

Paper was first made in North America.

Berlin taxed unmarried women.

The *commode* becomes popular.

Yale College was established in 1701 in New Haven, Connecticut.

Captain Kidd was hanged for piracy.

Denmark outlawed serfdom in 1702.

A company was founded for the slave trade between America and Africa.

Horseracing for cash awards—*sweepstakes*—began in England

In 1703, work began on Buckingham Palace.

Peter the Great laid out the foundations for St. Petersburg.

Residents of Deerfield, Connecticut, were killed by French troops and Indians in 1704.

Boston published the first weekly newspaper in America that endured, *The Boston News-Letter*.

Edmund Haley accurately predicted the return appearance of a comet peridiodically documented in history, in 1705.

Benjamin Franklin was born in 1706. He began publishing *Poor Richard's Alamanac* in 1732; invented the lightning conductor in 1752; wrote *Observations Concerning the Increase of Mankind, Peopling of Countries* in 1755. He also invented a stove, bifocals, contributed to the writing of the *Declaration of Independence,* and served as an ambassador to France.

An *evening newspaper* was first published in London.

Carriage springs were invented.

With the Act of Union in 1707, Scotland and England unite under the name Great Britain.

Mount Fuji in Japan erupted for the last time.

Patrons of Berlin coffee houses began playing *billiards.*

Samuel Johnson was born in 1709. The essayist, critic, and lexicographer was known for his sharp mind, conversation, and command of writing. His works included *Rasselas, The Lives of the Poets,* and of course, his dictionary.

The *pianoforte* was invented in Italy.

Eau-de-cologne was produced in Cologne.

Russian prisoners were sent to Siberia for the first time.

Britain enacted its first Copyright Act. It also regulated postage rates according to distance.

■ **1710**: Russia creates its first budget.

Three-color printing began.

■ The Ascot races were established by Queen Anne in **1711**.

■ *The Spectator* was published daily by Richard Steele and Joseph Addison from **1711** to **1712** and then later again in **1714** by Addison. Its essays and commentary were witty and pointed.

■ Jean-Jacques Rousseau, French philosopher, was born in **1712**. His philosophical inspiration for the French Revolution included novels, essays, and his autobiography, *Confessions*. He wrote of property, the social contract, and liberty.

The last execution for witchcraft took place in Britain.

New York City experienced a slave rebellion.

■ In **1713**, the Spanish Royal Academy in Madrid was founded.

The Prussian Army established *pigtails* as its standard hairstyle.

■ The *fine-pointed syringe* for surgical use was invented in **1714**.

D. G. Fahrenheit made the *mercury thermometer*.

■ The first company of English actors arrived in Williamsburg, Virginia, in **1716**.

China prohibited the teaching of Christianity.

The first Italian newspaper was published.

■ **1717** saw the first performance of the German composer George Frideric Handel's *Water Music*, on the Thames River. It was written for George I of England. Handel spent most of his life in England, and was known, in addition to his operas in the Italian style, for his English oratorios.

Inoculations against smallpox were introduced in England due to the efforts of Lady Mary Wortly Montagu, who learned of the concept from Turkish physicians.

Prussia made school attendance mandatory

■ **1718**: New Orleans was founded.

■ England declared Ireland an inseparable part of its lands in **1719**.

Russia expelled the Jesuits.

Cricket was first played in England.

■ Texas was occupied by Spain in **1720**.

Novels were serialized in a newspaper.

■ In **1722**, journalists were forbidden to report on Parliamentarian debates in England.

■ Gin became popular in Britain, around **1724**.

■ Rome's Spanish Steps were finished after four years of construction, begun in **1725**.

Casanova was born.

■ Brazil planted its first *coffee*

trees in **1727**.

The first *marriage advertisement* appeared in a newspaper in Manchester, England.

John Gay's *Beggar's Opera* was performed in **1728**.

Opium smoking was banned in China in **1729**.

Salzburg, Germany, banished Protestants in **1731**.

Philadelphia's Independence Hall was built. A subscription library was started by Benjamin Franklin in the city.

The *sailor's quadrant* was invented.

The prime minister's residence at 10 Downing Street in London was built.

Franz Joseph Haydn was born in **1732**.

London's Covent Garden Opera House opened.

Prussia instituted conscription for its army in **1733**.

The flying shuttle loom was patented.

The first horse race in America was run, **1734**.

Paul Revere was born in **1735**.

In a landmark trial, John Peter Zenger, the publisher of the *New York Weekly Journal,* was acquitted of seditious libel, with far-reaching implications for freedom of the press.

Georgia prohibited the sale of alcohol.

Patrick Henry was born in **1736**.

In **1737**, the last of the Medici line died.

Thomas Paine was born.

London issued the Licensing Act, which included a section that said all plays were open to censorship by the Lord Chamberlain before performance.

Excavation began in **1738** of the ancient Roman city of Herculaneum, buried alongside the ruins of Pompeii.

Germany's Black Forest region produced the first cuckoo clocks.

1740, and the University of Pennsylvania was founded.

Berlin had a smallpox epidemic.

Freedom of the press and freedom of worship were granted in Prussia under Frederick the Great.

Dubliners of **1742** were the first to hear a performance of Handel's *Messiah*.

Thomas Jefferson was born in **1743**. He died on July 4, 1826, the same day as John Adams died.

South Dakota's first settlement dated to 1743.

In **1744**, the ruling Arab family, the Sa-Udi, adopted the teachings of Abd-al-Wahhab, forming the basis of the Wahhabi beliefs.

London founded its Madrigal Society.

Tartans were prohibited in Great Britain in **1746**.

In the Paris of **1748**, hostess Marie-Thérèse Geoffrin started a *salon* for conversation among international men of letters.

Diphtheria was described by John Fothergill.

Charleston, South Carolina, opened a *subscription library,* among the first in the U.S., along with the Boston Athenaeum, the New York Society Library.

▨ *Sign language* was invented in in Portugal in **1749**.

▨ In **1750**, the first *playhouse* opened in New York City.

Glue was made from fish in Britain, circa 1750. Other types of glues soon followed.

▨ China invaded Tibet in **1751**.

▨ Jews were permitted naturalization in England, as of **1753**.

Weddings by unauthorized persons were forbidden by England's Marriage Act.

▨ The first female physician matriculated in Germany in **1754**.

▨ In **1755**, the University of Moscow was founded.

Jane Austen, author of *Sense and Sensibility, Pride and Prejudice, Emma,* and other *novels of manners,* was born.

▨ **1756** saw the birth of Wolfgang Amadeus Mozart, whose great works included the operas the *Magic Flute, Figaro,* and *Don Giovanni*; chamber works such as *Eine Kleine Nachtmusik*; and arguably his masterpiece, the *Requiem Mass,* completed in **1791**, the year of his death.

Germany's first *chocolate* factory began operations.

▨ Philadelphia enjoyed a *public concert* for the first time in **1757**.

▨ Lexicographer Noah Webster was born in **1758**.

▨ In the mid-eighteenth century, *schools for the deaf* were opened in France, Germany, and Britain (in Edinburgh).

The year **1760** is often used to mark the beginning of the Industrial Revolution in Britain.

Josiah Wedgwood's pottery shop opened in **1760**.

▨ Samuel Johnson met his friend and biographer James Boswell in **1763**.

▨ Brown University was founded in **1764** in Providence, Rhode Island.

London began numbering houses.

▨ Paris had the first public restaurant in the form of a soup business belonging to A. Boulanger, in **1765**. Boulanger advertised his soups as *restoratives*, from which *restaurants* derived.

▨ **1766** was the year that Czarina Catherine the Great granted freedom of religious worship in Russia.

Westminster, England, builds the first paved *sidewalk*.

▨ Mapmaker and engraver James Spilsbury created the first *jigsaw puzzle* out of a map in England in **1767**. They were used to teach geography to children.

▨ In **1768**, Boston residents refused to house British soldiers.

Austria introduced a new, more humanistic *criminal code*.

▨ Ludwig van Beethoven was born in **1770**. Probably the greatest of all Western composers, he bridged the Classical tradition to the new Romanticism. His music was innovative structurally and philosophically.

Scottish explorer James Bruce discovered the source of the Blue Nile.

▨ The first edition of the *Encyclopaedia Britannica* was published in **1771**.

▨ A British judge decided in **1772** that slaves landing in Britain were free.

■ **1773** saw the Boston Tea Party.

The *waltz* became the popular dance in Vienna.

■ *Hypnosis*, or Mesmerism, after the Viennese physician Franz Mesmer who advanced its use, was first used for health reasons in **1774**.

■ In **1778**, the importation of slaves into the U.S. was prohibited by Act of Congress.

London established the first children's clinic.

■ American Academy of Sciences was founded in Boston in **1780**.

■ Uranus was discovered by William Herschel in **1781**.

Construction of the Siberian highway began.

■ The first hot-air balloon took flight in France in **1783**.

■ Thomas Jefferson introduced "potatoes, fried in the French manner"—*french fries*—to the U.S. from France in the **late 1700s**.

■ The first working *parachute* was demonstrated in **1783** by Sebastien Lenormand.

■ The first *school for the blind* opened in Paris in **1784**.

■ Bread riots broke out in France in **1788**.

New York was named the capital of the U.S.

George Lord Byron was born. In addition to his poetry, he became a "personality" of the Romantic era.

■ The Continental Congress met in New York in **1789**.

The storming of the Bastille marked the beginning of the French Revolution.

H.M.S. Bounty mutineers settled on Pitcairn Island.

■ The capital of the U.S. changed to Philadelphia in **1790**, and the year also marked the founding of Washington, D.C.

Jews were granted civil liberties in France.

John Carroll of Baltimore became the first Roman Catholic Bishop consecrated in America.

The first *patent law* went into effect in the U.S.

The U.S. Supreme Court held its first session.

■ A general strike took place in Hamburg in **1791**.

Wolfe Tone and others began the Society of United Irishmen to fight for reforms, including universal suffrage and Roman Catholic emancipation. By **1794**, he was a leader in looking to France to help end English rule. In **1798**, rebellion broke out in Ireland, with French aid, but the battle was lost and soon after, Britain imposed an Act of Union on Ireland. The Irish who went into exile were known as the Wild Geese.

■ Poet Percy Bysshe Shelley was born in **1792**. He left his marriage to run away with the author of *Frankenstein*, Mary Wollstonecraft Godwin.

■ The Reign of Terror began in France in **1793**.

At 11 years of age, Niccolò Paganini debuted as a violin prodigy.

Escaped slaves were compelled to return to their owners under a new U.S. law.

■ The U.S. Navy was instituted in **1794**.

In **1795**, France adopted the metric system.

The Conservatoire de Musique was founded in Paris.

Freedom of worship was granted in France.

Lyric poet John Keats was born. His works included *Endymion*, "Ode on a Grecian Urn," "Ode to Melancholy," and "To Autumn."

Edward Jenner, in **1796**, introduced his smallpox vaccine.

Freedom of the press began in France.

William Wordsworth and Samuel Taylor Coleridge published *Lyrical Ballads,* which signalled the beginning of the Romantic era in English literature, in **1798**.

The Rosetta Stone was discovered in **1799**, and provided the key to interpreting *hieroglyphics*.

A perfectly preserved *mammoth* was found in Siberia.

Alessandro Volta demonstrated the *electric battery,* of zinc and copper plates, in **1800**.

Ottawa was established.

The slave trade was prohibited in England in **1807**.

England used gas to light streets.

Excavations began at Pompeii in **1808**.

Abraham Lincoln was born in**1809**.

Edgar Allan Poe was born. Louis Braille was born.

1810, Sir Walter Scott published *The Lady of the Lake.*

Charles Dickens was born in **1812**. He became the extraordinarily popular author of novels such as *David Copperfield, Tale of Two Cities,* *Bleak House,* and many others.

United States declared war on Britain because of its interfering, oppressive practices against neutrals on the high seas during the Napoleonic Wars.

Napoleon's Russian campaign was disastrous: Only 20,000 out of 550,000 soldiers returned.

Montreal's McGill University was founded in **1813**.

Richard Wagner, German composer, was born. His music was a revolutionary and came to be controversial for its role in German history. His operas included *The Flying Dutchman, Lohengrin, Tristan und Isolde,* and *The Ring of the Nibelung.*

In **1814**, Francis Scott Key wrote the poem that later became "The Star Spangled Banner."

In **1815**, London forbade unqualified physicians from practicing medicine with the Apothecaries Act.

Britain's income tax ended.

The *U.S.S. Fulton* was constructed, the first warship powered by steam.

Napoleon was defeated at Waterloo.

When in **1816** the British Museum obtained the Elgin Marbles, a collection of Greek statues, a controversy arose. Some, including the poets George Lord Byron and John Keats, thought such treasures should never have been removed from Greece.

David Brewster, a Scottish physicist who worked with optics, invented the kaleidoscope in **1816**.

Construction began on the Vatican Museum and on the Ērie Canal in **1817**.

Henry David Thoreau was born.

Karl Marx was born in **1818**.

Madrid's Prado Museum was founded.

"Silent Night" was composed.

A *steamship* crossed the Atlantic in 26 days.

Walt Whitman was born in **1819**.

A Sanskrit-English dictionary was published.

England passed laws requiring a maximum of a 12-hour work week for children.

Florence Nightingale and Susan B. Anthony were born in **1820**.

Uranium was discovered in Russia's Ural Mountains.

The Venus de Milo was discovered.

Jesuits were driven out of Rome.

Rubber was re-devised into *elastic*, particularly for use in fastenings, and patented in Britain by Thomas Hancock in **1820**.

Fedor Dostoevsky was born in **1821**. His novels included *Crime and Punishment* and *Brothers Karamazov*.

Boston streets were lit by *gas* in **1822**.

Louis Pasteur was born. He proved living organisms cause fermentation in **1857** and discovered the chicken cholera vaccine in **1880**.

Mexico became a republic in **1823**.

The Monroe Doctrine closed America to foreign colonization.

Waterproof fabric was invented by Charles Macintosh.

In **1824**, it was discovered that a sperm is vital to fertilization.

British workers were allowed to form *unions*.

English scientist Michael Faraday developed *toy balloons* to use in hydrogen experiments.

Sacrilege became a capital offense in France in **1825**.

Rochester, New York, was home to the organized Baseball Club.

The first of the Baedeker *travel guides* was published in **1827**.

J. J. Audubon published *Birds of North America*.

Photographs were produced on a metal plate.

London's water supply was purified by means of a *sand filter*.

Jules Verne was born in **1828**.

Webster published the *American Dictionary of the English Language.*

Construction of the Baltimore and Ohio railroad began, the first to transport both freight and passengers.

In **1829**, slavery was abolished in Mexico.

Britain's Catholic Emancipation granted Roman Catholics the right to sit in Parliament and hold most public offices.

A method of treating diseases with water, *hydropathy*, is developed.

James Smithsonian, a British chemist, bequeathed £100,000 pounds to found the Smithsonian Institution in Washington, D.C.

The first American *cooperative stores* opened in New York and Philadelphia.

A *typewriter* patent was granted in the U.S.

The new style in men's fashion in 1830 was stiff collars.

The *cell nucleus* discovered in plants.

Emily Dickinson was born.

A prototype of the *sewing machine* was invented.

French author Stendhal wrote *The Red and the Black*.

The **1831** cholera pandemic began in India, spread to Russia, Central Europe, and Scotland.

Horse-drawn *buses* began operations in New York.

Darwin sailed on the *H.M.S. Beagle* to begin his expedition, which led to *Origin of the Species*.

A method was discovered to make *matches* ignite easily.

Founding of New England's Anti-Slavery Society in Boston took place in **1832**.

1833 marked the end of slavery in the British Empire.

1834 saw the end of the Spanish Inquisition.

English mathematician Charles Babbage invented the *analytical engine*, on the principles behind modern computers.

The last Holy Roman Emperor died in **1835**.

Mark Twain was born.

P.T. Barnum embarked on his colorful career by hyping George Washington's alleged nurse, said to be more than 160 years old.

Melbourne, Australia, was founded.

The earliest *photographic negative* was taken.

In **1836**, Dutch Boer farmers begin their Great Trek across Africa.

Sitting Bull was born in 1837.

Birth registration was introduced in Britain.

The U.S. Congress passed a *gag law* to suppress debate on slavery.

Queen Victoria was crowned in **1838**.

The first Opium War was fought between China and Britain in **1839**.

Celtic was recognized as an Indo-European language.

Ancient Mayan culture was discovered in Central America.

Goodyear devised the process of *vulcanization*.

The first electric clock was made.

The first bicycle was built, in Scotland.

The first British-Afghan War ended in **1840** with the surrender of Afghan troops.

Building on the Houses of Parliament commenced; it was completed 20 years later.

Penny postage was established in Britain.

In **1841**, Scottish surgeon James Braid experimented with and advanced hypnosis.

The *New York Tribune* debuted.

The first American university degrees were granted to women.

The *polka* became fashionable in **1842**.

An American physician used *ether* as an anesthetic.

The New York Philharmonic Society was founded.

The first *minstrel show* was performed in **1843**.

Dorthea Dix reported on the terrible conditions in prisons and asylums.

Le Bal des Anglais, the world's first nightclub, debuted in Paris.

Norwegians started *skiing* as a sport.

England opened its first *public bath houses* in **1844**.

Samuel Morse's *telegraph* was used for the first time between Washington and Baltimore.

The Young Men's Christian Association (YMCA) was founded in England.

Victor Hugo published *The Hunchback of Notre Dame* in 1831.

The first *underwater cable* was laid across the English Channel in **1845**.

1846 saw the first painted *Christmas card.*

A potato crop failure caused famine in Ireland.

Evaporated milk was made for the first time in **1847**.

Marx and Engels issued the *Communist Manifesto* in **1848**.

The U.S. sees a rise in the popularity of Spiritualism.

The first *appendectomy* was performed.

Austria abolished serfdom.

The year saw the first Public Health Act in Britain.

First settlers arrived in New Zealand.

The slave Harriet Tubman escaped to Philadelphia in **1849**. She went on to help 300 or more slaves escape on what came to be called the *underground railroad.*

Women's dress reform was promoted by Amelia Bloomer.

Old-age insurance became available in France in **1850**.

In **1851**, Cuba declared its independence from Spain.

In **1852**, the United States brought in *sparrows* from Germany to counteract *caterpillars.*

Bandages were saturated with plaster by a Dutch army surgeon.

Small arms manufacturing was revolutionized by Samuel Colt in **1853**.

A *hypodermic syringe* for injections under the skin was used for the first time.

A *railroad* ran through the Alps for the first time.

Chloroform was administered during the birth of Queen Victoria's seventh child.

Smallpox vaccination was made mandatory in Britain.

In **1854**, a German watchmaker invented the first type of *electric bulb.*

Le Figaro began publishing in Paris.

The Republican Party formed in the U.S.

The *printing telegraph* was invented in 1855.

London modernized its *sewer system* after a cholera outbreak.

Florence Nightingale introduced modern *hygienic standards* into military hospitals.

Pure *cocaine* extract was taken from cocoa beans in **1856**.

A neanderthal skull was uncovered in Germany.

The Fenians, a nationalist organization, began in Ireland in **1857**.

Speculation in U.S. railroad shares caused financial crisis in Europe.

Czar Alexander II began the emancipation of serfs in Russia.

Transatlantic cable was laid; it was finished in **1865**.

In 1859, Niagara Falls was crossed by a tightrope walker.

Scotsman Samuel Smiles published *Self-Help,* a manual to help achieve success in life.

The British took soccer (football) to Argentina in the **1860s** and to Prague and Graz in the **1880s**.

1860: *Baseball* became popular in New York and Boston.

A Food and Drug Act was implemented in Britain.

1861 marked the outbreak of Civil War in America.

Britain began daily weather reports.

German corporation Krupp, founded earlier in the century to manufacture steel, began arms production in 1861.

The U.S. *passport system* started.

The *speed of light* was successfully measured in **1862**.

Earth's *currents* were discovered.

The idea for the Red Cross was introduced in Switzerland.

Paper dress patterns came into use in **1863**.

The National Academy of Sciences was founded.

London began building the *underground*.

Free city mail delivery was established by U.S. Congress.

The Travelers Insurance Company was founded in Hartford, Connecticut.

America was introduced to roller skating.

Baseball's first base was stolen.

Pasteurization for wine was introduced in **1864**.

The Geneva Convention established the neutrality of military hospitals.

In God We Trust appears on U.S. coins.

American Admiral David Farragut exclaimed, "Damn the torpedoes! Full speed ahead!"

Joseph Lister introduced the concept of *antiseptic surgery* in **1865**.

The *ice machine* was invented.

The Massachusetts Institute of Technology (MIT) was founded.

Gregor Mendel expounded his *law of heredity.*

The first U.S. *oil pipeline* was laid.

The first *carpet sweeper* was used.

The Ku Klux Klan was founded.

Pullman sleepers are introduced.

A train was held up for the first time in the U.S.

Chicago's Union stockyards opened.

1866 was the year of the invention of *dynamite* by Alfred Nobel.

Charles Ives was born in **1874**. He anticipated many of the developments of modern music in the twentieth century, including the use of popular music mixed with sophisticated dissonance.

Japanese art was introduced to the West at the Paris World Fair in **1877**.

A diamond field was discovered in South Africa.

In **1868**, a skeleton of Cro-Magnon man was found in France.

The Suez Canal opened in **1869**.

Britain abolished *debtors' prisons*.

In Austria, *postcards* were introduced.

Jules Verne published *Twenty Thousand Leagues Under the Sea*, in **1870**.

The Standard Oil Company was founded by John D. Rockefeller.

Rasputin was born in **1871**.

Through the Looking Glass was published by Lewis Carroll.

England and Wales introduced bank holidays.

Barnum's the *Greatest Show on Earth* opened in Brooklyn, New York.

The Great Fire broke out in Chicago.

Britain introduced secret balloting in **1872**.

An international soccer game was first played.

1873 saw the first development of color photos.

Production of typewriters began at E. Remington and Sons, a gunsmith firm.

Hungary united the towns of Buda and Pest to form its capital.

Germany adopted the mark as its official currency.

To treat bed sores, Neill Arnott devised a *waterbed*, used in St. Bartholomew's Hospital in London in **1873**

Winston Churchill was born in **1874**.

Staphylococci and *streptococci* were identified.

Canning foods was made easier with introduction of *pressure cooking*.

In New York, the Society for the Prevention of Cruelty to Children was founded.

Philadelphia opened the first American zoo.

Tennis was introduced to America.

Mark Twain's *The Adventures of Tom Sawyer* was published in **1875**.

Prussia abolished religious orders.

London's Medical School for Women was founded.

Albert Schweitzer was born.

Matthew Webber was the first officially to swim the English Channel, from England to France. Not until **1923** did Enrico Tiraboschi become the first to swim it in the other direction.

Queen Victoria was proclaimed Empress of India in **1877**.

Giovanni Virginio Schiaparelli observed the *canals of Mars*.

Wimbledon held its first championship tennis match.

Public telephones became operable in the U.S.

Europe received first shipments of *frozen meat*, from Argentina.

In **1878**, historian Heinrich Treitschke promoted an anti-semitic movement in Germany as part of his support of authoritarian politics.

Bicycles were manufactured in the U.S.

David Hughes invented the *microphone*.

London introduced *electric street lights*.

Joseph Stalin was born in **1879**.

Leon Trotsky was born.

In the **1880s**, Cecil Rhodes

gathered smaller *diamond companies* into his South African De Beers Consolidated Mines.

Helen Keller was born in **1880**.

Uncle Remus was published.

The *malarial parasite* was discovered.

Bingo was created.

Japan formed political parties in **1881**.

Russia persecuted Jews.

The Vatican archive opened to scholars.

The first U.S. Lawn Tennis Championship was held.

In **1882**, Chinese immigrants were banned from the U.S. for ten years.

The Hague Convention established a three-mile limit for territorial waters.

Sigmund Freud used *hypnosis* to treat *hysteria* in Vienna.

A patent was given to the *recoil machine gun*.

The American Baseball Association was organized.

Synthetic fiber was produced in Britain in **1883**.

Anthrax inoculation was described.

Chicago built the first *skyscraper*—10 stories.

New York's Brooklyn Bridge opened to traffic.

Johannesburg, South Africa, booms with the discovery of gold in the Transvaal in **1884**.

Mormons split into polygamous and monogamous sects in **1885**.

The individuality of *fingerprints* was established.

Golf was introduced to America

Karl Marx's *Das Kapital* was published in English in **1886**.

The Statue of Liberty was dedicated.

Auguste Rodin created *The Kiss*.

1888, America's Football League was founded.

The *Financial Times* launched in London.

Belgium held the world's first beauty contest.

1889, Adolph Hitler was born. Charlie Chaplin was born.

Japan held its first general election in **1890**.

Charles de Gaulle was born.

The first *moving-picture* was shown in New York.

Rubber gloves were used for the first time in surgery.

Influenza outbreaks took place on a global scale.

The Daughters of the American Revolution were founded.

In **1891**, Henri Toulouse-Lautrec created music hall *posters*.

Russia experienced widespread famine.

An *early zipper,* called a *slide fastener,* was invented by Whitcomb L. Judson.

The *escalator* began as a ride at Coney Island. It was devised as a steam-driven machine in **1892** by Jesse Reno and appeared at the amusement park three years later. Commercial use came a few years later, through the Otis Elevator Company.

Scotsman James Dewar, a chemist and physicist, invented the first *thermos* in **1892**, in experiments with liquid hydrogen and oxygen.

Ta-ra-ra-boom-de-ray was sung for the first time in an English music hall in **1892**.

In **1883**, Karl Benz constructed his four-wheel car.

Britain introduced an inheritance tax in **1894**.

Cuba fought Spain for independence, in **1895**.

Pyotr Tchaikovsky's ballet *Swan Lake* was performed in its entirety for the first time, in St. Petersburg.

Wilhelm Conrad Röntgen discovered *X-rays*.

Guglielmo Marconi invented *radio telegraphy*.

King Camp Gillette invented the *safety razor*.

The first modern Olympic Games were held in Athens in **1896**. The first winter games were held in **1924**.

Prospectors were off on the start of the Klondike *gold rush*.

In **1897**, the *electron* was discovered.

Ernest Hemingway was born in **1898**.

An *airship* designed by Ferdinand, Graf von Zeppelin, was built. The first trial flight was in **1900**.

The Paris Métro opened.

1899 witnessed the first magnetic recording of sound.

The Commonwealth of Australia was created in **1900**.

Excavations in Crete uncover the Minoan culture.

A dance called the *cake walk* became fashionable.

Oil was first drilled in Persia, modern Iran, in **1901**.

1902 was the date of the first recording by opera star Enrico Caruso. The first recording of a complete opera, Giuseppe Verdi's *Ernani*, occurred the following year.

An early version of an Aswan Dam opened. In **1970**, a modern dam was opened to great fanfare.

French chemist and inventor Georges Claude developed the *neon light* in **1902**.

The periscope was invented by Simon Lake in **1902** for American submarines. It was much improved for the British by Irishman Howard Grubb, whose family factory made high-quality telescopes.

The U.S. was first crossed coast-to-coast by car in **1903**.

The Tour de France began.

The first after-season baseball series took place.

Music was first transmitted via *radio* in **1904**.

The first *ultraviolet lights* were made.

Digging on the Panama Canal began.

Photographs were transmitted by *telegraph*.

New York's Hudson River *tunnel* was dug, for trains.

Trench warfare was used in the Russo-Japanese war.

The first regular cinema established in **1905**.

London has its first *motor buses*.

Neon lights appeared.

Theodore Roosevelt became the first American president to travel outside the U.S. during his term.

The term *allergy* was created.

The Grand Prix *motorcar race*

started its engines.

The *two-way mirror*, or transparent mirror, was invented by Emil Bloch and patented in the U.S. in **1906**.

In **1907**, Eugene Schueller invented synthetic *hair dye* in France and called it *Aureole*, or *halo*, and it eventually became L'Oreal.

Mr. Mutt; first daily comic strip debuted. It later became *Mutt and Jeff*.

Berlin built the first steel and glass building, in **1908**.

Bakelite was manufactured in **1909**, ushering in the Plastic Age.

Permanent waves were given ladies in London.

Weekend became a popular concept in the U.S.

The individual U.S. *federal income tax* began in **1913**. A corporate tax had been imposed four years earlier.

George Bernard Shaw's play, *Pygmalion*, was produced.

The first woman magistrate was sworn in, in London.

Successful *heart surgery* was performed on a dog in **1914**.

Paramount Pictures was created. Its stars will soon include Rudolph Valentino, Clara Bow, and Gloria Swanson. The same year, Charlie Chaplin appeared in Mack Sennet's Keystone film, *Making a Living*.

The first *fighter plane* was constructed in **1915**, during World War I.

The first *transcontinental telephone call* is made.

A book on *birth control* results in the author jailed. The following year, the first birth control clinic opens in New York.

Motorized *taxis* arrive.

In **1916**, the first *sneakers*, Keds, were marketed, as a result of the development over 25 years of rubber-soled shoes.

Daylight savings time starts in Britain.

Jazz recordings debuted in **1917**. Women *bobbed* their hair.

Czar Nicholas II of Russia abdicated and the Duma named a provisional government. By the end of the year, the Czar and his family had been executed, and Russia had become one of the Union of Soviet Socialist Republics.

Women over 30 got the vote in Britain in **1918**.

The first showing of Joan Miro's work occurred.

Daylight savings time was put in place in the U.S.

The year saw the first delivery of *airmail* between Chicago and New York.

1919 marked the first nonstop flight across the Atlantic.

A British woman was elected a Member of Parliament for the first time.

In the U.S. the Nineteenth Amendment gave the vote to women.

The true structure of the Milky Way was observed in **1920**.

A regular *radio program* was transmitted in the U.S. in **1921**.

In **1922**, *insulin* was first administered to diabetics.

A *birth control clinic* opened in **1923** in New York.

The U.S.S.R. established a station at the North Pole.

A *liquid fuel rocket* was fired in **1926**.

The first 16mm *movie film* was produced.

Crop dusting by airplane began in **1927**.

The first *vehicular tunnel* opened in New York City, the Holland Tunnel.

Charles Lindbergh flew solo across the Atlantic Ocean. The next year Ameila Earhart crossed as a passenger, and flew solo in **1932**.

1928 gave rise to the first scheduled *television* broadcasts. *Color motion pictures* arrived.

The term *apartheid* was formulated in **1929**.

The U.S.S.R. began its first *five-year plan* in **1930**.

The *photoflash bulb* was invented.

The northface of the Matterhorn was conquered.

Cellophane tape was invented.

Franklin Delano Roosevelt (FDR) coined the term *New Deal* in **1932**. The program for economic relief during the Great Depression was in place from **1933** to **1939**.

Unemployment insurance was enacted in Wisconsin.

The Nazis erected concentration camps in **1933**.

Positrons were discovered.

The first boycott of the businesses of Jews took place in Germany.

Plastic wrap, or Saran, was discovered and developed in **1933** by Ralph Wiley, who worked for Dow chemicals. In **1956**, it was deemed safe for use in wrapping foods.

Road reflectors, called *cat eyes* by their British inventor Percy Shaw, came into being in **1934**.

FDR signed the first Social Security Act in **1935**.

An *artificial heart* was invented in **1936**.

A *transcontinental radio program* was broadcast in **1937**.

The *ballpoint pen* was invented in **1938** in Hungary by journalist Laszlo Biro.

Remarkable examples of *prehistoric art* were discovered in France's Lascaux Caves in **1940**.

The first successful helicopter flight in the U.S. took place.

The *automatic computer* was developed in the U.S. in **1942**.

The year also saw the first American all-star bowling tournament.

In **1944** came a nonstop flight between Canada and London.

Newman Darby developed the *sailboard*, in **1948**. The first patent wasn't issued until **1968**, however, to two Californians who dubbed it a Windsurfer.

In **1951**, *color television* was introduced in the U.S.

A link between weather and *death rate* was first posited and published in **1952**.

The first *computer game* with graphics, tic-tac-toe, was developed at Cambridge University in **1952**. The first *video game* followed in **1958**, a tennis game devised at Brookhaven National Laboratory. Spacewar! followed in **1962**. The first to be played on a television, in **1967**, was Chase. The first *arcade game* was **1971**'s Computer Space, a permutation of Spacewar!

Links between smoking and lung cancer began to become clear in **1953**.

Newport, Rhode Island, held its first annual Jazz Festival in **1954**.

The *solar battery* or *cell* was invented. It was based on the discovery that when sunlight hits silicon a large quantity of free electrons results, and can be turned into electrical energy. Today, solar cells run everything from calculators to satellites.

Tetracycline, which became the most widely prescribed antibiotic in the U.S., was invented in **1955** by Lloyd Conover.

The U.S.S.R. launched Sputnik I and II, the first satellites, into space in **1957**.

Stereophonic recordings were the latest technology in **1958**.

Parking meters appeared in London.

Life peerages were first conferred in Britain.

Gordon Gould began to build the first optical *laser* (Light Amplification by the Stimulated Emission of Radiation) in **1958**.

The *snowmobile* was designed by Joseph-Armand Bombadier, in **1958**, although a related earlier snow vehicle was patented in **1921**.

In **1959**, the U.S. launched a nuclear-powered merchant vessel.

In **1960**, the U.S. launched a weather satellite.

The same year came the first underwater *circumnavigation* of the globe.

Alan Shepard was the first American in *space flight*, in 1961.

A hotline between the U.S. and U.S.S.R. was proposed in **1963**.

An artifical heart was used to cleanse blood during surgery. The first human heart transplant happened in **1967**.

1965 saw the first flight around the world over both poles.

France joined the space race and launched a satellite.

The techniques of *gas chromatography* advanced.

People's Republic of China exploded a hydrogen bomb in **1967**.

After many years and much controversy, the first U.S. troops were withdrawn in the war in Vietnam in **1969**.

Humans landed on the moon.

The SST Concorde was tested.

The battery-operated, home *smoke detector* was patented in **1969**.

The first complete synthesis of a gene was accomplished in **1970**.

Swiss women were at last granted the right to vote in **1971**.

The *New York Times* published the Pentagon Papers and the complexities of the Watergate crisis had begun.

For the first time, a woman athlete, Billie Jean King, earned $100,000 in a single year.

A shortage of petroleum products first was seen as possible in the U.S. in **1972**.

In **1973**, Tom Bradley became the first black mayor of Los Angeles, a city that was primarily white.

Frank Robinson became the

first black to manage a major league baseball team in **1974**.

▨ **1975** saw the first U.S. strike by physicians.

Sarah Caldwell became the New York Metropolitan Opera's first woman conductor.

▨ Detailed radar observations of Venus' surface were made in **1976**. Viking I and II sent back close-up photos of Mars' surface.

The Concorde, a *supersonic passenger flight*, was inaugurated.

The first of South Africa's black homeland attained independence.

U.S. vice-presidential debates took place for the first time.

The Ebla civilization in northern Syria—4,400 years old—was discovered.

▨ **1977** saw a woman ordained as a priest in America's Episcopal Church.

The structure of the sun's magnetic field was determined.

▨ The first *test-tube baby* was born in England in **1978**.

A pope visited a Communist country for the first time.

▨ A giant panda was born in captivity for the first time in **1980**.

A woman ran the mile in under four and a half minutes.

▨ In **1981**, fish were cloned by Chinese scientists.

The maiden voyage of the space shuttle *Columbia* took place.

Sandra Day O'Connor became the first woman appointed to the U.S. Supreme Court.

▨ The *STM* (scanning tunneling microscope) was invented in **1981** by Gerd Binnig and Heinrich

Rohrer. It provides images of metal surfaces at atomic levels.

▨ **1982**, a female priest first preaches in Canterbury Cathedral, England.

▨ Ronald Reagan spoke of the Evil Empire in **1983**, referring to the Soviet Union.

First U.S. woman went into space.

A woman became Lord Mayor of London.

An artificial chromosome was created.

The first compact disc was made.

A fossil of a land mammal was discovered in Antarctica.

▨ **1984** brought the first production of a Handel opera at the Metropolitan Opera in New York.

▨ Catalytic converters were made in **1985**.

A general election first took place in Zimbabwe, Africa.

Lasers cleaned clogged arteries.

▨ Desmond Tutu became the first Black Archbishop of Cape Town in **1986**.

John Paul II became the first pope to visit a synagogue.

The first triple transplant—heart, lung, liver—was performed in Britain.

An American won the Tour de France.

▨ The *high-temperature superconductor* was invented in **1986** by Georg Bednorz and Alex Mueller, for IBM.

▨ **1987** saw the first-trillion-dollar budget in the U.S.

▨ An aerospace engineer named

Lonnie Johnson invented the water blaster, later named *Super Soaker,* in **1988**. Johnson was an expert in thermodynamics.

A plutonium pacemaker was implanted in **1988**.

Mikhail Gorbachev became the first Soviet leader to meet a Pope, in **1989**.

Colin Powell was the first black American to become Chairman of the Joint Chiefs of Staff.

Mysterious *crop circles* appeared in Great Britain.

Female Anglican priests were ordained in the U.K. in **1990**.

After the fall of the Soviet Union and the Berlin Wall: Romania held its first free elections. Czechoslovakia held its first free elections since World War II. Boris Yeltsin became the first elected president in Russia.

A female president was elected in Ireland.

The first human received *gene therapy*.

A *low-calorie fat substitute* was marketed.

France elected a female premier in **1991**.

The spacecraft probe *Galileo* visited an asteroid.

Carbon nanotubes were discovered.

Queen Elizabeth II became the first British monarch to address the U.S. Congress.

Carol Moseley-Braun became the First African American woman elected to the U.S. Senate in **1992**.

Janet Reno was named the first female attorney general in **1993**.

Mongolia held its first direct presidential election.

Intel Pentium chips debuted and were shipped

A complete Australopithecus afarensis skull was found in Ethiopia in **1994**.

The tunnel under the English Channel between France and Britain officially opened.

Blacks were permitted the vote for the first time in South Africa.

A solo flight across the Pacific Ocean in a balloon was successful in **1995**.

A preventive *treatment for sickle cell anemia* was announced.

In **1996**, the computer chess program Deep Blue defeated Grand Master Garry Kasparov.

Dolly the sheep, the first c*loned mammal,* was born.

The comet Hale-Bopp was observed with the naked eye.

Madeleine Albright was the first woman to appointed U.S. Secretary of State, in **1997**.

A space burial took place.

Evidence was found of frozen water on the moon in **1998**.

An anthrax vaccination was given to American soldiers in Iraq.

Ambient calculus was devised. It describes and theorizes about mobile systems.

The Earth's population first exceeded 6 billion in **1999**.

A woman crossed the Atlantic Ocean alone in a rowboat.

The same year a non-stop world trip took place in a balloon.

In Finland in **2000**, the first female president was elected.

Hilary Rodham Clinton became

the first first lady elected to United States Senate.

Survivor launched a new genre: reality TV.

■ The World Trade Center and the Pentagon were attacked by terrorists, in **2001**.

A spacecraft landed on an asteroid for the first time.

The Netherlands produced a legal document allowing same-sex couples to marry.

A blind man reached the summit of Mount Everest.

A first annual Towel Day is held in honor of Douglas Adams's *The Hitchhiker's Guide to the Universe*.

A self-contained *artificial heart* was implanted in a human patient.

A *genetic map* was completed for a laboratory mouse.

■ In **2002,** a drug was approved by the U.S. Food and Drug Administration for reducing the risk of suicidal behavior.

■ A cloned deer and cloned horse were born in **2003**.

The People's Republic of China launched a manned space mission.

SARS, an extremely contagious respiratory virus, originated in China.

■ The U.S. started fingerprinting foreign visitors in **2004**.

George Bush called for another landing on the Moon. Rovers landed on Mars, sending back pictures. Yet another craft took pictures of Saturn.

Gay couples married in San Francisco, Boston, and other locations around the U.S. The legal response was a ban on the marriages.

Sedna, a planetoid in our solar system, was discovered.

Construction began at Ground Zero in New York.

Physicist Stephen Hawking reversed his theory about black holes, coming to believe that it will be possible to obtain information from them.

Research Pitfalls & How to Avoid Them

By Paula Morrow

Nonfiction can be not only bread and butter but even chocolate cake for the professional writer. Fact-based articles provide a consistent and reliable income stream as well as an ever-growing list of credits. When editors recognize your name and trust your work, you'll find yourself increasingly in demand. Eventually, you may reach the point where it's no longer necessary to query; an editor with a specific need will contact you directly to commission an article or even a book.

Such a position must be earned, of course, and several factors contribute to this kind of writer-editor relationship. First and foremost is trust. The editor wants to know that you write well, that you meet deadlines—and above all that your nonfiction is accurate.

Editors know what they want; they also know what they don't want. The following list is an editor's-eye view of research pitfalls, top turnoffs that will lead to a form rejection, as well as remedies to help you achieve that most-favored-author status.

Lists of Facts Masquerading as an Article

Every editor says it: "Don't send me an encyclopedia article!" What does that mean? For a reliable, authoritative overview of a topic, the encyclopedia is a great place to start—a compendium of facts about your subject. Your article, however, is not the facts themselves. It's what you do with the facts.

You've identified a fascinating topic that suits an upcoming theme in one of your favorite magazines. You've visited the local library, used *Readers' Guide to Periodical Literature* (or one of its subject-specific sister indexes) to identify appropriate magazine articles, and checked out at least one recent book to read. You've done a Google search, found over a hundred websites that relate to the topic to a greater or lesser degree, and spent several hours browsing sites and downloading or printing the most pertinent pages. You've even organized your notes into a logical order or outline. Now what?

Tempting as it may be, this is not the time to start writing. Collecting excellent information is your first step. Now your job as a writer is to understand the material, process it, and come up with your own unique, focused, individual presentation.

A red flag that you may be simply repeating information you've gathered, without internalizing it, is the use of many passive verbs in your manuscript. Scholarly writing has a distinctive style, with formal vocabulary, complex sentence structure, and heavy use of passive voice. ("The subjects were divided into groups." "The results were recorded.") This works for academia—not for kids. You need to know your topic well enough to explain it in your own words in order to write about it.

Give your article a solid introduction, making clear why the information it contains is important to your targeted readers. Identify your main point. Sort through your notes and select the material that relates directly to your focus; other information, no matter how fascinating or fun, should be saved for a different article. Use appropriate transitions between thoughts. Wrap up with a logical conclusion flowing out of everything you've said. Congratulations! You have a real article.

Internal Inconsistency

One offshoot of the list-of-facts article is the internally inconsistent article. I once received a lively, appealing submission about a common but little noticed animal with a funny name and amusing habits. In discussing the creature's diet, the author called it a *vegetarian*. Two pages later in the manuscript, the animal ate an earthworm. How could this be? The obvious inference is that in consulting several sources, the author had picked up conflicting material and had failed to notice the discrepancy.

A responsible author reconciles any apparent conflicts by doing further research. If the writer can't explain the discrepancy, then the manuscript is not ready to submit. Note, though, that it's not fair to eliminate information just because it seems contradictory; your readers deserve accuracy. Sometimes it's not possible to say which of two or more conflicting sources is correct. It's better to present them both and explain that opinions differ, rather than to delete one for simplicity, resulting in an article that's misleading and possibly wrong.

Shallow Research

It's been said that a job applicant might have 10 years' experience or he might have the same year of experience 10 times. By the same token, a bibliography might have 10 sources or might have the same source 10 times. I've seen bibliographies that contain 14 or 15 references without a single authoritative, in-depth source. A profile of a historical figure accompanied by a bibliography listing 10 different biographical dictionaries (or 10 .com websites) will not inspire confidence in an editor and is not likely to result in a sale.

Thanks to interlibrary loans, researchers are no longer limited to materials accessible by mouse click or within driving distance. Online catalogues open up the world's libraries. One of the best places to start is the Online Computer Library Center, or OCLC. The resources of OCLC are searchable from your home computer (or any other location) but require an authorization code and password. Check with your local library or community college for access.

Through FirstSearch, OCLC offers seamless electronic access to dozens of databases and more than 10 million full-text and full-image articles. Underlying FirstSearch is the WorldCat database, containing 54 million records from libraries worldwide. After identifying the resources you need, make a trip to your local library, introduce yourself to the librarians, and ask them to help you obtain the materials. Lending libraries set their own policies about the materials that may be loaned, and may charge photocopying fees if you need information from noncirculating journals or books, but the value of the service is far greater than the cost.

In addition to libraries, you'll find a wealth of information by seeking out appropriate museum collections, archives, societies, and other organizations dedicated to your topic. If you're writing about nineteenth-century clothing, it's worth visiting a costume museum to examine samples. For a story featuring a printing press, make the trip to see one in action, hear the clatter, smell the ink. To complete an article about training guide dogs, interview an actual trainer and meet her dogs. Librarians, curators, and experts in the field are usually delighted to answer thoughtful, intelligent questions.

Strings of Quotes

Interviews are a great way to obtain primary source material by talking with an expert in your area of interest, a person who has traveled in the country you're investigating, or someone who has experienced a historical event you're researching. If your topic is cutting-edge, it can be valuable to interview a researcher or other expert for the most up-to-date information. Books and articles will help you identify who is currently publishing on your topic. Credible publishers include the person's affiliations in the author biography or jacket flap copy, making it easier to track down your expert.

Before requesting an interview, be sure you have prepared by reading widely on the topic—especially the works of the person to be interviewed—and that you thoroughly understand the subject. I've noticed an unfortunate trend recently: Writers who claim to be professionals will cold-contact an expert (often by email) with a list of questions. If the expert is kind enough to respond, the so-called writer then simply strings together a series of quotes and submits it as an article. It's the adult equivalent of copying an encyclopedia article and turning it in as a class report. The author never achieves any personal competence in the subject and is unable to provide any depth or integration.

The author is responsible for giving the article a clear focus. It's wise to consult more than one expert for a broader view of the subject. Be alert for differences of opinion and understand how or why they occur. Quotes always need to be set in a well-researched and clearly explained context.

Conflict of Interest

Another well-written submission I received described the history, manufacture, and success of a popular seasonal candy. Built-in child appeal? You bet! But the bibliography listed only one source: the candy company's website.

In this age of the infomercial, the line between journalism and advertising is very blurred. When writing for children, it's particularly important to be aware of hidden messages in your sources, messages that may creep into your manuscript.

Corporate websites and publications are not the only sources that should be vetted for possible bias. Many researchers have ties to commercial firms, especially in the fields of science and technology. Working for a certain company does not automatically mean the

researcher is biased, but a conscientious writer is aware of the possibility. Consulting a variety of impartial sources will yield a richer and more balanced manuscript.

Unverified Web Sources

A colleague read a manuscript that seemed like a winner. Dealing with a familiar historical character and containing little-known, surprising details, it was sure to fascinate middle-grade readers. Even the bibliography looked good: a mix of books, articles, and websites.

Still, my colleague felt uneasy for reasons she couldn't quite explain. She began tracking the sources and discovered that the unusual facts all came from a single online news article. The website was professional in appearance, but the credits were vague. Following the trail led, in a roundabout way, to a radical fringe group with a specific agenda. The editor managed to find a phone number for one of their heavily quoted "experts," interviewed him herself, and discovered that he was neither a scientist nor a historian. The "facts" quoted were theories that had subsequently been debunked by reputable researchers.

But the website looked so credible! Don't be sucked in by a slick presentation; investigate the authority of your sources. Questions to answer include:

▨ Who are the author and the publisher?
▨ What are their credentials?
▨ How comprehensive is the

coverage?

▓ Is this an impartial site or one that emphasizes paid links? Be aware that Web publishers may change policies; a formerly impartial site may switch to sponsored links.

▓ What is the original date of the information? Has it been updated? How many times? How recently? Some first-rate sites are no longer being updated, and while they contain good, reliable information, they may be lacking the most recent advances in a field.

▓ What is the historical context of the information?

▓ Can the information be verified through another reputable source?

Research advice articles sometimes claim that sites ending in .edu or .gov are reliable because they're sponsored by universities or government agencies, respectively. Even these sites need to be used judiciously. For example, an .edu address may lead to material posted by faculty members, students, members of the clerical staff—anyone associated with the university.

One science manuscript I received quoted a surprising statistic and gave a university Web address. I checked the source and sure enough, the figure had been quoted accurately. The page looked odd, though, so I worked backward from there to determine the context. As it turned out, the page was part of a university-sponsored science fair project prepared by an 11-year-old child. Elsewhere in the presentation, he explained that he couldn't find statistics he needed, so he made what he called an "educated guess."

Accepting facts without verifying them can be disastrous. Another author sent me a piece on a certain species of animal on a small island. When asked to document a statement about the animal's behavior, she phoned a naturalist on the island and learned that, in fact, that species doesn't exist on that island. Her response was to suggest simply changing the name of the species in her manuscript. She seemed genuinely surprised when I rejected the submission.

Never accept a Web page at face value; always check context. If the page includes a *home* button, click there to learn the sponsoring organization or individual of the site. Then I attempt to navigate from the home page to the cited page in order to see the intermediate steps. The site map can be useful in figuring out the trail. In the case of the science fair project, nothing on the statistical page indicated that the figures were not based on fact, but the context made this clear.

For a dense or complex site, it's not always possible to figure out the navigation from home page to cited page. In that case, I truncate the URL, dropping letters and/or numbers following the final slash to move up in the hierarchy. This doesn't always work, but I move from right to left, deleting slash by slash, until I reach a working page.

Another alternative for checking Web sources is a *whois* search: At NetworkSolutions, it's possible to learn the owner of a domain name. American Registry for Internet Numbers provides the information by IP address. Finding out who owns the site doesn't necessarily attest to its reliability, but does give a name and contact information for further investigation.

Incomplete Bibliographic References

A fact-checker must be able to find your original sources, and that means a careful, complete bibliography is imperative. Citations for print sources are fairly standard across the different style manuals available: all include author, title, publisher, date, etc. Unless your target market specifies a preferred style, it's fine to go with the manual that makes you most comfortable. Your style manual will also tell you how to cite interviews and other non-print sources.

Website references are trickier. You would never cite a magazine article source as just *Time*, without giving the article's author, title, issue date, and page numbers, yet a surprising number of writers will give an Internet citation leading only to the site's home page. An editor trying to fact-check your manuscript will follow a direct link but won't search an entire site hoping to stumble across the needed information.

While there's no one standard format for citing Internet sources,

most editors will be satisfied if you give the title of the article, the author's name (if known), and the site name and/or sponsor, as well as the exact URL and the date you accessed the page. Web content comes and goes, so you can't always put a publication date, but you're at least documenting that the page was available on the particular day you used it. For example:

Holm, Janis Butler, "Word-play on the Web." Rx for Writers, July 2, 2004. Retrieved July 15, 2004 from the Institute of Children's Literature. < http://www.institutechildrenslit.com/rx/wt08/holm.shtml >

or

Holm, Janis Butler, "Word-play on the Web." Rx for Writers. Institute of Children's Literature, July 2, 2004. < http://www.institutechildrenslit.com/rx/wt08/holm.shtml > [Accessed July 15, 2004.]

Because of the highly dynamic nature of the Internet, URLs may change without notice. Just in case the source should change or even disappear next week, print out the most important pages. If an editor contacts you to verify your source and the direct URL no longer works, you'll be able to provide backup.

Information Old or New

The best source is the most recent

one, right? Not necessarily. Much depends on the topic of your research. In general, current topics need current references, and historical articles are enriched by careful reading of period sources. However, a piece on ancient civilizations will be incomplete if the author is unaware of the latest archaeological discoveries, while an explanation of a current scientific experiment may well require reference to earlier research leading up to the present study. As a careful writer, you'll need to search *longitudinally*: Work both backward and forward from your starting point.

Go back to a reputable encyclopedia and look at the list of sources for the article on your topic. Depending on the encyclopedia, this may be at the end of the article or in a separate section in the last volume of the set. These references will lead you back to the sources used in writing the encyclopedia article, which is, after all, a summary. Books and magazine articles contain bibliographies, too, and you owe it to yourself to check them for other sources you need to consider.

Bibliographies and source lists work backward, of course, leading to material published earlier than the work in your hand. It's also important to find newer sources. The most authoritative and up-to-date information often appears in professional journals before it filters down to popular magazines. Reference works such as *Science Citation Index, Social Science Citation Index,* and *Arts and Humanities Citation*

Index allow you to look up an older article and find out where it has been cited in more recent work. In other words, you can trace subsequent research and writing on your chosen topic.

Electronic databases and Internet searching may seem like an ideal way to cover vast collections of information, but they can be misleading. When searching electronically, check just how far back the backfiles go. While libraries, museums, and research institutions routinely put new data online, retrospective conversion is another matter. Of the more than 5,000 journals available through the OCLC, for example, the majority cover issues from the nineties and later. ISI Document Solution is an online document delivery system thta offers 8,700 journal titles, with back files from 1997 to the present. For earlier materials, the serious researcher still has to use a library or archive.

Ineffective Use of the Internet

The Internet is both a blessing and a curse for the researcher. It's quick, it's easy, it's even fun to run a Web search. Using advanced searching techniques and accessing the "hidden" Web, I can find information on literally any topic. Find it, yes; trust it, not necessarily. I need to know that what I've found is reliable, current, and complete.

As you search online, be aware that the Internet consists of several layers. Most apparent is the *surface Web*, consisting of sites accessible

Sources

Library Indexes

Readers' Guide to Periodical Literature. New York: H. W. Wilson Co. Back files to 1901.

· Related indexes from H. W. Wilson Company include:
Applied Science & Technology Index
Art Index
Biological & Agricultural Index
Business Periodicals Index
Education Index
General Science Index
Humanities Index
Index to Legal Periodicals
Social Sciences Index

Science Citation Index Expanded. Philadelphia: Institute for Scientific Information. Back files to 1945.

Social Sciences Citation Index. Philadelphia: Institute for Scientific Information. Back files to 1956.

Arts and Humanities Citation Index. Philadelphia: Institute for Scientific Information. Back files to 1975.

Online Search Tools

American Registry for Internet Numbers: http://www.arin.net

First Search, OCLC Online Computer Library Center: http://www.oclc.org/firstsearch/

Search Engine Watch: http://www.searchenginewatch.com/

through standard search tools such as Google. Other layers are more difficult to access.

The *shallow Web* contains sites that could be indexed but aren't, due to some idiosyncrasy, such as an odd tag. Think of these sites as a misfiled sheet of paper in a five-drawer filing cabinet. The *hidden Web* or *invisible Web* has sites that are not indexed because they are not known—for example, good sites that aren't linked anywhere. Finally, the *deep Web* consists of information buried below the threshold of a standard search tool. These may be sites with secure access such as a firewall, authentication code, or password. They may also be sites in nonstandard formats; many search engines do not index PDF files, for example. Searching only on the surface Web may return hundreds or even thousands of hits, but the re-

Sources

Search Engine Showdown: http://www.searchengineshowdown.com/
Document Solution: Thomson Scientific, 2004. http://www.isinet.com/journals/
Whois: Network Solutions: http://www.networksolutions.com/en_US/whois/index.jhtml

Online Articles

Note: Article links often change. In case of a bad link, use the publication's search facility, which most have, and search for the headline.

Sullivan, Danny. "Invisible Web and Database Search Engines." Search Engine Watch, February 20, 2002. http://www.searchenginewatch.com/links/article.php/2156181 [Accessed July 27, 2004.]

"Top 4 Top Places to Search the Invisible Web: Guide Picks." About.com, Primedia, Inc. http://websearch.about.com/od/invisibleweb/ [Accessed July 26, 2004.]

Tortorella, Dawne. "Research Engines and the Hidden Web." BellCow, Inc., April 6, 2003. http://www.bellcow.com/search.html [Accessed July 7, 2004.]

Tyburski, Genie. "Get Smart About Web Site I.Q." Search Engine Watch, April 4, 2002. http://searchenginewatch.com/searchday/article.php/34711_2159621. [Accessed July 15, 2004.]

sults will not be the most complete or reliable information.

Growing in popularity are *blogs*, or *weblogs*, which offer quick commentary or information. In checking the references for a manuscript on an unusual travel article, I found a fascinating first-person account online. The material intrigued me, and I continued searching beyond the references in the article. Soon I discovered that same story repeated on four other sites and attributed to four different authors, each of whom claimed to have experienced it firsthand.

Before accepting online information as fact, evaluate the source. You'll find it worthwhile to check out a site such as Search Engine Watch or Search Engine Showdown, both of which provide industry news and review different search engines. Links to services that search the invisible Web may be found at several sites, including Search Engine Watch and About. com.

When searching invisible Web directories, it's important to determine the selection process for including each resource, whether the resource is reviewed or evaluated, and the targeted consumer of the directory listing. This allows you to select sources appropriate to your specific purpose.

The Good News

Editors are seeing a lot of quick and easy research that's superficial and, frankly, suspect in many cases. We urge authors to overcome their shyness or inexperience or whatever holds them back and get out there to do the necessary legwork. It may seem like extensive effort (which it is), but research can produce more than one article, which makes the time and effort worthwhile. It also builds credibility with editors, and believe me, that writer will be nurtured as a most-favored author.

Kids' Culture: Finding Clothing & Toys to Bring Your Story to Life

By Sue Bradford Edwards

Boy Scout equipment from 1935. A pickle board from colonial America. Decorations on the clothes of the Plains Indians. A toy train in 1888 Scotland. The first set of Legos. And where can you locate a doll from Missouri in the year 1910?

Textual primary sources mention children's hobbies, toys, and clothes, but seldom go into detail about them, the kind of detail that brings them to full life. This was the problem for Deborah Heiligman while researching *High Hopes: A Photobiography of John F. Kennedy.* "We have a picture of the letter Kennedy wrote his father asking for a raise," she says. "He asked for the raise to buy more Boy Scout equipment." While the letter stated Kennedy's hope to purchase scouting equipment with an increase in his allowance, it didn't give any details. If Heiligman needed to know specifically what the equipment looked like, she would have to go elsewhere to locate an image.

Fortunately, many useful images can be found online. "In my view, it's okay to use all online sources if an extensive bibliography is included," says Rosanne Tolin, Editor of the ezine *Guideposts for Kids Online.* "So much info is found on the Web now, that if it's from a reliable source, hard copy data isn't always necessary. That's because much hard copy data has been put in Web format, like *Britannica* online or other trusted periodicals." From historic photographs and etchings to photographs of toys, clothing, and other artifacts, a wealth of data is available to the researcher who knows how to find it.

Think Globally

Sometimes locating a specific image is as easy as using a search engine such as Yahoo or Google. "I would first go to a search engine," says Senior Editor Summer Dan Laurie of Tricycle Press.

This was how Heiligman found the Kennedy letter as well as many of the other images she referenced in studying her topic. She *googled*

"John F. Kennedy" and found some 2,020,000 sites. While this is daunting but doable in the early stages of research, it is more than a writer wants to go through to fill in a detail about a doll in chapter three. That is when a focused search comes into play.

One way to focus is to search only for visual images. To select an image search on Google, click images above the space where the search term is entered. To do this in a Yahoo search, start at the main search page and choose the *Images* tab instead of the preselected *Web* tab. A sample search on Yahoo for "historic toys" turned up 109 images including dolls, dollhouses, and tractors. Many of these were images from dealers and collectors but also obvious were the more desirable URLs from several historical societies and museums.

Image searches such as the one on Yahoo don't locate every online image so it is often necessary to find a searchable database to give your child character a particular doll, toy airplane, or picture their clothing in your mind. "The Library of Congress website is also a fantastic resource for all things historical," says Laurie.

National museums with extensive collections online may have what you need. Check the Library of Congress' American Memory Collection (memory.loc.gov/) and the Smithsonian National Museum of American History (americanhistory.si.edu/ scienceservice/012046.htm).

What types of images can you find at these sites? A quick search of the American Memory collection for "children" and "1880s" brought 500 results. This listing included photographs of a boarding school, a Yakama group standing on a porch, a child holding an alligator, and children riding burros outside of Santa Fe—each group of children wearing clothing specific to their culture and place.

Five hundred images are a lot to pick through while looking for something specific. Searches can be broadened or narrowed to yield more or less information as needed. A search on "toys" in the American Memories collection turned up everything from dolls to airplanes, farm equipment, board games, and cradle boards. Use such a broad search when more specific searches like "tin toys" or "tops" bring no results.

Act Locally

Unfortunately, relying on national online collections has drawbacks in the eyes of some editors. "If you go only with what is online, such as at the Library of Congress, you will get only what other people have likely used," says Carolyn Yoder, Editor of Calkins Creek, a new line of books from Boyds Mills Press that focuses on history. To offset this, Yoder suggests, you might need to visit the museum or library. Or search for museums or historical societies in the area in which the story is set.

Looking at such locally specific sites can help with another potential problem. A photograph may show a girl in dress common to the 1870s, but will it be the correct costume for your setting? If you are looking for what a child in Arizona might be wearing in 1887, this might vary from what a child in Missouri or New Hampshire would be wearing in 1888. Ethnic, religious, economic, and environmental factors all played a role in what clothing children wore and what toys they might have had. Solve this problem by visiting sites for institutions with a geographic specialization (Arizona history) or with a specialization in a certain artifact (mechanical banks or dollhouses). To find these sites requires more time and energy, but can be worth the effort when you find a donkey cart played with by a boy in the same location and time as your story.

Mine Historical Periodicals

Still can't find a clear enough photograph of a child in play clothing from 1912? Or an appropriate museum display? Turn to historical periodicals online. After all, editors look for a variety of resources in bibliographies. "I like to see a mix of websites and books, magazines, and periodicals, etc.," says *Wee Ones* Editor Jennifer Reed. With more and more periodical data available online, researchers can consult even these sources from home.

Some magazines have already been mined for what you need and the findings organized into a coherent site. "Dressing Baby" (www.history. rochester.edu/ godeys/readers/ kh/db-1850 /index.htm), which features Victorian children's clothing, contains information pulled from issues of *Godey's Lady's Book*, a Victorian women's magazine.

Treat these sources as you would print sources, however. Just reworking or rewording information doesn't make for a unique interpretation and does come across as secondhand. "We used to rail against authors submitting bibliographies with encyclopedia entries or other children's books only," says *Cricket* Executive Editor Deborah Vetter. "We now feel a need to add Internet research to that list. Even with extensive secondary sources from online locations, writers should dig deeper, seeking out primary, firsthand, material."

Seek out archived periodicals to supplement websites based on periodicals. Search for archived publications either by name (*Godey's Lady's Book*) or by searching for "historical

311

periodicals." If you search for "historical magazines" you will likely find magazines that discuss topics of interest to history buffs.

Many of the searchable databases of historical periodicals are fully available to subscribers only, although some, such as Newspaper Archive (www.newspaperarchive.com) and Historical Newspapers (www.classicnewspapers.com), have free trial periods. Though useful for an immediate search, these databases are unavailable for repeat viewing.

Others, such as Archiving Early America (www.earlyamerica.com) and the Olden Times (www.theoldentimes.com) are always free. Some articles are accompanied by photographs or other images while others are not. The very best are the scanned images of pages. If you are lucky enough to locate such a newspaper from an appropriate time and place, check advertising, which may include line drawings of clothing or toys. These are the same goods that parents of that time would have considered for their children.

Answered Questions

If you find an image but are uncertain whether this particular yo-yo or woolen coat was available within the area in which your story or article is set, you may need to find someone who does know. Contact someone from an appropriate local museum or historical society. "You can call them up. Supplement with personal contact," says Yoder. "It's not hard

to contact experts. Most of them are eager to share their knowledge and present children with the most accurate and fair information. Personal contacts are often the best research. I'm impressed if a bibliography includes expert reviews and contacts."

Either call or email using the contact information from their website. If you can refer them to a URL from another site such as the Library of Congress, they could visually verify that the item in question is similar to something from their own collection.

Fran Kennedy had to make inquiries to verify information for *The Pickle Patch Bathtub*. She started out online. "I went to look at cucumbers and pickles and found factories. I found an advertisement to tell how they were made throughout history." But Kennedy had a girl in rural Missouri growing cucumbers for pickles: What tools would this child have been using? Would the pickle board be the same? She found experts still using these techniques. "I contacted the Amish community," Kennedy said. "I called a restaurant." An expert can also describe how a game was played, how a particular toy was constructed, or when a song became popular.

If you are willing to take the time to look up a last detail online, take the time to back up what you have found. The necessary email or phone call may take a little longer but it is worth the effort. Such a search, even if time-consuming, may yield the doll that would have

Where to Start

From clothing to sheet music, many details necessary to recreate a child's world are available online. Here is a sampling of databases available to research last-minute facts on children's culture.

General Sites
American Memory Collection: memory.loc.gov
Digital representations of more than 7 million primary sources dealing with American history and culture found within the Library of Congress's collections.
Art Resource: www.artres.com/c/htm/Home.aspx
Worldwide fine art photo archive.
Picture History: www.picturehistory.com
Archive of images and film sponsored by the Kohlberg Foundation.

Toys
Smithsonian National Museum of American History: americanhistory.si.edu/ scienceservice/012046.htm
La Porte County Historical Society Museum, Antique Toy Collection: www.lapcohistsoc.org/oldtoys.htm
Collection found in La Porte, Indiana.
The Delaware Toy and Miniature Museum: www.thomes.net/toys
Collection includes dollhouses, dolls, and boats.
Evans Toy Museum: www.evanstoys.com
Evans Toy Store and Farm Toy Museum, Stover, Missouri.
Toy and Miniature Museum of Kansas City: www.umkc.edu/tmm/index.html
Mechanical Bank Collectors of American: www.mechanicalbanks.org/index.html
The Mego Museum: www.megomuseum.com
Graphic site on Mego Corporation action figure toys from the 1970s.
Marx Toy Museum of Glendale, West Virginia: www.marxtoymuseum.com
Images range from Rock 'Em Sock 'Em Robots to a world of miniatures set on farms and in the Wild West, and Army toys.
Marvin's Marvelous Mechanical Museum: www.marvin3m.com
Private museum of coin-operated toys and oddities.

continued

Where to Start

Children's Clothing

Just the Arti-FACTS:
www.chicagohs.org/AOTM/Jan98/jan98artifact.html
Sponsored by the Chicago Historical Society.

Boy's Historical Clothing: www.histclo.hispeed.com/intro.html
Private site that, while accurate, frequently requests "memberships" and donations.

Dressing Baby, Victorian Children's Clothing:
www.history.rochester.edu/godeys/readers/kh/db-1850/index.htm
Materials from *Godey's Lady's Book*.

18th Century Children's Clothing:
www.colonialwilliamsburg.com/history/clothing/children/index.cfm

Northampton Museum, Boot and Shoe Collection:
www.northampton.gov.uk/museums/Collections/Boot_and_Shoe/Boot
_and_Shoe.htm
International exhibit with a variety of photographic images. Not searchable.

Traditional Korean Clothing:
www.lifeinkorea.com/culture/clothes/clothes.cfm

Victorian and Edwardian Children:
www.costumegallery.com/virgini3.htm
Sponsored by The Costume Gallery.

Children's Garments: dept.kent.edu/museum/exhibit/kids/1750.htm
Sponsored by Kent State University.

Music

Popular Songs in American History: www.contemplator.com/america
Sound files (Musical Instrument Digital Interfaces or Midis) of actual songs.

Historic American Sheet Music:
lcweb2.loc.gov/ammem/award97/ncdhtml/hasmhome.html
Part of the Library of Congress' American Memory Collection.

KIDiddles: www.kididdles.com/mouseum/traditional.html
Lyrics to 2,000 children's songs, including those under the *traditional* subject category.

Where to Start

Historical Periodicals

Newspaper Archive: www.newspaperarchive.com
Offers a trial subscription.

Historical Newspapers: www.classicnewspapers.com
Offers a trial subscription.

Paper of Record, Newspapers:
www.paperofrecord.com
Subscription required.

The Toronto Star, **Pages of the Past:** thestar.pagesofthepast.ca
Subscription required.

Archiving Early America: www.earlyamerica.com
Free.

The Olden Times: www.theoldentimes.com
Free.

been the perfect birthday present complete with a little girl dressed up to receive her. And it is all based on visual data from times past either in the form of historic photographs or more recent photographs of modern museum collections. Primary data that editors seek.

Research & Science Writing

By Ellen Macaulay

I'm the first to admit that I'm an unlikely science writer. Outside of a fairly moldy psychology degree, I don't have a science background. Plus, when I have had something scientific published, something for children no less, I'm not even any good at explaining to people what it is I just wrote about. ("What's your latest article about, Ellen?" "Rainbows." "Really, how do rainbows form anyway?" "Um, well, they kind of, um . . . ") It can be downright embarrassing!

You don't have to be a science whiz to write science. If you can write for children, then, you can write science for children too. You just have to be a good researcher.

Specific Angle

I started my science writing career querying editors regarding articles on animals with bad public relations—sharks, wolves, snakes, you know the type. Quite a few editors were interested, as long as the article had some kind of special *thread* to it. For the most part, editors don't want a general, all-about-something-or-other article. They want a focused article with a specific angle, as evident in this succinct *Highlights for Children* guideline: "Focused articles are more successful than broad factual surveys."

My comparison of a real life wolf to the fictional one in "Little Red Riding Hood" was the specific angle of a cover article published by *Child Life*. The specific angle of my *Disney Adventures* piece on snakes was more subtle, but it was there. It was: "I'm going to tell you about dangerous snakes through the people actually involved in studying and handling these snakes." I have discovered that this one-on-one, up close and personal approach is more often than not the specific angle for science pieces.

Focus is the key to successful nonfiction. But it's not only your writing that needs to be focused; your research does too. Suppose you're interested in writing an article about electricity. That's a big subject to tackle, so you decide to write about a type of electricity—lightning. All of a sudden your research task is much less daunting. But you narrow your focus even more. Perhaps the piece is about how to tell how close lightning is striking during a storm. There's where you want to focus your research. You will find that you save considerable time and aggravation if you can pinpoint what it is you're about to research.

Researching Ideas

As you've probably discovered, many magazines seek science articles. So, it must be hard work to find a good, focused idea to pitch to these magazines, right?

Some of you are going to like my first idea (on how to get an idea). Because a great idea can often come from plopping down on the couch—reading a magazine or a newspaper or watching TV or a video. Look and listen to what's going on around you in the media. You may be surprised at the extent of scientific information you will find. There are science programs like *NOVA* and those on the Discovery Channel. Animal shows like that nutty Australian guy that dangles alligators or barges in on rattlesnake nests (research, if not common sense, will reveal that that's not a good plan).

Rent a documentary. Watch the news. Suppose there's a news report on a beached whale a community is desperately trying to save. There's a focused idea right there: Why do whales beach themselves?

Magazines like *Popular Science* and books can often spark ideas. Generally, use adult sources. Peruse kids' magazines and books just to gauge the type of material being published, length, and so on.

Once you've depleted the couch potato opportunities, visit toy stores to see what cool science products they're selling these days. Ask teachers and librarians. What materials would they like to see? Talk to the kids you know. What are they interested in?

Museums, zoos, and aquariums are also available resources in most areas. But even if you live in the most isolated, rural area in the world, there's bound to be something science-related nearby. How about a dam (man-made or beaver), an interesting bridge, a breeding area (elk, bald eagles), a waterfall, a meteor hole, tornado or earthquake or other natural disaster facility, a tar pit, a hot spring, a mystery spot, an eccentric doctor, an old-timer who witnessed something weird. There's something everywhere worth writing about. Do some research in your local paper or local library and find it.

Internet to Start

Chances are once you have your fine, focused, scientific idea with kid appeal and a specific angle, you're going to start your writing research where most of us do these days—the Internet.

Now, the Internet is a wonderful tool. You can find just about anything you want—phone numbers, addresses, contacts, web pages, products, information, services, links, etc.—all related to the topic you plan on covering. Using the Internet can save you valuable time. Certainly, most nonfiction writers today couldn't live without it.

But there are definite problems with relying on a source like the Internet. Anyone at all—from a renowned scholar to a frantic teenager fudging a report—can set up a web page to present information. As a result, the information online, no matter how official looking, is fraught with errors. Trusting people repeat these errors in their own work, and the cycle continues. You will need to make sure, by checking other reliable sources, such as those listed in the sidebar, that any *facts* you get off the Internet are indeed facts.

Consider the Internet a good launching pad for your research, one of many possible launching pads, and not your sole source. Other initial possibilities include the library reference table, biographies, newspapers/magazines (old and new), TV/videos, and, of course, books. Be sure to check out the bibliographies of books you're skimming. That'll help you move ahead with your research process.

What Editors Want

You could stop there, with your initial sources. But, most likely, you will want to dig further. The amount of research necessary depends on the editor's needs of the publication you're going for. Be

forewarned: Even general interest magazines that are not specifically science or education-oriented often have stringent research requirements for science pieces.

Andy Boyles, Science Editor for *Highlights for Children,* offers an editor's perspective on research: "To write well, the author should have his or her own understanding of the subject. I can usually

tell when an author does not have such an understanding. Either the science sounds downright wrong or the author's voice changes dramatically from one paragraph to another."

It's a given that most publishers require sources that go above and beyond basic sources, such as the Internet or an encyclopedia. It also makes perfect sense. If your source is so readily available that anyone could access it, why do they need you to write the piece? (This question is one every writer should be prepared to answer no matter what they're working on.)

Get Me Mr. Rot

Editors like the reader to feel connected to the outside world. The best way to do that is to present material through the eyes of an

Getting a Scientist to Talk to You

▦ "You can't be shy about calling. That's part of being a writer. You have to say, '*Hi, I'm here!*'" says Pat Murphy, Publications Director of San Francisco's Exploratorium and a science author.

▦ Mention up front that you're writing for children. If an editor has already expressed interest in your project, mention that as well.

▦ You're coming from a position of strength because you are writing for children. Murphy says, "It's a pretty Scrooge-like character who will say: 'I don't care about the little rugrats!'"

▦ Make the meeting convenient for the interviewee's schedule, not necessarily yours. The interview can be conducted either on the phone or in person.

▦ Have all your questions prepared in advance. Don't overstay your welcome.

▦ Come to the interview prepared: Have a tape recorder with extra batteries, notepad, and camera. When I wrote an article for *Disney Adventures* article, the editor requested photos of each of the three scientists I interviewed, just for documentation purposes. I couldn't believe it when they actually used one of my shots in the magazine!

▦ Take notes while recording, as a back-up. (Writers have been known to forget to turn the machine on! No comment from me on which writers.) You *must* always inform the person that you are recording, on the phone or in person. If they object, you must turn off the recorder.

▦ Here's a little secret: Most scientists have big egos. They like to be interviewed. They like to have their work covered. They like to have

expert—a living, breathing person who knows what they're talking about. It's your job to provide the conduit, the go-between, to that person. You bring the expert to the reader. (And that's why you're the person who should write the article!)

Just as everyone, everywhere, can find a suitable idea for a science piece, everyone, everywhere, has access to an expert. Check out universities, zoos, academies, aquariums, museums, and the like.

All these institutions have educational programs, which means they have people who are knowledgeable about particular things.

Pat Murphy is Publications Director for the Exploratorium, a San Francisco museum of science, art, and human perception, and is also a writer of science and award-winning science fiction (*Adventures in Time and Space with Max Merriwell*), and my co-writer on a new children's science book, *Exploratopia*

Getting a Scientist to Talk to You

their picture taken. And, they're often competitive with other scientists. Use this little secret any way you see fit.

■ You have to work a bit harder if you don't have a science background. Have your scientist slow down or re-explain in kid terms if you don't understand something. Blame it on your readers! Because you're writing for kids, the material must be simplified.

■ Andy Boyles of *Highlights for Children* recommends, "For your own understanding, read the original scientific papers written by the scientists themselves. Try your best to understand them before the interview. The points you don't understand may lead to good questions for the interview, which reveal the care you have taken. Just about any scientist will respect the effort, and you may even end up with a better interview as a result."

■ Murphy says, "Many scientists are worried that you will get things wrong. That's a reasonable concern. People have had their research misinterpreted. It's easy for writers to get the science just a little bit wrong. To make sure this doesn't happen to you, ask your scientist if they'd be willing to review anything you write. Tell them that you'd be happy to show them the quotes to make sure you've gotten it right. That kind of assurance is often needed."

■ If you do a good job and your scientist is happy with the published piece, your scientist will most likely help you with another article or even refer you to some of their scientist friends.

(Little, Brown, 2006). She also recommends supporting your local facility: "Let's say the local museum is having an exhibit on bats. Well, bats are cool. Visit the exhibit. From there, you'll probably learn enough to write your general query. Your next step is to call the museum and find out who worked on that exhibit. There's your expert. Call that person and say, 'Hey, I want to write a kids' article on bats. Can I interview you?'"

Odyssey, for example, stresses research with experts. Its guidelines say that it is "interested in articles rich in scientific accuracy and lively approaches to the subject at hand. The inclusion of primary research (interviews with scientists focusing on current research) is of primary interest."

Highlights's guidelines also specify a preference for primary sources: "Firsthand experience or research based on consultation with experts is preferred." And: "Biographies of individuals who have made significant artistic, scientific, or hu-

manitarian contributions are strengthened by the inclusion of formative childhood experiences. Those that are rich in anecdotes and place the subject in a historical and cultural context are preferred." Boyles adds: "Interviewing an expert on the subject at hand is an excellent tool for gathering direct quotations, telling details, and anecdotes—the main things editors look for that give an article *life*."

Murphy shares a firsthand experience: "I'd advise anyone who wants to write a science article to seek out an expert in their area of interest. I love finding experts on some obscure topic. These folks don't get called often for interviews and they're usually delighted to share their knowledge with you.

"One time I was working on seeing what the weather was like in the past by looking at the rings of a tree now. I had these great pictures of logs on the forest floor that were rotting. I needed to know how long they were rotting. I searched the In-

ternet until I found probably the only expert on rotting logs. I e-mailed him and he said: 'Yeah, I'm pretty much it. I'm Mr. Rot!' I think that talking to Mr. Rot is a much better and easier way to proceed than to go to the library and check out books on the chemistry of rotting logs. That's harder to sort through and if you want to get to the original source matter, which you should, it's often difficult if you don't have a science background, and even if you do."

The Art of Extraction

A final way of working with science information is to extract from a community of information. An example is the way Murphy and I are composing *Exploratoria*. Murphy provided the science background (among many other things) and I was the official children's writer. She provided me with all the research I would need to do the writing. The Exploratorium is a renowned educational facility and, as such, they have a tremendous amount of existing, credited, published material. So, with them, I didn't have to find information or interview experts who worked in the field. Their finished articles, experiments, book excerpts, conclusions, and web pages were simply handed over to me, chapter by chapter.

But most of their material was designed for an adult audience. My job was to extract interesting stuff from all that research—topic by topic—and translate it for a kid audience. Because I had science research experience, I was used to dealing with gobs of material, most of which I would end up not using. This experience helped me extract the stuff of interest to kids, which fit the focus of the section I was working on. The point is if you show you can research effectively, it may just lead to writing jobs where you no longer have to do all the research yourself. There may be someone in your community you can team up with.

While working on the book, I was amazed at all the intriguing material we included. I boasted to my son that this was the greatest book ever written because everything possible under the sun was covered. A typical middler schooler, he had to challenge me. "What about brain freeze? You know, an ice cream headache?" Dang! That wasn't in there. I talked to Pat. And brain freeze is now in the book. Now I'm careful to say that *practically* everything is in the book.

This brain freeze episode confirmed two things for me: One, the world is an interesting place filled with wonder, all of which probably has some sort of scientific base. And two, there's always something out there in this wonderful, scientific world that you've overlooked. So there's always something to research, which means there's always something to write about.

Do your research. You can stop when you thoroughly know your topic or your focus. But, don't worry; you can never research too much. Even if you overdo it for your current needs, you can always break the research up into several pieces—here's one article, here's another, hey, here's a how-to piece, here's an activity, or if you're so inclined, sections for a future book.

If you prove yourself to be a writer who can be counted on to provide accurate, fascinating, and timely scientific information, your services will always be in demand.

Science Websites

American Library Association:
www.ala.org/parentspage/greatsites/science.html
This page of the American Library Association site provides multiple science links in specific categories (i.e., biology, chemistry, astronomy, geology, experiments, environmental).

American Museum of Natural History:
www.amnh.com
The science at New York City's American Museum of Natural History ranges from anthropology to zoology to the physcial sciences.

Bill Nye the Science Guy: www.billnye.com
A beloved science expert and TV personality makes learning fun for kids and adults. Site includes impressive graphics and sound effects.

Carnegie Science Center: www.csc.clpgh.org
A Pittsburgh museum, the Carnegie Science Center and its site are dedicated to presenting science programs to educate and inspire all ages.

Discovery Channel:
www.discovery.com
http://school.discovery.com/schrockguide/sci-tech/scigs.html
The "Web Universe" of the Discovery Channel. Search for the subjects of its science shows and follow links to such pages as its Global Education Partnership. The Discovery Channel School's Kathy Schrock Guide For Educators provides website links, lesson plans, and study starters for numerous science categories, including earth science, physics and optics, biological science, chemical science, and others.

Exploratorium: www.exploratorium.edu
San Francisco museum of science, art, and human perception. It won the Webby Award for a best science site.

Federal Resources for Educational Excellence:
www.ed.gov/free/index.html
This government site includes a page linking to science websites in such popular fields as space, paleontology, and oceanography, but also in botany, chemistry, engineering, pharmacology, and others.

Kidsastronomy: www.kidsastronomy.com
A site on space and the stars. Explore distant worlds and galaxies, play games, take free online classes.

Lawrence Livermore National Laboratory: www.llnl.gov
A U.S. Department of Energy National lab operated by the University of California at Berkeley, this facility is known for its dinosaur research.

Science Websites

Monterey Bay Aquarium Research Institute: www.mbari.org

Ocean observations, research and development, data and images are available at this site of an institute known for its shark research.

NASA: www.nasa.gov/home/index.html

Information, current events, links to websites, educational resources and centers of the National Aeronautics and Space Administration.

National Geographic Society: www.nationalgeographic.com

The website of the Society, its magazines, and programs.

National Weather Service: www.nws.noaa.gov

Information about U.S. official weather conditions, access to an Information Center, Education Outreach, and more.

National Zoo: www.nationalzoo.si.edu

Overview of the National Zoo's science, animal, and conservation programs.

Physics Central: www.physicscentral.com

The American Physical Society produces this site with weekly physics articles, photo archive, news, links, questions and answers.

Popular Science: www.popsci.com

The website of the venerable publication lists articles and numerous links related to the many branches of science.

Sandlotscience: www.sandlotscience.com

General information and demonstrations of "optical illusions and visual oddities."

Slooh: www.slooh.com

Astronomy site. "A live online astronomy experience" that provides real telescope viewings. Membership.

Smithsonian Institution: www.si.edu

A site devoted to public education and national service in the arts, science, and history.

Worldwide Science Facilities: www.cs.cmu.edu/~mwm/sci.html

This page is older, last updated in 1999, but it still has pointers to public museums around the world that emphasize interactive science education.

A Closer Look at Websites for Children's Writers

By Mary Northrup

Just type "writing for children" into your favorite search engine. Over 8 million hits! Finding information is great, but this may be too much of a good thing. Let us help you sort through those sites and give you some of the best for children's writers.

All About Writing & Publishing

Do you need good, solid information on improving your writing for current markets? How about tips on how to bolster your article sales? Do you need questions answered on how to market your book? All this and more is available on these sites, which are packed with information for novice and veteran writers.

▓ **Writing, Illustrating, and Publishing Children's Books: The Purple Crayon**
www.underdown.org/
This excellent site, well organized, and easy to use, is full of everything that children's writers need. Lots of basic information is provided, as well as advice on cover letters and queries; lists of children's books, including award-winners; and links to other sites on children's writing, children's literature, general writing sites, reference sites, and sources for images. You can even find an editor or consultant to work with you. And discover why this site is called "The Purple Crayon"!

▓ **Institute of Children's Literature**
www.institutechildrenslit.com
An abundance of writing information awaits you at this useful site, belonging to the publisher of this book. From the site menu, connect to articles that will help writers, a chatroom that features interviews with authors and editors, an open forum where you can get your questions answered, and links to the Institute's newsletter *Children's Writer,* the Writer's Bookstore, and writing contests.

▓ **Highlights Foundation**
www.highlightsfoundation.org
Highlights for Children magazine sponsors this site, with information

about its Chautauqua workshop and other sessions that can help the children's writer. In the "Writers Resources" section, find many helpful articles searchable by topic, author, or title, and written by children's writers and editors.

Kid Magazine Writers
www.kidmagwriters.com

Created specifically for children's magazine writers, this site features articles by writers, market information, interviews with editors, techniques, and market reports on specific magazines.

Publishing Central
www.publishingcentral.com

Although designed for all writers, this site contains a section on "How to Get a Children's Book Published" and links to websites connecting you to children's authors, book awards, publishers, and products. The main page contains many links to topics of interest to all writers: agents, marketing, editing, associations, and more. It also has special pages for book, magazine, and audio publishing.

Writing-world.com
www.writing-world.com/children

Find useful information presented by children's writers in articles about writing, marketing, specific genres, school visits, controversial subjects, rhyming stories, and more. Also check out the links to a variety of online resources for writers and a list of book reviewers for those writers submitting their own books for review.

Raab Associates
www.raabassociates.com

Susan Salzman Raab is founder of Raab Associates, specializing in promoting and marketing children's books. This site can help you in publicizing your children's book. The "To Market" page answers dozens of questions on public relations, working with publishers, niche marketing, sales, self-publishing, and more. Also find help on designing a website.

Writers' Periodicals

Whether you are a beginning writer or have been writing for years, you can always use information on improving your work. These online sources feature tips, interviews with writers, instruction in the craft of writing, and links that will help you as you seek to make your writing the best it can be.

SmartWriters.com
www.smartwriters.com

Choose "Writing for Children," which will take you to information that answers questions that beginning writers often have. The main site provides much information, including articles by writers on writing, links to publishers and their writers' guidelines for books and magazines, conferences, and contests. "Writing Resources" links to sites on writing, specific genres, chat, message boards, newsletters, and marketing.

The Writer Magazine

www.writermag.com

The online version of the popular print magazine offers the table of contents and teasers for the current issue and back issues. In addition, you can access news, discussions, and links. You can register to become a member, which gains you free access to articles, postings, newsletters, and market information.

▨ **Writer's Digest**

www.writersdigest.com/topics/
childrens.asp

Another popular writer's magazine, *Writer's Digest* provides a section especially for children's writing, where you can find tips and articles by children's writers. Other helpful features include links to 101 best websites, lists of books for writers (many books in general categories, but also "Writing for Children"), and a discussion forum.

Style and Grammar

If you need help with those pesky pronouns, dangling modifiers, and run-on sentences, you may want to check these out.

▨ **Big Dog's Grammar**

www.aliscot.com/bigdog

Subtitled "A barebones guide to English," this site is written from the point of view of a dog, but behind the cuteness is some serious grammar. You may even want to take the self-tests to reinforce your learning.

▨ **The Elements of Style**

www.bartleby.com/141

The full text of this classic by William Strunk, Jr., is now online to guide you in the rules of usage and composition.

▨ **Guide to Grammar and Style**

www.andromeda.rutgers.
edu/ ~ jlynch/Writing/

Written by an English professor, Jack Lynch, this guide gives you the rules—and the explanations and examples. Searching for specifics is easy; you can jump directly to whatever you are looking for in the alphabetical listing at the top of each page.

▨ **Guide to Grammar and Writing**

www.ccc.commnet.edu/grammar

In addition to the information on grammar at this website, you can find short articles on unbiased language, writer's block, tone, editing, and vocabulary building. You can even send your tough questions to "Ask Grammar."

Author Websites

Many authors create websites to provide information on their work and life for their fans and as a means of publicity. Some also offer information for aspiring writers. Valuable because they are from someone who has "made it," these tips run the gamut from where ideas originate to getting published.

General

▨ **Meet Authors and Illustrators**

www.childrenslit.com

An extensive list of links to authors and illustrators of children's literature.

▢ Yahoo! Directory of Children's Authors

dir.yahoo.com/Arts/Humanities/
Literature/Authors/Children_s

Another list containing links to numerous children's authors' home pages.

Individual sites

▢ Haemi Balgassi

www.haemibalgassi.com

Explore this site to find "Advice for Beginning Children's Writers" and "Books for Beginning Children's Writers." Her colorful, easy-to-read site is practical and personal.

▢ Judy Blume

www.judyblume.com/menu

Click on "On Writing" to read what Blume—the most recent winner of the National Book Foundation Medal for Distinguished Contribution to American Letters—has to say to those who want to write: on style, rewriting, rejection, getting published, and more. She is honest and open about the frustrations and joys of writing.

▢ Mem Fox

www.memfox.net

Just like a book, Fox's website is divided into chapters. Turn to "Chapter 5: For Writers (and Potential Writers)," where you can find out what makes a good picture book, where ideas come from, why writers write, audience, story essentials, and much more, with examples of stories.

▢ Ellen Jackson

www.ellenjackson.net

Go to the "For Writers" section to find lots of information on creating plots and characters, writing dialogue, handling rejection, conflict, setting, titles, and story hooks. Jackson's well-organized site is very easy to read, with large type.

▢ Linda Sue Park

www.lindasuepark.com

This Newbery Medal award-winner's site provides a Writing link that leads to information on writing and getting published. An interesting section is on understanding *editorese*.

▢ Aaron Shepard

http:/aaronshep.com/kidwriter/

This easy-to-navigate site provides information on all aspects of writing for children: how to write, the publishing world, books on writing and publishing for children, the business of writing for children, and links to other sites on this subject.

▢ Cynthia Leitich Smith

www.cynthialeitichsmith.com

Click on "Writing" for personal, yet solid information on a number of topics. Check out "Reading List" to find books for writers under both "inspiration" and "perspiration."

▢ Jane Yolen

www.janeyolen.com

Click on "For Writers" to find Yolen's speeches, interviews, frequently asked questions, and links.

Author of more than 200 books, she shares her views on the muse, intuition, serendipity, and the joy of writing.

Children's Literature

Children's writers should be aware of children's literature as an academic subject and as it is used in school curricula. Many sites cover these areas. Here are some of the best.

Carol Hurst's Children's Literature Site

www.carolhurst.com

This is one of those superb websites that shows up as a link on many other sites. An excellent source for teachers, it is valuable for children's writers to see how books are used in the classroom, to read reviews of recent children's books, to find information on authors and illustrators, and to keep up-to-date on professional education topics. An online newsletter is also included.

ISLMC (Internet School Library Media Center) Children's Literature and Language Arts Resources

falcon.jmu.edu/ ~ ramseyil/ childlit.htm

To discover the types of books that teachers and librarians use in their work, explore this well-stocked site, which includes book awards, reviews of books and media, authors and illustrators, book genres, and topics in language arts and literature of interest to teachers. Also find a link to an extensive list of book fairs and literary festivals.

Kay E. Vandergrift

www.scils.rutgers.edu/ ~ kvander

Vandergrift, a professor of children's literature, presents information on children's and young adult books as a scholarly study. Read about the history of the field, gender and culture in picture books, censorship, and how to combine literature with learning.

Once Upon a Time

www.bsu.edu/classes/vancamp/ ouat.html

This site, created by college professor Dr. Mary Ellen Van Camp, is a collection of links to many other sites pertaining to children's books, language, reading, libraries, authors and illustrators, and book awards, and her own courses of children's literature.

Major Publishers for Children

On their sites, many publishers provide their catalog, writers' guidelines, author information, resources for teachers, featured books, and other information pertinent to readers and authors interested in their books.

Here are some of the big ones. But almost all children's publishers have a website. To find others, simply type their name into Google or another search engine. Or find publisher's links on some of the websites included in this article.

Farrar, Straus & Giroux Books for Young Readers

www.fsgkidsbooks.com

▓ **Front Street Books**
www.frontstreetbooks.com

▓ **Harcourt Children's Books**
http://www.harcourtbooks.com/
childrensbooks/

▓ **HarperCollins Children's Books**
http://www.harperchildrens.com/
hch/

▓ **Henry Holt and Company Books
for Young Readers**
www.henryholtchildrensbooks.
com

▓ **Holiday House Books
for Young People**
www.holidayhouse.com

▓ **Houghton Mifflin Books**
www.houghtonmifflinbooks.com/
hmcochild

▓ **Hyperion Books for Children**
www.hyperionbooksforchildren.
com

▓ **Lee and Low Books**
www.leeandlow.com/home

▓ **Little, Brown & Company Books
for Young Readers**
www.twbookmark.com/children

▓ **Penguin Putnam Books
for Young Readers**
us.penguingroup.com
Click on "Young Readers."

▓ **Random House Children's Books**
www.randomhouse.com/kids

▓ **Scholastic**
www.scholastic.com

▓ **Simon & Schuster**
www.simonsayskids.com

Publishers Plus

▓ **Colossal Directory of Children's
Publishers**
www.signaleader.com/childrens-
writers

This site is exactly what it says it is: a comprehensive listing of publishers, arranged alphabetically and all providing a link to the publishers' websites. Submissions guidelines are also often available by direct link. And there's more. If you need to find an agent, an appropriate publisher, general information on writing for children and illustrating, or help in formatting a manuscript, it can all be found here. You will also want to check the list of writing reference books, some specifically for children's writers.

▓ **Publishers' Catalogues**
www.lights.com/publisher/index.
html

On this site for all writers, there is a link for children's books under "All Topics." There you can click on a publisher and be taken to their website. In addition, the site lists recommended books on publishing and writing, plus links to sites for self-publishing.

Online Bookstores

Buy the books you want for information and inspiration without leaving your spot in front of the computer. These sites enable you to search by title, author, subject, ISBN, publisher, date, and sometimes even age group and price.

- www.amazon.com
- www.barnesandnoble.com
- www.booksamillion.com
- www.booksense.com
- www.powells.com

Organizations

These professional and trade associations are influential in the publishing and education communities. On their sites you will find useful information for children's writers, including directories of members, book awards, and reviews.

- **ALAN, The Assembly on Literature for Adolescents of NCTE (National Council of Teachers of English)**
www.alan-ya.org

- **American Booksellers Association**
www.bookweb.org

- **American Library Association**
www.ala.org

- **Association of Booksellers for Children**
www.abfc.com

- **Canadian Children's Book Centre**
www.bookcentre.ca

- **Canadian Society of Children's Authors, Illustrators and Performers**
www.canscaip.org

- **Children's Book Council**
www.cbcbooks.org

- **International Board on Books for Young People**
www.ibby.org

- **International Reading Association**
www.reading.org

- **Society of Children's Book Writers and Illustrators**
www.scbwi.org

- **United States Board on Books for Young People**
www.usbby.org

At the National SCBWI Conference

By Marjorie Flathers

When Jon Scieszka, acclaimed author of *The Stinky Cheese Man* and *The True Story of the Three Little Pigs*, approached the podium at the Society of Children's Book Writers and Illustrators' (SCBWI) summer conference, he told the audience he was there to give them the secret to getting published.

"I don't know why all of you haven't already figured this out," he added, pausing dramatically while we sat on the edges of our chairs, pencils poised, eager to learn what to do. "The secret is," he said, *"Be a celebrity!"*

Laughter and knowing nods filled the room, but since this easy road to fame and fortune wasn't an option for most us who had signed up for the thirty-third annual conference, the speakers, workshops, panels, consultations, and related events offered during those four days were the next best thing.

Children's writers at all levels— multi-published, newly published, and wannabe published—gathered in Los Angeles at the Century Plaza hotel, where there was something for everyone. This pricey hotel is one of the few that can accommodate such a large group. Factor in the food and tuition fees and a struggling writer needs to weigh the advantages against the amount spent. This year, nearly 1,000 SCBWI members from around the country and the world decided that the advantages were important and they attended to obtain the ideas and insights that could help them towards success in children's literature.

The conference presents successful writers and illustrators giving how-to-do-it advice, agents seeking clients, and editors and publishers offering expertise and tips. Often, agents and those editors whose houses are closed to unsolicited or unagented submissions will accept manuscripts from writers who have attended the SCBWI conference.

Tears & Elan

This year's meeting began on a somber note. Well-loved children's author Paula Danziger had recently passed away, and Friday evening, the first night of the conference, a tribute to her was held. Amid tears and personal reminiscences of this unique woman and her very popular books, members said a fond and final farewell.

The format of the conference is divided between the main sessions, which touch on a variety of topics, and breakout sessions, divided into tracks for beginners, professionals, illustrators, and general interest. Danziger had been scheduled as a presenter, and Bruce Coville took her place at the last moment. He rose to the occasion with élan.

"The way to make a good story a great one," Coville said, "is to give your character a moral dilemma and have him or her make the right choice, the tough choice." Since, Coville said, most stories revolve around desire meeting obstacle (who wants what and why they can't have it), how this problem is fixed should be described by the writer "so clearly that the reader must pay attention." He added, "The perfect ending to a book should be inevitable, yet a surprise." His words received a standing ovation.

David Levithan, Editor of the PUSH imprint at Scholastic Books, began his remarks by listing classic *teen lit* (a term he prefers to *young adult*) authors, including S. E. Hinton, Judy Blume, and Robert Cormier. He stated that anyone who is attempting to write in this field should begin by reading their works, in addition to looking through teen magazines and watching movies and TV geared to this age group.

Levithan said he considered "the Eighties and Nineties a dead phase in this genre, but today we are in the golden age of teen lit," and that this is a good market for anyone who can write the cutting-edge stories teens want. He also cautioned that "at present, the picture book market is saturated," and few books of this type by new authors are being accepted.

Jodi Reamer, Writer's House agent, noted that two elements are necessary in a successful manuscript: "engaging characters and a strong voice." She added that she is open to any manuscript that contains these two important ingredients, emphasizing that before work is submitted to her, or to any agent or editor, it needs to be evaluated by a strong, working writers' critique group.

"Know your voice," Reamer said. "Not every author can write for every genre." She personally prefers YA and middle-grade novels that are not too serious. She also doesn't care for stories that are "sexy," preferring those that are more wholesome, although not old-fashioned.

Karen Cushman, award-winning historical author (*Catherine, Called Birdy* and *The Midwife's Apprentice*), told her audience that she is often a victim to procrastination. "The most difficult part for me," she said, "is getting the words down the first time. I often wonder how I will ever stretch my ideas to fill a whole book, but I try to remember that the first draft is not the finished product." Revising, she added, is "reading what you've said and beginning to see what you are really trying to say."

Cushman cautioned writers not to be so hemmed in by others' opinions that "you don't have room for your own," and concluded by stating that her goal is "to inspire passion and caring" in her readers.

Research was the subject of prolific writer Donna Jo Napoli's speech. "We are defined by the world in which we live, so it's crucial to know and understand our characters' environment." Whether a book is historical or contemporary, Napoli says a writer must immerse him or herself in that period. "Study the music, art, and other literature of the times," she recommends, "and, if possible, visit where the main character lived, to acquire sensory impressions of the area."

Humor and adventure writer Gordon Korman and Hyperion Books Editor Alessandra Balzer discussed the relationship between writer and editor. Korman noted that "an editor can bring things out in your writing that you didn't know were there," and he advised "writing about what bugs you."

Connie Epstein presented her meticulous yearly market report. This overview of the publishing scene provides up-to-the-minute news about changes in staff at pub-

Must Reads

Reading children's books is as much an integral part of being a children's writer as the writing itself. Nearly every speaker at the annual conference of the Society of Children's Book Writers and Illustrators recommended it at some point.

Young adult author Richard Peck said, "We write by the light of every book we've ever read."

Dutton Children's Books Editor Mark McVeigh added a short but eclectic list of books he believes every children's writer should know intimately:

- *Little Bear*, by Else Holmelund Minarik
- *Where the Wild Things Are*, by Maurice Sendak
- *The Contender*, by Robert Lipsyte
- *I'll Get There; It Better Be Worth the Trip*, by John Donovan
- *Weetzie Bat*, by Francesca Lia Block

And picture book writer Jon Scieszka succinctly proclaimed, "Read everything!"

lishing houses along with detailed synopses of what each house is seeking. By studying these requirements and needs, writers can direct their submissions to a receptive editor and increase their odds of acceptance. As in previous years,

Epstein strongly stated that publishers often close their doors to unsolicited or unagented submissions because writers fail to do market research.

Breakout Sessions

Breakout sessions focused on such varied topics as marketing, negotiating contracts, your first picture book, fantasy, poetry, and Q&A sessions with editors.

Computer guru Bruce Balan offered useful skills and tips on computer use for writers. His friendly and understandable presentation made it easy for even computer illiterates (like me) to put these ideas to work.

Among many choices, illustrators could hear Katie Davis give cautionary words about getting into licensing, Loren Long speaking on the relationship between artist and writer, and Kristine Brogno listing "10 Things Not to Send an Art Director."

Beginners learned basics from veteran children's writers Stephanie Gordon Jacob and Judith Ross Enderle and the best way to submit that first manuscript from Dutton Children's Books Editor Mark McVeigh.

Also of interest was the "First Time, Big Time" panel, moderated by Arthur Levine, Editorial Director of his own imprint at Scholastic. This presentation of authors whose first books were recently published included middle-grade novelist Lisa Yee, author of *Millicent Min, Girl Genius*; YA writer Libba Bray, *A Great and Terrible Beauty*; picture book author Melinda Long, *How I Became a Pirate* (illustrated by David Shannon); and poet Billy Merrell, *Talking in the Dark*. The authors spoke about seeing their work in print and their hopes for the future.

"To be on a panel with my editor, Arthur Levine, was amazing," Yee said. "Now I know how people feel when Oprah makes their dreams come true."

In another breakout session, Bray went straight to the hearts of many writers when she discussed dealing with the Inner Critic, who, she said, "exists to keep you from telling the truth." She advised writing a letter to this Critic to release all the things you want to say to it.

Bray also recommended using her Madman/Editor theory. Both qualities exist in a writer, she believes. "The Madman is the free creative spirit. It must go first and get everything down so the Editor has something to work with."

A panel for professionals titled "Sustaining and Maintaining Your Career" was moderated by Barbara Seuling, and featured authors Richard Peck, Katie Davis, Bruce Coville, and Karen Cushman. Coville received nods of agreement from other panelists when he stated that "we all get in our own way, especially with unrealistic expectations about our writing and our goals. We need, always, to trust the process."

Coville and Cushman spoke about learning to say *no* to requests for school visits and other speaking engagements when they use up too much time and energy. Cushman added that she believes writing is "a dream job. You can work at home, listen to music, take naps, and go on walks to explore what it means to be human."

In Addition

An important part of the conference is the opportunity (for an additional fee) to have an individual evaluation of a manuscript by an editor, agent, or professional author. The results of these consultations can vary from being advised to rethink and revise the manuscript to being invited to submit this work for possible representation or publication, but most writers report that the results are positive experiences.

Optional evening sessions provided a change of pace for attendees eager for additional motivation. Open mike sessions; small critique groups devoted to specific genres, such as picture books or historical fiction; and even yoga for writers were offered.

Saturday night, writers put down their pens and notebooks and took up their dancing shoes to sparkle at the Glitter Ball. Children's writer and former Regional Advisor Collyn Justus remarked, "I had a fabulous time. The dance floor was packed with participants who enjoyed getting way down!" This popular break from concentration, with a different theme each year, has become a tradition and is always attended with enthusiasm.

Chat and laughter filled the huge

Golden Kite Award Winners

▪ **Fiction:** Jerry Spinelli, *Milkweed*
Honor Book: Donna Jo Napoli, *Breath*.
▪ **Nonfiction:** Robert Byrd, *Leonardo: Beautiful Dreamer*
Honor Book: Carmen Bredeson, *After the Last Dog Died: The True-Life, Hair-Raising Adventure of Douglas Mawson and his 1911–1914 Antarctic Expedition*
▪ **Picture Book Text:** Amy Timberlake, *The Dirty Cowboy* (illustrated by Adam Rex)
Honor Book: Jacqueline Briggs Martin, *On Sand Island* (illustrated by David A. Johnson)
▪ **Picture Book Illustration:** Loren Long, *I Dream of Trains* (text by Angela Johnson)
Honor Book: Yuyi Morales, *Just a Minute* (author and illustrator)

---

ballroom on Sunday at the Golden Kite Awards luncheon. These awards are presented yearly and each recipient delivered a short and heartfelt speech.

Of special interest was the presentation of the newly created Sid Fleishman Humor Award. This year's honoree was Lisa Yee for *Millicent Min, Girl Genius*. Yee commented that winning this award came as a "total shock, since I didn't set out to write a funny book and didn't know my publisher had submitted it." But she termed the award "a wonderful gift, and to receive it from Sid Fleishman himself made it even more special."

A great perk of the conference is reconnecting with friends from previous years and making new ones. You never know who you'll run into next. This network is not only satisfying but also can lead to interesting working relationships. Most people at the conference are willing to help with information and ideas. As Justus said, this is a "second family—the children's book community."

The shopping experience isn't neglected, either. A bookstore is set up at one end of the main meeting room and offers a wide selection of books by the authors on the faculty. In addition to books, many can't resist buying the annual SCBWI T-shirt or sweatshirt, book bag or pen.

On the last day, weary writers listened up as the final speaker, Richard Peck, offered inspiration that we could all take home with us. "The greatest cause," he said, "is creating something out of nothing to place in the hands of those who will be here after we are gone." He said, "Ours is a higher calling because we are held to higher standards than are writers for adults." Peck's concluding words were "Thank you for what we do." He received a sustained standing ovation.

An autograph party followed where books were signed and attendees even had the opportunity for a few words with a favorite writer.

A personal reaction to the

SCBWI conference, after totalling up what was spent on room, food, and tuition: Contacts made—*priceless*!

Writers' Conferences

Conferences Devoted to Writing for Children— General Conferences

BYU Writing for Young Readers Workshop

230 Harman Continuing Education
  Building
Brigham Young University
Provo, UT 84602
http://ce.byu.edu/cw/

This five-day workshop is designed for people who want to write for children or young adults. It features daily four-hour workshops where participants will focus on a single market: picture books, book-length fiction, fantasy/science fiction, general writing, beginning writing, and illustration.

Date: July.

Subjects: Sample workshops include "Early Chapter Books," "Starting Out as an Illustrator," "Folktales," and "Networking."

Speakers: Previous conference speakers include Tracy Hickman, Laura Curtis, Chris Crowe, and Virginia Euwer.

Location: Provo, Utah.

Costs: Full workshop registration is $399. Afternoon-only registration is $200. University credit is available for an additional fee.

Celebration of Children's Literature

Tracy Singleton
Montgomery College Continuing
  Education
51 Mannakee Street
Rockville, MD 20850
www.childrensbookguild.org

This one-day workshop features several workshops for writers, book signings, and networking sessions. It targets librarians, teachers, reading specialists, writers, booksellers, and artists. The conference is open to 150 participants. Early registration is recommended.

Date: April.

Subjects: Past workshops included "Expanding Visual Expression," "I Hear America Laughing," and "An Oxymoron No Longer."

Speakers: Last year's speakers included Elizabeth Levy, Michael Cart, and Floyd Cooper.

Location: Montgomery College in

Rockville, Maryland.
Costs: $90; $75 for early registration (fees include breakfast).

Central Ohio Writers of Literature for Children

Jim Mengel, Development Director
Saint Joseph Montessori School
933 Hamlet Street
Columbus, OH 43201
http://sjms.net/conf/contact.html

This one-day conference is open to all writers. Previous writing experience is not required. The conference features keynote speakers, manuscript evaluations, and writing and illustrating workshops. Editors and published authors make up its faculty.
Date: April 23, 2005.
Subjects: Topics include poetry, easy readers, picture books, and workshops on how to pitch ideas.
Speakers: This year's speakers include Margaret Peterson Haddix, Anna Grossnickle Hines, Robert Pottle, and Jan Mader.
Location: Columbus, Ohio.
Costs: $110; $95 for early registration; $120 for late registration.

Highlights Foundation Writers Workshop at Chautauqua

814 Court Street
Honesdale, PA 18431
www.highlightsfoundation.org

In its 21st year, this conference includes seminars, small-group workshops, and one-on-one sessions with accomplished authors, il-

lustrators, editors, critics, and publishers in the field of children's literature. It is open to writers at all levels of experience.
Date: July 16 through July 23, 2005.
Subjects: This year's workshops include "Conflict/Tension," "Beginnings and Endings," "Creating a Rebus," and "From Manuscript to Picture Book."
Speakers: Last year's conference faculty included Linda Sue Park, Jerry Spinelli, Barbara Joosse, and Kristi Holl.
Location: Chautauqua, New York.
Costs: TBA.

The Loft Festival of Children's Literature

Suite 200, Open Book
1011 Washington Avenue South
Minneapolis, MN 55415
www.loft.org

This two-day program offers concurrent morning and afternoon sessions led by established authors, editors, and publishers. The program also features panel discussions, manuscript critiques, and keynote speeches and lectures.
Date: April.
Subjects: Past workshops have included writing nonfiction for young children, editing young adult novels, and writing for middle-grade readers.
Speakers: Speakers from past workshops have included Marsha Qualey, John Olive, and Kristen McCurry.
Location: Minneapolis, Minnesota.
Costs: Workshops cost between $120 and $135 for the two-day event.

Pacific Northwest Children's Book Conference

Portland State University Haystack
 Summer Program
P.O. Box 1491
Portland, OR 97207-1491
www.haystack.pdx.edu

Focusing on the craft of writing and illustrating for children and young adults while working with an outstanding faculty of acclaimed editors, authors, and illustrators, this conference features small-group critique workshops, private review sessions, lectures, and panel discussions.

The conference covers all aspects of writing for children including plot, characters, revision, and voice.
Date: July.
Subjects: 2004 workshops included "Five Things Every Writer Should Think About (and Probably Doesn't)"; "They Must Be Easy—They're So Short! Defining the Picture Book"; and "They Love It! They Bought It! Now What?"
Speakers: 2004 speakers included Arthur Levine, Ellen Howard, Marla Frazee, and Susan Fletcher.
Location: Portland, Oregon.
Costs: Commuter cost: $585 (non-credit); $855 (3 credits). On-Campus Package: $745 (non-credit); $1,015 (3 credits). Individual manuscript reviews are $45.

Perspectives in Children's Literature Annual Conference

University of Massachusetts
School of Education
226 Furcolo Hall
813 North Pleasant Street
Amherst, MA 01003-9308
www.umass.edu/childlit

This one-day conference features morning and afternoon workshops on several topics of interest to children's writers. Visit the website or send an SASE for updated fee information and workshop topics for the 2005 conference.
Date: April 2, 2005.
Subjects: Workshops from the 2004 conference included "Magical Moments—The Evolution of a Book," "Once Upon a Time—Writing and Illustrating Fairy Tales," and "Thoughts on At-Risk Teens."
Speakers: 2005 keynote speakers include Jacqueline Woodson and Robert Sabuda.
Location: Amherst, Massachusetts.
Costs: TBA.

Conferences Devoted to Writing for Children—
Society of Children's Book Writers & Illustrators

Alabama
Writing and Illustrating for Kids

Southern Breeze Region-SCBWI
Jo Kittinger, Co-Regional Advisor
P.O. Box 26282
Birmingham, AL 35260
www.southern-breeze.org

In its 14th year, this conference offers full-day workshops with something for everyone from beginners to the well-published author. Keynote speakers include authors, editors, agents, and illustrators.
Date: October 15.
Subjects: The 2004 keynote address was titled, "What Makes a Good Children's Book?" Workshops were offered on poetry and picture book writing.
Speakers: Past speakers include Faye Gibbons, Diana Shore, Carol Mader, and Melanie Jones.
Location: Birmingham, Alabama.
Costs: Conference fees range from $85–$100 and include lunch.

California
Asilomar Conference and Retreat

Jim Averbeck, Regional Advisor
www.scbwinorca.org

This annual three-day retreat features presentations and workshops by prominent editors, art directors, illustrators, and authors in the children's publishing business, as well as a portfolio show. Critiques are also available to participants for an extra fee.
Date: February.
Subjects: Workshops from the 2004 retreat included "Building a Fantasy World," "Dealing with Change," and "Working Together: The Illustrator/Editor Relationship."
Speakers: Past speakers include Lois Lowry, Christopher Paul Curtis, and Gerald McDermott.
Location: Montery, California.
Costs: $350 includes a shared room and all meals.

Los Angeles Annual Retreat

P.O. Box 1728
Pacific Palisades, CA 90272
www.scbwisocal.org

This four-day retreat promises a mix of inspiration, market information, networking, keynote speeches, and interactive workshops designed to focus on special interests.
Date: August.
Subjects: Workshops from the 2004 conference included "What Goes on in Acquisitions Meetings," "Remember Me? Creating Lasting Characters with Depth and Humor," and "Writing a Humorous Picture Book."
Speakers: Speakers from the 2004 retreat included Mark McVeigh, Bruce Hales, Jessica Hatchigan, Wendy Loggia, and Jodi Reamer.
Location: Los Angeles, California.
Costs: Conference fees range from

$400 to $500. University credits are available for added fees.

Canada
SCBWI Canada Conference
Noreen Kruzich Violetta, Regional
Advisor
www.scbwicanada.org

In its seventh year, this one-day conference provides a forum for new and emerging writers to meet and share their work and get constructive criticism and feedback. One-on-one critiques are also available. It features workshops, book sales, and silent auctions.
Date: May.
Subjects: Workshops from the 2004 conference included "Character/Setting," "Insights from a New York Editor," and "A Step-by-Step Guide to Producing Illustrated Nonfiction."
Speakers: Speakers from the 2004 conference included Linda Aksomitis, Lionel Bender, Sydell Waxman, and Stephanie Lane.
Location: Ottawa, Ontario.
Costs: Contact Noreen Kruzich Violetta via email at Noreen@scbwicanada.org.

SCBWI Rocky Mountain Chapter Spring Conference
www.rmcscbwi.org

The Rocky Mountain Chapter of SCBWI presents this three-day conference each spring that offers a chance for new and experienced writers to meet with authors, editors, and agents to discuss their craft. Manuscript and art critiques

are available to participants who register early for an extra fee of $25.
Date: October.
Subjects: Workshops from the 2004 conference included "Beyond the Bookshelf: Developing Your Career by Diversifying Your Portfolio," "How to Become an Overnight Sensation in Only Fifteen Years," and "Characters for Hire."
Speakers: Past speakers include Mary Lee Donovan, Julie Anne Peters, Ronnie Ann Herman, and Jane Maday.
Location: Golden, Colorado.
Costs: Conference fees range from $95 to $130.

Kentucky/Tennessee
SCBWI-Mid-South Annual Conference
Tracy Barrett, Regional Advisor
P.O. Box 120061
Nashville, TN 37212
www.scbwi-midsouth.com

This annual day-long event features authors, illustrators, editors, and agents sharing tips and advice for beginners, as well as experienced writers and illustrators. The conference is limited to 100 participants and registration is accepted through the day of the conference. Manuscript critiques are available for an extra fee. All attendees are invited to bring a manuscript and/or art portfolio to share in a group critique. The conference also features a contest for illustrators.
Date: September.

Subjects: Past workshops included "Trends in Publishing for Children and Youth," "Worse for Your Characters Means Better for Your Plot," and "What in the Pattern Has Changed?"

Speakers: Among the 2004 conference speakers were Elaine Marie Alphin, Chuck Galey, Marie Bradby, and Randi Rivers.

Location: University School of Nashville, Nashville, Tennessee.

Costs: Registration fee, $65 for SCBWI members; $79 for non-members.

Maryland/Delaware/ West Virginia Annual Summer Conference

3377 Littlestown Pike
Westminster, MD 21158
www.boo.net/ ~ becka/scbwi.htm

This annual one-day conference features two editors, four authors, and an illustrator on its staff. It is attended by writers and illustrators for writing workshops and critique sessions. Check the website for 2005 conference updates and keynote speakers.

Date: July.

Subjects: Past workshops have included fiction, nonfiction, writing for young children, and marketing advice.

Speakers: The 2004 faculty included Joy Peskin, Lara Zeises, Lois Szymanski, and Melanie Greenberg.

Location: McDaniel College, Westminster, Maryland.

Costs: $70 for members of SCBWI; $80 for non-members.

New England SCBWI New England Annual Conference

Sally Riley, Regional Advisor
www.nescbwi.org

The New England Chapter of SCBWI presents their annual conference for 2005 titled, "Home Is Where You Start From." It deals with writing and illustrating from our core being. The three-day conference features programs for both new and experienced writers, one-on-one critiques, and breakout sessions led by authors, editors, and illustrators.

Date: May 20–22.

Subjects: Workshops for the 2005 conference include "A New Way of Seeing," "First Pages," and "First Looks."

Speakers: Past keynote speakers have included Jane Yolen, Gregory Maguire, Patricia Polacco, and Patricia Reilly Giff.

Location: Nashua, New Hampshire.

Costs: TBA.

Oregon SCBWI Oregon Retreat

www.sparpungent.com

This one-day event is jam-packed with keynote presentations, workshops, individual critique opportunities, and portfolio shows. Oregon members and subscribers will receive a registration brochure with complete conference information in March, 2005. Non-members should email robink@sparpungent.com to get on the mailing list.

Date: May 21, 2005.
Subjects: 2004 workshops included "Team Work and Collaboration," "The Art of the Edgy YA Novel," "Revision: Only God Gets It Right the First Time."
Speakers: Melissa Hart, Carolyn Digby Conahan, Kathryn Galbraith, and Ellen Howard were among the 2004 keynote speakers.
Location: Holiday Inn Conference Center, Wilsonville, Oregon.
Costs: Check the website for fees.

Texas
Austin Fall Conference
Debbie Dunn, Regional Advisor
www.austinscbwi.com

The Austin Chapter of SCBWI presents an annual fall conference for writers and illustrators of all levels of experience. Among the activities of this one-day event are one-on-one personal critiques and several workshops on all facets of writing. Visit the website for 2005 conference information.
Date: October.
Subjects: TBA.
Speakers: Past speakers have included Judy O'Malley and Sarah Ketchersid.
Location: Austin, Texas.
Costs: TBA.

Brazos Valley Winter Workshop
Janet Fox
5602 Polo Road
College Station, TX 77845
www.scbwi-brazosvalley.org

This annual winter workshop is a one-day event featuring an acclaimed author who works in various genres of writing for children. It offers writing workshops and one-on-one critiques.
Date: January.
Subjects: Past workshops included "Trends in Nonfiction," "Where's Your Story," and "Self-Editing without Self-Destructing."
Speakers: The 2005 speakers are Robin Conley and Carmen Bredeson.
Location: College Station, Texas.
Costs: $75 for SCBWI members; $85 for non-members. One-on-one critiques, $25 for members; $35 for non-members.

Washington
Annual Writing and Illustrating for Children Conference
P.O. Box 799
Woodinville, WA 98072-0799
www.scbwi-washington.org

In its 14th year, this annual conference features manuscript consultation, portfolio reviews, and an art show. In a one-day format, this conference also offers several workshops for both beginning and established children's writers and illustrators.
Date: April 30, 2005.
Subjects: Among the subjects covered are picture books, writing nonfiction for early readers, and magazine stories and articles.
Speakers: Past speakers have included Kim T. Griswell, Alvina Ling,

Reka Simonsen, and David Diaz.
Location: Seattle Pacific University, Washington.
Costs: Check website or send an SASE for 2005 fees.

Wisconsin
SCBWI Wisconsin Fall Retreat
www.scbwi-wi.com

Writers, editors, and illustrators come together at this three-day conference to share their craft, forge friendships, and share industry news. The retreat includes lectures, breakout sessions, and one-on-one critiques.

Interested participants can check the website for updated information or email regional advisor Ann Angel at aangel@aol.com for more information.
Date: October, 2005.
Subjects: Among the 2004 subjects covered were the picture book market, and writing for young adults.
Speakers: Phyllis Root, Lauren Myracle, Julia Straus-Gabel, and Hannah Rodgers were among the 2004 retreat faculty.
Location: Siena Center, Racine, Wisconsin.
Costs: Check the website for 2005 fees. 2004 fees were $350 and included room and board and a one-on-one critique.

Conferences with Sessions on Writing for Children— University or Regional Conferences

Aspen Summer Words

Aspen Writers' Foundation
Suite 116
110 E. Hallam Street
Aspen, CO 81611
www.aspenwriters.org

This writing retreat and literary festival offers five days of literary explorations led by award-winning and best-selling authors. The conference is the ideal venue for anyone with a passion for words. It features hands-on workshops, readings, industry panels, and social receptions. To be considered for admission, an applicant must submit a writing sample, a cover letter explaining why you would like to attend, and a completed application form.
Date: June.
Subjects: Workshops will include the topics of fiction, essay, memoir, and writing for children.
Speakers: Past speakers have included Erica Jong, Alison Berkley, Anita Shreve, and Lynn York.
Location: Aspen, Colorado.
Costs: Visit website for current price list.

Harriette Austin Writers Conference

Georgia Center for Continuing Education
University of Georgia
Athens, GA 30602-3603

This annual conference is open to writers of all levels and presents intensive workshops, book signings, manuscript critiques, lectures, social gatherings, and panel discussions.
Date: July.
Subjects: Workshops from the 2004 conference included "Selling Short Fiction," "Get an Agent, Or So You've Been Told," "Making a Setting Come Alive," and "De-Mystifying the Children's Book Business."
Speakers: Past speakers have included Patrick LoBrutto, Nancy Steinbeck, Penny Warner, and Andrea Brown.
Location: Athens, Georgia.
Costs: Send an SASE for 2005 conference fees.

Bear River Writers Conference

Department of English Language & Literature
3187 Angell Hall
University of Michigan
Ann Arbor, MI 48109
www.lsa.umich.edu/bearriver

This four-day workshop features morning workshops, afternoon writing sessions, and evening readings. The emphasis of this conference is on creative writing and the environment. All participants will receive a complete conference packet with a schedule of workshops two weeks prior to the event.
Date: May/June.

Subjects: Writing subjects including children's literature, fiction, nonfiction, and poetry will be covered.
Speakers: Speakers from the 2004 conference included Elizabeth Cox, Jerry Dennis, Rhian Ellis, and Thomas Lynch.
Location: Walloon Lake, Michigan.
Costs: $600 (includes meals and lodging, $500 (includes meals only).

Canadian Authors Association Annual Conference

Box 419
Campelford, Ontario K0L 1L0
Canada
www.canauthors.org

Celebrating Canadian literature, this conference provides an educational forum for professional and emerging writers from across Canada, and supports writers in the development and promotion of their work. It features workshops, panel discussions, and lectures. Manuscript critiquing sessions and contests are optional features available to participants.
Date: June 23–26.
Subjects: 2005 workshops will include storytelling, business writing, writing for children, and writing memoirs.
Speakers: 2005 speakers include Chris Banks, Veronica Ross, Kelley Armstrong, and Erin Noteboom.
Location: Kitchener, Ontario.
Costs: Member fees range from $150 to $175; fees for non-members range from $190 to $225.

Cape Cod Writers' Conference

P.O. Box 408
Osterville, MA 02655
www.capecodwriterscenter.com

This annual conference for aspiring and published writers offers practical guidance to enable writers to hone their skills, network with other writers, and meet with agents and editors. It is a week-long event, but participants are given the option of signing up for one day of the event.
Date: August.
Subjects: Subjects from the 2004 conference included "Writing Unique Dialogue," "Don't Tell Your Audience What It Already Knows," and "Writing Life Stories."
Speakers: Past speakers include Bill Roorbach, Hallie Ephron, Peter Abrahams, and Greg Greenway.
Location: Craigville Beach, Massachusetts.
Costs: Visit the website for 2005 conference fees.

Columbus Writers Conference

Angela Palazzolo, Producer/Director
P.O. Box 20548
Columbus, OH 43220
www.creativevista.com

The goal of this annual conference is to be an educational and networking opportunity, featuring a wide variety of topics aimed at writers who range from beginners to seasoned professionals. The conference features workshops presented by successful writers, editors, and literary agents.

Date: August.
Subjects: Past topics covered included finding and working with a literary agent, writing science fiction, memoirs, plays, and humor, and targeting markets to sell your work.
Speakers: Past conference presenters include Jerry Gross, Brenda Copeland, David Baker, and Lee K. Abbot.
Location: Columbus, Ohio.
Costs: Visit the website for 2005 conference fees.

A Day for Writers

Steamboat Springs Arts Council
P.O. Box 774284
Steamboat Springs, CO 80477
www.steamboatwriters.com

This annual event looks to encourage a sharp focus within a short time frame. It is open to both novice and professional writers and features workshops, lectures, book signings, and book sales.
Date: July.
Subjects: Subjects from the 2004 conference included "Letting the Words Out," "Stories and Lines: Why Use Verse to Create Characters and Tell Stories," and "The Plot Thickens: How and Why to Plot."
Speakers: Last year's speakers included David Mason and Connie Willis.
Location: Steamboat Springs, Colorado.
Costs: $45.

Flathead River Writers Conference

P.O. Box 7711
Kalispell, MO 59904

This affordable writers' conference is open to writers of all levels. Proof of writing ability is required to attend three-day workshops preceding the regular conference. The conference features consultations with faculty, lectures, workshops, and scheduled readings. Workshops are led by established writers, editors, agents, publishers, and publicists.
Date: October.
Subjects: Subjects covered in past conferences included children's writing, fiction, horror, humor, mystery, publishing, and screenwriting.
Speakers: Past speakers include Bill Brooks, Marc Hernandez, Jacky Sach, and Gary Ferguson.
Location: Whitefish, Montana.
Costs: TBA.

Gig Harbor Writers' Conference

P.O. Box 826
Gig Harbor, Washington 98335
www.peninsulawritersassociation.org

This three-day conference offers manuscript consultation, workshops, readings, keynote speakers, and social gatherings. The conference focuses on a variety of topics including young adult and children's literature, romance, science fiction, mystery, and nonfiction. The conference is limited to 75 participants so early registration is recommended.
Date: April/May.

Subjects: Past workshops include "Juvenile Historicals," "The Art of Essay," "Plotting," and "Personal Mythology."
Speakers: Keynote speakers for the 2005 conference include Tad Bartimus, Jill Barnett, and Pete Fromm.
Location: Gig Harbor, Washington.
Costs: $275 includes fees for all three days. Participants just attending on Saturday and Sunday pay $175.

Indiana University Writers' Conference

464 Ballantine Hall
Bloomington, IN 47405
www.indiana.edu/ ~ writecon

Participants in this five-day conference join faculty-led workshops in fiction, nonfiction, and poetry, and take classes on various aspects of writing. One-on-one manuscript consultations, social events, and scheduled readings are also part of this event that is open to both new and experienced writers. Interested participants must send an application form to be considered for this conference. Application forms are available at the website or with an SASE.
Date: June 5–10, 2005.
Subjects: Classes focus on all aspects of fiction, nonfiction, and poetry.
Speakers: 2005 speakers to be announced on website.
Costs: $350. Attendees wishing to take specialized workshops must pay an additional $150.

Iowa Summer Writing Festival

University of Iowa
199 Oakdale Campus W310
Iowa City, IA 52242-5000
www/continuetolearn.uiowa.edu

Each year, the University of Iowa presents this summer writing festival that offers week-long and weekend workshops and classes to explore, enhance, and market one's writing. It is open to those over the age of 18 only.
Date: June/July.
Subjects: Past workshops have included "Narrative Journalism," "Elements of a Novel," "Teaching Your Prose to Sing," and "Introduction to the Craft of Fiction."
Speakers: Speakers from past festivals include Sandra Scofield, Lisa Chavez, Geoff Becker, and Maudy Benz.
Costs: Costs range from $435 to $500 per week and $200 to $250 per weekend.

Kentucky Women Writers Spring Conference

251 West Second Street
Lexington, KY 40507
www.carnegieliteracy.org

This four-day conference was established in 1979 by the University of Kentucky. The focus of the event is on women's literature and writing, and it includes workshops on children's literature, fiction journalism, memoirs, poetry, and playwriting. It also features panel discussions, scheduled readings, manuscript critiques, writing sessions, and social events. Early registration is recommended as this conference has a limited space for 100–200 participants.

Date: TBA.

Subjects: Past workshops have included "The Politics of Publishing," "Women Teaching Women," and "Reading Women's Literature."

Speakers: Past faculty has included Marita Golden, Gwyn Hyman Rubio, Michelle Parkerson, and Bell Hooks.

Location: Lexington, Kentucky.

Costs: $120.

Manhattanville Writers' Week

Manhattanville College
School of Graduate and Professional Studies
2900 Purchase Street
Purchase, NY 10577
www.mville.edu/graduate/writers_week.htm

This week-long program offers the opportunity to spend an intensive week of writing and working closely with well-known writers and teachers of writing. The program is open to all writers and features keynote speakers, sessions with editors and agents, readings by distinguished faculty, and workshops on various aspects of writing and editing. Participants may either be beginning a new work or completing a project they have already started.

Date: June.

Subjects: Subjects from the 2004 conference include "Fiction: Begin-

ning with Craft," "Personal Narrative: The Art of Experience," and "Nonfiction: The Traveler's Eye."

Speakers: Workshop leaders from the 2004 event included Mark Matousek, Ann Jones, Valerie Martin, and Linda Oatman High.

Location: Purchase, New York.

Costs: $980 (includes 2 graduate credits); $650 for non-credit. Registration fee is $35 extra.

Maui Writers Conference

P.O. Box 968
Kihei, HI 96753
www.mauiwriters.com

The conference prides itself with bringing prominent authors and editors together with writers of all levels for close personal interaction. The conference offers many opportunities for emerging writers to further their careers. The three-day event is sponsored by the Maui Writers Foundation and includes consultations with faculty, contests, keynote speakers, lectures, discussion panels, workshops, readings, and writing sessions.

Date: Labor Day Weekend.

Subjects: Workshops on literary and commercial fiction, nonfiction, and screenwriting are among the subjects to be covered.

Speakers: Speakers from the 2004 conference included Elizabeth George, John Saul, Terry Brooks, and Dorothy Allison.

Location: Wailea, Hawaii.

Costs: $495–$695.

New England Writers' Conference

P.O. Box 5
Windsor, VT 05089
www.newenglandwriters.org

This one-day program includes lectures, workshops, panel discussions, readings, and writing sessions. It is open to writers at all levels and prides itself on being an affordable opportunity for writers.

The conference is limited to 150–200 participants and features a faculty of established writers, editors, and publishers.

Date: July.
Subjects: The conference will cover writing for children, fiction, nonfiction, marketing, and getting published.
Speakers: Speakers from the 2004 conference included Peter Filkins and Elizabeth Graver.
Location: Windsor, Vermont.
Costs: $20.

Northeast Texas Writer's Organization Spring Conference

P.O. Box 411
Winfield, TX 75493
www.netwo.org

This two-day event is sponsored by the North Texas Writer's Organization and offers lectures, question-and-answer sessions, and personal interaction with prominent authors, editors, and agents.

Date: April 29–30, 2005.
Subjects: Past conferences have covered the subjects of children's fiction, humor, marketing, mystery, and young adult novels.
Speakers: The 2004 faculty included Jane Roberts Wood, Greg Garrett, and Charles Backus.
Location: Winnsboro, Texas.
Costs: $60.

Oklahoma Writers' Federation Conference

P.O. Box 2654
Stillwater, OK 74076
www.owfi.org

This annual conference features writers, editors, agents, and informative programs to help writers improve their craft and find success in publishing their work. It also provides an opportunity for writers to network with their peers and receive constructive criticism and feedback.

Date: April 29–30, 2005.
Subjects: Subjects to be covered at the 2005 conference include mystery, romance, writing contests, and working with literary agents.
Speakers: Speakers for the upcoming event include William Bernhardt, Barry Friedman, Anna Myers, and Carolyn Wall.
Location: Stillwater, Oklahoma.
Costs: $100 for registrations received prior to April 15th; $125 thereafter.

Philadelphia Writers' Conference

D. O. Haggerty
535 Fairview Road
Medford, NJ 08055
www.pwcwriters.org

Open to writers over the age of 18, this conference looks to bring writers together for instruction, counsel, and the exchange of ideas. Workshops are led by established writers, editors, and agents. The conference also offers manuscript critiques and consultations, and lectures.

Date: June.

Subjects: Subjects covered at the 2004 conference included literary short story, mystery, novel, theme and plot, and creative essay.

Speakers: Past speakers include Molly Cochran, William Lashner, Michael Elkin, and Jen Bryant.

Location: Philadelphia, Pennsylvania.

Costs: Visit the website for 2005 conference fees.

Seven Hills Writers' Conference

Tallahassee Writers' Association
2636 W. Mission Road #146
Tallahassee, FL 32304
www.tallahasseewriters.net

Expanding to a two-day event in 2005, this conference offers more than 25 workshops presented by experts in their field. Participants are able to meet and talk with several agents and editors during faculty consultations. Discussion panels, lectures, and social events are all part of the 2005 line-up. Interested writers should send an email to conference@tallahasseewriters.net.

Date: April 8–9, 2005.

Subjects: Workshops will include sessions on the craft of writing, children's literature, memoirs, mystery, and poetry.

Speakers: Speakers from past conferences include Michael Lister, Adrian Fogelin, Judge Terry Lewis, and John Pekins.

Location: Tallahassee, Florida.

Costs: TBA.

SkylineWriters Conference

P.O. Box 33343
North Royalton, OH 44133
www.skylinewriters.com

In its 22nd year, this conference offers workshops, manuscript critiques, readings, keynote speakers, and a writing contest. Its faculty consists of established authors, editors, and agents, and also offers programs and workshops specifically geared toward young adults.

The one-day event is limited to 75 participants per year. Early registration is recommended.

Date: September.

Subjects: Workshops from the 2004 conference included "The Power of Writing," "Journaling Your Journey," "The Best on Children's Literature," and "The Creative Soul."

Speakers: Tricia Springstubb, Claudia Taller, Ted Schwartz, and Sandie King were all workshop leaders at the 2004 conference.

Location: Parma, Ohio.

Costs: $50 for members; $65 for non-members; and $40 for students.

Southern California Writer's Conference

Michael Steven Gregory, Coordinator

1010 University Avenue #54
San Diego, CA 92103
www.writersconference.com

This three-day event offers a tiered workshop structure with one session always devoted to the reading and critiquing of manuscripts. Among the other program highlights are late night rogue workshops, keynote speakers, lectures, discussion panels, writing sessions, and social events. It is open to all writers, but limits the program to 250 participants. Early registration is recommended. Visit the website for updated program information.
Date: June 10–12, 2005.
Subjects: Among the subjects to be covered at the 2005 conference will be writing for children, marketing, humor, horror, religion/self-help, and science fiction.
Speakers: TBA.
Location: Palm Springs, California.
Costs: $275–$345. Manuscript critiques are available for an extra fee.

Willamette Writers Conference

9045 SW Barbur Boulevard #5A
Portland, OR 97219
www.willamettewriters.com

This three-day conference is sponsored by the Willamette Writers, a non-profit writing group in the Pacific Northwest. It offers consultations with editors, workshops, lectures, and a banquet. The conference is open to 300 participants. Early registration is recommended.
Date: August.

Subjects: Subjects covered in past conferences include humor in young adult writing, memoirs, mysteries, and screenwriting.
Speakers: Past speakers have included Cynthia Whitcomb, Donald Maass, and Barbara Gislason.
Location: Portland, Oregon.
Costs: $375.

Write on the Sound Writers' Conference

Frances Chapin, Coordinator
700 Main Street
Edmonds, WA 98020

This two-day conference consists of 28 individual workshops that are presented by noted authors, educators, and trade professionals who will share their secrets, talents, and literary visions. Manuscript critiques, panel discussions, and a writing contest are also offered.
Date: October.
Subjects: Past workshops have included "Beyond Journaling: The Art of Memoir," "Writing Fiction That Sells," and "Writing for the Stage."
Speakers: Keynote novelist Diana Abu-Jaber spoke at the 2004 conference.
Location: Edmonds, Washington.
Costs: $125. Early-bird registration, $99. Manuscript critiques, $20.

The Writers Institute Annual Conference

Room 621
610 Langdon Street
Madison, WI 53703
www.dcs.wisc.edu/lsa/writing/awi

This annual two-day conference provides a forum for both fiction and nonfiction writers to get inspired and learn the latest techniques for writing and marketing. The conference also features book sales, a writing contest, and take-home materials.

Date: July.

Subjects: The 2004 conference subjects included writing book proposals, poetry writing, effective foreshadowing, and being a columnist.

Speakers: Past speakers include Danielle Egan-Miller, Scott Edelstein, Chitra Divakaruni, and Doug Moe.

Location: Madison, Wisconsin.

Costs: $225.

Conferences with Sessions on Writing for Children— Religious Writing Conferences

Association for Mormon Letters Annual Conference

P.O. Box 51364
Provo, UT 84605-1364
www.aml-online.org

Sponsored by the Association for Mormon Letters, this annual conference features panel discussions, lectures, keynote speakers, and workshops for beginning through advanced writers. Representatives from several local publishing companies will also be at the conference to discuss their current wants and needs in the publishing field.

Writers will gain hands-on experience through the "Lucky 13" workshops where participants bring the first 13 lines of their story, 13 lines of setting or characterization, or 13 lines of a synopsis or plot outline for a workshop complete with feedback from other writers.

Date: October.
Subjects: Workshops from the 2004 conference included "Writing Children's & Young Adult Fiction: Realism or Fantasy?" "Writing Mysteries," and "Plots and Characters."
Speakers: Speakers from the 2004 conference included Shannon Hale, Mari Jorgensen, Caleb Warnock, and Anne Perry.
Location: Salt Lake City, Utah.
Costs: $45 for members and students; $55 for non-members.

East Texas Christian Writers Conference

East Texas Baptist University
1209 N. Grove Street
Marshall, TX 75670
www.etbu.edu

This one-day conference features four breakout sessions with four options for each time block. Its faculty members are available for manuscript consultations, and the conference will also feature keynote speakers and a catered luncheon.

Date: June.
Subjects: Workshops from the 2004 conference included "E-Publishing: The Ins, Outs, Ups, and Downs of Going Electronic," "Writing for Scholarly Publications," "Keeping the Focus in Writing," and "Writing and Marketing Your Work."
Speakers: Speakers from the 2004 event include Jim Pence, Marv Knox, Bill O'Neal, Archie McDonald, and Carolyn Pedison.
Location: Marshall, Texas.
Costs: $60; $90 per couple.

Florida Christian Writers Conference

2344 Armour Ct.
Titusville, FL 32780
www.flwriters.org

Editors, agents, and freelance writers join together to create a superb professional faculty for this annual conference. Open to beginning and advanced writers it offers an opportunity to hone your craft, realize your publishing goals, and provide marketing opportunities and networking within the publishing industry. It features 56 one-hour workshops, special interest group meetings, and one-on-one appointments with editors, agents, and authors.

Date: March 3–6, 2005.

Subjects: Workshops for the 2005 conference include "Creating a Manuscript to Meet Market Needs," "The ABC's of Sketch Writing," and "How Does the Author/Editor Relationship Really Work?"

Speakers: This year's speakers include Katrina Cassel, Dottie Russ, Rosemary Upton, Christine Tangvald, and Denise George.

Location: Bradenton, Florida.

Costs: $775.

Glorieta Christian Writers Conference

P.O. Box 66810
Albuquerque, NM 87193
www.classservices.com

This conference is structured to provide a balance of education, inspiration, and relaxation. Morning sessions feature devotional, music, and a panel discussion of a variety of different writing subjects. Evening lectures are also offered. Workshops designed specifically for children's writers are regularly featured.

Date: October.

Subjects: Workshops from the 2004 conference included "Writing Filler to Establish Yourself as a Writer," "How to Package Your Passion," and "The Nine Secrets of Successful Interviews."

Speakers: Speakers from the 2004 conference included Beth Clayton, Ed Rowell, Jack Cavanaugh, and Judi Perry.

Location: Glorieta, New Mexico.

Costs: From $275 to $325.

Jewish Children's Literature Conference

6150 Mount Sinai Drive
Simi Valley, CA 93063
www.jewishchildrensbookfest.org

Sponsored by Mount Sinai Memorial Parks Association, this annual conference features keynote speakers, lectures, workshops, discussion panels, and social events with a focus in the areas of children's literature and the publishing industry.

Date: November.

Subjects: Past workshops have included "Teaching Tolerance through Young Adult Historical Novels," "Everything You Ever Wanted to Know about Publishing Jewish Books But Didn't Have a Chance to Ask," and "Picture Book Holiday Tales."

Speakers: Past speakers have included Bernie Saltzberg, Len Levitt, and Rabbi Ed Feinstein.

Location: Los Angeles, California.

Costs: $55.

Mount Hermon Writers' Conference

P.O. Box 413
Mount Hermon, CA 95041
www.mounthermon.org

For 35 years, this conference has offered a place for new and emerging writers to get together with experienced authors, editors, and agents to showcase their work. It presents 65 individual workshops on all aspects of writing.

The five-day event provides writers an opportunity to check their skills under the guidance of professional writers, to test their message alongside Jesus' teachings as proclaimed by the keynote speakers, and to challenge the marketplace by sharing their manuscripts with others.

Date: April.
Subjects: Workshops from the 2004 conference included "The Power of Imaginative Language in One's Faith and Witness," and "The Power of Christian Fiction in an Increasingly Secular World."
Speakers: Dr. Rosalie de Rosset, Ted Deker, and Jeff Adams were among the 2004 conference speakers.
Location: Mount Hermon, California.
Costs: TBA.

This annual conference offers small group coaching classes, writing seminars, workshops, critiques, and editor appointments. It is open to all writers, but limits itself to 250 participants to ensure small group classes. It invites participants to bring writing proposals for meetings with editors.

Date: October.
Subjects: Past subjects covered include writing fictional characters, writing for children, self-publishing, and submitting book proposals.
Speakers: Speakers from the 2004 event include Francine Rivers, Karen Ball, and Sally Stuart.
Location: Canby, Oregon.
Costs: $500.

Oregon Christian Writers Conference

1075 Willow Lake Road North
Salem, OR 97303
www.oregonchristianwriters.org

Writers' Contests & Awards

Jane Addams Children's Book Award

Donna Barkman, Chairperson
Jane Addams Peace Association
777 United Nations Plaza
New York, NY 10017
www.janeaddamspeace.org

The Jane Addams Children's Book Award has been presented annually since 1953 to a children's book that most effectively promotes the cause of peace. All eligible books will have been published in the year preceding the contest. Book themes may include solving problems non-violently, overcoming prejudice, and accepting responsibility for the future of humanity. Entries must also meet the conventional standards of literary and artistic merit.

Books may be submitted by the publishers or requested by the committee. Only books targeting children ages preschool through fourteen are eligible.

Deadline: December 31.
Representative winners: *Harvesting Hope: The Story of Caesar Chavez,* Kathleen Krull; *Out of Bounds: Seven Stories of Conflict and Hope,* Beverley Naidoo.
Announcements: Winner is announced in April.
Award: Winner receives an honorary certificate and cash award that are presented at an awards dinner in New York.

Amazing Kids! Annual Essay Contest

PMB 485
1158 26th Street
Santa Monica, CA 90403
www.amazing-kids.org

Sponsored by the Internet publication *Amazing Kids!,* this essay contest is held annually. It is open to children and young adults ages five to seventeen and consists of a different theme each year.

Prefers email submissions sent to essays@amazing-kids.org. Will accept photocopies and computer printouts. Entries must include author's name, address, and a parent or guardian's written permission to enter the contest.

Deadline: August 15.

Representative winners: "Spring," Caroline Hanna; "Nature Walk," Shree Nadkarni.

Announcements: Winners are announced 60 days after the deadline on the website.

Award: Winners receive publication of their essays in the September issue of *Amazing Kids!*

American Association of University Women Award for Juvenile Literature

North Carolina Literary and
  Historical Association
4610 Mail Service Center
Raleigh, NC 27699-4610

Established in 1953, this award celebrates the creativity involved in the writing of juvenile literature. It is presented for the year's best work of juvenile literature by a writer from North Carolina. Only books published in the year preceding the contest are eligible.

All entries must contain subject matter relevant to North Carolina, and feature an imaginative quality.

Deadline: July 15.

Representative winners: *Jasper,* Michelle Groce; *Remember the Bridge,* Carole Boston Weatherford; *A Perfect Friend,* Reynolds Price.

Announcements: Winners are announced in November.

Award: Winners are honored at the annual meeting with an awards ceremony.

American Book Cooperative Children's Picture Book Competition

11010 Hanning Lane
Houston, TX 77041-5006
www.americanbookcooperative.org

Open to writers living in the U.S. and over the age of 21, this competition is sponsored by the American Book Cooperative. Ten finalists are chosen by the judges and then posted on the ABC website for others to vote on the winner. The competition accepts original, unpublished manuscripts only.

No entry fee. Limit 5 entries per competition. Critique sheets for each entry are available by request with SASE after July 1. Accepts photocopies and computer printouts. Manuscripts will not be returned.

Deadline: April.

Announcements: Winner is announced in September.

Award: Winner receives publication of their manuscript along with a marketing plan and initial PR launch.

Américas Book Award for Children's and Young Adult Literature

Consortium of Latin American
  Studies Programs
c/o Center for Latin America
University of Wisconsin–Milwaukee
P.O. Box 413
Milwaukee, WI 53201
www.uwm.edu

This award is presented in recognition of works of fiction, folklore, poetry, and nonfiction written in the U.S. during the year preceding the contest. Winners are chosen based on distinctive literary quality, cultural contextualization, exceptional integration of text, illustration and design, and potential for classroom use.

This award looks to reach beyond geographic borders, as well as multicultural-international boundaries, focusing instead on cultural heritages within the hemisphere. Entries may be written in either English or Spanish. Send an SASE or visit the website for complete information and guidelines.

Deadline: January 15.

Representative winners: *Just a Minute: A Trickster Tale and Counting Book,* Yuyi Morales; *The Meaning of Consuelo,* Judith Ortiz Cofer.

Announcements: Winner is announced in the spring.

Award: A letter of citation to the author and publisher, and a cash prize of $200 are awarded.

Hans Christian Andersen Awards

International Board of Books for
  Young People
IBBY Secretariat, Nonneweg 12
Postfach, CH-4003
Basel, Switzerland
www.ibby.org

These awards are presented every other year to an author and an illustrator whose complete works have made a lasting contribution in the field of children's literature.

Nominations are made by the National Sections of IBBY and recipients are selected by a distinguished international jury of children's literature specialists. Send an SASE or visit the website for complete guidelines.

Deadline: August 15.

Representative winners: Martin Waddell, Aidan Chambers, Ana Maria Machado.

Announcements: Winners are announced at the Children's Book Fair in Italy.

Award: Winners receive a gold medal and a diploma at an awards reception.

ASPCA Henry Bergh Young Adult Book Award

ASPCA Education Department
424 East 92nd Street
New York, NY 10128-6804
www.aspca.org/bookaward

This annual award honors a book that best promotes the humane ethic of compassion and respect for all living creatures through young adult literature. It is presented to an author of the most distinguished young adult book for readers ages 13 through 17. Works of fiction, nonfiction, and collections of short stories, essays, or poetry by one author are eligible. All entries must have been published during the year preceding the contest in either Canada or the U.S. Visit the website or send an SASE for complete guidelines.

Deadline: October 31.
Representative winners: "Working Like A Dog: The Story of Working Dogs through History," Gena K. Gorrell; "The Deliverance of Dancing Bears," Elizabeth Stanley; "Seldovia Sam and the Sea Otter Rescue," Susan Woodward Springer.
Announcements: Winner is announced in December.
Award: The Henry Bergh Young Adult Book Award will be presented to the winner.

Atlantic Writing Competition

Writers' Federation of Nova Scotia
1113 Marginal Road
Halifax, Nova Scotia B3H 4P7
Canada
www.writers.ns.ca

The Writers' Federation of Nova Scotia sponsors this annual competition that encourages writers living in Atlantic Canada to explore their talents by sending their original, unpublished work in the categories of novel (to 10,000 words); short story (to 3,000 words); poetry (to 6 poems); writing for children (to 20,000 words); or magazine article/essay (from 1,200 to 2,500 words).

Entrants are asked to choose a pseudonym to ensure impartiality of the judges. Limit one entry per category. All entrants must be residents of the Atlantic Provinces for at least six months prior to submitting their entry.

Entry fees: novels, $25 for nonmembers; $20 for members. All other categories, $15 for non-members; $10 for members. Manuscripts are not returned. Send an SASE or visit the website for complete category and submission information.
Deadline: August 1.
Representative winners: *Wanting the Day,* Brian Bartlett; *Opening Island,* Anne Compton.
Announcements: Winners are announced in the fall.
Award: Cash prizes ranging from $50 to $250 are awarded in each category.

AuthorMania.com Writing Contests

Cindy Thomas
Rt. 4 Box 201-A
Buna, TX 77612
www.authormania.com

AuthorMania.com sponsors a fiction contest and poetry contest each year. The contests are open to writers living in the U.S. and look for original, unpublished material. Entries may be on any subject, but should not include violence or hate. Submissions must be written in English. Visit the website for more information.
Deadline: May 31.
Representative winner: Molly Varnum.
Announcements: Winners will be announced in June.
Award: Winner of the fiction contest receives a cash award of $1,000. Winner of the poetry contest receives a cash award of $400.

AWA Contests

Cumberland College
6000 College Station Drive
Williamsburg, KY 40769

Open to members of the Appalachian Writers Association, these contests present several awards in categories that include short story, essay, and playwriting. They accept previously unpublished material only.

No entry fee. Word lengths vary for each category. Submit two copies of each entry. Accepts photocopies and computer printouts. Manuscripts are not returned.
Deadline: June 1.
Representative winners: "Story Suite," David Lee Kirkland; "Red, White & Jesus," Janice Willis Barnett; "A Long Summer," Dan Leonard.
Announcements: Winners are announced in the fall.
Award: First-place winners in each category receive a cash prize of $100. Second- and third-place winners receive cash awards of $50 and $25, respectively.

Baker's Plays High School Playwriting Contest

Baker's Plays
P.O. Box 699222
Quincy, MA 02269-9222
www.bakersplays.com

This annual contest accepts submissions from high school students only and looks to encourage the art of playwriting among young people.

No entry fee. All entries must be accompanied by the signature of a sponsoring high school English teacher. It is recommended that all entries have a public reading or production prior to submission. Accepts photocopies and computer printouts. Include an SASE for return of manuscript. Visit the website or send an SASE for complete guidelines.
Deadline: January 30.
Announcements: Winners are announced in May.
Award: Cash prizes ranging from $100 to $500 are awarded. First-place winner will also receive a production of their play.

John and Patricia Beatty Award

California Library Association
Suite 200
717 20th Street
Sacramento, CA 95814
www.cla-net.org

This award honors the author of a distinguished book for children or young adults that best promotes an awareness of California and its residents. A committee of librarians selects the winning title from books published in the U.S. during the year before the contest.

This award is sponsored by the California Library Association and is gaining in reputation and prestige due to the excellence of the books it has honored. Send an SASE or visit the website for further information.
Deadline: February 10.

Representative winners: *Cecile Poole: A Life in the Law,* James Haskins; *Ansel Adams: America's Photographer,* Beverly Gherman.
Announcements: The winner is announced during National Library week in November.
Award: Winner receives a cash award of $500 and an engraved plate.

Geoffrey Bilson Award for Historical Fiction

The Canadian Children's Book Center
Suite 101, Lower Level
40 Orchard View Boulevard
Toronto, Ontario M4R 1B9
Canada
www.bookcentre.ca

This annual award recognizes the writing of an outstanding work of historical fiction for young people, written by a Canadian author. Entries must be historically authentic and look to inform the reader significantly. All entries must be published in the year preceding the contest.

Entrants should submit 6 copies of each entry. Winners are chosen by a jury that is appointed by the Canadian Book Centre.
Deadline: January 15.
Representative winners: *The Word for Home,* Joan Clark; *If I Just Had Two Wings,* Virginia Frances Schwartz.
Announcements: Winner is notified in June.
Award: Winner is presented with a cash award of $1,000 and a certificate.

The Irma Simonton Black and James H. Black Award for Excellence in Children's Literature

Linda Greengrass
610 West 112th Street
New York, NY 10025
http://streetcat.bankstreet.edu

This award honors an outstanding book for young children in which text and illustrations are inseparable, each enhancing and enlarging on the other to produce a singular whole.

Children will be the final judges of this competition. Librarians and educators choose 20 to 25 books from the many children's books published each year that they consider the best candidates for the award. These books are then sent to classrooms at the Bank Street School for Children. The children then read the books and vote on their favorites.
Deadline: December 15.
Representative winners: *How I Became a Pirate,* Melinda Long; *Bubba and Beau, Best Friends,* Kathi Appelt; *The Three Pigs,* David Wiesner.
Announcements: Winners are announced in May.
Award: A scroll with the recipient's name and a gold seal designed by Maurice Sendak will be given to the winning author and illustrator.

Waldo M. and Grace C. Bonderman Youth Theatre Playwriting Competition

Dorothy Webb, Contest Chair
1114 Red Oak Drive
Avon, IL 46123
www.indianarep.com/Bonderman

This competition is open to all writers and encourages the creation of artistic scripts for young audiences. All entries must be previously unpublished.

It accepts scripts in two categories: grades 1–3 (approximately 30 minutes in length); and grades 3 and up (minimum length of 45 minutes). Scripts must not be committed to publication at the time of submission. Musicals will not be accepted.

Submit 3 copies of each manuscript. Author's name must not appear on manuscript. Entries must include a brief synopsis and cast list. A manuscript critique will be returned with each entry if an SASE is provided.

Deadline: October 6.
Announcements: Winners will be contacted in January.
Award: The top four winners receive cash awards of $1,000 and a staged reading of their play.

The Boston Globe-Horn Book Awards

Suite 200
56 Roland Street
Boston, MA 02129
www.hbook.com

These awards recognize and reward excellence in literature for children and young adults. Entries must be submitted by publishers, although judges reserve the right to honor any eligible book. All entries must have been published in the U.S. Winners will be selected in the categories of fiction, nonfiction, picture book, and poetry. Honor books may also be awarded.

Deadline: May.
Representative winners: *The Man Who Walked Between the Towers,* Mordicai Gerstein; *The Fire-Eaters,* David Almond.
Announcements: Winners are announced in May.
Award: Winners in each category receive a cash award of $500 and an engraved silver bowl. Honor recipients receive an engraved silver plaque.

Ann Connor Brimer Award

P.O. Box 36036
Halifax, Nova Scotia B3J 3S9
Canada
www.nsla.ns.ca/awards.html

Established in 1990 by the Nova Scotia Library Association, this award is presented annually to the author living in Atlantic Canada who has made an outstanding contribution to children's literature. It is named for the late Ann Connor Brimer who was a strong advocate for Canadian children's literature and saw the need to recognize and reward children's writers.

The competition is open to authors residing in Atlantic Canada

who have published a book intended for young readers up to the age of 15 that was published in the year preceding the contest.
Deadline: April 30.
Representative winners: *The First Stone,* Don Aker; *Shoulder the Sky,* Lesley Choyce; *Where I Live,* Francis Wolfe.
Announcements: Winner is announced in September.
Award: Winner receives a cash award of $1,000.

Marilyn Brown Novel Award
Association of Mormon Letters
125 Hobble Creek Canyon
Springville, UT 84663
www.aml-online.org/awards/

This award is presented every other year, and looks for well-written, unpublished entries that reflect the values and culture of the Mormon faith.

No entry fee. Limit one entry per competition. Accepts photocopies and computer printouts. Author's name should not appear on manuscript itself. Include a cover sheet with author's name, address, and telephone number. Send an SASE or visit the website for complete guidelines.
Deadline: July 1.
Representative winners: Shannon Hale, Janean Justham, Coke Newell.
Announcements: Winners are notified by mail.
Award: Winner receives a cash award of $1,000.

ByLine Magazine Contest
ByLine Magazine
P.O. Box 5240
Edmond, OK 73083-5240
www.bylinemag.com/contests.html

ByLine Magazine sponsors several contests that are designed to motivate writers by providing a forum for competition. Open to all writers, the contests are presented in several categories including short story, inspiration article, juvenile short story, and short humor.

Entry fees and word lengths vary for each category. Multiple entries are accepted. Send an SASE or visit the website for current category list and guidelines.
Deadline: Deadlines vary.
Announcements: Winners are announced in *ByLine Magazine.*
Award: Winners receive cash awards ranging from $10 to $70.

Randolph Caldecott Medal
American Library Association
50 East Huron
Chicago, IL 60611
www.ala.org/alsc/caldecott.html

This prestigious award is presented annually by the Association for Library Services to Children, a division of the American Library Association, to the artist of the most distinguished American picture book for children.

The contest is open to citizens of the U.S. and all illustrations must be original work. Necessary criteria include excellence in execution of the

artistic technique and of pictorial interpretation of the story, theme, or concept and illustration style.
Deadline: December 31.
Representative winner: *The Man Who Walked Between Two Towers,* Mordicai Gerstein.
Announcements: Winner is announced at the ALA Mid-Winter Meeting.
Award: The Caldecott Medal is presented at an awards banquet.

California Book Awards

The Commonwealth Club of
   California
595 Market Street
San Francisco, CA 94105
http://commonwealthclub.org

These annual book awards honor the exceptional literary merit of writers from California. Nominated entries must be written by an author from California, and published during the year preceding the contest. Awards are presented in the categories of fiction, nonfiction, first work of fiction, poetry, juvenile, and young adult. All books are nominated and voted on by members of the Commonwealth Club of California.
Deadline: December 31.
Representative winners: *Evidence of Things Unseen,* Marianne Wiggins; *River of Shadows: Eadweard Muybridge and the Technological Wild West,* Rebecca Solnit.
Announcements: Winners are announced in May.
Award: Winners receive a cash award of $300 and a plaque.

Calliope Fiction Contest

Calliope
Sandy Raschke, Fiction Editor
P.O. Box 466
Moraga, CA 94556-0466

Sponsored by *Calliope,* this annual contest accepts entries of short fiction that display creativity, good storytelling, and appropriate use of language for the target audience.

Entry fee, $2 for non-subscribers; first entry free for subscribers. Limit 5 entries per competition. Entries should not exceed 2,500 words in length. Accepts photocopies and computer printouts. Enclose an SASE for winners' list.
Deadline: Entries are accepted between April 15 and September 30.
Award: First-place winner receives a cash award of $75. Second- and third-place winners receive cash awards of $25 and $10, respectively. All winners will be published in *Calliope* and receive honorary certificates and a 1-year subscription to *Calliope.*

Canadian Library Association's Book of the Year for Children Award

Canmore Public Library
950-8th Avenue
Canmore, Alberta T1W 2T1
Canada
www.cla.ca

Sponsored by the Canadian Library Association, this annual award honors the best children's book published in the year preceding the contest, by a Canadian author.

Any work that is an act of creative writing, including fiction, poetry, and re-tellings of traditional literature are eligible for nomination.
Deadline: Nominations must be made by January 1.
Representative winners: *Boy O'Boy,* Brian Doyle; *Hana's Suitcase,* Karen Levine.
Announcements: Winners are announced in June during the annual CLA conference.
Award: Winners are presented with a medal at the annual conference.

CAPA Competition
Connecticut Authors and Publishers Association
223 Buckingham Street
Oakville, CT 06779
http://aboutcapa.com

Open to residents of Connecticut, this annual competition accepts entries in the categories of children's short story and adult short story (to 2,000 words); personal essay (to 1,500 words), and poetry (to 30 lines). It accepts original, unpublished entries only.

Entry fee, $3 for one story/essay or up to 3 poems. Multiple entries are accepted. Submit 4 copies of each entry. Visit the website or send an SASE for complete guidelines.
Deadline: June 30.
Representative winners: "Playing for the Mob," John Goodwin; "The Organist's Apprentice," Kathryn J. Lord.
Announcements: Winners are announced in the fall.
Award: First-place winner in each

category receives a cash prize of $100. Second-place winners receive cash awards of $50.

Rebecca Caudill Young Readers' Book Award
P.O. Box 6536
Naperville, IL 60526
www.rebeccacaudill.org

This annual award is presented to the author of a book for young readers that was voted most outstanding by students from participating schools in Illinois. The award is given in recognition of Rebecca Caudill's literary talent.

Books are nominated by students, teachers, and librarians. A committee votes on the top 20 books to be read by children in grades four through eight. Schools in Illinois must register to participate in the competition. Students read the nominated books and vote on their favorites.
Deadline: Tallied votes must be received by February 28.
Representative winner: *Stormbreaker,* Anthony Horowitz.
Announcements: Winner is announced in March.
Award: Winning author receives a plaque and a cash prize of $500.

Children's Writer Contests
Children's Writer
93 Long Ridge Road
West Redding, CT 06896-1124
www.childrenswriter.com

Each year *Children's Writer* sponsors two writing contests that are open to all writers on various themes. The competition accepts original, unpublished work only and entries are judged on originality, writing quality, characterization, plot, and age-appropriateness. Visit the website or send an SASE for current themes and guidelines.

Entry fee, $10 for non-subscribers (includes an 8-month subscription); no entry fee for subscribers. Multiple entries are accepted. Manuscripts are not returned.

Deadline: February and October of each year.

Representative winners: "High-Tech Treasure Hunt," Nancy Humphrey; "The Reed Whistle," Maurissa Guibord.

Award: Winners are awarded cash prizes.

Mr. Christie's Book Award

Nabisco Ltd.
95 Moatfield Drive
Toronto, Ontario M3B 3L6
Canada
www.nabisco.ca

This annual award is sponsored by Nabisco and looks to honor excellence in the writing and illustration of Canadian children's literature and to encourage the development and publishing of high-quality children's books that will promote a love of reading. The competition is open to all Canadian writers, and accepts books published in the year preceding the contest.

Entries are judged on intellectual and emotional values, high integrity, and their effectiveness in reflecting and exploring the world of childhood. Send an SASE for complete competition guidelines and further information.

Deadline: January 31.

Representative winners: Jean Litte, Werner Zimmerman.

Announcements: Winners are announced in June.

Award: The grand-prize winner receives a cash award of $7,500. Other winners receive a gold or silver seal on their books and are honored at an awards dinner.

Christopher Awards

The Christophers
12 East 48th Street
New York, NY 10017
www.christophers.org

Each year these awards are presented in several categories including books for young people, books for adults, and feature films. The awards were established in 1949 and look to celebrate the humanity of people in a positive way. Entries must be original titles published in the year preceding the contest. Send 4 copies of entry with press kit, press release, or catalogue copy.

Submissions are reviewed year round. Send an SASE or visit the website for further guidelines.

Deadline: November.

Representative winners: *A Human Being Died That Night,* Pumla

Gobodo-Madikizela; *If I Get to Five,* Fred Epstein.

Announcements: Winners are announced in February.

Award: Winners are presented with bronze medallions.

CIPA National Writing Contest

Colorado Independent Publishers Association
5476 Mosquito Pass Drive
Colorado Springs, CO 80917
www.cipabooks.com

The purpose of this annual competition is to provide new and emerging writers with an opportunity to show their work to experienced authors and publishers and receive feedback on how their work fits into the publishing market. The competition is open to all writers and accepts entries in the categories of children's books, business, self-help, health, and cookbooks.

Entry fee, $25. Entries should not exceed 20 pages in length. Send 3 copies of each entry. All entries must include a cover letter that lists the title, category, author's name, and contact information. Visit the website or send an SASE for complete guidelines.

Deadline: January 15.

Representative winners: "The Monster Solution," Sara Zimet; "Pushing Water Uphill," Steve Baker.

Announcements: Winners are announced in the spring.

Award: First-place winners in each category receive a cash award of

$100 and membership in CIPA.

CNW/FFWA Florida State Writing Competition

CNW/FFWA
P.O. Box A
North Stratford, NH 03590
www.writers-editors.com

Held annually, this competition is open to all writers and presents awards in several categories including unpublished short story; previously published article or essay; unpublished children's story; and poetry. Entries are judged on presentation, suitability, clarity, structure, and logic.

Entry fees vary for each category but range from $10 to $25. Multiple entries are accepted under separate cover. Manuscripts should not be stapled; use paper clips only. Manuscripts are not returned.

Entries are judged on format, grammar, clarity, structure, transitions, and impact. Author's name should not appear on manuscript. Include a cover sheet with author's name, address, telephone number, and email address. Visit the website or send an SASE for complete list of categories and further guidelines.

Deadline: March 15.

Representative winners: "Last Light of Hope," Timothy G. Sebastian; "You Are My Sunshine," Richelle Putnam; "Regina's Closet," Diana M. Raab.

Announcements: Winners are announced by May 31.

Award: First- through third-place

winners in each category receive cash prizes ranging from $50 to $100. Winners also receive honorary certificates. Honorable mention certificates may also be awarded at the judges' discretion.

Delacorte Dell Yearling Contest

Random House, Inc.
9th Floor
1745 Broadway
New York, NY 10019
www.randomhouse.com

This annual competition is open to writers who have not yet published a middle-grade novel. Its purpose is to encourage the writing of contemporary and historical fiction set in North America for readers ages 9 to 12. The competition is open to writers living in the U.S. and Canada and manuscripts should be between 96- and 160- typewritten pages in length.

Include a cover sheet listing author's name, address, telephone number, and brief plot summary. Limit two entries per competition. Accepts photocopies and computer printouts. Send an SASE or visit the website for complete guidelines and further information.

Deadline: Manuscripts must be postmarked between April 1 and June 30.

Announcements: Winners will be announced no later than October.

Award: Winner receives a standard book contract with $7,500 against royalties and $1,500 in cash.

Delacorte Press Contest for a First Young Adult Novel

Random House, Inc.
9th Floor
1745 Broadway
New York, NY 10019
www.randomhouse.com

Open to writers living in the U.S. and Canada, this contest is open to submissions of high-quality young adult fiction in a contemporary setting for readers ages 12 to 18. Entrants should not yet have published a young adult novel to be eligible for this award.

Manuscripts should be between 100- and 224- typewritten pages. Include a cover sheet listing the author's name, address, telephone number, title of manuscript, and brief synopsis. Limit two entries per competition. Accepts photocopies and computer printouts. Include an SASE for return of manuscript. Visit the website or send an SASE for complete guidelines.

Deadline: Manuscripts must be postmarked between October 1 and December 31.

Representative winners: *Wings,* Julie Gonzalez; *Ostrich Eye,* Beth Cooley; *Bringing Up the Bones,* Lara M. Zeises.

Announcements: Winners will be announced no later than April 30.

Award: Winner receives a standard book contract covering world rights for a hardcover and paperback edition, $7,500 against royalties, and a cash award of $1,500.

Distinguished Achievement Awards

The Association of Educational
   Publishers
201 Mullica Hill Road
Glassboro, NJ 08028
www.edpress.org

Honoring and promoting educational publishers, these awards are presented annually in 64 categories including short story, short nonfiction, and software for children and young adults.

All entries must be published in the year preceding the contest. Visit the website or send an SASE for complete category list and further guidelines.
Deadline: January.
Announcements: Winners are announced in the spring.
Award: Winners in each category are presented with a plaque at the annual EdPress awards banquet.

Margaret A. Edwards Award

Young Adult Library Services
   Association
50 E. Huron
Chicago, IL 60611
www.ala.org/yalsa

This annual award recognizes authors whose book or books have provided young adults with a window through which they can view their world and that will help them to grow and to understand themselves and their role in society.

Nominations may be submitted by young adult librarians and teenagers. Authors must be living at the time of nomination. Books must have been published in the U.S. no less than five years prior to nomination.
Deadline: December 31.
Representative winners: Nancy Garden; Paul Zindell; Robert Lipsyte.
Announcements: Winner is announced at the American Library Association's Mid-Winter Meeting.
Award: A cash award of $2,000 is presented to the winner.

Arthur Ellis Awards

Crime Writers of Canada
Box 113
3007 Kingston Road
Scarborough, Ontario M1M 1P1
Canada
www.crimewriterscanada.com

Sponsored by the Crime Writers of Canada, this competition accepts entries in the categories of best crime novel, best true crime, best juvenile crime, best crime short story, and best French language crime novel. All entries must be published in the year preceding the contest, and be written by Canadian authors. Send an SASE or visit the website for further information.
Deadline: January 31.
Representative winners: *Acceleration,* Graham McNamee; *Just Murder,* Jan Rehner.
Announcements: Winners are announced in June.
Award: Winners receive a hand-carved "Arthur" statue.

Empire State Award

Mendon Center Elementary School
110 Mendon Center Road
Pittsford, NY 14534
www.nyla.org/yss/empire.html

Sponsored by the Youth Services Section of the New York Library Association, this award honors a body of work that represents excellence in children's or young adult literature that has made a significant contribution to literature for young people.

The competition is open to writers living in New York only. Send an SASE or visit the website for more information.

Deadline: November 30.
Representative winners: Seymour Simon, Jerry Pinkney, Jean Fritz.
Announcements: Winner is announced in May.
Award: Winner receives an engraved medallion.

William Faulkner Creative Writing Competition

64 Pirate's Alley
New Orleans, LA 70116-3254
www.wordsandmusic.org

This annual competition presents awards in seven divisions: novel; novella; novel-in-progress; short story; essay; poetry; and high school short story. It accepts previously unpublished work only.

Entry fees range from $10 to $35 depending on divisions entered. Accepts photocopies and computer printouts. All submissions must include an entry form and cover letter including author's name, address, telephone number, category, and word count. Manuscripts will not be returned. Send an SASE or visit the website for complete list of category requirements and entry forms.

Deadline: April 30.
Representative winners: "The Goat Bridge," T. M. McNally; "That Social Jones," Brian Rogers; "Incompatible with Life," Thomas Jay Berger.
Announcements: Winners will be notified by October 1.
Award: Winners receive cash prizes ranging from $250 to $7,500.

Shubert Fendrich Memorial Playwriting Competition

Pioneer Drama Service
P.O. Box 4267
Englewood, CO 80155-4267
www.pioneerdrama.com

Open to writers who have not been published by Pioneer Drama Service, this playwriting contest accepts entries on any subject that is appropriate for family viewing.

Entries should have a running time of between 20 and 90 minutes. Include a cover letter with title of entry, synopsis, cast list breakdown, proof of production, number of sets and scenes, and if applicable, musical score and tape. Accepts photocopies, computer printouts, disk submissions (text files or Microsoft Word) and email of entries to editors@pioneerdrama.com.

Deadline: March 1.

Representative winners: "Larceny & Old Lace," Van Vandagriff; "Chateau La Roach," Lauren Wilson.

Announcements: Winner is announced in June.

Award: Winner receives a contract for publication with Pioneer Drama Service and a cash advance of $1,000.

Focus on Writers Contest

Friends of the Sacramento Public Library
3rd Floor
828 I Street
Sacramento, CA 95814
www.saclibrary.org

The purpose of this annual contest is to offer writers the opportunity to test their talents against other writers, and to give recognition and encouragement to the winners. The contest is open to residents of California and accepts entries in the categories of short story, nonfiction article, books/articles for children, first chapter of a young adult novel, first chapter of an adult novel, and poetry. Send an SASE or visit the website for word length limits and additional category information and guidelines.

Entry fee, $5. Limit five entries per competition. Accepts photocopies and computer printouts. Author's name should not be included on manuscript. Include a 3x5 index card with author's name, address, and title of entry.

Deadline: August 31.

Representative winners: "The Tex-ture of Hope," Ann Newton Holmes; "Remember My Name," Joanna Kraus; "What's On TV?," Leslie New Kranz.

Announcements: Winners are announced in November.

Award: First-place winners in each category receive a cash prize of $200. Second- and third-place winners in each category receive cash prizes of $100 and $50, respectively.

H. E. Francis Award

Department of English
University of Alabama at Huntsville
Huntsville, AL 35899
www.uah.edu/colleges/liberal/
english/whatnewcontest.html

Sponsored by the Ruth Hindman Foundation and the UAH English Department, this competition is open to all writers and accepts previously unpublished entries only.

Entry fee, $15. Multiple entries are accepted. Manuscripts should not exceed 5,000 words in length. Entries are subject to blind judging. Author's name should not appear on manuscript itself. A cover sheet containing author's name, address, title of entry, and word count should accompany each entry.

Deadline: December 31.

Representative winners: "Planet Ernest," Bill Lamp; "Depreciation," Morgan M. McDermott.

Announcements: Winner is announced in March.

Award: Winner receives a cash award of $1,000.

Don Freeman Memorial Grant-In-Aid

Society of Children's Book Writers
and Illustrators
8271 Beverly Boulevard
Los Angeles, CA 90048
www.scbwi.org

This grant-in-aid was established by SCBWI to enable picture book artists to further their understanding, training, and creative work in the picture book genre. It is available to both full and associate members of SCBWI, who as artists seriously intend to make picture books their chief contribution to children's literature. Applications and procedures are posted on the website or are available with an SASE.
Deadline: Entries must be postmarked between February 1 and March 1.
Representative winners: Matt Phelan, Anik McGrory, David Udovic, Theresa Smythe.
Announcements: Grant winners will be announced in August.
Award: Winner receives a cash grant of $1,500. One runner-up grant of $500 will also be awarded.

Friends of the Library Writing Contest

130 North Franklin
Decatur, IL 62523
www.decatur.lib.il.us

Open to all writers, this competition accepts previously unpublished and published entries in the categories of essay (to 2,000 words); fiction and juvenile fiction (to 3,000 words); and rhymed and unrhymed poetry (to 40 lines). All entries must be typed. Author's name should not appear on manuscript. Include a cover sheet with author's name, address, telephone number, and title of entry.

Entry fee, $3. Limit five entries per person. Visit the website or send an SASE for more information.
Deadline: September 25.
Representative winners: "Soap Gets In Your Eyes," Sharon Whitehill; "Garden Rows In the Air," Barbara Deming; "Skipping Stones," Mary Chandler.
Announcements: Winners will be announced in December.
Award: First-place winners in each category receive a cash award of $50. Second- and third-place winners receive cash awards of $30 and $20, respectively.

Frontiers in Writing Contest

Panhandle Professional Writers
P.O. Box 8066
Amarillo, TX 79114

Held annually, this contest presents awards in several categories including juvenile/young adult short story; juvenile/young adult novel; historical novel; and screenplay. The competition is open to all writers and accepts previously unpublished material only.

No entry fee. Accepts photocopies and computer printouts. Author's name must not appear on manuscript. Each entry must include an entry form with author's

name, address, and telephone number. Entry forms are available at the website or with an SASE.
Deadline: March 1.
Representative winners: "Mystery at Rogue Theatre," Scott Williams; "Inhale," Marcy McKay; "Polo," Sharon T. Hinton.
Award: First-place winners in the short story categories receive $75; novel category winners receive $100. Second- and third-place winners receive cash prizes ranging from $25 to $35.

Danuta Gleed Literary Award

The Writers' Union of Canada
Suite 200
90 Richmond Street East
Toronto, Ontario M5C 1P1
Canada
www.writersunion.ca

Celebrating the genre of short fiction, this award is presented annually to a Canadian writer for the best collection of short fiction written in the English language. All entries must have been published in the year preceding the contest.

Entrants should submit four copies of each entry. Visit the website or send an SASE for guidelines.
Deadline: January 31.
Representative winners: "The Broken Record Technique," Lee Henderson; "Silent Cruise," Timothy Taylor.
Announcements: Winners are announced on Canada Day, April 23.
Award: Winner receives a $5,000 prize.

The Golden Kite Awards

SCBWI Golden Kite Coordinator
8271 Beverly Boulevard
Los Angeles, CA 90048
www.scbwi.org

Open to members of the Society of Children's Book Writers and Illustrators, the Golden Kite Awards are presented annually to the most outstanding children's books published in the year preceding the contest. The awards are presented in four categories: fiction, nonfiction, picture book text, and picture book illustration.

Publishers should submit four copies of each entry. Visit the website or send an SASE for further information.
Deadline: December 15.
Representative winners: *Milkweed,* Jerry Spinelli; *The Dirty Cowboy,* Amy Timberlake; *I Dream of Trains,* Loren Long.
Announcements: Winners will be notified by March 1.
Award: Golden Kite Statuettes are presented to the winners in each category. Plaques are presented to honorable mentions.

Gold Medallion Book Awards

Evangelical Christian Publishers Association
Suite 2
1969 East Broadway Road
Tempe, AZ 85282
www.ecpa.org

These awards are presented

annually by the Evangelical Christian Publishers Association and serve to recognize excellence in evangelical Christian literature. Eligible books must have explicit Christian content or a distinctly Christian worldview.

It presents awards in 22 categories including fiction, nonfiction, preschool children, youth, elementary children, and biography/autobiography. Books should be submitted by publishers.

Entry fee, $125 per title for ECPA members; $275 for non-members. Send an SASE or visit the website for complete list of categories and guidelines.

Deadline: December.

Representative winners: *Boom: A Guy's Guide to Growing Up,* Michael Ross; *The Trouble with Jesus,* Joseph M. Stowell; *Next Door Savior,* Max Lucado.

Announcements: Winners are announced in the spring at the Gold Medallion Book Awards Banquet.

Award: Plaques are awarded to the winners in each category.

Governor General's Literary Awards

The Canada Council for the Arts
Writing and Publishing Section
P.O. Box 1047
350 Albert Street
Ottawa, Ontario K1P 5V8
Canada
www.canadacouncil.ca

These awards are given annually to the best English-language and French-language book in each of the seven categories of fiction, literary nonfiction, children's literature (text), children's literature (illustration), poetry, drama, and translation (from French to English). Books must be foreign or first Canadian edition trade books that have been written, translated, or illustrated by Canadian citizens or permanent residents of Canada. Titles must be published in the year preceding the contest and must be at least 48 pages with the exception of picture books, which must be a minimum of 24 pages. Books with more than one author/illustrator are not eligible. Send an SASE or visit the website for further information.

Deadline: April 15.

Representative winners: *Stitches,* Glen Huser; *Elle,* Douglas Glover.

Announcements: List of nominated books is announced in October; winners are announced in November.

Award: Each winner is presented with $10,000 and a specially bound copy of their book.

Lorian Hemingway Short Story Competition

P.O. Box 993
Key West, FL 33041
www.shortstorycompetition.com

Writers of short fiction are encouraged to enter this competition that is open to writers whose works of fiction have not yet appeared in a nationally distributed publication with a circulation of 5,000 or more.

It accepts original, unpublished

stories of 3,000 words or less. No theme restrictions. Entry fee, $10 for entries postmarked before May 1 and $15 for entries postmarked between May 1 and May 15. Author's name should not appear on manuscript itself. Include a cover letter with author's name, address, email address, and title of entry. Manuscripts will not be returned.
Deadline: May 15.
Representative winners: "Light Skinned-ed Girl," Heidi Durrow; "Beggars," Patrick Roscoe.
Announcements: Winners will be announced in July.
Award: First-place winner receives a cash award of $1,000. Second- and third-place winners each receive cash awards of $500.

Highlights for Children
Fiction Contest
803 Church Street
Honesdale, PA 18431
www.highlights.com

With a commitment to raising the quality of writing for children, *Highlights for Children* sponsors this annual fiction contest with a different theme each year. The 2005 theme will be funny stories that have fewer than 500 words. The contest looks for stories for children ages two to twelve that do not contain violence, crime, or derogatory humor. Manuscripts should clearly be marked Fiction Contest.

Multiple entries are accepted. Accepts photocopies and computer printouts.

Deadline: February 28.
Representative winners: "Go Kerplunk," Janet Costa Bates; "Six Seconds of Lightning," Claudia Cangilla McAdam.
Announcements: Competition is announced in September; winners are announced in June.
Award: Winning entries are published in *Highlights for Children* and three cash prizes of $1,000 are awarded.

Insight Writing Contest
Insight Magazine
55 West Oak Ridge Drive
Hagerstown, MD 21740-7390
www.insightmagazine.org

Offering prizes in the categories of general short story, student short story, and student poetry, this competition is annually sponsored by *Insight Magazine*. Entrants in student categories must be under the age of 22. The competition accepts previously unpublished work with a strong spiritual message. The use of biblical texts is encouraged but not required.

No entry fee. Entries should not exceed 7-typed pages for short stories and 1 page for poetry. Multiple entries are accepted. Author's name should not appear on manuscript. Include a cover sheet with author's name, address, phone number, and title of entry. Send an SASE or visit the website for more information.
Deadline: May 28.
Announcements: Winners are announced in a special winner's issue

of *Insight Magazine.*
Award: First- through third-place winners in each category receive cash prizes ranging from $50 to $250.

IRA Children's Book Awards
International Reading Association
P.O. Box 8139
Newark, DE 19714-8139
www.reading.org

These awards are presented for an author's first or second published book targeting children or young adults. Awards will be given for both fiction and nonfiction books in the categories of primary, intermediate, and young adult. All entries must be published in the year preceding the contest.

Books may be entered into the competition by either the author or publisher. Entries should be free of racism, and sexism, and should help to encourage young people to read by providing them with something they will delight in and profit from. Official guidelines and application forms are available at the website or with an SASE.
Deadline: November 1.
Representative winners: *Mary Smith,* Andrea U'ren; *Sahara Special,* Esmé Raji Codell; *Buddha Boy,* Kathe Koja.
Announcements: Winners are announced in January.
Award: Winners in each category receive a cash award of $500 and a a medal.

Barbara Karlin Grant
Society of Children's Book Writers and Illustrators
8271 Beverly Boulevard
Los Angeles, CA 90048
www.scbwi.org

Established to recognize and encourage the work of aspiring picture book writers, this grant is available to members of SCBWI who have not yet published a picture book. The competition is open to picture book manuscripts of fiction, nonfiction, or re-tellings of fairy tales, folktales, or legends. Manuscripts should not exceed 8 pages.

Request for applications may be made beginning October 1 of each year. Instructions and complete guidelines are sent with application form.
Deadline: Completed applications are accepted between April 1 and May 15.
Representative winners: Deborah Diesen, Jann Johnson, Kimberley C. Young.
Announcements: Winners are announced October 1 of each year.
Award: Winners receive a cash grant of $1,500. Runners-up receive cash grants of $500.

Coretta Scott King Award
American Library Association
50 E. Huron Street
Chicago, IL 60611-2795
www.ala.org

Named for the widow of Dr. Martin Luther King Jr., this competition is open to writers of African American descent whose distinguished books promote an understanding and appreciation of the "American Dream."

Send 3 copies of each entry. Visit the website or send an SASE for complete information.

Deadline: December 1.

Representative winners: *The First Part Last,* Angela Johnson; *Bronx Masquerade,* Nikki Grimes.

Award: Winner receives a framed citation, an honorarium, and a set of Encyclopaedia Brittanica or World Book Encyclopedia.

Magazine Merit Awards

SCBWI
8271 Beverly Boulevard
Los Angeles, CA 90048
www.scbwi.org

Open to members of the Society of Children's Book Writers and Illustrators, these awards look to honor previously published fiction and nonfiction. The purpose of these awards is to recognize outstanding original magazine work for young people published during the calendar year.

No entry fee. Submit 4 copies of the published work showing proof of publication date. Include 4 cover sheets with member's name, mailing address, telephone number, entry title, category, name of publication, and date of issue.

Deadline: Entries are accepted between January 31 and December 15 of each year.

Representative winners: "Noah and the Cow," Susan R. Anderson; "Railroad Raid," Tracy E. Fern; "Fishing Cat," Phyllis Hornung.

Announcements: Winners are announced in April.

Award: Winners in each category receive a plaque. Honor certificates are also awarded.

Milkweed Fiction Prize

Milkweed Editions
Suite 400
430 First Avenue North
Minneapolis, MN 55401-1473
www.milkweed.org

Presented to the most exemplary work of literary fiction that is accepted by Milkweed Editions each year, this contest is held annually. Manuscripts can be a collection of short stories or individual stories previously published in magazines or anthologies.

No entry fee. Manuscripts previously submitted to Milkweed Editions should not be resubmitted.

Deadline: Ongoing.

Announcements: Winners are announced no later than October 1.

Award: Winner receives a $10,000 cash advance.

Mythopoeic Awards

Mythopoeic Society
P.O. Box 320486
San Francisco, CA 94132-0486
www.mythsoc.org

These annual awards offer prizes in the categories of fantasy for adults and fantasy for children. Books must be single-author novels or single-author story collections.

Nominations and winners are chosen by the Mythopoeic Society. Send an SASE or visit the website for complete competition information and category guidelines.
Deadline: February 28.
Representative winners: *Sunshine,* Robin McKinley; *The Hollow Kingdom,* Clare B. Dunkle.
Announcements: Winners are announced in July or August.
Award: Winners are presented with a statuette of a seated lion, intended to evoke Aslan from C. S. Lewis's *Chronicles of Narnia.*

National Book Award for Young People's Literature

National Book Foundation
Suite 709
95 Madison Avenue
New York, NY 10016
www.nationalbook.org

Recognizing an outstanding contribution to children's literature, these awards look to enhance the public's awareness of exceptional books written by Americans and increase the popularity of reading overall.

Books are accepted in all genres of young adult literature. Translations and anthologies will not be accepted. Entry fee, $100. Books must be submitted by publishers. Send an SASE or visit the website for further guidelines.
Deadline: July.

Representative winners: *The Great Fire,* Shirley Hazzard; *Waiting for Snow in Havana: Confessions of a Cuban Boy,* Carlos Eire.
Announcements: Winners are announced in October.
Award: Winner receives a cash award of $10,000. Sixteen other finalists also receive cash awards of $1,000.

National Children's Theatre Festival

Actors' Playhouse at Miracle Theatre
3140 S. Peoria #295
Aurora, CO 80014
www.actorsplayhouse.org

Open to the submission of original musical scripts targeting children ages 5 to 12, this competition is sponsored by the Actors' Playhouse. Entries are judged on originality, content, and music.

Entry fee, $10. Entries should have a running time of 45–60 minutes. Scripts must have a maximum of 8 adult roles. Multiple submissions are accepted under separate cover. Accepts photocopies and computer printouts. Include an SASE for return of manuscript. Send an SASE or visit the website for further guidelines.
Deadline: August 1.
Announcements: Winners are announced in November.
Award: Winner receives a cash award of $500 and a full production of their play (requires performance rights for a limited time).

Native Writers' Circle of the Americas First Book Award Competition

English Department
University of Oklahoma
Norman, OK 73019-0240

This competition is open to writers of Native American heritage and accepts entries in the categories of prose and poetry.

Manuscripts must be at least 100 pages for prose and 50 pages for poetry, and may be on any subject.

Include a brief biographical note with entry that includes place of residence, professional background, tribal background, and publishing credits, if any. Send an SASE for complete guidelines.

Deadline: January 1.
Representative winners: *The Power of a Name,* Susan Supernaw; *Wild Plums,* Marion D. Sherman.
Announcements: Winners are notified in March or April.
Award: Winners receive a cash award of $500.

NESFA Short Story Contest

P.O. Box 809
Framingham, MA 01701-0809
www.nesfa.org

This short story contest is sponsored by the New England Science Fiction Association. It accepts original entries of science fiction or fantasy from writers who have not yet sold a story of any length to a professional publication.

No entry fee. Entries should not exceed 7,500 words. Accepts photocopies, computer printouts, and email submissions to storycontest@nesfa.org. Author's name should not appear on manuscript itself. Include a separate cover sheet with author's name, address, and title of entry. Visit the website or send an SASE for further guidelines.

Deadline: October 15.
Representative winner: "White Like Me," Tony Reidy.
Announcements: Winners are announced in February.
Award: Winner receives a plaque and a $50 gift certificate to the NESFA Press.

The John Newbery Medal

Association for Library Services to Children
50 E. Huron Street
Chicago, IL 60611
www.ala.org/alsc

The Newbery Medal honors the author of the most distinguished contribution to American literature for children. The competition is open to citizens of the U.S. and permanent residents. Entries must be published in the year preceding the contest and may be fiction, nonfiction, or poetry. Reprints and compilations are not eligible. Entries should display respect for children's understandings, abilities, and appreciations and should target children up to the age of fourteen.

Nominations can be made by ALSC members only.
Deadline: December 31.

Representative winners: *A Tale of Despereaux: Being the Story of a Mouse, A Princess, Some Soup, and a Spool of Thread,* Kate DiCamillo; *Crispin: Cross of Lead,* Avi.

Announcements: Winners are announced at the ALA Mid-Winter Meeting.

Award: The Newbery Medal is presented to the winner at an annual banquet.

New Voices Award

Lee & Low Books
95 Madison Avenue
New York, NY 10016
www.leeandlow.com

Open to writers of color living in the U.S. who have not yet published a picture book, this competition is sponsored by Lee & Low Books. It accepts entries of both fiction and nonfiction picture books and looks for publishability of story, uniqueness of theme/plot, and a distinct author's voice.

Manuscripts should address the needs of children of color by providing stories with which they can identify and relate, and that promote a greater understanding of one another. Entries should target children ages 5 to 12 and should not exceed 1,500 words in length. Send an SASE or visit the website for complete guidelines.

Deadline: October 31.

Representative winner: "Sixteen Years in Sixteen Seconds—The Story of Dr. Sammy Lee, Olympic Gold Medalist," Paula Yoo.

Announcements: Winners are announced in January.

Award: Winner receives publication of their manuscript by Lee & Low Books and a cash award of $1,000. Honorable mention receives a grant of $500 and possible publication.

Ursula Nordstrom Fiction Contest

HarperCollins Children's Books
1350 Avenue of the Americas
New York, NY 10019
www.harpercollins.com

Open to writers living in the U.S., over the age of 21, who have not yet been published, this annual first fiction contest is named for the legendary children's editor. It looks to encourage new talent in the writing of innovative and challenging middle-grade fiction. All entries must be suitable for children ages 8 to 12.

No entry fee. Entries should range between 100 and 300 pages in length. Limit one entry per competition. Accepts photocopies and computer printouts. Include an SASE for return of manuscript. Send an SASE or visit the website for complete information.

Deadline: Entries are accepted between March 15 and April 15.

Representative winner: *Letters from Rapunzel,* Sarah Holmes.

Announcements: Winner is announced in June.

Award: Winner receives a book contract for a hardcover edition, a $7,500 advance, and a $1,500 cash prize.

NWA Nonfiction Contest

National Writers Association
3140 S. Peoria #295
Aurora, CO 80014
www.nationalwriters.com

The National Writers Association sponsors this annual competition that looks to recognize high-quality work in the field of nonfiction. It accepts original, unpublished material only.

Entry fee, $18. Multiple entries are accepted under separate cover. Entries should not exceed 5,000 words. Accepts photocopies and computer printouts. All entries must be accompanied by an official entry form (available with an SASE or at the website).

Deadline: December 31.
Announcements: Winners are announced in October.
Award: First-place winner receives a cash prize of $200. Second- and third-place winners receive $100 and $50, respectively.

NWA Novel Contest

National Writers Association
3140 S. Peoria #295
Aurora, CO 80014
www.nationalwriters.com

This annual competition encourages the development of creative skills. It looks to recognize and reward outstanding ability in the area of novel writing, and accepts previously unpublished novel entries in any genre.

Entry fee, $35. Entries should not exceed 100,000 words. Accepts photocopies and computer printouts. Include an SASE for return of manuscript. Guidelines are available at the website or with an SASE.

Deadline: April 1.
Announcements: Winners are announced in June.
Award: First-place winner receives $500. Second- and third-place winners receive $250 and $150, respectively. Fourth- through tenth-place winners receive a book and an honor certificate.

NWA Short Story Contest

National Writers Association
3140 S. Peoria #295
Aurora, CO 80014
www.nationalwriters.com

This annual contest looks to encourage the development of creative skills, and to recognize and reward outstanding ability in short story writing. It accepts previously unpublished entries only.

Entry fee, $15. Multiple entries are accepted under separate cover. Entries should not exceed 5,000 words. Accepts photocopies and computer printouts. All entries must be accompanied by an official entry form (available at the website or with an SASE).

Deadline: July 1.
Announcements: Winners are announced in the fall.
Award: First-place winner receives a cash prize of $250. Second- and third-place winners receive $100 and $50, respectively.

Scott O'Dell Award for Historical Fiction

1700 East 56th Street
Chicago, IL 60637
www.scottodell.com

This annual award is presented each year to a high-quality book of historical fiction published in the year preceding the contest. It is open to submissions of both children's and young adult literature. The award was established in 1982 to encourage writers to focus on the important genre of historical fiction.

Entries are usually submitted by publishers, although authors may submit their own work. Send an SASE or visit the website for complete list of guidelines and entry form.

Deadline: December 31.
Representative winners: *A River Between Us,* Richard Peck; *Trouble Don't Last,* Shelley Pearsall; *The Land,* Mildred D. Taylor.
Award: Winner receives a cash award of $5,000.

Once Upon a World Award

Museum of Tolerance
1399 S. Roxbury Drive
Los Angeles, CA 90035-4709
www.wiesenthal.com/library/award.cfm

The mission of this award is to support and perpetuate the values and mandate of the Simon Wiesenthal Center & Museum of Tolerance by honoring children's books targeting the 6 to 10 age group. Entries should deal with the issues of tolerance, diversity, human understanding, and social justice. Entries may be fiction, nonfiction, or poetry.

No entry fee. All entries must have been published in the year preceding the contest. A nomination form must accompany each entry. Guidelines and nomination forms are available at the website or with an SASE.

Deadline: April.
Representative winners: *Thank You, Sarah,* Laurie Halse Anderson; *Freedom Summer,* Deborah Wiles and Jerome Lagarrigue.
Announcements: Winner is announced each June.
Award: Winner receives a cash award of $1,000.

Orbis Pictus Award for Outstanding Nonfiction for Children

National Council of Teachers of English (NCTE)
64 Juniper Hill Road
White Plains, NY 10607
www.ncte.org

The National Council of Teachers of English sponsors this annual award promoting and recognizing excellence in the writing of nonfiction for children.

Nominations of individual titles may come from the membership of NCTE and from the educational community at large. Each nomination should meet the following criteria: accuracy; organization; attractive design; interesting style; and enthusiastic writing. All submissions must be useful in classroom teaching for kindergarten through eighth-grade classrooms and should encourage children to think outside the box.

Send nominations to the committee chair and include the author's name, book title, publisher, copyright date, and a short explanation of why you liked the book.

Deadline: November 30.

Representative winner: *An American Plague: The True and Terrifying Story of the Yellow Fever Epidemic of 1793,* Jim Murphy.

Announcements: Winners are announced in April.

Award: Winners receive a plaque presented during the Books for Children Luncheon at the annual NCTE Convention. Five honor books will receive certificates of recognition.

Pacific Northwest Writers Literary Contest

P.O. Box 2016
Edmonds, WA 98020-9516
www.pnwa.org

This annual literary contest presents awards in 10 categories including romance, adult genre novel, juvenile short story or picture book, and juvenile/young adult novel. Send an SASE or visit the website for complete list of categories and word length information.

Entry fee, $35 for members; $45 for non-members. Limit one entry per category. Submit two copies of each entry. Author's name should not appear on manuscript. Include a 3x5 index card with author's name, address, telephone number, and title of entry.

Deadline: February 28.

Representative winners: "The Faistine: A Very Big Scottish Secret," Christy Raedeeke; "Is That You, Pumpkin?" Anne Mini.

Announcements: Winners are announced in July.

Award: Winners in each category receive cash prizes ranging from $150 to $1,000.

PEN Center USA Literary Awards

PEN Center USA
Suite 41
672 S. Lafayette Park Place
Los Angeles, CA 90057
www.penusa.org

Open to authors and translators who live west of the Mississippi River, including all of Minnesota and Louisiana, these literary awards are presented to books of outstanding literary merit in 10 categories including fiction, nonfiction, poetry, children's literature, and translation. All entries must have been published in the year preceding the contest.

Entry fee, $35. Submit 4 copies of each entry. All entries must include a completed entry form. Send an SASE or visit the website for complete list of categories and specific guidelines.

Deadline: December 31.

Representative winners: *Zipped,* Laura McNeal; *Crescent: A Novel,*

Diana Abu-Jaber; *Body of Faith,*
Luis Alfaro.
Announcements: Winners are announced in the spring.
Award: Winners in each category receive a cash award of $1,000.

PEN/Phyllis Naylor Working Writer Fellowship

PEN American Center
Suite 303
588 Broadway
New York, NY 10012
www.pen.org

This fellowship is presented to a writer of children's or young adult literature in financial need, who has published at least two books, and no more than five, during the past 10 years, which may have been well-reviewed and warmly received by literary critics, but which have not generated sufficient income to support the author.

Writers must be nominated by an editor or a fellow writer. It is strongly recommended that the nominating party write a letter of support, describing in some detail how the candidate meets the criteria for this fellowship. Send an SASE or visit the website for complete submission information.

Deadline: For works published between January 1 and April 30, submit entry by April 30. For works published between May 1 and August 30, submit entry by August 30. For works published between September 1 and December 31, submit entry by December 31.

Representative winners: Deborah Wiles, Franny Billingsley, Lori Aurelia Williams.
Announcements: The fellowship is awarded each May.
Award: Winner receives a $5,000 fellowship.

Pikes Peak Writers Conference Annual Contest

Angel Smits, Contest Coordinator
P.O. Box 63114
Colorado Springs, CO 80962
www.pikespeakwriters.org

Encouraging emerging writers to focus on producing a marketable manuscript, this contest is sponsored by the Pikes Peak Writers Group. It accepts manuscripts in several categories including children's, young adult, mystery, historical fiction, creative nonfiction, and contemporary romance.

Entry fee, $25 (a $40 entry fee includes a manuscript critique). Word lengths vary for each category. Accepts photocopies and computer printouts. All entries must be accompanied by an entry form, a cover letter, and copies of manuscript. Guidelines and category information are available at the website or with an SASE.

Deadline: November 1.
Representative winners: "Dear Lizzie," John Sisson; "Digging Holes in a Lake," Christian Lyons; "Scent of a Killer," Kendra Wartnaby.
Announcements: Winners are announced in February.

Award: First-place winner in each category receives a cash prize of $100. Second-place winner receives a cash prize of $50.

Please Touch Museum's Book Awards

210 N. 21st Street
Philadelphia, PA 19103
www.pleasetouchmuseum.org

These prestigious awards recognize books for children that are imaginative, exceptionally illustrated, and that help encourage a child's life-long love of reading. One award is presented to a picture book, published in the year preceding the contest, that is particularly imaginative and effective in exploring concepts for children ages 3 and under. A second award is presented to a book of the same high quality targeting children ages 4 to 7. All entries must be written by an American author.

Send four copies of each entry. Entries will not be returned. Send an SASE or visit the website for further information.

Deadline: September 17.
Representative winners: *Babies on the Go,* Linda Ashman; *One Dark Night,* Lisa Wheeler.
Announcements: Winners will be notified by December 1.
Award: Winners will receive a press release and are encouraged to hold a book signing at the museum. The winners are celebrated at an awards presentation and dinner.

Pockets Annual Fiction Contest

Pockets Magazine
Box 340004
1908 Grand Avenue
Nashville, TN 37203-0004
www.pockets.org

The purpose of this contest is to discover emerging writers who would add a new perspective to children's literature. It accepts previously unpublished short stories of 1,000 to 1,600 words. Include an SASE for return of manuscript. Visit the website or send an SASE for further information.

Deadline: August 15.
Representative winners: Catherine Goodwin, Sue Silvermarie, John McGranaghan.
Announcements: Winner is announced November 1.
Award: Winner receives a cash award of $1,000 and publication in *Pockets.*

Edgar Allan Poe Awards

Mystery Writers of America
6th Floor
17 E. 47th Street
New York, NY 10017
www.mysterywriters.org

Sponsored by Mystery Writers of America, this annual competition looks to enhance and promote visibility of the mystery genre. It presents awards in 12 categories including best fact crime; best young adult mystery; best juvenile mystery; best first novel by an American author; and best motion picture screen play.

No entry fee. All entries must have been published or produced in the year preceding the contest. Submit one copy of entry to each member of the appropriate judging committee. Official entry form and committee information are available with an SASE or at the website.
Deadline: Varies for each category.
Representative winners: *Acceleration,* Graham McNamee; *Bernie Magruder & the Bats in the Belfry,* Phyllis Reynolds Naylor; *Dirty Pretty Things,* Steve Knight.
Announcements: Winners are announced in April.
Award: An "Edgar" is presented to each winner. Cash prizes may also be awarded.

Michael L. Printz Award for Excellence in Young Adult Literature

American Library Association
50 East Huron
Chicago, IL 60611
www.ala.org/yalsa/printz/index.html

This annual award is presented to a book that exemplifies literary excellence in young adult literature. Entries may be fiction, nonfiction, poetry, or an anthology. All entries must be published in the year preceding the contest. Submissions should target young adults ages 12 to 18 and must have been published during the year preceding the contest.

ALA committee members may nominate any number of titles. All nominations are kept confidential. Judges note that winning titles won't necessarily have a profound message, and that controversy is not something they avoid. Judges are looking for books that get young people talking and encourage them to continue reading.
Deadline: December 31.
Representative winners: *The First Part Last,* Angela Johnson; *No Man's Land,* Aidan Chambers.
Announcements: Winner is announced at the ALA Mid-Winter Conference.
Award: Winner is honored at an ALA awards ceremony.

Science Fiction/Fantasy Short Story Contest

Science Fiction Writers of the Earth
P.O. Box 121293
Fort Worth, TX 76121
http://home.flash.net/~swfoe

Held annually, this contest looks to promote the art of writing quality science fiction and fantasy. Open to all writers who have not yet received payment for publication in these genres, it accepts original material only.

Entry fee $5 for first entry; $2 for each additional entry. Manuscripts should be between 2,000 and 7,500 words in length. Accepts photocopies and computer printouts. Visit the website or send an SASE for further guidelines.
Deadline: October 30.
Representative winner: "Mirror,

Mirror," Genevieve Kierans.
Announcements: Winners are announced in February.
Award: First-place winner receives publication on the SFWOE website. First- through third-place winners receive cash awards ranging from $50 to $200. Special awards are also presented for outstanding work from younger authors.

Seven Hills Writing Contest

Tallahassee Writers Association
P.O. Box 32328
Tallahassee, FL 32315
www.twaonline.org

Sponsored by the Tallahassee Writers Association, these annual contests accept entries in the categories of short story, memoir, and children's literature. It accepts previously unpublished entries only.

Entry fee, $15 for members; $20 for non-members. Multiple entries are accepted. Accepts photocopies and computer printouts.
Deadline: October 1.
Announcements: Winners are announced in January.
Award: Winning entries will be published in *Seven Hills* and receive honor certificates.

Seventeen Magazine Fiction Contest

13th Floor
1440 Broadway
New York, NY 10018
www.seventeen.com

Seventeen Magazine sponsors this annual fiction contest that is open to writers ages 13 to 21. It accepts original, unpublished entries on any subject of interest to young adults.

No entry fee. Entries should not exceed 3,500 words. Multiple entries are accepted. Accepts photocopies and computer printouts.
Deadline: April 30.
Announcements: Winners are announced during the summer.
Award: Winner receives a cash award and publication in *Seventeen Magazine*.

Side Show Anthology Fiction Contest

Somersault Press
404 Vista Heights Road
El Cerrito, CA 94530

Side Show, a fiction anthology, promotes this annual contest that accepts entries of fiction in any genre. The competition looks for work of high literary merit to award with publication and prizes.

Entry fee, $12.50. One entry fee covers several manuscripts provided they are included in the same envelope. Accepts photocopies and computer printouts. Submissions that include an SASE will be returned with a manuscript critique if requested.
Deadline: Ongoing.
Award: First-place winner receives publication of their story in *Side Show* and a cash prize of $100. Second-place winner receives a cash prize of $75 and third-place winner receives a cash prize of $50.

Skipping Stones Awards

Skipping Stones
P.O. Box 3939
Eugene, OR 97403
www.skippingstones.org

These annual awards look to cultivate awareness of our multicultural world without perpetuating stereotypes or biases. Entries should promote cooperation, non-violence, and an appreciation of nature. Entries may be published magazine articles, books, or educational videos.

Entry fee, $50. Send 4 copies of each entry. Entries must have been published in the year preceding the contest to be eligible. Send an SASE or visit the website for complete guidelines.
Deadline: January 15.
Representative winners: *Alice Yazzie's Year,* Ramona Maher; *Okomi and the Tickling Game,* Helen and Clive Dorman.
Announcements: Winners are announced in April.
Award: Cash prizes are awarded to the first- through fourth-place winners. Winning entries are reviewed in the summer issue of *Skipping Stones.*

Kay Snow Writing Contest

Willamette Writers
Suite 5A
9045 SW Barbour Boulevard
Portland, OR 97219-4027
www.willamettewriters.com

This annual writing contest is sponsored by Willamette Writers and presents awards in several categories including juvenile short story or article, fiction, nonfiction, and student writer. It accepts original, unpublished material only.

Entry fee, $10 for members; $15 for non-members. Word lengths vary for each category. Submit 3 copies of each entry. Author's name should not appear on manuscript. Include a cover letter with author's name, title of entry, and contact information. Send an SASE or visit the website for more information.
Deadline: May 15.
Representative winners: *This and That,* Carol Coven Grannick; *Round,* Jill Hedgecock; *Talking with My Water God,* Judi Blaze.
Announcements: Winners are announced in August. Finalists will be notified by mail prior to the announcement of winners.
Award: Cash prizes ranging from $50 to $300 are awarded in each category. A Liam Callen award will also be presented to the best overall entry with a cash prize of $500.

Society of Midland Authors Awards

P.O. Box 10419
Chicago, IL 60610
www.midlandauthors.com

Open to writers living in the Midwest, these awards look to encourage writers to practice their craft in the heartland. Awards are presented in the categories of adult fiction and nonfiction, biography, poetry, and children's fiction and nonfiction. All entries must be published in the year preceding the contest and book entries must be at least 2,000 words. Multiple submissions are accepted. Send an SASE or visit the website for further guidelines.

Deadline: January 30.

Representative winners: *Buddha Boy,* Kathe Koja; *Jack: The Early Years of John F. Kennedy,* Ilene Cooper; *I Sailed with Magellan,* Stuart Dybek.

Announcements: Winners are announced in May.

Award: Winners in each category receive cash prizes and a recognition plaque.

Southwest Writers Annual Contest

Southwest Writers Workshop
Suite A
3721 Morris Street NE
Albuquerque, NM 87111-3611
www.southwestwriters.org

The purpose of this annual contest is to encourage, recognize, and honor distinctiveness in writing. It accepts entries in the categories of novel, short story, short nonfiction, book-length nonfiction, children's book, screenplay, and poetry. Send an SASE or visit the website for complete category requirements and subcategories.

Entry fee, $45 for non-members; $25 for members. Multiple entries are accepted under separate cover. Submit 2 copies of each entry. Include a 9x12 SASE for return of manuscript.

Deadline: June 1.

Representative winners: "The Ruby Cage," Madison David Link; "Jake and the Boys," Vince Anderson; "The Herb Lover," April Radbill.

Announcements: Competition is announced in January; winners are announced in the fall.

Award: First-place winner receives a cash award of $2,000.

The Spur Awards

Paul Andrew Hutton, Awards Chair
University of New Mexico
Dept. of History
1080 Mesa Vista Hall
Albuquerque, NM 87131-1181
www.westernwriters.org

The Spur Awards, given for distinguished writing about the American West, are among the oldest and most prestigious in American literature. The awards are offered in the categories of Western novel (short novel), novel of the West (long novel), short story, short nonfiction, contemporary nonfiction, biography, history, juvenile fiction and nonfiction, TV or motion picture drama, and first novel. The awards are open to all writers, and entries must have been published in the year preceding the contest.

Send one copy of entry along with completed entry form (available with an SASE or at the website).

Deadline: December 31.

Representative winners: *Prairie Nocturne,* Ivan Doig; *Seeing the Elephant: The Many Voices of the Oregon Trail,* Joyce Badgley Hunsaker.

Announcements: Winners are announced in the spring.
Award: Winners in each category receive a cash award of $2,500.

Stanley Drama Award
Wagner College
Dept. of Theater and Speech
631 Howard Avenue
Staten Island, NY 10301
www.wagner.edu/stanleydrama.html

These awards were established to encourage and support aspiring playwrights. They accept entries of original full-length plays, musicals, or series of two or three thematically related one-act plays that have not been professionally produced or received tradebook publication.

Limit one submission per playwright. Entry fee, $20. Musical entries must be accompanied by an audio cassette with all the music to be included in the play.
Deadline: July 31.
Announcements: Winners are announced approximately 60 days after the deadline.
Award: First- through fourth-place winners receive cash prizes ranging from $10 to $80.

Stepping Stones Writing Contest
P.O. Box 8863
Springfield, MO 65801-8863

This annual contest promotes writing for children by giving writers an opportunity to submit their work for competition. Entries are judged on clarity, punctuation, grammar, and imagery that are suitable for children. Entries may be either fiction (to 1,500 words) or poetry (to 30 lines) and must be unpublished, original material.

Entry fee, $8 for first entry; $3 for each additional entry. Accepts photocopies and computer printouts. For additional information and entry forms, send an SASE.
Deadline: July 31.
Announcements: Winners are announced approximately 60 days after the deadline.
Award: First-place winner receives a cash award of $140 and publication in *Hodge Podge*. Second- through fourth-place winners receive cash awards ranging from $15 to $50.

Tall Tales Press Hidden Talents Short Story Contest
20 Tuscany Valley Park NW
Calgary, Alberta T3L 2B6
Canada
www.talltalespress.com

This annual contest offers writers a chance to gain the experience that publishers demand. It accepts manuscripts in several categories for both adult and young adult writers and accepts previously unpublished material only.

Entry fee, $10 for adults; $5 for junior categories. Multiple entries are accepted. Send an SASE or visit the website for complete list of categories and word length guidelines.
Deadline: May 31.

Representative winners: "My Favorite Housekeeper," David W. Silva; "Silence Speaks Volumes," Michelle Chen.

Announcements: Winners are announced after the contest deadline in *Writers' Journal* and on the website.

Award: Winners and honorable mentions receive cash awards ranging from $10 to $500 and possible publication.

Peter Taylor Prize for the Novel

Knoxville Writers Guild
P.O. Box 2565
Knoxville, TN 37901-2565
www.knoxvillewritersguild.org

Sponsored by the Knoxville Writers Guild, this contest is held annually and is open to both published and unpublished writers living in the U.S. It looks to identify, promote, and publish novels of high literary quality.

Entry fee, $20. Entries should be a minimum of 40,000 words. Multiple submissions are accepted. Entries must be on standard white paper. Include an SASE for contest results. Manuscripts will not be returned. Send an SASE or visit the website for complete competition guidelines.

Deadline: Entries must be postmarked between February 1 and April 30.

Representative winners: *Minyan: Ten Jewish Men in a World That Is Heartbroken,* Eliezer Sobel; *Blue,*

Sarah Van Arsdale.

Announcements: Winners are announced in the summer.

Award: Winner receives a cash award of $1,000, publication of the novel by the University of Tennessee Press, and a standard royalty contract.

Sydney Taylor Manuscript Competition

Association of Jewish Libraries
315 Maitland Avenue
Teaneck, NJ 07666
www.jewishlibraries.org

Established in 1985, this manuscript award is presented for the best fiction manuscript appropriate for children ages eight through eleven. Entries must be previously unpublished and a minimum of 64 pages, with a maximum of 200 pages in length. Eligible entrants must have not yet published a book of fiction as this competition is intended for beginning authors.

No entry fee. Limit one manuscript per competition. Manuscripts will not be returned. Visit the website or send an SASE for complete competition guidelines.

Deadline: December 15.

Representative winners: "Cara's Kitchen," Brenda A. Ferber; "A Pickpocket's Tale," Karen Schwabach.

Announcements: Winner is announced by April 15.

Award: Winner receives a cash award of $1,000.

Utah Original Writing Competition

617 East South Temple
Salt Lake City, UT 84102
http://arts.utah.gov/literature/
comprules.html

Established in 1958, this annual competition looks to promote and reward excellence from Utah's finest writers. The competition presents awards in several categories including juvenile book, juvenile essay, short story, and general nonfiction. It accepts previously unpublished material from Utah writers only.

No entry fee. Word lengths vary for each category. Limit one entry per category. Accepts photocopies and computer printouts. Manuscripts will not be returned. Send an SASE or visit the website for category list and further guidelines.
Deadline: June 25.
Announcements: Winners are notified in September.
Award: Winners receive cash prizes ranging from $300 to $5,000.

Vegetarian Essay Contest

The Vegetarian Resource Group
P.O. Box 1463
Baltimore, MD 21203
www.vrg.org

Held annually, this contest looks to educate young people on the vegetarian and vegan lifestyles. The competition is open to students in 3 categories: ages 14–18; 9–13; and 8 and under. Students need not be vegetarians to enter the contest.

Entrants should base their submissions on interviews, research, or personal opinion.

No entry fee. Entries should be between 2–3 pages in length. Limit one entry per competition. Accepts photocopies, computer printouts, and handwritten entries. Visit the website or send an SASE for further guidelines.
Deadline: May 1.
Announcements: Winners are announced at the end of the year.
Award: Winners in each category receive a $50 savings bond and publication in *The Vegetarian Journal* (requires all rights).

Jackie White Memorial National Children's Playwriting Contest

Columbia Entertainment Company
309 Parkade Boulevard
Columbia, MO 65202
http://cec.missouri.org

Put in place to encourage the writing of family-friendly plays, this contest is held annually. It seeks top-notch scripts suitable for children's theater with roles that will challenge and expand the talents of actors. Entries should be a full-length play (1 to 1.5 hours running time) with speaking roles for at least seven characters.

Entry fee, $10. Multiple entries are accepted. Include a 3x5 card with name of play, author's name, mailing address, telephone number, character descriptions, synopsis, résumé, and a cassette or CD of

music if the play is a musical.
Deadline: June 1.
Representative winners: "The Klemperer's New Clothes: A Home-spun Tale," William Squier; "Dragon Ribbons," Jane Alden.
Announcements: Winners will be announced no later than August 31.
Award: Winner receives a $500 cash award and possible publication or staged reading of their winning entry.

William Allen White Children's Book Award
Emporia State University
Box 4051
1200 Commercial Street
Emporia, KS 66801
www.emporia.edu

Established to honor one of the state's most distinguished citizens by encouraging the boys and girls of Kansas to read and enjoy books, this award is presented annually to two books: one for third- through fifth-grade students and one for students in sixth through eighth grade.

The contest is open to residents of North America only. It accepts entries that were published in the year preceding the contest.
Deadline: May.
Representative winners: *Ghost Sitter,* Peri R. Griffin; *Surviving Hitler: A Boy in the Nazi Death Camps,* Andrea Warren.
Announcements: Winners are announced in the fall.
Award: Winners receive a cash prize of $1,000 and a bronze medal.

Laura Ingalls Wilder Medal
Association for Library Services to Children
50 E. Huron Street
Chicago, IL 60611
www.ala.org/alsc

Presented every other year, this medal honors an author or illustrator whose books through the years have made a lasting contribution to literature for children. All books must have been published in the U.S. The recipient is selected by a committee of children's librarians. Nominations can be made by ALSC members only.
Deadline: Ongoing.
Representative winners: Eric Carle; Milton Meltzer.
Announcements: Winners are announced in January.
Award: A medal is presented to the winner at an annual banquet.

Tennessee Williams One-Act Play Competition
Tennessee Williams New Orleans Literary Festival
UNO Lakefront
New Orleans, LA 70118
www.tennesseewilliams.net

Open to previously unpublished playwrights, this competition accepts entries of one-act plays with strong literary merit.

Entry fee, $15. Multiple entries are accepted under separate cover. Accepts photocopies and computer printouts. All entries must be typed and must include an entry form

(available at the website or with an SASE). Send an SASE or visit the website for complete guidelines.
Deadline: December 5.
Announcements: Winners are announced by April.
Award: Winner receives a cash prize of $1,000 and a reading and staging of their winning entry.

Paul A. Witty Short Story Award

International Reading Association
P.O. Box 8139
Newark, DE 19714-8139
www.reading.org

This annual award recognizes an author whose original short story is first published in a children's magazine or periodical. Entries should serve as a literary standard that encourages young people to read periodicals. Limit three entries per competition.

Authors and publishers may nominate a short story and send it to the designated Paul A. Witty Subcommittee Chair. No entry fee. For additional information and award guidelines, send an SASE or email exec@reading.org.
Deadline: December 1.
Representative winners: "Noah and the Cow," Susan R. Anderson; "Blizzard," Patricia Baehr; "Medicine Hattie," Dayton O. Hyde.
Announcements: Winner is announced in the spring.
Award: Winner receives a cash award of $1,000 presented at the IRA annual convention.

Women in the Arts Annual Writing Contest

P.O. Box 2907
Decatur, IL 62524

Open to all writers, this contest accepts entries in the categories of essay, fiction, and nonfiction for children (up to 1,500 words); plays (one-act); and rhymed and unrhymed poetry (up to 32 lines). All entries must be original work and may be previously published or unpublished.

Entry fee, $2. Multiple entries are accepted under separate cover. Entries are subject to blind judging. Author's name should not be included on manuscript. Include a cover sheet with author's name, address, telephone number, email address, title of entry, category, and word count. Do not staple entries. Manuscripts will not be returned. Send an SASE for complete category information and further guidelines.
Deadline: November 1.
Representative winners: "The Cookie Sale," Melody Bills; "All's Fair," Marilyn Voorhees; "Mister Is Missing," Elizabeth Drummer.
Announcements: Winners will be notified by March 15.
Award: First-place winners in each category receive a cash award of $50. Second- and third-place winners receive cash awards of $35 and $15, respectively.

John Wood Community College Creative Writing Contest

1301 S. 48th Street
Quincy, IL 62305
www.jwcc.edu

John Wood Community College sponsors this annual creative writing contest that accepts entries in several categories including nonfiction, fiction, traditional rhyming poetry, and non-rhyming poetry. The competition focuses on promoting the work of beginning writers.

Entry fees range from $5 to $7 depending on category. Accepts photocopies and computer print-outs. Author's name should not be included on manuscript. Include a 3x5 index card with author's name, address, and telephone number. Send an SASE or visit the website for specific category information.
Deadline: April 2.
Announcements: Winners are announced in the summer.
Award: Cash prizes are awarded to first- through third-place winners. All winners may also receive publication of their winning entries.

Carter G. Woodson Book Awards

National Council for the Social Studies
Suite 500
8555 16th Street
Silver Spring, MD 20910
www.socialstudies.org

These awards are presented to the most distinguished social science books appropriate for young readers that depict ethnicity in these United States. The purpose of the awards is to encourage the writing, publishing, and dissemination of outstanding social science books for young readers that treat topics related to ethnic minorities and relations sensitively and accurately.

All submissions must be published in the year preceding the contest. Submit one copy of each nominated title to the full Carter G. Woodson Book Award Subcommittee, which ranges from 14 to 20 members. Send an SASE or visit the website for complete guidelines.
Deadline: February.
Representative winners: *Sacagawea,* Lisa Erdich; *In America's Shadow,* Kimberly and Kaleigh Komatsu; *Early Black Reformers,* James Tackach.
Announcements: Winners are announced in the spring.
Award: Certificates are presented to the winners at the annual NCCS conference in November.

Work-in-Progress Grants

Society of Children's Book Writers
and Illustrators
8271 Beverly Boulevard
Los Angeles, CA 90048
www.scbwi.org

The Society of Children's Book Writers and Illustrators presents these grants each year to assist children's book writers in the completion of a project. Grants are awarded in the categories of Gen-

eral Work-in-Progress; Contemporary Novel for Young People; Nonfiction Research; and Unpublished Author. Requests for applications may be made beginning October 1 of each year. Instructions and complete guidelines will be sent with application forms. Applications should include a 750-word synopsis and writing sample from the entry that is no longer than 2,500 words.
Deadline: Applications are accepted between February 1 and March 1.
Representative winners: Heather Doran Barbieri, Mary Ikagawa.
Announcements: Winners of the grants are announced in September.
Award: Cash grants of $1,500 and $500 are awarded in each category.

Writers at Work Fellowship

P.O. Box 540370
North Salt Lake, UT 84054-0370
www.writersatwork.org

This annual competition is open to writers who have not yet published a book-length volume of original work. It accepts entries in the categories of fiction and nonfiction (to 5,000 words); and poetry (up to 6 poems).

Entry fee, $15. Multiple entries are accepted under separate cover. Accepts photocopies and computer printouts. Indicate category on outside envelope. Manuscripts will not be returned. Send an SASE or visit the website for further information.
Deadline: March 1.
Representative winners: "A Lesson in Manners," Misty Urban; "Finding Father," Deidre Elliot.
Announcements: Winners are announced in April.
Award: Winners in each category receive a cash prize of $1,500 and publication in *Quarterly West*. Honorable mentions are also awarded.

Writer's Digest Annual Writing Competition

4700 East Galbraith Road
Cincinnati, OH 45236
www.writersdigest.com

Open to all writers, this competition accepts work in several categories including children's fiction, feature article, genre short story, memoir/personal essay, and stage play script. The competition accepts original, unpublished work only.

Entry fee, $10. Multiple entries are accepted under separate cover. Accepts photocopies and computer printouts. Author's name, address, phone number, and category should appear in the upper left corner of the first page. Manuscripts are not returned. Visit the website or send an SASE for complete category list, word length requirements, and additional guidelines.
Deadline: May 31.
Announcements: Winners are announced in the November issue of *Writer's Digest*.
Award: Grand-prize winner receives a cash award of $1,500. Cash prizes and books from *Writer's Digest* are also awarded to winners in each category.

Writers' Journal Writing Contests

P.O. Box 394
Perham, MN 56573-0374
www.writersjournal.com

These contests are sponsored by *Writers' Journal* and offer prizes in several categories including short story, ghost story/horror, romance, travel, fiction, and poetry. Word lengths and guidelines vary for each contest.

All entries must be previously unpublished. Multiple entries are accepted. Submit two copies of each entry. Accepts photocopies and computer printouts. Entry fees range from $5 to $10 depending on the category. Enclose a #10 SASE for winners' list.

Deadline: Varies for each category.
Representative winners: "Giving Rides," Benjamin T. Nickol; "The Ladies of High Wine Street," Jennifer C. Martin.
Announcements: Winners are announced after each contest deadline in *Writers' Journal* and on the website.
Award: Winners receive cash prizes and publication of their winning entry.

The Writing Conference Writing Contests

P.O. Box 664
Ottawa, KS 66067-0664
www.writingconference.com

Open to children and young adults, these contests accept entries of short stories, short nonfiction, and poetry. The goal of these contests is to encourage a love of writing among young people.

No entry fee. Limit one entry per competition. Accepts photocopies and computer printouts. Visit the website or send an SASE for further information.

Deadline: January.
Announcements: Winners are announced in February.
Award: Winners in each category receive publication in *The Writer's Slate*.

Writing for Children Competition

The Writers' Union of Canada
Suite 200
90 Richmond Street East
Toronto, Ontario M5C 1P1
Canada
www.writersunion.ca

Open to citizens of Canada who have not yet published a book, this competition looks to discover, encourage, and promote new and emerging writers. Entries must target children and may be either fiction or nonfiction.

Entry fee, $15. Multiple entries are accepted. Entries should not exceed 1,500 words. Accepts photocopies and computer printouts. Send an SASE or visit the website for further information.

Deadline: April.
Representative winners: Susan John Yasar, Candace Mitchell, Amanda Seals.

Announcements: Winner is announced in June.
Award: Winner receives a cash prize of $1,500 and the Writers' Union of Canada will submit the winning entry to several children's publishers.

Paul Zindell First Novel Award

Hyperion Books for Children
114 5th Avenue
New York, NY 10011
www.hyperionchildrensbooks.com

Formerly called the New Worlds Award, this award is presented annually for a work of contemporary or historical fiction set in the United States that reflects the diverse ethnic and cultural heritage of our country. Entries should be intended for readers ages 8 through 12.

Submissions should be a book-length manuscript of between 100- and 240-typewritten pages. Manuscripts must be accompanied by an entry form (available at the website or with an SASE). Accepts photocopies and computer printouts. Limit two entries per competition.
Deadline: April 30.
Representative winners: *Little Cricket,* Jackie Brown; *Blue Jasmine,* Kashmira Sheth.
Announcements: Winners will be notified after July 15.
Award: Winner receives a book contract with Hyperion Books for Children, covering world rights including but not limited to hardcover, paperback, e-book, and audio book editions with an advance against royalties of $7,500. Winner also receives a cash prize of $1,500.

Zoo Press Award for Short Fiction

Zoo Press
P.O. Box 22990
Lincoln, NE 68542
www.zoopress.org

Sponsored by Zoo Press, this competition is open to all writers. It accepts previously unpublished, original entries of collections of short fiction. Collections must total 40,000 words.

Entry fee, $25. Multiple entries are accepted. All entries must include a cover letter. Manuscripts will not be returned. Send an SASE or visit the website for complete guidelines and further information.
Deadline: February 14.
Announcements: Winners are announced in late spring.
Award: Winning entry will be published by Zoo Press and winner receives a $5,000 advance against royalties.

Index

K

L